From the Secret Files of J. Edgar Hoover

EDITED WITH COMMENTARY BY
ATHAN THEOHARIS

Elephant Paperbacks
IVAN R. DEE, PUBLISHER, CHICAGO

FROM THE SECRET FILES OF J. EDGAR HOOVER. Copyright ©
1991, 1993 by Athan Theoharis. This book was originally published in
1991 by Ivan R. Dee, Inc. This paperback edition contains a new
Appendix on Secret Files, Secret Records Systems.

First ELEPHANT PAPERBACK edition published 1993 by Ivan R.
Dee, Inc., 1332 North Halsted Street, Chicago 60622. Manufactured in
the United States of America and printed on acid-free paper.

Library of Congress Cataloging-in-Publication Data:
Theoharis, Athan G.
    From the secret files of J. Edgar Hoover / edited with commentary
by Athan Theoharis.
        p.   cm.
    "Elephant paperbacks."
    Includes index.
    ISBN 1-56663-017-7 (acid-free paper)
        1. Internal security—United States—History—20th century.
    2. Anti-communist movements—United States—History—20th
century.   3. Subversive activities—United States—History—20th
century.   4. Hoover, J. Edgar (John Edgar), 1895–1972—Archives.
    5. United States. Federal Bureau of Investigation—Archives.   I. Title.
    [E743.5.T48   1993]
    353.0074—dc20   92-41197

55153

For Nancy, Jeanne, George, and Elizabeth—
their commitment to peace and social justice
inspire and justify this effort

Acknowledgments

I have incurred a number of debts—financial, research, and editorial—in compiling this book of documents. I could not have defrayed the substantial costs required to obtain FBI documents under the Freedom of Information Act without the financial assistance of the Field Foundation, Warsh-Mott Funds, C. S. Fund, Fund for Investigative Journalism, Webster Woodmansee Fund, and Marquette University. I am indebted to numerous individuals who shared their research findings with me, including Kenneth O'Reilly, Stephen Leahy, Chris Span, Seth Rosenfeld, Alex Charns, Jim Rowen, Tony Mauro, and Laura Kalman. The staff of the FBI's Records Management Division, and particularly its chief Emil Moschella, processed my numerous FOIA requests with dispatch and a high degree of professionalism. At a critical time Judy Klawitter provided invaluable typing assistance while Jeffrey Shulman and John Muscato offered helpful editorial direction at the initial stage of this project. I am particularly indebted to my editor, Ivan R. Dee, whose demanding editorial criticisms and suggestions made this a better book. I can never fully acknowledge the support of my wife, Nancy, and my children, Jeanne, George, and Elizabeth. Not sharing my compulsive—they would claim *obsessive*—interest in the FBI (as well as Marquette basketball and their soccer playing), they forced me to adopt a more balanced perspective. Their principled commitment to a more just social order has inspired my own work.

A. T.

Contents

From the Secret Files of
J. Edgar Hoover

Introduction

ATTORNEY GENERAL CHARLES Bonaparte's July 1908 order creating a permanent investigation division within the Department of Justice, the Bureau of Investigation (formally renamed the FBI in 1935), marked a new phase in the nation's political history. Until then, libertarian and states' rights values had defined law enforcement as a local and state responsibility. In 1907–1908, when Secret Service agents (temporarily hired by the Justice Department) uncovered evidence of land fraud which led to the indictment of two U.S. congressmen, Congress was incensed by this "targeting." Members likened the actions to those of a tsarist secret police and voiced fears of a "national secret police" and its threats to a government of checks and balances. In January 1909, the outgoing attorney general sought to allay these concerns, heightened by his unilateral action in creating the Bureau of Investigation. He denied in congressional testimony that the newly created Bureau would pose any such threat. Bonaparte assured the congressmen that Bureau investigations would be confined to enforcing the antitrust and interstate commerce laws. The Bureau was not about to monitor political dissent or target members of Congress at the request of their partisan adversaries in the White House.

U.S. involvement in World War I in April 1917 proved that the alarmist concerns of 1907–1908 were prescient. During the period 1917–1921, Bureau of Investigation agents compiled more than 200,000 dossiers on American organizations and residents (including the pacifist Jane Addams, antiwar Senator Robert LaFollette, civil libertarian Roger Baldwin, and Irish nationalist Eamon deValera) because of their opposition to the Woodrow Wilson administration's foreign policy. Agents continued to monitor the activities of radical trade unionists and socialists even after the armistice of November 1918. Lacking the authority to use the acquired information for prosecutive purposes, the Bureau shared it with state police officials and private employers who had an interest in identifying union organizers and activists. The extent of this extralegal and covert assistance acquired a new dimension with the disclosure in 1923 that Bureau agents had monitored those congressional critics of the administration of Warren G. Harding who had exposed the Teapot Dome scandal. This monitoring had included breaking into and wiretapping the offices of these congressmen.

To calm the resulting furor, in May 1924 Attorney General Harlan Fiske Stone initiated a massive housecleaning of the Bureau, naming J. Edgar Hoover to replace the discredited Bureau director William J. Burns. At the same time, Stone announced a series of restrictions on Bureau investigative activities, including the banning of wiretapping and the confining of future investigations to the prosecution of federal law violators. "A secret police," Stone then warned, "may become a menace to free government . . . because it carries with it the possibility of abuses of power which are not always quickly apprehended or understood." Stone assured the public and Congress that the recently disclosed abuses would not recur, for the reconstituted Bureau "is not concerned with political or other opinions of individuals. It is concerned only with their conduct and then only such conduct as is forbidden by the laws of the United States."

At the time of his appointment, Hoover was keenly aware of the tenuous nature of his position. He knew that revelations of Bureau abuses might result in his dismissal and provoke calls for the Bureau's termination. The newly appointed acting director (Hoover's probationary appointment ended in December 1924 when Stone made the appointment permanent) publicly affirmed his intent to limit the Bureau's activities to federal statutory violations. At the same time, he initiated a public relations campaign to refurbish the image of Bureau agents as honest, efficient, God-fearing professionals. Despite his initial success in dispelling concerns, Hoover remained fully aware that his stewardship would be closely monitored and that his continued tenure would depend on his ability to keep tight rein on the conduct of Bureau agents and officials.

Hoover's most predictable course of action would seem to have been to honor Stone's ban against Bureau surveillance of personal and political activities. Instead, Hoover directed his agents to continue such monitoring—but subject to his approval if he concluded that such investigations could be conducted without danger of discovery. Cannily, the director required that Bureau officials obtain his written approval before conducting any sensitive investigation, and then report, also in writing, what they discovered and how they secured the information. These oversight requirements demanded written records and thus posed a potentially serious political problem. Theoretically, Bureau records were subject to congressional subpoena, court-ordered discovery motion, and requests from Justice Department officials (notably the attorney general) and the White House. Hoover surmounted this records problem, first, by specifying that certain records were to be filed in his own office and, second, by outlining how sensitive information was to be reported. From the time of his appointment as director, Hoover, as he himself described it, maintained "in the office of [his administrative assistant Helen] Gandy a confidential file in which are kept various and sundry items believed inadvisable to be included in the general files of the Bureau." At the same time, Hoover refined a reporting procedure called "personal and confidential" letters, which he had inherited from his predecessor. These had been designed to call important communications to the director's attention. Hoover specified that "personal and confidential" letters were to be used only when "there is some matter that you [heads of FBI field offices, special agents in charge, or "SACs"] wish to be brought to my personal attention before correspondence is opened and indexed in the file room." In other words, Hoover's procedure ensured that these communications would not be serialized in the Bureau's central records system.

His own office file and the "personal and confidential" letters procedure enabled Hoover to circumvent Attorney General Stone's ban on the monitoring of radical activities. When forwarding reports with information about "subversive activities," SACs were to use "personal and confidential" letters. In August 1936, however, President Franklin Roosevelt verbally authorized Hoover to investigate "communistic and fascist" activities. With presidential authorization for what had been an ongoing but risky practice, Hoover now advised SACs that in "ordinary cases it is [no longer] necessary that these data [on "subversive activities"] be carried in personal and confidential files [in the SAC's office] but may be carried among the regular pending or closed files of an office." But Hoover did not abandon "personal and confidential" letters; he stipulated that henceforth they be used only "if the communication pertains to official matters of a highly confidential nature which are deemed of sufficient importance to be brought to the Director's personal attention."

Hoover's secret office files and special submission procedures permitted the Bureau to collect and maintain noncriminal information (such as the monitoring of homosexual activities, which dated from 1937, and the submission of "obscene or indecent" information, which dated from 1925), without fear of discovery. Sensitive reports (such as those that recorded the FBI's resort to illegal investigative techniques—break-ins, wiretaps, bugs), because they were forwarded to office files and not serialized in the central records system, enabled FBI officials to affirm truthfully in legal proceedings that their "central records system" contained no record of suspected illegal conduct.

"The secret files of J. Edgar Hoover" comprise several different sets of sensitive records. The most relevant and extant is Hoover's Official and Confidential File. Excerpts from that file in this book offer insights into Hoover's hidden agenda. His conservative political philosophy and judgmental moralism led him to actions in striking contrast to his public claims of professionalism, political neutrality, and respect for the law and for rights of privacy. But this was not the only file that Hoover maintained in his office during his forty-eight years as FBI director. There were at least five other such secret files.

First, Hoover was able to disguise his interest in certain files by returning them to the central records system. He was able to request the file of a named individual or of an ongoing or closed investigation, then return it to central records when it no longer interested him. Returning these unneeded files enabled him to keep his routine office file to a manageable limit and not arouse suspicion that he maintained it as a secret office file.

This practice of Hoover's is documented by a Justice Department review of the index to his Official and Confidential file in 1972, before the department incorporated this file into the FBI's central records system following Hoover's death that May. The department review noted three folders listed in the index to this file that were apparently missing. A follow-up search confirmed that these folders had been returned to the FBI's central records system but that Hoover's administrative assistant, Helen Gandy, had simply forgotten to destroy the index cards which she had created when she temporarily placed them in Hoover's office file.

We also know of at least one instance of the destruction of a folder "maintained in the Director's Office." This folder contained a brief on Harry Dexter White, an accused "subversive," which Hoover had ordered his aides to prepare in November 1953 and then to update periodically. Preparation of this brief had been prompted by Republican Attorney General Herbert Brownell's assertion in November 1953 that former Democratic President Harry Truman had in 1946 appointed White to a sensitive government position despite having received FBI reports about White's disloyalty. When Truman challenged Brownell's remarks, the attorney general and FBI Director Hoover appeared before a Senate subcommittee to repeat and document the charge. Hoover's overtly partisan action infuriated many Southern Democrats. From time to time they raised Hoover's support of Brownell as reason to reduce FBI appropriations or end Hoover's tenure as FBI director. By October 1966, though, the White case had waned as a political issue, so Hoover authorized destruction of this brief, having concluded that it had "served its purpose."

Second, in October 1941 Hoover decided to create "a confidential file [to] be maintained [henceforth] in the office of [FBI assistant director Louis] Nichols, under his direction and supervision." In authorizing the Nichols File, Hoover aimed to restrict the contents of his own office file "to confidential items of a more or less personal nature of the Director's and items which I might have occasion to call from time to time, such as memoranda to the Department on the Dies Committee, etc." He transferred to the Nichols File specific documents "such as confidential information on [name withheld], Communist infiltration into the Department of

Justice, etc." At the same time he shifted to the FBI's National Defense Division another broad range of documents from his office file, asking that they "be maintained in an up to date manner and immediately available to me should I desire the same." These documents included "confidential memoranda on undercover and SIS [Special Intelligence Service*] employees; name, number and brief biography of confidential informants; list of surveillances maintained on diplomatic representatives at the sanction of the State Department, and other similar items."

Third, after Hoover's death, Justice Department officials discovered "about a drawer and a half of Bureau files which were kept in [Hoover's] office under lock and key." These were in addition to the Official and Confidential File. When members of a House subcommittee inquired why these documents had been kept separate from other FBI records, Helen Gandy replied "for safekeeping," because they "were highly confidential Bureau information." Because they are now fully incorporated in the FBI's central records system, we cannot determine what made these files so sensitive and, further, why Hoover maintained direct control over them.

Fourth, still another office file was Hoover's so-called Personal and Confidential File. Within weeks after Hoover's death, and pursuant to his instructions, Helen Gandy destroyed this file and the index cards identifying its contents. Why would Hoover order the destruction of his Personal and Confidential File but not his Official and Confidential File? Documents in the latter file, after all, were politically explosive. They documented, for example, Hoover's interest in derogatory information on prominent Americans (such as Eleanor Roosevelt and John Kennedy), his willingness to authorize illegal investigative techniques, and his obsessive efforts to retain the FBI directorship and to discredit his critics.

While a destroyed file cannot be re-created, we can describe the general character of the Personal and Confidential File. We can also understand why Hoover wanted to retain the Official and Confidential File and why he did not want his successor (let alone members of Congress, Justice Department officials, or the news media) to have access to the Personal and Confidential File. Memoranda in the Official and Confidential File indirectly describe the contents of the

*This FBI division was created in September 1940 when President Roosevelt directed the FBI to collect foreign intelligence information in South America.

destroyed Personal and Confidential File as a repository for even more sensitive information about prominent political and civic leaders. When FBI officials, for example, were asked by Hoover to prepare a summary of information on Senator George McGovern, they noted that they had reviewed all references to McGovern in the FBI's central records system and then conducted "a review of the personal records in the Director's Office."

Hoover's Official and Confidential File includes another memorandum which Hoover had written "for personal files," recording his June 4, 1971, conversation with Attorney General John Mitchell. At the time, the columnists Rowland Evans and Robert Novak had somehow secured a copy of a confidential memorandum which Mitchell had written to Hoover. Denying that the FBI was the source of the leak, Hoover asserted, "I don't think I have that kind of disloyalty in the Bureau." He then confided to Mitchell how he safeguarded sensitive communications: "What I have done in view of leaks to these scavengers [Hoover's derogatory term for investigative journalists], I have filed many of the memoranda I have sent back and forth in a Personal and Confidential file in my office and not in the main Bureau [files] so that the great majority of file clerks don't get to them unless it is a case they personally are handling."

The title of this file, Personal and Confidential, derived from Hoover's letters procedure instituted earlier and later refined. Such letters had originally been incorporated in one office file; at some point, when Hoover decided to create the Nichols File, he directed Helen Gandy to create two discrete files in his office with their own separate indices—an Official and Confidential File and a Personal and Confidential File.

In October-November 1971, Hoover began to review the contents of his Personal and Confidential File. He soon transferred eight folders from it to his Official and Confidential File. These folders now allow us to understand the kinds of documents that had originally been filed in the now-destroyed Personal and Confidential File.

The most revealing of these eight folders is captioned "Black Bag" Jobs. Memoranda in this folder summarize the procedures instituted by Hoover in 1942 to ensure that FBI agents could conduct break-ins, subject to his personal authorization, without risk of discovery. While the other seven folders are not as politically incriminating, they are no less sensitive. They include a folder on Fred Black, recording Hoover's 1966 efforts to force then Attorney General Nicholas Katzenbach to defend the FBI's illegal bugging of Black, subject of a criminal investigation. Hoover pressed Katzenbach by exploiting the anti–Robert Kennedy biases of President Lyndon Johnson, Senator Edward Long, and former Republican Attorney General William Rogers.

In addition to the eight transferred folders, other memoranda scattered through Hoover's Official and Confidential File bear a notation that a copy was filed in the Personal and Confidential File. Still other memoranda—like the one about the leak to Evans and Novak—are captioned "for personal files." That Helen Gandy filed some "personal files" memoranda in the Official and Confidential File suggests that she had the authority to decide which of these two files to use for specific "personal" memoranda.

The "personal" memoranda and the transferred folders confirm that Hoover's criterion for routing memoranda to his Official and Confidential File was their potential value to his continued tenure as FBI director. That file was considered less threatening than the Personal and Confidential File. This is indirectly confirmed by the timing of Hoover's decision to transfer the "Black Bag" Jobs folder.

Originally written in 1966 and 1967, the memoranda in this folder record Hoover's authorization of "clearly illegal" activities. They also document the Do Not File procedure he devised to ensure the undiscoverable destruction of documents recording FBI break-in practices. When they were written, these memoranda were potentially explosive, and accordingly they were filed in the Personal and Confidential File. By 1971, however, they had acquired a different character: they could document that Hoover had banned break-ins but had acceded to pressure from the Nixon White House.

When the memoranda were created in 1966 and 1967, Hoover became concerned that discovery of his authorization since 1942 of FBI break-ins could effect his forced retirement,* and thus wrote on the bottom of a 1966 memorandum describing ongoing FBI break-in

---

*Hoover had reached the mandatory retirement age of seventy in January 1965 and was able to continue as FBI director because of President Johnson's 1964 executive order waiving this requirement. Despite Johnson's order, Hoover worried that any disclosure which raised questions about his administration of the Bureau could result in his involuntary retirement.

policy his ban against continued "use of this technique." In a second memorandum in this folder, dated January 1967, Hoover expressed displeasure that SACs continued to request his authorization to conduct break-ins despite his July 1966 ban. This evidence Hoover wished to preserve, so he ordered its transfer to the Official and Confidential File.

In this case, what changed Hoover's mind was pressure from the Nixon White House. Because of it, in 1970 Hoover verbally authorized FBI agents in New York City to conduct break-ins during an investigation of the radical Weather Underground. Worried by various efforts to relieve him of the FBI directorship, Hoover decided to preserve a permanent record of his written order of July 1966 banning future break-ins. At the time, in September-October 1971, White House aides and Attorney General John Mitchell were pressing President Nixon to request Hoover's resignation. Hoover also discovered that FBI Assistant Director William Sullivan, whom Hoover had dismissed in late September, had (without Hoover's knowledge) delivered to the Nixon White House certain sensitive wiretap records which Hoover had asked Sullivan to maintain. They documented that the FBI's wiretapping of National Security Council and White House aides, and four leading Washington reporters, had been conducted pursuant to a request from the Nixon White House.

Fifth and finally, Hoover authorized another secret office file to be maintained by his long-time aide and the second most powerful FBI official, Clyde Tolson. The Tolson File consists of memoranda which Hoover addressed to Tolson with further attention of specific FBI assistant directors.

Dating from at least February 1941, Hoover had two "recording instruments" installed in his office: one was attached to the telephone of his administrative assistant Helen Gandy, and the second to the telephone room. By taping all incoming calls to his office, Hoover ensured that a written record could be created of any request requiring his attention (for example, a 1970 Nixon White House request for a report listing those members of the Washington press corps who were homosexuals "and other stuff"). Hoover's memos recording these requests were addressed to Tolson and then to identified FBI assistant directors. They were to get the desired information and report through Tolson.

In March 1953 Hoover ordered the Tolson File memoranda to be regularly destroyed every six months, as were other office files maintained by other FBI assistant directors. For reasons unknown and unknowable, memoranda routed to Tolson's office that were written during the period 1965 through 1972 were *not* destroyed. The partially complete Tolson File thus offers insights into Hoover's directorship of the FBI.

To sum up, Hoover's extant Official and Confidential File, Nichols's Official and Confidential File, and the Tolson File are only part of "the secret files of J. Edgar Hoover." Because they were purposefully maintained separate from the FBI's central records system, they represent those matters which Hoover considered important—but he did not wish to have his interest in them known outside the FBI. As a record of decisions and actions which were purposefully kept secret, these files document the perils which unelected officials can pose to constitutional government. Hoover had access to the FBI's vast resources and could operate without accountability.

The reprinted documents that follow are representative samples from Hoover's massive (17,700 pages) Official and Confidential File and from the Nichols and Tolson files, with selected clarifying documents from the FBI's central records system. I have identified by ellipses those sections of the original documents which have not been reprinted, and by brackets those sections which the FBI has withheld. I have also provided, in brackets or in footnotes, background information about matters or individuals referred to in the documents or about the event that prompted the creation of a particular document. Whenever a document is not from Hoover's Official and Confidential File, I have identified its source (Nichols or Tolson files, or FBI case file number).

Owing to their sensitivity, these reprinted documents were never to have been disclosed, whether or not other records in the FBI's central records system became publicly available. My ability to obtain these documents stems from the mandatory disclosure provisions of the Freedom of Information Act (FOIA). This act requires the FBI, like any other federal agency, to conduct a full search of its records and release all documents relating to a specified FOIA request. Yet the opportunity poses a Catch-22 situation. Those who invoke the FOIA must be able to identify specific FBI files and thus know that specific office or policy files had been created—even though such files had originally been created with the intent of their never being discovered.

My ability to identify and thus request specific files (at least those which remain extant) came from references in published congressional hearings or released FBI memoranda. For example, I learned of the Tolson File from a memo in the FBI's files on Alger Hiss. It reported FBI officials' response to Hoover's inquiry as to where specific sensitive memoranda had been located—in "Tolson's Personal File." A further source was summary memoranda prepared by FBI officials and incorporated in the FBI's files. When preparing such memoranda, FBI officials often identified code-named programs or cited FBI files from which the summarized information was obtained.

A close reading of FBI memoranda, then, provided revealing insights into where especially sensitive FBI records were maintained. Nonetheless, while I discovered the existence of the Hoover, Nichols, and Tolson office files, I also found that similar office files maintained by FBI assistant directors Cartha DeLoach and W. Mark Felt are no longer extant, and that the memoranda predating 1965, which had been filed in Tolson's office, had been destroyed.

No doubt future FOIA requests will uncover further examples of FBI activities during Hoover's forty-eight-year tenure as FBI director. But the reprinted documents that follow will remain an accurate record of the politics and priorities that governed Hoover's directorship and of his ability to immunize his own (and FBI officials') conduct from public scrutiny. The consequence of this secrecy was the forging of an independent, virtually autonomous agency with its own political agenda, capable of influencing public opinion and national politics.

PART ONE
PERSONALITIES AND POLITICS

1: John F. Kennedy

IN HIS FICTIONAL *account of Hoover's secret files, popular mystery writer Robert Ludlum has one of his characters in* The Chancellor Manuscript *describe the FBI director's methods: "Every paper, every insert, every addendum related to Security crossed Hoover's desk. And as we know, 'Security' took on the widest possible range. Sexual activities, drinking habits, marriage and family confidences, the most personal details of the subjects' lives—none were too remote or insignificant. Hoover pored over these dossiers like Croesus with his gold. Three Presidents wanted to replace him. None did."*

Ludlum's fictional Hoover was purely speculative, but the author's suspicions were not wholly off the mark. The FBI's investigation of Inga Arvad offers a case in point.

Inga Arvad was an immigrant from Denmark who was employed as a gossip columnist by the Washington Times-Herald *(a conservative, anti–New Deal, and isolationist paper) in the early forties. She became a target of FBI interest in January 1942 owing to unsubstantiated rumors that she was a German spy. The resulting FBI investigation uncovered no evidence of Arvad's involvement in espionage. But her regular contact with prominent Washingtonians as a columnist who wrote about the personal side of Washington led Hoover to conclude that she engaged in a "most subtle type of espionage activity." He requested Attorney General Francis Biddle's authorization to wiretap her.*

Biddle accepted Hoover's characterization of Arvad's espionage activities at face value and approved the tap. He never inquired whether the FBI investigation and wiretap confirmed the

*suspicion of espionage (they did not). Biddle had his own
reasons to suspect the loyalty of an employee of the isolationist
Times-Herald, so he willingly gave Hoover broad latitude.*

*While the Arvad wiretap failed to uncover her participation in
espionage, it did reveal a romantic liaison with navy Ensign
John F. Kennedy in Charleston, South Carolina. The Office of
Naval Intelligence had advised the FBI that Arvad and
Kennedy were having an affair, but Hoover demanded a discreet
investigation to uncover the nature of the relationship. He
stressed the delicacy of this operation in view of Arvad's
employment and the inevitable damage should this anti–New
Deal paper discover and publicize the FBI surveillance.*

*The FBI's Charleston office was cautious. Its head informed
Hoover that an FBI bug installed in the Arvad-Kennedy hotel
room during two weekend visits disclosed that they "engaged in
sexual intercourse on a number of occasions." Further, Arvad
had advised Kennedy during the second weekend visit that she
might be pregnant. Thus a "security" investigation had
uncovered evidence of illicit sexual activities.*

*The records of the FBI's surveillance of Arvad were originally
maintained in FBI assistant director Louis Nichols's office
file. By 1960, however, these records acquired a quite different
importance. On July 13, the date John Kennedy won the
Democratic presidential nomination, Hoover was briefed on
derogatory information of Kennedy's wartime affair with
Arvad. On July 14, 1960, the folder on the FBI's "espionage"
investigation of Arvad was immediately forwarded, on
Hoover's order, to his office file—a real-life confirmation of
Robert Ludlum's fictional account of Hoover's ability to use
such information.*

■ **Memo, SAC Washington S. K. McKee to FBI Director,
December 12, 1941**
On the afternoon of December 12, 1941, Mr. Frank Waldrop, Associate
Editor, Washington Times Herald, called at this office with Miss [name
withheld], a reporter of that paper, and Inga Arvad, columnist for the
Times Herald. . . . Mr. Waldrop stated that he had brought these two

young ladies to our office upon the instructions of Eleanor Patterson,
Editor in Chief, Washington Times Herald.

Briefly, Miss [name withheld], several days ago, stated to Miss Kathleen
Kennedy, a reporter of the Times Herald, and the daughter of former
Ambassador [Joseph] Kennedy, that she would not be surprised if Inga
Arvad was a spy for some foreign power . . . [and] that one of her friends
had been going through some old Berlin newspapers and had noted a
picture of Inga Arvad taken with Hitler at the [1936] Olympic games in
Berlin. This picture . . . bore a caption stating, in substance, that Miss
Inga Arvad of Copenhagen was doing work for the German propaganda
ministry. Miss Kennedy, a very close friend of Inga Arvad, told [Arvad] of
Miss [name withheld's] statements.

Miss Arvad then contacted Eleanor Patterson and complained about such
rumors. Eleanor Patterson was quite worried about this matter, stating to
Miss Arvad that it might reflect unfavorably upon the Times Herald, an
isolationist paper, if it became known that they had been employing a
person suspected of being a spy; however, Eleanor Patterson professed to
have complete faith in Miss Arvad and instructed Mr. Waldrop to take both
of the young women to the Federal Bureau of Investigation, so that a
complete report might be made.

Miss Arvad heatedly denied the accusations and professed to detest the
Germans. Miss Arvad stated that she wanted an investigation made and
then wanted a letter from the Federal Bureau of Investigation, stating that
she was not a spy. It was diplomatically pointed out to Mr. Waldrop and
Miss Arvad that this would be impossible and Mr. Waldrop stated that he
could understand our reasons for declining such a letter.

Mr. Waldrop stated that Inga Arvad has been an entirely satisfactory
employee; that she writes a small column for the Times Herald, consisting
almost entirely of what he termed "personal interest interviews" with
prominent persons in Washington, D.C. . . .

After giving the background of this matter, Mr. Waldrop left our office
and the two young ladies remained and were interviewed separately by
Agent [C. A.] Hardison. . . . [During their separate interviews, the two
reporters repeated the above account, Arvad explaining that her earlier
contacts with Hitler and other Nazi officials were in her capacity as a
reporter for a Danish newspaper.]

The files of the Washington Field Office do not reflect any information
concerning Inga Arvad or Paul Fejos [her estranged husband]. . . .

■ **Personal and Confidential Letter, FBI Director J. Edgar Hoover
to SAC Washington S. K. McKee, December 24, 1941**
. . . This will confirm my instructions . . . to the effect that a discreet

investigation should be instituted to determine the truth of the allegations against Miss Arvad. It is suggested that the [phrase withheld] angle be followed through and that other sources which can be checked discreetly be run down along this same line. As of possible assistance, . . . a syndicated column in one of the local papers several weeks ago had an item to the effect that [Arvad] had at one time been Hitler's publicity agent.

I shall expect a report from you in this matter in the near future and wish to caution that should it be necessary to direct undeveloped leads to other [FBI] field offices, they be accompanied by appropriate advice as to the discreet nature of this investigation.

■ **Memo, FBI Liaison Agent George Burton to FBI Assistant Director D. Milton Ladd, January 17, 1942**
[FBI supervisor R. P.] Kramer advised the writer that information has come to the Bureau that Inga Arvad has been carrying on an affair with a young ensign of the United States Navy reported to be the son of the former American Ambassador to London, Joseph P. Kennedy. Mr. Kramer instructed the writer to discretely [sic] confer with ONI [Office of Naval Intelligence] and determine if this were true and if it were true to determine what action had been taken against the ensign. While discussing other matters with Lieutenant J. N. Horan [of ONI], I broached the subject casually. Lieutenant Horan . . . advised that it had come to ONI's attention that Ensign Kennedy had been "playing around" with Inga Arvad and that steps had been taken to put an end to this relationship. Lieutenant Horan stated that Kennedy would probably not be disenrolled but it was anticipated that he would be transferred out of Washington. . . .

■ **Memo, FBI Assistant Director D. Milton Ladd to FBI Director, January 17, 1942**
I thought you would be interested in the following information which has been developed in the investigation to date concerning [Inga Arvad]. . . . You will recall that the original information received in this case was an expression of suspicion . . . that Inga Arvad was engaged as a Nazi agent and that one [name withheld] had stated he had seen a picture of her posed with Adolf Hitler. . . . Mr. Waldrop subsequently furnished the picture which turned out to be a typical studio photograph posed alone by Miss Arvad. It was a Press Service picture which had been received from Europe and distributed through the International News Photos and bore the caption: "Copenhagen, Denmark . . . Meet Miss Inga Arvad, Danish beauty, who so captivated Chancellor Adolf Hitler during a visit to Berlin that

he made her Chief of Nazi Publicity in Denmark. Miss Arvad had a colorful career as a dancer, movie actress and newspaper woman before Herr Hitler honored her for her 'perfect Nordic beauty'." This photograph was dated March 16, 1936. . . .

Continued inquiry developed that [Arvad's] husband [Paul Fejos] is the secretary of Axel Wenner-Gren, the well known Swedish financier. . . .

It appears that [Arvad's] mother has told other occupants of the apartment building that Inga Arvad intends to divorce Fejos and . . . it has been learned that two young men wearing the uniform of ensigns in the U.S. Navy call on [Arvad] fairly regularly and that one of them, whose identity has not been established as yet, apparently has intimate relations with her. There is some indication this latter individual may be the son of former Ambassador Joe Kennedy and this is being checked at the present time.

The field offices have been instructed to follow through on all pertinent leads expeditiously and particularly to cover the matter of the Naval ensigns and several telephone calls to persons of Germanic sounding names in New York. I shall advise you immediately of further developments of interest.

■ **Memo, FBI Director J. Edgar Hoover to Attorney General Francis Biddle, January 21, 1942**

It is requested that authorization be granted to install a technical surveillance on the telephone of Mrs. Paul Fejos, nee Inga Arvad.

For your information [Arvad] is the wife of Paul Fejos, secretary of Axel Wenner-Gren, the Swedish financier, who has just recently been placed on the American black list. Mr. Fejos returned to the United States December 9, 1941, after having spent two years in Western Pan America in charge of a scientific expedition for Wenner-Gren.

It is further of interest to note that Mrs. Fejos, who is presently employed as a reporter by the Washington Times-Herald, was prior to her arrival in this country in February 1940, for several years a reporter for the Berlingske Tidens, a member of the Copenhagen press. A photograph has been located date lined Copenhagen, Denmark, but reportedly released from Berlin, Germany, under date of March 16, 1936, which depicts [Arvad] in a studio pose over the caption: "Meet Miss Inga Arvad, Danish beauty, who so captivated Chancellor Adolf Hitler during a visit to Berlin that he made her Chief of Nazi Publicity in Denmark."

In the current investigation of this woman as an espionage suspect, it has been determined that in the short period she has been in Washington, she has established close social and professional contacts with persons holding important positions in the Government departments and bureaus vitally concerned with the national defense, and in particular, has become very friendly with several Naval ensigns. It has been found that she is carrying on an affair with one such Naval officer who is a repeated visitor at her apartment, and it is reported that another man in a similarly commissioned position has indicated he is engaged to marry her. The combination of these facts indicates a definite possibility that she may be engaged in a most subtle type of espionage activities against the United States.

■ **Personal and Confidential Letter, FBI Director J. Edgar Hoover to SAC S. K. McKee, January 30, 1942**
     This is in reference to the [Arvad] case . . . in which you have previously been advised of my desire that it receive continuous attention and your close personal supervision. . . . I shall expect the Washington Field Office as office of origin to be fully cognizant of the potentialities involved here and handle the development of the facts accordingly. In order that the Bureau may be currently advised at all times, each office is instructed to submit reports not less frequently than weekly.

■ **Memo, FBI Assistant Director Edward Tamm to FBI Director, February 3, 1942**
     SAC McKee called . . . and advised that they are dealing with Mr. Rhea Whitley of ONI on [the Arvad] matter. He stated they have learned definitely that Jack Kennedy is the Naval Ensign [believed to be associating with Arvad]. I told Mr. McKee it was my understanding that Kennedy had been transferred to Charleston, South Carolina. Mr. McKee stated . . . that Kennedy is restricted to a 70 mile limit from his station down there but it looks as though Inga Arvad is going down there this coming weekend. . . .
     Mr. McKee stated that Mr. Whiteley has an interest in a microphone surveillance out there [in Charleston] if it is possible to have one set up. In answer to his inquiry as to what I thought about this I told him I could see no objection to it.

■ **Personal and Confidential Letter, SAC S. K. McKee to FBI Director Hoover, February 3, 1942**
     . . . At 10:18 p.m. [Arvad] received a call from "Jack" in Charleston, South Carolina, . . . this individual is probably the Naval Ensign referred to in previous reports in this case as "Jack" and who is apparently the

paramour of Miss Arvad. He is evidently Jack Kennedy, the son of former Ambassador Joseph P. Kennedy. . . .

They then had an argument as to whether she should come to Charleston or whether he should come to Washington for the following weekend and it was agreed that he would come to Washington this time inasmuch as she had made the last trip to see him. (Inasmuch as Miss Arvad was out of town on January 24, and 25, 1942, it is believed that she was probably with Jack in Charleston, South Carolina.) . . . Miss Arvad stated that in the event his work detained him in Charleston, that she would come down.

During the latter part of the conversation Miss Arvad inquired of him as to the date of his sailing and he stated that they were not sailing at any time in the immediate future. Miss Arvad told him that she didn't believe that he would tell her when he was going to sail, to which he replied that he would tell her as he had promised in the past. . . .

A copy of this letter is being furnished to the Savannah Field Division. . . . The Savannah Field Division is requested to make no further investigation concerning Kennedy other than to determine his name, due to his evident employment with the United States Navy. The purpose of this inquiry should be merely to establish his identity. . . .

■ **Transcript, Wiretap Conversation, Inga Arvad and John Kennedy, February 3, 1942, 11:00 PM**

. . . Kennedy: I have been trying to get away from here this weekend.

Arvad: You can't.

Kennedy: You must get permission to go more than 70 miles from Charleston. My commanding officer lives in the same house. Why don't you come here?

Arvad: I may.

Kennedy: Don't say you may. I know I shouldn't ask you to come here twice in a row but I'll be up there as soon as I get permission.

Arvad: Isn't that sweet. I'll come maybe.

Kennedy: I hate for you to come all this way just to see me.

Arvad: Darling, I would go around the world 3 times just to see you.

Kennedy: I heard you had a big orgy up in New York.

Arvad: I'll tell you about it. I'll tell you about it for a whole weekend if you like to hear about it. My husband has his little spies out all over the place.

Kennedy: Really.

Arvad: No, he doesn't. But he told me all sorts of things about you, none of which were flattering. He knew every word you had said to your Father about me. It made me look like ——, it amused me very much.

Kennedy: What does he mean by "every word I said to my Father about you."

Arvad: Somebody who knows your family well and also knows my husband but I don't know who it is. The person had known you since you were a child and I think they live in New York.

Kennedy: What about it?

Arvad: He said, "JACK KENNEDY shrugged his shoulders and said I wouldn't dream of marrying her. She's just something I picked up on the road." It's very amusing, darling. Tell me, when are you going away?

Kennedy: I'm not leaving for quite a while yet. What all did your husband say?

Arvad: Why, he said I could do what I wanted. He said he was sad to see me doing things like this. I'll tell you about it and I swear that he is not bothering us and that you need not be afraid of him. He is not going to sue you though he is aware what he could do by suing you. . . . Do you want me to come this weekend very much.

Kennedy: I would like you to.

Arvad: I'll think it over and let you know. So long my love.

Kennedy: So long.

■ **Personal and Confidential Letter, SAC Washington S. K. McKee to FBI Director, February 5, 1942**

This is to advise that on the morning of February 5, 1942, at 9:45 A.M., I telephonically contacted Special Agent in Charge J. R. Ruggles of the Savannah Field Division, advising him that . . . Inga Arvad would leave Washington, D.C., via the Atlantic Coast Line Railroad at 7:05 P.M., for Charleston, South Carolina, where she will arrive at 8:30 A.M. on the following morning, February 6, 1942.

Mr. Ruggles was advised that the Bureau had instructed that a 24 hour, very discreet surveillance be maintained on Inga Arvad at all times. In this connection, it was emphasized that the utmost discretion should be used, and that the surveillance was to be dropped if there was any indication that it was being made.

Mr. Ruggles was further advised that permission had been granted by [FBI assistant director] E. A. Tamm of the Bureau for a technical surveillance, and it was suggested to the Savannah Field Division that if their previous contacts with the Fort Sumter Hotel in Charleston (where Arvad indicated she would stay) were of such a nature that their discretion could be relied upon, that perhaps Miss Arvad could be given a room where arrangements had been made for such a confidential coverage.

Advice was also furnished that . . . Arvad would remain in Charleston, Friday, Saturday and Sunday. This [wiretap of Arvad's Washington, D.C., residence] and others [sources] have indicated that she is "having an affair" with John Kennedy . . . and further, that Kennedy would contact her at the Fort Sumter Hotel after 4:00 P.M. on Friday, when he finished work for the weekend at the Charleston Navy Yard. . . .

Mr. Ruggles was informed that in Washington, the Office of Naval Intelligence was interested in this matter, and has been cooperating with the FBI on a 24 hour surveillance. . . . Mr. Ruggles was advised that the Office of Naval Intelligence in Washington was not aware of the technical surveillance on Arvad, with the exception of the supervising officer in Washington, formerly a Special Agent in Charge with the Bureau, and who has stated that he would not let this information leak out.

The Savannah Field Division was instructed that this was an investigation of Inga Arvad, and not of John Kennedy, whose activities as a Naval Ensign are not within the investigative jurisdiction of the FBI. . . .

To emphasize the degree of discretion necessary in this investigation, . . . Miss Arvad is a close personal friend and protege of Miss Eleanor (Cissie) Patterson, owner of the Washington Times-Herald, and from an editorial which appeared in the Times-Herald, evidently written by Miss Patterson, a striking analogy was drawn between a fictitious person in the Times-Herald with a person evidently Miss Arvad, in which Miss Patterson set out that probably the career of such a person would be ruined if an indiscreet investigation were conducted of her by the FBI. From this association, it is believed that the Times-Herald would be quick to expose any investigation of the FBI. . . .

■ **Memo, FBI Assistant Director D. Milton Ladd to FBI Director, February 6, 1942**
I thought you would be interested to know that through the surveillance now in use on [Arvad], it has been determined that Jack Kennedy, the son of former Ambassador Joseph P. Kennedy, is the individual to whom she is supposed to be engaged and who has apparently been the ensign observed leaving her apartment in the morning on several occasions after having been there with her all night. He is now stationed at Charleston, South Carolina and she has been there at least once to visit him.

It has also been developed that [Arvad] visited her husband in New York apparently to arrange with him for her to secure a divorce. Subsequently, in a conversation with Jack Kennedy concerning her husband's reactions in this matter, it transpired that young Kennedy had discussed her with his father in a manner she felt indicated her to be immoral. In another conversation, Arvad accused young Kennedy of telling someone that he had no intentions of marrying her, that it was merely a passing incident.

As you will recall, Arvad is a close friend of Jack Kennedy's sister,

Kathleen, but it has been indicated that their father would probably be opposed to Jack's marriage to Arvad should she divorce Fejos since he is known to be a very strict adherent to his religion.

■ **Memo, FBI Assistant Director D. Milton Ladd to FBI Assistant Director Edward Tamm, February 6, 1942**
SAC McKee of the Washington Field Office informed me . . . that the Savannah Office put the microphone surveillance into effect yesterday. It has been ascertained that Inga Arvad was at Charleston, South Carolina on January 24 and 25, 1942, using the name Barbara White, and she is using that name again. . . .

With regard to the technical equipment which is being installed by the Washington Field Office relative to this case, Mr. McKee advised that they have made the portion of the installation in Arvad's apartment, they have made the hookups throughout the building, and all they have to do now is put the other end in and they will be ready to operate.

■ **Personal and Confidential Report of Special Agent Savannah Office to Washington Office, February 9, 1942.**
Synopsis of facts:
Surveillance maintained upon [Arvad] from the time of her arrival in Charleston, S.C. at 8:20 A.M. on 2-6-42 until her departure therefrom on 2-9-42 at 1:09 A.M. to return to Washington, D.C. While there, John Kennedy, Ensign U.S. Navy, spent each night with subject in her hotel room at the Fort Sumter Hotel, engaging in sexual intercourse on numerous occasions. . . . Only information gained by [Arvad] of possible espionage value, fact that Kennedy proceeding to Norfolk, Va. soon for training, fire control work, also serious illness of Harry Hopkins, Presidential Advisor. . . .

At Charleston, South Carolina
At 8:20 A.M. on February 6, 1942, [Arvad] arrived at the Union Station in Charleston, South Carolina, where she was met by John Kennedy. . . . Mrs. Fejos registered at the Fort Sumter Hotel approximately at 8:55 A.M., on the same date as her arrival, using the name Barbara White. A twenty-four hour surveillance was maintained from that point on until the subject departed from Charleston. . . .

From a strongly confidential source [a bug in their hotel room], a great deal of the conversation which passed between [Arvad] and Kennedy in the hotel room was obtained. The majority of this conversation was of little interest in this particular case. . . .

Shortly prior to subject's departure on the evening of February 8, Kennedy made out a check payable to [Arvad] in an amount which could not be ascertained. After he made out this check, he asked [Arvad] if it were sufficient, to which she replied in the affirmative. From this same [microphone installation] it was determined that Kennedy and Mrs. Fejos engaged in sexual intercourse on a number of occasions from February 6, 1942, until February 9, 1942. Kennedy spent the nights of February 6, 7, and 8th in the subject's hotel room, staying all night there after she had left for Washington D.C., as set out above.

The only information pertaining to Kennedy's official movements that was obtained from their conversation was the fact that he expected to go to Norfolk, Virginia within the next four or five days for a period of three weeks to study fire control. She did not press him further as to his future plans, or for any information concerning the movements of any vessels belonging to the United States Navy. As to her movements, she stated that she was going to return to Washington to go back to work and was seriously considering going to Reno to get a divorce from her present husband and marry Kennedy. . . .

■ **FBI Wiretap Summary, John Kennedy to Inga Arvad, February 17, 1942, 11:00 P.M.**

Jack Kennedy, Charleston, S.C., contacted Arvad. . . . She asked for news about his week-end. . . . She asked when he expects to leave . . . and he thought he would be stuck in Charleston for some time—remarking that all of his plans seem to fall through. She called him Honey, Darling, Honeysuckle, Honey Child Wilder, and said "I love you." . . . She asked about the church stuff and he said he talked to a Priest about it and has written for a book to see if he is right. . . . He asked when she is coming back (to Charleston), and she said "in 3 or 4 months—or when you really want me very much to come." He said that is now. . . . They talked again about where he was going, . . . and she wanted to know why the Singapore trip went down the drain, and if "Big Joe" couldn't help him get it. He said when he learned about it it was all over, but he tried to call him (his Father) tonight but he wasn't in. He said he was to have left in a couple of weeks. He applied for transfer but fears he can't get it for six months. . . . He wants very much to see her. She may go down soon but they will make arrangements later. . . .

2-16-42
11:35 P.M.
. . . [Kennedy] asked [Arvad] to come down as soon as possible and she agreed to do so this weekend, and she promised to let him know about all her plans. She said she might fly down and will decide after counting her money.

2-16-42
11:40 P.M.
Arvad reserved Lower 5, Car R53, on Atlantic Coast Line train leaving Washington Friday 2/20/42 at 7:05 P.M. going to Charleston, S.C., and asked them to get similar accommodations on train leaving Charleston on Sunday, 2/22/42 at 1:09 P.M. for Washington. . . .

■ **Personal and Confidential Letter, SAC Savannah J. R. Ruggles to FBI Director, February 23, 1942**
. . . From a strictly confidential source [bug], of which the Bureau has been previously advised, a great deal of conversation which passed between [Arvad] and Kennedy in the hotel room was obtained. It was learned that the subject was quite worried about becoming pregnant as a result of her two previous trips to Charleston, and she spoke of the possibility of getting her marriage annulled. It was noted that Kennedy had very little comment to make on the subject. . . .

From the same confidential source mentioned above, it was learned that [Arvad] and Kennedy engaged in sexual intercourse on a number of occasions; that he spent the nights of February 20 and 21 with the subject in room 926 at the Francis Marion Hotel, and that he remained in this room on the night of February 22, 1942 after [Arvad] had departed for Washington on Sunday morning, February 22, 1942. . . .

On the same evening, [Arvad] and Kennedy had another discussion in regard to her worries over becoming pregnant. She accused Jack of "Taking every pleasure of youth but not the responsibility." . . .

Just before [Arvad] left on the night of February 22, 1942, she asked Kennedy if he would tell her when he left the country, stating she did not believe he would tell her. He replied, "Why wouldn't I tell you" and she then stated "I don't know, maybe you would. You wouldn't tell me ahead of time, you would tell me when you left." . . .

Under separate cover there is being forwarded to the Bureau recordings which were made of the conversations between [Arvad] and Kennedy in room 926 at the Francis Marion Hotel.

Particular attention is called to records 8 and 9 which contain the telephone conversation between Kennedy to the home of Joseph P. Kennedy on the night of February 22, 1942.

■ **Memo, FBI Assistant Director D. Milton Ladd to FBI Assistant Director Edward Tamm, March 2, 1942**

SAC McKee of the Washington Field Office telephonically contacted me, advising that the information which has been obtained from the maintenance of the technical surveillance on Inga Arvad indicates that she is aware of at least part of the surveillance which is being maintained on her, and it appears that she obtained this information from ONI. . . .

Mr. McKee suggested in view of the fact that Arvad is apparently aware that a surveillance is being maintained of her that the microphone be removed from her room as soon as possible. Mr. McKee stated that there is no way in which the technical surveillance can be traced. I told Mr. McKee this would be advisable, that a physical surveillance should be placed on Arvad and then when the opportunity presents itself the microphone should be removed from her room.

Mr. McKee stated that the only person in ONI with whom he had discussed this surveillance was Rhea Whitley; and he inquired if he should talk to Whitley for the purpose of finding out if Whitley had discussed this matter with anyone else. I told Mr. McKee that he should not talk to Whitley about this matter, that we would handle it at the Bureau.

Mr. McKee mentioned the fact that Arvad will leave soon for Reno. He stated that he would send to the Bureau immediately, marked for my attention, the log which was maintained of the technical surveillance on Arvad. . . .

[Hoover's handwritten note: "I think for time being we should discontinue." FBI supervisor J. K. Mumford's handwritten note: "SAC McKee was instructed by Mr. Tamm—see (indecipherable) memo."]

■ **Personal and Confidential Letter, SAC Washington S. K. McKee to FBI Director, March 5, 1942**

. . . On February 25, 1942, at 9:41 A.M., Inga [Arvad] told Kathleen Kennedy . . . she might go down [to Charleston] to see Jack soon. Inga stated she would probably see Jack on the weekend of March 6, 1942, and go from there to Reno.

At 10:45 A.M., on February 25, 1942, Inga made a reservation on the Eastern Airlines 3:45 P.M., plane March 6, 1942, for Charleston, South Carolina. . . .

At 9:49 A.M., [February 27] Inga sent the following telegram: "Ensign John F. Kennedy, District Security Building, Charleston, South Carolina. Working Saturday. If possible flying to Charleston Friday, sixth. Love, Barbara."

At 9:59 A.M., Inga conversed with her mother . . . about her visit with

Paul [Fejos] and emphasized the fact that her husband, Paul, had been so terribly sweet when she saw him in New York City. She added that Paul was going to give her $730 with which to get the divorce. . . .

At 11:50 P.M., on [March 1], Inga conversed with Dr. Paul Fejos, New York City, and . . . remarked "I hear that our friends, those that have been looking for me the whole time, you know whom I mean, they are still on my trail. Very much so apparently. I hear they have a dictaphone in my room. I hope they have so they can listen to my interesting conversations." Dr. Fejos advised, "Don't be listening to such silly talk." Inga, "That is what I hear and from very reliable sources on account of my attachment to the Naval Intelligence Service. So I'm quitting that acquaintance." Fejos, "What? I don't get that." Inga, "I am not going to see that person anymore. I'm tired of all that nonsense. I want some peace for God's sake." Fejos, "What happened?" Inga, "Nothing happened. I just made up my mind. You know how I function." (From the fact that this technical has indicated that Inga Arvad, up until the time of this conversation, was apparently madly in love with Jack Kennedy and was planning to go to Reno to divorce Dr. Fejos so she could marry him. Due to the fact that Jack Kennedy had left town only one hour previously after having seen Inga Arvad, it is believed Jack Kennedy had broken off relations with Inga Arvad, giving the reason that some friend of his, probably the Naval Intelligence, had told Kennedy the Naval authorities were watching him and apparently had a microphone in her room. This seemingly was the reason given by Jack in breaking off these relations with Inga.) . . .

■ **Transcript, Wiretap Conversation, John Kennedy to Inga Arvad, March 6, 1942, 10:15 PM**

Kennedy: Surprised to hear from me?

Arvad: A little maybe.

Kennedy: It's about time.

Arvad: Kathleen [Kennedy] says everyday that yoy [sic] will call me.

Kennedy: I have been in bed with a bad back. . . . What did you decide?

Arvad: I don't do anything more. . . . I talked to Frank Waldrop and told him that I was going to Nevada. He said that . . . it will be all right for me to go as soon as I am 2 weeks ahead. I called up Eastern Airlines today and cancelled my reservation to Charleston.

Kennedy: Why didn't you come?

Arvad: What a question. Don't you remember that we talked it over Sunday? . . . You're not giving up what we promised last Sunday, are you?

Kennedy: No, not till the next time I see you. I'm not too good, am I?

Arvad: I think you're perfect, dear. We'll probably meet again.

Kennedy: You mean, next week.

Arvad: I'm not coming. I don't know. I'm not trying to be stubborn. I'm only trying to help you. You know that, don't you. . . . Did you think I was coming to Charleston?

Kennedy: I had big hopes. . . . All that talk you hear but I don't know anything about it. All this gab going around.

Arvad: You don't think they're trying to scare you. That's what I think. Personally, I think it is coming from Miami Beach [Joseph Kennedy].

Kennedy: I talked to him Sunday night and he spoke to me about it. He said he got the report. He said . . . things aren't quite right up there. I said I didn't believe that. He said he was just telling me what he heard.

Arvad: What is it they say?

Kennedy: I guess the thing isn't quite O.K. for some reason. You are mixed up in something.

Arvad: I wonder what it is?

Kennedy: It's probably me but I don't know. Evidently you got something. You're not holding out on me, are you?

Arvad: You know that I'm not, don't you?

Kennedy: I'm quite sure of it. I don't know. It might have been something you said. . . .

Arvad: But what could the conversation be about except you and me? There's nothing illegal that they can put their hands on. What's illegal about being in love?

Kennedy: But maybe there is some background on you. You can see that.

Arvad: Yes I can. Then it would be much better for me to get a divorce because the only thing they have on me is that my husband works for Wenner-Gren.

Kennedy: I think that would be about the best subject—they can always say, well that da da da. I wouldn't get it for that reason. . . . It's up to you whether you get. I don't want to influence on you in any way in getting it.

Arvad: That's childish. I'm still going to get it [a divorce] and we decided not to see each other anymore, didn't we. So what do you have to do with it. . . . I'll do it because I want to do it. Have you any doubts?

Kennedy: My point is that you hadn't hesitated on account of me.

Arvad: That's not the point, what are you afraid of? . . .

Kennedy: You just go ahead and keep me posted. You'll probably be seeing me as soon as you get back.

Arvad: I think so. I hope so. . . . I don't think things are at all like you think. I am going to see [FBI Director] Hoover. I made an appointment for Monday.

Kennedy: What did they say to you?

Arvad: I talked to Miss Gandhi [sic, Helen Gandy], his private Secretary, and she said "Howdy do Miss Arvad, it is very nice to talk to you again. How are you?"

Kennedy: Did she ask what you wished to see Mr. Hoover about?

Arvad: No. I said I would like to see Mr. Hoover for a few minutes and she said delighted.

Kennedy: What are you going to say to him?

Arvad: I'm going to say "Now look here Edgar J., I don't like everybody listening in on my phone." You know that somebody is always listening in on this phone.

Kennedy: How do you know?

Arvad: Why on earth does it always cut. Don't you notice when we talk there is some cut in it. We were cut off for a fraction of a second . . . and the same thing happened when I just talked to New York.

Kennedy: They must have little to do if they are listening to us. They must have had a pretty dull week.

Arvad: If they listen to us, then yes. I'm going to tell him that I would like to know a little bit about the whole thing myself because I hear nothing but a fantastic amount of rumors from everybody and I am after all, the chief actress in the play.

Kennedy: Do you think he'll tell you?

Arvad: I think so. Why shouldn't he? I'll say it's spoiling my career here—which it is.

Kennedy: I guess nothing.

Arvad: Do you think I am going to hush you up—to try to catch you.

Kennedy: Yes.

Arvad: JACK!

Kennedy: I was just kidding.

Arvad: You know how I think about marrying you and everything like that.

Kennedy: Of course. But I was thinking you don't know about your job. Frank Waldrop might make [sic] up some morning and decide to cut that column out. There you would be—without a job and all these other things holding over. It's a point you have to consider.

Arvad: But as long as I am well I can get a job of some kind. I know that I will never go back to him [Paul Fejos].

Kennedy: I just wanted to be sure that this is what you want to do. From what you have said, I didn't have anything to do with you getting the divorce.

Arvad: You pushed the last stone under my foot but that doesn't hold you responsible for anything. Meeting you 2½ months ago was the chief thing that made up my mind. As far as I am concerned, you don't exist any more. That's how I felt an hour ago. I still love you as much as always and always will. But you don't figure in my plans whatsoever. . . . I'm still going to do it.

Kennedy: O.K.
Arvad: Drop me a line.
Kennedy: I will and I'll call you next week.

■ **Memo, FBI Assistant Director Edward Tamm to FBI Director, March 6, 1942**

I called SAC McKee of the Washington Field Office and instructed that all investigation and activity in connection with the [Arvad] matter, in Washington and elsewhere, cease. I asked that a closing report be submitted to the Bureau.

[Although Hoover had ordered the discontinuance of the FBI's wiretapping and bugging of Arvad's Washington residence on March 6, the FBI reinstalled this wiretap on May 4, 1942, at the request of President Roosevelt. This resumed investigation also uncovered no information suggesting that Arvad was engaged in espionage activity.]

INFORMATION ON KENNEDY'S affair with Inga Arvad, and other political activities, did not simply repose in FBI files. When Kennedy became the Democratic presidential nominee, FBI officials summarized the personal and political information that had been collected on him—and the next day Hoover ordered the Arvad folder transferred to his office file.

■ **Summary Memo, FBI Supervisor Milton Jones to FBI Assistant Director Cartha DeLoach, July 13, 1960**

. . . The purpose of this memorandum is to briefly summarize high lights of pertinent available information concerning Senator John F. Kennedy and his favorable attitude toward the Bureau in connection with the strong probability that he will be nominated as the Democrat candidate for the Presidency. [Indeed, Kennedy won the nomination that very day, July 13.] . . .

Friendly relations with Bureau:

The Bureau and the Director have enjoyed friendly relations with Senator Kennedy and his family for a number of years. . . .

West Virginia Primary Elections:
In connection with the recent hotly contested primary elections in West Virginia, several charges of improper actions were made to the Bureau, including allegations that votes were bought, that a polling place in Logan County was moved to prevent qualified West Virginians from voting, and that voting officials in Logan County pulled voting machine levers for local citizens. With regard to Senator Kennedy's religion, improperly labeled anti-Catholic literature was distributed by a nonexistent organization called the "Protestant Information Center."

Political Views:
In a syndicated column datelined Washington, D.C., 1-14-57, Fulton Lewis, Jr., described Kennedy as "conscientious and sincere" in his Senate duties and stated, "Kennedy tempers his political liberalism with enough realistic conservatism that the Walter Reuther–Americans for Democratic Action leftists mistrust his independence. . . ."

The 6-30-59 issue of "The Washington Post and Times-Herald" contained an article reflecting that Senator Kennedy urged "swift repeal of the loyalty oath requirement of the National Defense Education Act." This Act required students getting a Federal scholarship loan to sign a loyalty oath. . . .

In connection with civil rights matters, Senator Kennedy has been particularly interested in Federal legislation to curb bombings of religious and educational institutions. In 86th Congress he was cosponsor of Kennedy-Ervin Bill designed to deal with hate bombings whose provisions were substantially the same as bombing provisions of Civil Rights Act of 1960 which has increased FBI jurisdiction in this field. . . .

With regard to subversive matters, it is interesting to note that in March, 1960, Governor Wesley Powell of New Hampshire (a staunch Nixon supporter) accused Senator Kennedy of "softness toward communism." Kennedy called upon the Vice President to repudiate Powell's accusation, and Nixon's press representative issued a statement in Washington saying "the Vice President has known and worked with Senator Kennedy since they served together on the House Labor Committee in 1947. While they have differences on some issues, they have always been in complete agreement in their unalterable opposition to communism at home and abroad." . . .

Miscellaneous:
As you are aware, allegations of immoral activities on Senator Kennedy's part have been reported to the FBI over the years. These allegations are not being treated in detail in this memorandum. They include, however, data reflecting that Kennedy carried on an illicit relationship with another man's wife [Inga Arvad] during World War II; that (probably in January, 1960) Kennedy was "compromised" with a woman in Las Vegas; and that Kennedy and Frank Sinatra have in the recent past been involved

in parties in Palm Springs, Las Vegas and New York City. Regarding the Kennedy-Sinatra information, "Confidential" magazine is said to have affidavits from two mulatto prostitutes in New York.

Allegations also have been received concerning hoodlum connections of Senator Kennedy. Again, in the interest of brevity, no effort is being made to list these allegations in full detail—much of the information being unsubstantiated. [Four lines withheld on personal privacy grounds.]

Regarding Kennedy's book, "Profiles in Courage," [syndicated columnist] George Sokolsky advised [FBI assistant director] L. B. Nichols in May, 1957, of a rumor circulating in New York to the effect that Arthur Krock actually wrote the book. According to Sokolsky, a group of New York people were attempting to verify whether Krock did, in fact, write the book—and if Krock did, they were going to charge fraud in connection with the awarding of a Pulitzer Prize to Kennedy. . . .

(It is reiterated that the above is not a complete summary of all information in Bufiles concerning Senator Kennedy. It is, instead, a summary of high lights of pertinent available data—with particular regard to recent information and material concerning his relationship with and views toward the Bureau.)

■ **Memo, FBI Supervisor H. N. Bassett to FBI Assistant Director Nicholas Callahan, February 13, 1975**
An article on page A1 of the 2/7/75 issue of the Washington Star-News stated Charles W. Colson, former [Nixon] White House Aide, appeared on NBC's "Today" program on 2/7/75. He stated while he was a White House aide the FBI furnished extensive information to the [Nixon] White House in 1971 or 1972 concerning former President John F. Kennedy while he was a United States Navy Lieutenant during WW II. It concerns information picked up while the FBI was investigating a female Nazi agent. "Lieutenant Kennedy was being followed by FBI Agents." Colson characterized the data as "personal gossip." . . .

Background
The case file captioned "Mrs. Paul Fejos, nee Inga Arvad; Internal Security-Espionage-G" concerns our investigation of . . . [Inga Arvad] and apparently is the matter referred to by Colson. . . . It is believed the entire file was maintained in [FBI assistant director Louis] Nichols' office as routing slips dated 4/16/42 and 5/7/42 indicate. The file was probably sent to the Director's office in July, 1960, as exhibits to this file were sent to Miss Gandy of the Director's office on 7/14/60. Almost all correspondence in this file was marked "Personal and Confidential." . . .

A complete review of the above file fails to indicate any data concerning

John F. Kennedy's affair with Mrs. Fejos in 1942 was ever disseminated by the FBI either orally or by memorandum to anyone at anytime including the White House in 1971 or 1972 as implied by Mr. Colson. . . .

[The above conclusion was based simply on the *absence* of any record reporting that information on Kennedy's affair was disseminated outside the Bureau. Because the Arvad investigation documents were tightly held separate from other FBI "espionage" investigation records—between 1942 and 1960 in Nichols's confidential office file, and after July 14, 1960, in Hoover's office—Colson could only have learned of this affair from senior FBI officials. It is unlikely that a record of this briefing would have been created.]

WHILE THE DEROGATORY information about John Kennedy's 1942 affair with Inga Arvad had been incidentally obtained, Hoover was nonetheless keenly interested in such information, even if it was mere rumor or unsubstantiated allegation. As Milton Jones's July 13, 1960, memorandum confirms, after Kennedy became a prominent politician Hoover maintained in his office whatever derogatory information the FBI was able to collect on Kennedy, first as a U.S. senator and then after his election to the presidency. To service the director's interest, FBI officials willingly accepted information from interested citizens, attempted to confirm the more damaging allegations, and through the Bureau's own resources (including wiretaps) acquired additional information about Kennedy's alleged personal indiscretions.

The following documents both confirm this interest and offer insights into how Hoover safeguarded his interest and then, when convenient and safe, used such damaging information. On receipt of derogatory information, FBI agents were invariably directed to run down rumors and allegations, and to confirm or refute the charge (for example, the allegation of Kennedy's "marriage" to Durie Malcolm). This activity and attendant interest were closely guarded—Hoover wanted no one to learn that the FBI was in the business of collecting and

*investigating charges of personal misconduct. Yet at times he
alerted President Kennedy (either indirectly through his brother,
the attorney general, or directly to the president or White
House aides) that the FBI had received derogatory personal
information. He did so, however, only when no question
could be raised about how the FBI came to have such
information.*

*Hoover was an astute bureaucrat who recognized that a direct
attempt at blackmail could compromise his tenure as director.
So he volunteered information only after it was already public
(thus the belated timing of his briefing of Kennedy on the
Durie Malcolm allegation and on Florence Kater's charges) or
had been obtained incidental to a wiretap installed during an
authorized criminal investigation (such as the information
involving Kennedy's contacts with Judith Campbell, obtained
through a wiretap on organized crime leader John Roselli). A
sophisticated blackmailer, Hoover only hinted at the FBI's
ability to monitor personal misconduct. When he was moved to
use such information (as in the case of the oral briefing of
the Nixon White House in 1971 about Kennedy's affair with Inga
Arvad), he did so in such a manner that his actions could not
be documented.*

■ **Memo, FBI Assistant Director Cartha DeLoach to FBI Assistant
Director John Mohr, April 19, 1960**

Mr. James Dowd, Departmental Attorney who has been handling the
[James] Hoffa case in Florida, dropped by yesterday and . . . passed along
the following information concerning Senator Kennedy on a strictly confidential basis:

Dowd said that in July 1959, prior to leaving his practice in West
Orange, New Jersey, he had met [name and title withheld] . . . [who had]
expressed great concern over Senator Kennedy's presidential aspirations.
He said he felt Kennedy was extremely vulnerable and had shown "damn
poor judgment." [Two lines withheld on grounds of personal privacy.]
[Name withheld] said he was checking offices in the Senate Building one
night and noted on the top of Kennedy's desk a photograph openly
displayed. This photo included Senator Kennedy and other men, as well as
several girls in the nude. It was taken aboard a yacht or some type of

pleasure cruiser. [Name withheld] told Dowd that the thing that disturbed him was that the Senator would show such poor judgment in leaving the photo openly displayed and said that other members of the guard and cleaning forces were aware of the photograph and that Kennedy's "extra-curricular activities" were a standard joke around the Senate Office Building. . . .

■ **Airtel, SAC Los Angeles to FBI Director, April 1, 1960**
[The FBI withheld the contents of this one-page message on grounds of personal privacy, FBI sources and methods, and information related solely to the FBI's internal personnel practices. The message reported that an FBI informer in organized crime had learned that *Confidential* magazine had a copy of an affidavit of two mulatto prostitutes reporting on a party they had attended in New York at which Frank Sinatra and John Kennedy were present. In their affidavit, the prostitutes had expressed concern about Kennedy's sexual activities.]

■ **Airtel, SAC New Orleans Bachman to FBI Director, March 23, 1960**
[An individual being recruited by the New Orleans office as a criminal informant] furnished the following information:
[Five and one-half lines withheld on personal privacy grounds] he has met a number of well known hoodlums, such as Meyer Lansky, whom he described as a gambler operating in Miami and Havana, Cuba, and Joe Fischetti, Aka. Joe Fish, who [name withheld] believes is the dominant figure in the racketeering element in the Miami area. [Name withheld] claims that as a result of his contacts with these individuals, he has met socially a number of their associates, whose identities are not known to him, and whom he has not sought to identify, feeling that inquisitiveness on his part might be detrimental to his relationship with [name withheld].
In this connection, [name withheld] stated that on occasions he has overheard conversations between these individuals concerning their activities, . . . that he has never exhibited any inquisitiveness concerning these conversations because he felt "it would not be healthy for him." [Name withheld] related that within the past week he has returned from the Miami area and while there he learned from individuals, whom he declines to identify, but whom he claims are members of the underworld element, that Fischetti and other unidentified hoodlums are financially supporting and actively endeavoring to secure the nomination for the Presidency as democratic candidate, Senator John F. Kennedy. He stated as evidence of

this fact, Frank Sinatra is going to campaign for Kennedy in several of the primaries. . . . Sinatra is only booked to appear after clearance is obtained with Fischetti.

He advised that in addition to Sinatra, a song writer named Jimmy Van Husen is in Miami writing campaign songs for Kennedy. . . . [Name withheld] stated that it is his opinion that Sinatra and Van Husen are being made available to assist Senator Kennedy's campaign whereby Fischetti and other hoodlums will have an entre to Senator Kennedy. . . .

[Name withheld] stated when in Miami he had occasion to overhear a conversation which indicated that Senator Kennedy had been compromised with a woman in Las Vegas, Nevada. He stated that he knows that Senator Kennedy was staying at the Sands Hotel in Las Vegas about 6 or 8 weeks ago. . . . He stated that he observed Senator Kennedy in the night club of the Sands Hotel, during this period, but has no idea as to the identity of any possible female companion. He stated that when Senator Kennedy was in Miami, Fla., an airline hostess named [name withheld] who is a native of [city and state withheld] was sent to visit Sen. Kennedy. He stated that he learned this from an airline hostess whom he did not want to involve and whom he declined to identify. He stated that he had no idea of the date Sen. Kennedy was in Florida.

[Name withheld] stated that all of the above information has come from members of the hoodlum element he has met and their associates. . . . He stated that there is no way he can check the accuracy of this information as he is afraid to ask questions of any of these individuals, but he believes that this information is correct. [Name withheld] said that he was considerably disturbed when he learned this information, as he would hate to see a pawn of the hoodlum element such as Sinatra have access to the White House.

Although it is realized that the above information as furnished by PCI [potential criminal informant, name withheld] is to a great extent non-specific, it is being brought to the Bureau's attention in view of the prominence of Senator Kennedy. [Four lines withheld on personal privacy grounds.] Upon his return, [name withheld] will be followed closely to assure that any additional information received by him is made available to this office.

■ **Memo, FBI Assistant Director Cartha DeLoach to FBI Associate Director Clyde Tolson, June 10, 1959**
By letter of 6/4/59, the New York Office forwarded two letters which they had received from Stearn Publications, Inc., regarding [Senator] John F. Kennedy.

The letters in question, including a photograph, contain allegations regarding personal immorality on the part of Jack Kennedy. [In the letters, the writer, Florence Kater, charged that her photographing Kennedy leaving the apartment of his mistress had prompted Kennedy to threaten that her husband would be fired from his job.]

Apparently, this data has received rather widespread distribution—correspondent allegedly sent copies to "about thirty-five reporters."

Based on identifying data available, Florence Kater, who signed one of the letters, is not identifiable in Bufiles. Mrs. Kater indicates her husband is one Leonard Kater. In 1944 and 1945, we conducted an investigation of one Leonard Emil Kater who resided in Philadelphia and Washington. He was single at the time and had reportedly made pro-German remarks. No information of pertinency was developed, and under oath, Kater denied these allegations.

You will recall that some months ago, Luther Huston in the [Eisenhower Justice] Department said he had received from a reliable source information reflecting on Senator Kennedy's sex life. You will also recall that we have detailed and substantial information in Bufiles reflecting that Kennedy carried on an immoral relationship with another man's wife [Inga Arvad] during World War II.

Inasmuch as attached data has apparently received widespread distribution, it is recommended that copies of instant letters be brought to the attention of the Attorney General [William Rogers] for his information.

[Tolson's handwritten notation: "I see no need to refer this to A.G. (attorney general)." Hoover's handwritten notation: "I concur."]

■ **Registered Letter, Florence Kater to FBI Director J. Edgar Hoover, April 5, 1963**

I have personal knowledge and proof that Miss Pamela Turnure, press secretary in the White House to Mrs. John F. Kennedy, has an illicit sexual relationship with President John F. Kennedy.

Under the circumstances I feel it is in the national interest to call this matter to your attention as a very possible security risk. (enclosures) [The enclosures included a letter dated April 2, 1963, sent to Attorney General Robert Kennedy, numerous newspapers, syndicated columnist Drew Pearson, members of Congress, the Democratic and Republican national committees, and religious organizations, in which Kater claimed that President Kennedy was having an affair with Pamela Turnure and decried the press's refusal to report this affair.]

■ **Airtel, SAC Los Angeles to FBI Director, February 7, 1962**

. . . Sheila Lee Taylor [the subject of a white slave traffic investigation] interviewed in Los Angeles FBI Office 2/6/62 . . . [and] stated that [two names withheld individuals] had a suite of rooms at the Park Wilshire Hotel about the time of the [1960] Democratic Convention at Los Angeles. . . . Taylor, in her capacity as a Madam for [name withheld] sent prostitutes to [name withheld] after which she received telephone calls from these two individuals to send other girls to their associates whom she cannot identify. Taylor estimated that this occurred at a time just prior to the opening day of the Democratic Convention in Los Angeles in 1960. Taylor claims that either $200 or $300 was received by the two girls sent to [name withheld]. Taylor recalled that when Robert Kennedy and his wife moved into the Park Wilshire for the convention, [name withheld] and his staff then moved to the Biltmore Hotel in downtown Los Angeles, after which either [names withheld] called Taylor for more girls. Taylor accompanied five prostitutes to the Biltmore Hotel. She cannot recall the floor or the room number.

Taylor did recall that she and the girls ended up in the wrong suite of rooms after which they tricked the occupants of these rooms and then found [name withheld] and his party after which the five prostitutes turned their tricks then returned to the Park Wilshire Hotel. Taylor claims she does not recall the names of the girls she was using at this time.

During the course of the interview pertaining to [name withheld], Taylor remarked that she had heard rumors during the Democratic Convention that prostitutes had been obtained by [two names withheld] for parties thrown by them at which John F. Kennedy was alleged to have attended, but stated she had no further knowledge whatsoever along these lines. . . .

■ **Memo, FBI Assistant Director Courtney Evans to FBI Assistant Director Alan Belmont, February 12, 1962**

Kenneth O'Donnell at the White House was advised of the information which had been developed in [the Sheila Lee Taylor white slave traffic act] case particularly to allegations of Taylor and as to the furnishing of prostitutes to [name withheld] and his associates. O'Donnell advised that [name and title withheld] was in Los Angeles at the time of the Democratic Convention. O'Donnell could not identify the individual referred to as [name withheld] but was aware of the fact that [name withheld] had stayed at the Park Wilshire Hotel in Los Angeles. O'Donnell said he was most appreciative of being informed of the Taylor allegations and particularly since she is to testify on 2/13/62 in a state case wherein subjects are being tried on vice charges.

■ **Memo, FBI Assistant Director Courtney Evans to FBI Assistant Director Alan Belmont, March 20, 1962**

There is attached a restatement of information relating to telephone calls made to President's Secretary [Evelyn Lincoln] from Judith Campbell's Los Angeles residence.

This is being submitted as the Director may desire to bear this information in mind in connection with his forthcoming appointment [on March 22, 1962] with the President.

Enclosure Blind Memo Re Judith E. Campbell, March 20, 1962

Information has been developed that Judith E. Campbell, a free-lance artist has associated with prominent underworld figures Sam Giancana of Chicago and John Roselli of Los Angeles.

A review of telephone toll calls from Campbell's Los Angeles residence discloses that on November 7 and 15, 1961, calls were made to Evelyn Lincoln, the President's Secretary at the White House.

Telephone calls were charged to residence Campbell rented in Palm Springs, California, to Evelyn Lincoln at the White House on November 10, 1961, and November 13, 1961.

Campbell was also charged with a call to Mrs. Lincoln on February 14, 1962, from Cedars of Lebanon Hospital in Los Angeles, where Campbell was a patient at the time.

The nature of the relationship between Campbell and Mrs. Lincoln is not known.

[Name of FBI informer withheld] of questionable reputation, advised that he has seen Campbell with John Roselli. [Name withheld informer] referred to Campbell as the girl who was "shacking up with John Kennedy in the East."

[Hoover did brief President Kennedy about this matter on March 22 and also furnished this information to Attorney General Robert Kennedy.]

■ **Very Urgent Confidential Cablegram, FBI Legat, London Charles Bates to FBI Director, June 29, 1963**

[Paragraph withheld on grounds that information is national security classified but refers to recent disclosures involving British cabinet officer John Profumo's illicit sexual affair with Christine Keeler.] [Name withheld, but Maria Novotny] talked about President Kennedy and repeated a rumor that was going around New York that the President had many girl friends.

Complete report on interview presently being prepared and should be available to this office on Monday, July 1.

[Two lines withheld on grounds that information is national security classified.]

■ **Informal Memo, FBI Assistant Director Courtney Evans to FBI Assistant Director Alan Belmont, July 3, 1963**

The Attorney General was contacted and orally furnished the information which was received from a former informant, who is said to have received allegations from one [name withheld] to the effect that she has had illicit relations with highly placed governmental officials. It was stressed that the informant is of questionable reliability but that [two lines withheld on personal privacy grounds].

The AG [Attorney General Robert Kennedy] said he was appreciative of the Director's sending this information to him on a confidential basis, and that there always are allegations about prominent people that they are either homosexuals or promiscuous. It was noted the AG made particular note of [name withheld's] name. The AG was told that we propose to pursue this matter vigorously and he indicated his agreement with this course of action.

I also mentioned to the AG the information we had received from Los Angeles yesterday about [two lines withheld on personal privacy grounds]. The AG said he had always thought that [name withheld] was a motion picture actress, rather than a prostitute. I told him that, on the basis of Hollywood's moral reputation, this might be a question of semantics. He made note of the names and was informed that if we were able to secure any further information he would, of course, be advised.

The AG once again expressed his appreciation for the discreet manner in which this information was handled.

■ **Secret Memo, FBI Assistant Director Courtney Evans to FBI Assistant Director Alan Belmont, July 24, 1963**

The Attorney General was contacted last evening and orally advised of the information developed by the [phrase withheld on grounds information is national security classified but refers to British intelligence] that [name withheld] had lived with [Ellen Rometsch], a New York City call girl, and that one of her clients was alleged to be the then presidential candidate John F. Kennedy. He was further informed that Marie Novotny had allegedly gone to New York to take [Rometsch's] place, as she was traveling on pre-election rounds with the presidential candidate. As a matter of fact, Novotny did not enter the United States until December 14, 1960, nearly six weeks after the election.

The Attorney General was appreciative of our bringing this matter to his attention personally. He said it did seem preposterous that such a story would be circulated when a presidential candidate during the campaign travels with scores of newspapermen. He added that with the next presidential election now less than 18 months away, he anticipated there would be more similar stories and he would like for us to continue to advise him of any such matters coming to our attention on a personal basis, as he could better defend the family if he knew what was being said.

■ **Memo, SAC New York to FBI Director, November 13, 1961**

A rumor currently circulating in Brooklyn, New York, came to the attention of SA [special agent] Raymond T. Jackson who furnished the following information to the NYO [New York office]:

. . . Prior to his present marriage President John F. Kennedy had been married to a woman whose name was unknown but who was connected with a socially prominent family having the name of Blauvelt. The rumor, . . . alleges that the information is supported by an entry in a genealogy compiled by the Blauvelt family, a copy of which is available in the New York Public Library. In a private capacity and without identifying himself as a Bureau agent SA Jackson made inquiry at the NY Public Library concerning the Blauvelt study. He was advised that . . . a Photostat of certain pages were available to the general public. SA Jackson was able to see these Photostat copies and furnished to the NYO a brief description.

On 11/13/61, SA Charles W. Cavanaugh without identifying himself and in his private capacity proceeded to the Genealogy Section, . . . New York Public Library. . . . At this section a request was made for the Blauvelt Genealogy. SA Cavanaugh was advised that the Blauvelt Genealogy was at the binders and was not available. The clerk on duty suggested that if there were some specific information required the library might be able to assist in furnishing it. SA Cavanaugh advised the librarian that he had information that a Photostat had been prepared from the Blauvelt Genealogy and that he would like to review that Photostat. SA Cavanaugh was furnished a folder on the inside of which were stapled two Photostats purporting to be Photostats of pages 883 and 884 of the Blauvelt Genealogy. . . . Page 884 carries at the top of the page "Eleventh Generation." About half way down in the left hand column appears the following item: "(12,427) DURIE, (Kerr), MALCOLM, (Isabel O. Copper, 11304). We have no birth date. She was born Kerr, but took the name of her stepfather. She first married Firmin DesIoge, IV. They were divorced. Durie then married F. John Bersbach. They were divorced, and she married, third, John F. Kennedy, son of Joseph P. Kennedy, one time Ambassador to England. There were no children of the second or third marriages. . . ."

The above information is being furnished for the Bureau's information. The NYO intends to take no further action in this matter. Indices of the NYO contain no identifiable references to any of the individuals named in the genealogy.

■ **Personal and Confidential Memo, SAC New York to FBI Director, November 14, 1961**
[Name withheld, *Newark Star Ledger* reporter] made available the attached excerpts from what appears to be a genealogy of the Blauvelt family. . . .
[Name withheld reporter] said he was not going to publicize this information but he thought it was significant and that it should be called to the Bureau's attention. He did not advise where he had obtained the material, but he informed he knew of another person, unidentified, who had the information available, and he did not know whether or not the other person would attempt to publicize it. [Name withheld reporter] said he did not feel it would do the country any good to publicize the alleged first marriage. . . .

■ **Memo, FBI Director J. Edgar Hoover for Personal Files, November 22, 1961**
The Attorney General Robert Kennedy called and while talking to him I asked him if he had seen this thing being circulated about the first marriage of the President. The Attorney General stated he had. I advised him that it had come into the Bureau last week, a reprint of something. The Attorney General stated he had seen it and that a number of newspapermen have spoken to him about it. I remarked that they have apparently started wide circulation of it because it had come in here from three different sources.
The Attorney General stated that the fellow who put [this genealogy] together is dead, and the executor of the estate went through the material to find out where he got the information and all he found was a newspaper clipping saying the President had gone out with the girl. The Attorney General stated that the girl used to go out with his brother, Joe, and that the President, Jack, took her out once. He stated the newspaper people contacted the girl and, in fact, a lot of the facts regarding her were incorrect. I remarked it was a kind of smear. The Attorney General stated that as he had remarked, the fellow who put it together wrote it four or five years ago and is now dead, so they do not know what he intended. I stated what impressed me was that all of a sudden there is circulation of it. The

Attorney General stated the newspapermen come in and he tells them he hopes they print it because then "we" could all retire on what "we" collect.

I told the Attorney General that . . . apparently some individual is sending it out anonymously to people and that was what concerned me. The Attorney General expressed appreciation for my concern and said he supposed they will always come up with something. I stated I just wanted him to be alert to this.

■ **Memo, Legat Rome to FBI Director, January 30, 1961**

The January 31, 1961, issue of "Le Ore," a weekly magazine published in Turin, Italy, carries an article . . . [about] Alicia Purdom concerning her relations with President Kennedy in 1951.

The article (in Italian) states that she was engaged to President Kennedy and that she could have become the First Lady of America, except that the marriage was opposed on the basis of the fact that she is a Polish-Jewish refugee.

The article . . . also indicates that she is contemplating further releases in connection with her alleged relations with President Kennedy. . . .

Bureau is further requested to make available from the files any identifying data concerning [Alicia Purdom] which may be available. Further checks concerning her are being made in Italy since she is reported to have resided in Italy and to have indicated a desire to return to Italy.

[Hoover's handwritten notation: "Send memo to A. G. (attorney general)." Notation by unidentified FBI official: "Let to AG 2/6/61."]

■ **Memo, FBI Supervisor Milton Jones to FBI Assistant Director Cartha DeLoach, August 9, 1963**

On July 29, 1963, Senator [John] Tower called . . . to speak with someone [in the FBI] about a very unusual set of circumstances. . . .

Sometime during the third week of July (7-14–20) [Tower's administrative assistant H. Edward] Munden began to receive a series of telephone calls, allegedly from New York from an individual who would only identify himself as Robert Garden (phonetic). . . .

On July 22nd, . . . Senator Tower briefly spoke with Garden and thereafter directed that Munden should go to New York to meet with Garden . . . [who indicated] that his information concerns the indiscretions of "our foreign policy." No mention of the President's personal life was mentioned in these phone calls. . . . Munden reserved a room at the Waldorf and [met Garden]. . . .

Garden identified himself verbally as a private detective; . . . [and] was carrying a tan brief case from which he took some papers and gave them to Munden . . . [who] did not closely examine the documents especially so when he saw that they dealt with personal matters regarding the President and the Attorney General. The papers primarily consisted of what appeared to be legal documents in which an attorney (name unrecalled) was involved in a suit with a woman. The gist of the matter appeared to concern an affair between the President and a woman and as a result of which the woman became pregnant. This apparently occurred before his election. Munden did not observe whether this woman gave birth to the child and Garden did not volunteer the information. The type of suit involved was not evident to Munden nor could he recall how the President's name was set forth. Munden noted that as he scanned the papers, Garden was continuously talking, pointing out that he had done some work for the attorney and was paid a reasonable fee; however, he later learned that the attorney told everyone that he (Garden) received a much larger fee. . . . It appeared to Munden that Garden hoped to embarrass the attorney involved and . . . that Garden was hoping to receive some money for the papers.

Included in the documents was a photostat of a handwritten letter from the woman involved directed to the attorney in which it was stated that now that Mr. Kennedy has been elected President, "their" position was much better. Garden claimed to have compromising pictures and additional documents in safe deposit boxes in the midwest and west coast. . . .

Garden indicated that when the legal papers were filed, Attorney General Kennedy "got wind of it" and had representatives of his office "squash the entire matter." Garden claimed that the attorney was severely reprimanded for his part in the entire matter. Munden stated that as he perused the papers . . . it was quite obvious to him (Munden) that the entire supposed matter bore on the President's personal life and told Garden that he wanted nothing to do with such material. Garden was "strictly business" and when he realized that Munden meant what he said, he took the material and left. . . .

Munden at first declined to identify the supposed woman involved in the incident . . . [but eventually] identified the woman as the widow of a very high executive in the Singer Sewing Machine Company. He was not definitely sure of her name but thought it was Clark (phonetic). . . . This was all of the information [Munden] had regarding the contacts by Garden who has not called him since the meeting in New York City. . . . [But] should Garden again contact him he would immediately notify the Bureau. Munden . . . was at a loss as to why Garden continued to contact Senator Tower's Office other than the fact that Senator Tower has been rather outspoken on some phases of the present administration. . . . Munden . . .

has not discussed this matter with any one else other than Senator Tower and has not furnished the above information to the Attorney General's Office or the Secret Service.

The New York Office was directed to make a discreet check with the Division of Licenses, New York Police Department, . . . in an attempt to determine if Garden was a registered detective in New York. New York . . . checked several combinations of names . . . however were unable to identify Garden. A similar check with the Credit Bureau and State Division of Licenses met with negative results. . . . No contact was made with the Singer Sewing Machine Company. "Who's Who" reflects a Stephen Carlton Clark who is described as an industrialist and formerly on the Board of Directors at the Singer Manufacturing Company died 9-17-60. Bureau indices were checked under approximately 20 combinations of Garden . . . without identifying any logical suspects based on the limited identifying information.

Recommendation:

That in view of the nature of this information Assistant Director Evans verbally furnish it to Attorney General Kennedy.

[Hoover's handwritten notation: "No. Do so by memo to A.G."]

ADDENDUM, FBI Assistant Director Courtney Evans, August 9, 1963

This whole matter undoubtedly related to action taken by the State Court in New York in June, 1963, in censuring two veteran attorneys because of information contained in a Bill of Particulars filed in a suit for $1,200,000 by an attorney against Alicja Purdom Clark. Clark, the former wife of actor Purdom, married Alfred Clark, Singer Sewing Maching [sic] heir who died thirteen days later leaving her his $10,000,000 estate. We made inquiry concerning this matter in June on the basis of a report that [name withheld], a private detective in New York, had endeavored to sell these documents to James Hoffa.

Magazine articles have been published in Italy alleging that Alicja Purdom, . . . claimed that several years ago she was engaged to be married to John F. Kennedy but the latter's father vetoed the wedding because of Alicja's Polish-Jewish descent.

The Attorney General was kept informed by memoranda and on June 5, 1963, we wrote him we were taking no further action in the absence of a specific request because the court had sealed the record. We never did see the documents during the course of our inquiry.

It would seem advisable to let the Attorney General know that further efforts are being made to peddle copies of these documents even though the originals have been sealed in the court record.

[Hoover's handwritten notation: "Do so by memo to A.G."]

[By "personal" memorandum dated August 14, 1963, Hoover briefed Attorney General Robert Kennedy on this matter, observing that "the information furnished by Mr. Munden relates to events previously furnished to you" and adding that "no further action will be taken by this Bureau with regard to this matter in absence of a specific request. Any additional information which may be received will be brought to your attention." A note on the bottom of Hoover's copy of this memorandum reports that "because of the delicate nature of the information furnished, copies are not designated for other departmental officials. The same reasoning applies to this memorandum."]

2: Robert Kennedy

THE FBI DIRECTOR'S ability to uncover derogatory information about John Kennedy through the Bureau's contacts and illegal investigative techniques was not atypical. Through a bug installed during a criminal investigation, Hoover soon learned that Attorney General Robert Kennedy allegedly was having an illicit sexual affair. In this case, as in those instances when Hoover had briefed President Kennedy about similar allegations because no question could be raised about how the FBI had acquired the information, the director asked the FBI's liaison to brief the attorney general. The rumor had no basis in fact, so Kennedy was not intimidated. But he nonetheless felt compelled to refute allegations that he was having an affair with Marilyn Monroe, another matter of interest to the director.

■ **Memo, FBI Assistant Director Courtney Evans to FBI Assistant Director Alan Belmont, August 11, 1962**

A highly confidential source [bug] covering the residence of notorious hoodlum, Meyer Lansky, at Hallandale, Florida, recently furnished information to the effect that Lansky made an allegation that Attorney General Robert Kennedy is carrying on an affair with an El Paso, Texas, girl.

The source indicated that Lansky was alone with his wife and began a discussion of the Attorney General, mentioning that the latter has seven children but is carrying on the affair with the girl. Mrs. Lansky reportedly replied, "It's all [Frank Sinatra's] fault, he is nothing but a procurer of women for those guys. [Sinatra] is the guy who gets them all together." Lansky then replied to his wife, "It's not [Sinatra's] fault and it starts with the President and goes right down the line." We have received no information from the highly confidential source [bug] or by other means that Lansky has made this allegation to any other person. . . .

In view of the fact that this allegation involves the Attorney General and the President, I believe that it should be brought to the attention of the Attorney General. Because of the sensitive nature of this matter, I recommend that I be authorized to personally bring it to the attention of the Attorney General upon his return to the city.

[Hoover's handwritten notation: "Yes but make proper notation for files after you have done so."]

■ Memo, FBI Assistant Director Courtney Evans to FBI Assistant Director Alan Belmont, August 20, 1962

The Attorney General was contacted and advised of the information we had received alleging he was having an affair with a girl in El Paso. He said he had never been to El Paso, Texas, and there was no basis in fact whatsoever for the allegation.

He said he appreciated our informing him of it; that being in public life the gossip mongers just had to talk. He said he was aware there had been several allegations concerning his possibly being involved with Marilyn Monroe. He said he had at least met Marilyn Monroe since she was a good friend of his sister, Pat Lawford, but these allegations just had a way of growing beyond any semblance of the truth.

■ Airtel, SAC New York to FBI Director, July 2, 1964, FBI 77-51387—Not Recorded

On instant date, [Frank A. Capell] advised he is about to publish a 70 page paperback book dealing with the suicide of actress Marilyn Monroe. . . . Capell advised that the book should be ready for sale on or about 7/10/64, and that he will furnish a copy of this book for the Bureau's information.

He advised that the book will make reference to Attorney General Robert Kennedy and Kennedy's friendship with Miss Monroe. He advised that he will indicate that the evidence shows that Kennedy and Monroe were intimate and that Kennedy was in Monroe's apartment at the time of her death. He advised that he will attempt to show that some Communists were evidently working behind the scenes, inasmuch as a physician who signed the death certificate was a Communist. . . .

■ **Personal Memo, FBI Director to Attorney General Robert Kennedy, July 8, 1964, FBI 77-51387—Not Recorded**

Mr. Frank A. Capell . . . advised the New York Office of this Bureau on July 2, 1964, that he is publishing a 70-page paperback book . . . [that] will make reference to your alleged friendship with the late Miss Marilyn Monroe. Mr. Capell stated he will indicate in his book that you and Miss Monroe were intimate and that you were in Miss Monroe's apartment at the time of her death.

In recent years Capell has published "The Herald of Freedom," an anticommunist newsletter of an exposé type, which names names and organizations, [four lines withheld on grounds of FBI sources or methods].

Any additional information concerning the publication of the above book will be brought promptly to your attention.

[Note on bottom of copy of this memo: *"ATTENTION: SAC, NEW YORK.* Reurairtel 7/2/64. You are instructed to follow this matter very closely. Furnish two copies of the book to the Bureau promptly upon its publication in order that the Attorney General may be kept advised."]

■ **Memo, FBI Supervisor R. W. Smith to FBI Assistant Director William Sullivan, July 14, 1964, FBI 77-51387—Not Recorded**

. . . The New York Office has now furnished us with a copy of [Frank Capell's] 70-page book. The book claims that Miss Monroe's involvement with Kennedy "was well known to her friends and reporters in the Hollywood area," but was never publicized. It is alleged that "there are person-to-person telephone calls, living witnesses, tape recordings and certain writings to attest the closeness of their friendship."

The author suggests that Miss Monroe "was led to believe his intentions were serious," and that Kennedy had promised to divorce his wife and marry her. When he failed to do so, the book charges, she "threatened to expose their relationship," which would have ruined his presidential aspirations. It was then that Kennedy decided "to take drastic action."

Kennedy Had Communists "Murder" Miss Monroe

According to the book, Kennedy used "the Communist Conspiracy which is expert in the scientific elimination of its enemies" to dispose of Miss Monroe by making her murder appear to be a suicide. This could have been achieved without great difficulty, the author points out, because her personal physician, Dr. Hyman Engelberg, was a communist. . . .

It should be noted that the allegation concerning the Attorney General and Miss Monroe has been circulated in the past and has been branded as utterly false. . . .

By letter dated 7/7/64, we advised the Attorney General of the nature of Capell's forthcoming book, as well as background data on Capell. . . .
Recommendation:

That the attached letter be sent to the Attorney General enclosing a copy of the aforementioned book.

[Hoover's handwritten notation: "OK."]

3: Dwight D. Eisenhower

UNDENIABLY HOOVER HAD an obsession with the Kennedys. In his office he kept two massive folders containing derogatory personal and political information on John Kennedy, two folders on Robert Kennedy (the second pertaining to the autopsy following his assassination), two folders on their father Joseph, and one folder on their sister Patricia. For Hoover this information had value in helping to further his own bureaucratic and political goals.

Earlier, Hoover had also been interested in the personal and political activities of the relatively more conservative Republican President Dwight Eisenhower. Eisenhower at first posed a quite different challenge: he possessed a blank political past when he was drafted by Eastern Republicans in the spring of 1952 as part of a "stop-Taft" movement. Because Eisenhower had neither been active in national politics nor taken public stands on major domestic issues (excepting foreign policy), his attitude toward communism concerned Hoover and many other conservative activists. So Hoover directed his aides to monitor Eisenhower's principal campaign advisers and prospective cabinet appointees. As with John Kennedy, the director readily exploited the Bureau's vast resources, including wiretaps and conservative politicians, to acquire intelligence, including allegations of sexual misconduct.

■ Informal Memo, FBI Assistant Director Louis Nichols to FBI Associate Director Clyde Tolson, December 5, 1952, Nichols File

I was confidentially advised last night that Wesley Roberts has been selected to become the Chairman of the National Republican Committee. Colonel LeRoy Green, who has been [current Republican National Committee chairman and postmaster general–designate Arthur] Summerfield's Executive Assistant, has been approached to remain as the Executive Assistant to Roberts.

[Nichols's addendum later that day: "Roberts is from the State of Kansas, is a former newspaper publisher, was a college classmate of (President-elect Eisenhower's brother) Milton Eisenhower. We have no identifiable information on Roberts in our files."]

■ Memo, Frances Lurz [Secretary to FBI Assistant Director Louis Nichols] to FBI Supervisor Milton Jones, December 5, 1952, Nichols File

Please have a check made at once to find out if anything on [Republican National Committee chairman Wesley] Roberts since [FBI] check made in Aug, 1952.

[Lurz's handwritten insert: "see memo 8/12/52 Leonard Hall, Wayne J. Hood, Wesley Roberts, Robert Humphreys (all high-level officials on Eisenhower's presidential campaign staff) stating no info on Roberts." Jones's handwritten insert: "No references on Wesley Roberts since August 1, 1952. 12-5-52."]

■ Informal Memo, FBI Assistant Director Louis Nichols to FBI Director, December 31, 1952, Nichols File

[New York Herald-Tribune publisher and chairman of the 1952 Citizens for Eisenhower presidential committee] Odgen Reid . . . [met with President-elect Dwight Eisenhower] this morning. This was a follow up of a conversation that Reid had with the General immediately prior to the election at which time Reid cautioned the General about being taken in by Communists and talked at some length about secret Communists and the necessity of creating alertness in the new administration. . . .

Basically, Reid stated he made the point that the General should himself be aware of internal security threats, secret Communists, and methods of infiltration, that he in turn should seek at the very beginning to bring about a security awareness on the part of his top administrators. To prove his points on these, Reid cited the cases of [Roosevelt and Truman appointees] Lee Pressman, Laughlin Currie, Frank Coe, and Harry Dexter White.

Reid stated that the General indicated further surprise at some of these details and . . . was somewhat shocked to think that there were professional people such as lawyers, doctors, clergymen, and college professors who were Communists. The General stated he could not conceive, for example, the Board of Trustees of Columbia University keeping a professor who was a Communist.

Reid further related his survey of the Red menace in the United States when he did his series [in the *New York Herald-Tribune*] . . . and expressed his opinion that he thought one of the great difficulties in the past has been a failure on the part of top administrators to take seriously the manifestations of subversive activities and to be entirely too trusting.

The General concurred with Reid on this observation and then asked Reid what suggestions he had on getting the facts together. Reid told him that he felt certain the FBI would be the agency which knew most about the problem from an internal security standpoint and CIA would be the agency who knew most from an external standpoint. . . .

The General then asked Reid if he . . . [would arrange to have Hoover meet Eisenhower's] top people (and Reid inferred from this the Cabinet) for one hour on January 20 or shortly thereafter [Hoover instead submitted a lengthy briefing memo to assistant to the president Sherman Adams on January 28, 1953] to give them a briefing in general terms on the meaning of intelligence information, the difficulties in obtaining intelligence information, and give some picture of the influence of concealed members of the party both in the government and in civilian life. . . .

The General made the observation that he had noted in the papers the statement of Senator [Joseph] McCarthy about investigating education. He, the General, was inclined to think this was not the way to approach the matter, that the way to approach the matter was to supply trusted members of the Board of Trustees of a college or university with the facts and he had no doubt in his mind as to what they had to do.

Reid stated . . . he has on numerous occasions made it unmistakably clear to the General that he, Reid, feels the FBI is an example of good government, that it should have the support of good people, that it was the one agency that could be trusted and that stood as a bulwark in protecting the American way of life. . . .

Reid stated that no doubt the Director would see the General from time to time and it was his suggestion that the next time the Director saw the General that he merely let the General know he received his message through Reid and then leave the matter of the details for the meeting up to the General.

Reid also felt in view of the General's inclination to be naive on concealed members of the Party, that sometime in a private conversation the Director might mention a couple of shocking cases that have occurred: persons in either Government or civilian life. In this connection, perhaps, the best case I can think of would be the Robert Oppenheimer case and how he blocked the production of the H-Bomb for several years. . . .

Reid made the observation that he has never heard of a President following a course of action such as General Eisenhower suggested, namely, of having his top people together for an hour's briefing for a subject such as this and that he thinks this would be a wonderful thing for the Bureau and for the Director personally.

There is no question as to Reid's sincerity in fighting Communism in my mind and in his loyalty to the Bureau.

[Hoover's handwritten notation: "1. I regret the idea the General has for such a briefing. It places FBI in an undesirable position for its own long range good. 2. Get started *at once* on a memo for such a briefing in case the General goes through with it." Nichols's handwritten notation: "Being worked on."]

■ **Informal Memo, FBI Assistant Director Louis Nichols to FBI Director, January 8, 1953, Nichols File**

I had dinner with George Murphy and an individual whom he introduced as a close friend of his by the name of Fran Alstack [sic, Alstock], spelling phonetic.

Murphy and Alstack staged practically all of the large TV rallies wherein General Eisenhower spoke during the convention, along with Ed Birmingham and Bob Burroughs. . . . Burroughs is the president of a bank in New England and . . . will have a desk at the White House and will spend considerable time down here in an advisory capacity. Birmingham will also have a desk at the White House. They are both described as our type of people and both have blood in their eyes against the so-called pseudo-liberals. . . .

Alstack is [*New York Herald-Tribune* publisher] Jock Whitney's man and was with Jock Whitney when he was in Washington. Judging from the way Alstack talks, he is probably more rabid against Communists than Murphy, as he is more extreme and intemperate in his views as to what to do with them. . . .

Alstack and Murphy are both of the opinion that the Bureau should have its man at the White House. Both stated that . . . if we had any desire merely to give them the name of the individual we wanted and they would have him over at the White House after January 20 and become an important position. I chided Murphy a little bit on this. . . .

Another individual who is a part of this clique is a woman by the name of [Mary] Lord, who apparently is extremely able and extremely wealthy. She will sort of be a coordinator of women's activities in the new Administration and, in addition to taking Eleanor's [Roosevelt] place [as U.S. delegate to the United Nations], she will have a desk at the White House and will contact Oveta Hobby and the other [prominent Republican] women. George stated she is our type of people and he will get her over here in due time; that she could be very helpful. . . .

[The FBI withheld two paragraphs on personal privacy grounds; this withheld information pertained to Nichols's briefing of Murphy and Alstock on Eleanor Roosevelt's alleged "affair" with Joseph Lash.]

The General has a thorough distrust, distaste and dislike for Eleanor and told [Secretary of State–designate John Foster] Dulles to get her out of the picture [i.e., as a member of the U.S. delegation to the United Nations]. . . . Alstack reasoned that as long as Eleanor was in the picture, she would not become the subject of any Congressional investigation, but that sooner or later, there was going to be an investigation of her affair with Joe Lash.

Alstack made the observation that in his opinion the International Monetary Commission stunk to high heaven, was serving the interests of the Communists, that it is a brain child of Harry Dexter White, that he hoped we had good coverage of it and he was doing his best to get the new administration to tear it apart. . . .

■ **Informal Memo, FBI Assistant Director Louis Nichols to FBI Associate Director Clyde Tolson, January 27, 1953, Nichols File**

You will recall early in January I had dinner one evening with George Murphy and Francis Alstock. . . . [who had] stated that we of course should have somebody in the White House to look out for our interests and offered to be of assistance. I passed this off and did not pursue it further.

Alstock called me today and stated that everything was all set . . . [and] that Stan Rumbaugh, . . . is now the assistant to Walter Williams, undersecretary of Commerce; that he has had a long talk with Rumbaugh and Rumbaugh wanted a contact in the Bureau to whom he could come for advice and guidance. Alstock told Rumbaugh to contact me; that if I could not handle any situation that he brought I would either take it up with the Director or put him in touch with the Director. He stated that Rumbaugh is thoroughly briefed on the left-wing issue, the need of giving the Bureau what it needs in the way of support, etc. *Rumbaugh in turn is very close to Charlie Willis at the White House* and the matter which was discussed at dinner last week is now scheduled to be taken up at the next Cabinet meeting. Perhaps the Director or you will know what he was talking about. [Tolson's handwritten insert: "I don't know." Hoover's handwritten insert: "I don't know either."]

Alstock stated he is getting May Rabby assistant to [assistant to the president Sherman] Adams lined up just in case another person is needed; that he is going back to New York today and will be back in Washington next week and will call me and perhaps we can get together. I will plan on pursuing this further although I don't know exactly what his game is. . . .

■ **Informal Memo, FBI Assistant Director Louis Nichols to FBI Associate Director Clyde Tolson, May 13, 1955, Nichols File**
[Senator Joseph McCarthy's aide] Don Surine told me in confidence that in 1944 General Eisenhower wrote a personal letter to General [of the army George] Marshal[l] in longhand asking Marshal's advice as to what effect a divorce would have upon General Eisenhower's personal career. This occurred at a time when General Eisenhower was allegedly having an affair with Kay Summersby, the British WAC. General Marshal is reported to have squelched the idea of the divorce and to have engaged in maneuvering which broke up the affair with Kay Summersby. [Syndicated columnist] Drew Pearson, according to the scuttlebutt, allegedly has a photostatic copy of this letter which was given to him by Anna Rosenberg. While Surine did not spell it out, I concluded that from what he said that his source was John Henshaw, former leg man for Drew Pearson.

■ **Informal Memo, FBI Assistant Director Louis Nichols to FBI Associate Director Clyde Tolson, September 23, 1955, Nichols File**
Don Surine called at 4:30 p.m., 9/22/55, to confidentially advise that Kay Summersby, a former WAC Staff Officer assigned to President Eisenhower in Europe, has been staying at the [Washington] Shoreham Hotel for the last 30 or 45 days under an assumed name.

■ **Informal Memo, FBI Assistant Director Louis Nichols to FBI Associate Director Clyde Tolson, September 28, 1955, Nichols File**
Don Surine, of Senator [Joseph] McCarthy's Office, advised 9/22/55, that [Kay Summersby], a former WAC officer who was assigned as secretary, aid and chauffeur to President Eisenhower, while he was European Commander, was staying at the Shoreham under an assumed name. The Director indicated "See if we can discreetly get the name."
Surine was discreetly contacted re an attempt to procure name assumed by Summersby. He later called back, 9/27/55, and advised his confidential source. [Seven lines withheld on personal privacy grounds.] Surine did not reveal interest of FBI in matter and it has been indicated to him that

interest in this stems from personal curiosity and has no connection with the FBI.

Bureau files reflect little concerning Summersby. She was attacked by one Marion Bryant, Negro, 2/12/47, at WAC Officers Quarters, Hamilton Field, California. [Bryant] tried and convicted of intent to commit rape and sentenced to 15 years imprisonment. Summersby married on 11/20/52 to Reginald H. Morgan, of New Canaan, Connecticut, a Wall Street broker. She is currently 46 years of age, born in Ireland and served in British Armed Forces before becoming a WAC Captain in U.S. Army Auxiliary. While President Eisenhower was Supreme Allied Commander in Europe, Summersby served as confidential secretary, aid and driver. In 1948, she wrote and published a book entitled "Eisenhower Was My Boss."

Summersby has been married twice. Her first marriage ended in divorce in England, in July, 1943, when her husband, Gordon Summersby, brought charges of adultery. The third party involved was not mentioned. Her current husband, Morgan, has been married three times. His first wife died in 1943, and his second marriage ended in divorce in early 1952.

Summersby was naturalized 1/19/51, in New York. Her occupation on various records includes that of saleslady and housewife. Her address prior to marriage to Morgan was 155 East 49th Street, New York City.

Washington Field Office has made discreet check through contacts at Shoreham and has learned no individual is registered there under the name of Kay Morgan, Mrs. Reginald H. Morgan, or Kay McCarthy (maiden name). Other variances were checked with negative results.

The New York Office made a pretext telephone call to current residence of Reginald H. Morgan. There was no answer. A second attempt will be made during the evening hours.

All checks mentioned above were made with complete secrecy and it is felt that no interest has been aroused on the part of outsiders concerning this matter. You will be advised of the result of New York's pretext call they will make during the evening hours. . . .

ADDENDUM: 9/28/55

ASAC [assistant special agent in charge, New York] Simon advised at 5:12 p.m. that this afternoon second pretext call was made . . . and Mrs. Morgan (Kay Summersby) answered telephone. Conversation was carried on under pretext to some extent and Mrs. Morgan was most pleasant. There was no information received which would indicate whether she had recently been in Washington or not.

4: Eleanor Roosevelt

HOOVER DID NOT rely solely on the FBI's resources to acquire derogatory information on public officials and other prominent Americans. He unhesitatingly tapped the resources of other agencies, notably the staffs of the House Committee on Un-American Activities and of the Senate Internal Security Subcommittee, local and state police officials, and military intelligence agencies. Indeed, through the FBI's liaison to the Military Intelligence Division (MID), Hoover acquired (and then retained in his office) sixty-eight reports numbering approximately 450 pages detailing derogatory information on members of Congress and other prominent Washingtonians. One of the more explosive reports kept by Hoover in his office involved an alleged affair between then First Lady Eleanor Roosevelt and Joseph P. Lash. George Burton, Hoover's liaison to MID, had been the eager recipient of this information offered by his MID contacts.

Assigned to Chanute Air Base near Urbana, Illinois, in February 1943, Lash had almost immediately become the subject of an investigation conducted by the army's Counter-Intelligence Corps owing to his highly publicized radical activities during the 1930s and early 1940s. In the course of this investigation, MID agents wiretapped Lash's conversations, opened his mail, followed him during trips to Urbana and Chicago, and bugged his Urbana hotel room during a weekend visit with his fiancée, Trude Pratt.

When MID's monitoring of Lash's meeting with Mrs. Roosevelt in Chicago in March 1943 inadvertently came to her attention, she protested through White House aide Harry

Hopkins to General of the Army George Marshall. The scope of the military agents' "counterintelligence" investigation disturbed Marshall, and he eventually disbanded the Counter-Intelligence Corps and ordered the destruction of its domestic surveillance files. MID officials then offered these investigative reports to their contacts in the FBI—and Hoover willingly accepted. He retained these sensitive reports in his office file.

Having secured this information and made sure it could not be publicly compromised, Hoover could use it when he deemed it safe and convenient to do so. When rumors of an affair between Lash and Mrs. Roosevelt first surfaced in 1951, Hoover felt that his possession of this material ought to be kept a secret (Harry Truman, a Democrat, was president). With changed political circumstances following the election of a Republican president in 1952, Hoover was willing in 1953 and 1954 to share this derogatory information about Mrs. Roosevelt with officials in the Eisenhower administration.

■ **Do Not File Memo, FBI Liaison Agent George Burton to FBI Assistant Director D. Milton Ladd, December 31, 1943**

It has been apparent to the writer for several months that certain powerful interests within or near the War Department have undertaken an active program aimed at the dismemberment of the Counterintelligence Corps of G-2 [military intelligence]. It is now the writer's belief that this opinion is justified. . . .

Recently at a G-2 social function the writer had a long discussion with Colonel [Edgar] Kibler who is Officer in Charge of the Counterintelligence Corps. The Colonel stated quite frankly that the reason the Counterintelligence Corps had been wrecked was that Harry Hopkins and the Secret Service had ordered it to be so wrecked. Colonel Kibler stated that through some unknown means Harry Hopkins learned that the Counterintelligence Corps was investigating Joseph Lash and that in this investigation they had run upon Mrs. Roosevelt who had come to Chicago [on March 27–28] apparently for the purpose of meeting Lash. Colonel Kibler stated that he did not know exactly how Hopkins found out about this but believed it was through some indiscretion of Colonel Fubershaw who is the Director of Intelligence, Sixth Service Command, stationed in Chicago.

Colonel John Bissell [who had formerly been Kibler's superior, heading the Counterintelligence Corps] . . . [also reported to me] that he had been recommended for a promotion to Brigadier General on several occasions and on each occasion this recommendation had been stopped in the office of Lieutenant General McNarney, Deputy Chief of Staff.

Recently . . . [Bissell] learned that he had been blackballed by the White House . . . [and] would never advance any further in the Army and would probably never be sent out of the country with troops . . . because he had been connected with the Joe Lash–Eleanor Roosevelt investigation in Chicago.

[Colonel Leslie] Forney [Bissell's successor as chief of G-2] stated to Bissell that the facts of this investigation had been disclosed to the White House through some unknown means and that shortly after Bissell left [as chief of the Counterintelligence Corps], a call was received by General [George] Strong [head of the Military Intelligence Division, within which the Counterintelligence Corps was headquartered] and Colonel Forney to proceed to the White House with the complete records of this matter at approximately 10:00 p.m. at night. When they reached the White House they were received by the President, [White House aides] General [Edwin] Watson and Harry Hopkins and were ordered to produce the entire records in this case. Colonel Forney stated to Colonel Bissell that this was extremely embarrassing in as much as the material contained a recording of the entire proceedings between Lash and Mrs. Roosevelt which had been planted in the [Blackstone] hotel room. This recording indicated quite clearly that Mrs. Roosevelt and Lash engaged in sexual intercourse during their stay in the hotel room. Forney advised Bissell that after this record was played Mrs. Roosevelt was called into the conference and was confronted with the information and this resulted in a terrific fight between the President and Mrs. Roosevelt. At approximately 5:00 a.m. the next morning the President called for General [Hap] Arnold, Chief of the Army Air Corps, and upon his arrival at the conference ordered him to have Lash outside the United States and on his way to a combat post within ten hours.

After the conference was over it was learned that the President had ordered that anybody who knew anything about this case should be immediately releaved [sic] of his duties and sent to the South Pacific for action against the Japs until they were killed. Forney advised Bissell that everyone who is known to have any knowledge at all of this matter is on the permanent black list at the White House. Bissell stated that the only thing that kept these men from being sent to the South Pacific was that it was learned that there were too many of them to be treated in this manner. Colonel Bissell stated that the only reason that more was not done to him was that General Watson apparently came to his defense and assured the President that Bissell would not talk about this matter indiscriminately.

[Colonels Kibler's and Bissell's briefing of agent Burton was erroneous in every respect—and not only because Roosevelt would scarcely have insisted on hearing the CIC's recordings in the presence of these officers and then have had a public showdown with his wife.

First, General Marshall did order the dissolution of the army's domestic Counterintelligence Corps in 1943 in response to Harry Hopkins's discovery of the CIC's monitoring of Mrs. Roosevelt, but the catalyst to this was her relatively innocent protest. When she was advised by officials of the Blackstone Hotel in Chicago that she had been the subject of military surveillance during her stay, on her return to Washington the First Lady protested this surveillance. (Responsibility for protecting the president was vested in the Secret Service, and Mrs. Roosevelt objected even to this invasion of her privacy.) Hopkins in turn protested to General Marshall who concluded that the focus of CIC efforts should be on foreign agents, not American citizens.

While Marshall, Hopkins, and the Roosevelts learned of the Chicago surveillance, military intelligence officials had not briefed them on their earlier monitoring of Lash's contacts with Mrs. Roosevelt and his fiancée, Trude Pratt. Nor did the CIC's bug of Mrs. Roosevelt's Blackstone Hotel room record a sexual liaison between Lash and Mrs. Roosevelt. The only such recording of sexual intercourse involved the CIC's bugging of Lash's March 12–14 visit with Trude Pratt in Urbana, Illinois.

Second, Colonel Bissell was not blackballed for his role in supervising the CIC's investigation of Lash. Bissell was relieved of his responsibility as chief of the Counterintelligence Corps and transferred to Fort Sill, Oklahoma, in March 1943, *before* Mrs. Roosevelt's visit to Chicago and her subsequent protest to Hopkins of April 10. And, while Bissell might have been dissatisfied with his failure to have been promoted in 1943, he was promoted to lieutenant general in November 1944.

Third, not only was Lieutenant Colonel Paul Boyer (who headed the CIC's Chicago unit which conducted this surveillance of Lash) and the four other men of this unit not assigned to the South Pacific, but their army careers did not suffer. Indeed, Boyer's counterintelligence career after March 1943 reflected a strong progression in responsibility, including a stint as liaison to the Office of Strategic Service's (OSS) counterespionage and espionage branches, assignment to the army's extremely sensitive counterintelligence and decoding branch in Arlington Hall, Virginia, and help in planning postwar occupation policy for Germany.

Fourth, Lash (at the time an army air force recruit assigned to Chanute Air Base near Urbana) was suddenly transferred on April 23, 1943 (but not "within ten hours") for an assignment in the South Pacific. Lash's assignment, however, was not to a combat post but to a weather station in New Caledonia. The impetus for this transfer apparently had little to do with Mrs. Roosevelt's protest. Rather, it reflected his superior officer's concerns, based on CIC briefings, of Lash's radical political activities. Indeed, as early as March 27, 1943, Boyer had reported to Bissell that the commander of Chanute Air Base was "anxious to remove" Lash from his base and "would cooperate in any way to get him another assignment."]

■ **Informal Memo, FBI Assistant Director Louis Nichols to FBI Director, January 18, 1951**

[FBI Assistant Director D. Milton] Ladd and I have checked on the Joe Lash file.

With reference to the Mrs. Roosevelt incident, we of course never investigated this. It was investigated by CIC [Counterintelligence Corps] prior to 1943. We do have a photostat of the G-2 file [numbering one hundred pages and consisting of reports on Lash's correspondence, CIC agents' monitoring of his weekend trips to Urbana, and bugging of his hotel room during his weekend visit with Trude Pratt March 12–14, 1943].

There were no recordings in the Bureau files between Mrs. Roosevelt and Lash. Obviously, they did have a microphone because there were recordings of conversations between Lash and Mrs. Trudie W. Pratt which also reflected what transpired in the hotel room.

This information was given to George Burton by Colonel [Edgar] Kibler and Colonel Jack Bissell. It is recorded in a blue [Do Not File] memorandum dated December 31, 1943.

The blue memorandum and a photostat of the G-2 file are maintained by Miss [Helen] Gandy but have never been in the Files Section.

It is not believed that anyone in the Bureau has knowledge of this except Burton, Mr. Ladd, E. A. Tamm, me, and the stenographer whose initials are FIL and whose identity we are now trying to establish.

[Nichols's handwritten insert: "(Name deleted) stenographer resigned 8/24/44 No indication she would talk about incident."]

It is therefore believed thoroughly safe for [FBI assistant director Stanley] Tracy to tell [conservative Republican] Senator [Arthur] Watkins the FBI never investigated the Roosevelt-Lash incident. There is nothing from official sources on this in the FBI files.

Both Mr. Ladd and I do recall there have been newspaper articles linking Lash to Mrs. Roosevelt.

In 1949, Frank Waldrop of the [Washington] Times Herald told me they were on the trail of certain recordings that allegedly would show an illicit relationship between Lash and Mrs. Roosevelt. At that time I made a thorough check of all our files and there was nothing in the main files. The pink [Do Not File] memorandum [on Waldrop's inquiry] has never been circulated in the Bureau and is not known to anyone outside of Miss [Frances] Lurz in my office, Mr. Tolson, Miss Gandy, and you. Mr. Ladd was informed of my check this morning although he vaguely recalls when I was checking on this a year ago.

Mr. Tracy will be advised along the lines of our discussion this morning. . . . I think, as a tactic, Tracy should get across to Watkins and Watkins should carry the point to Anderson that he had checked at the FBI and FBI files do not contain any such information.

[Hoover's inserted comment: "Right." Nichols's inserted comment: "Tracy advised 1/19."]

■ **Informal Memo, FBI Assistant Director Louis Nichols to FBI Director, February 2, 1954**

The thought occurs that if the President [Dwight Eisenhower] does not know of the furor that was caused in G-2 some years ago as the result of G-2's investigation of Joe Lash and his connections with Mrs. Roosevelt, you might want to consider mentioning this incident to him.

Joe Lash is a close friend of [*New York Post* editor] Jimmy Wechsler and the last word I had was that Joe Lash was working for the New York Post which has been exceedingly critical of the President as well as of us. Wechsler, of course, is a kingpin in the Americans for Democratic Action along with Mrs. Roosevelt.

(Nichols's handwritten insert: "Lash had a signed article in N.Y. Post today.")

The attached memorandum details Lash's connections with Mrs. Roosevelt along with the G-2 investigation, the subsequent confrontation with Mrs. Roosevelt and the order issued by FDR that everyone knowing of this action should be sent to South Pacific until they were killed. . . .

This, of course, could have a relationship to the subsequent orders given to the Army to destroy the files on subversives.

We have photostats of the G-2 investigative reports on their coverage of Lash and there is no question about Lash's tie-in with Mrs. Roosevelt. G-2 files contain Mrs. Roosevelt's letters to Lash which invariably start with "Joe Dearest" and end with "All my love, ER." . . .

HOOVER WAS MOST interested in Mrs. Roosevelt's liberal political activities, a concern which dated from her days as First Lady and extended until her death in 1962. The scope of his interest is most revealingly documented by his response to a report that FBI agents in New York City had discovered and photocopied her correspondence with officials of the radical American Youth Congress during a break-in at the Congress's New York office in January 1942, when she was the First Lady.

■ **Do Not File Memo, FBI Assistant Director D. Milton Ladd to FBI Director, February 4, 1942, Nichols File**

Reference is made to your request that the attached correspondence [of Eleanor Roosevelt], made available by [FBI assistant director] P. E. Foxworth and obtained [through an FBI break-in] from the offices of the American Youth Congress in New York City, be reviewed and analyzed. . . . Correspondence contained therein was reviewed and the pertinent information set forth in a blue [Do Not File] memorandum . . . [which] was transmitted to your office with the developed photographs and the roll of negatives for whatever disposition deemed advisable.

[The referenced Do Not File memorandum analyzing Mrs. Roosevelt's correspondence with American Youth Congress officials is not extant. The two copies of this correspondence were safeguarded in the official and confidential files of FBI assistant director Louis Nichols, one copy in the American Youth Congress folder and the second in the Eleanor Roosevelt folder.]

5: Washington, D.C., Field Office Reports

HOOVER'S INTEREST IN the personal indiscretions of national leaders called for the FBI's Washington, D.C., field office to report derogatory personal information about diplomats, congressmen, and high-level government officials. One of the folders that Hoover kept in his office includes a series of reports—based on information obtained through FBI wiretaps, agent investigations, and informers—dated between June 5, 1958, and October 29, 1965. Because only one copy was prepared and the carbon destroyed, we do not know whether similar reports were submitted to Hoover before and after these dates, or whether this folder contains all reports submitted during the 1958–1965 period. Furthermore, because derogatory personal information was being reported, in releasing these documents the FBI has heavily edited their contents on personal privacy grounds.

We can nonetheless describe the general contents of this folder. When briefing Attorney General Edward Levi before his February 1975 congressional testimony about Hoover's Official and Confidential File, FBI officials described the folder's contents this way: "Contains almost entirely letters to Hoover from SACs in Washington Field Office containing general immoral or criminal activities on part of diplomats, government employees, politicians, sport figures, socially prominent persons, senators and congressmen."

The memoranda reprinted in this section convey Hoover's interest in derogatory information as well as his moralistic reaction. The reports underscore that the FBI intensively monitored developments in Washington and then forwarded to

Hoover for safekeeping derogatory information obtained through Bureau contacts and "national security" wiretaps and bugs.

■ **Letter, Acting SAC, Washington Thomas McAndrews to FBI Director J. Edgar Hoover, June 13, 1958**

There is set out below certain other material which has come to the attention of the Washington Field Office during the past week and in which you may be interested.

DIPLOMATIC ACTIVITIES

[Six paragraphs withheld on national security grounds.]

GOVERNMENT CIRCLES

On June 5, 1958, [name withheld reporter of name withheld] newspapers, was overheard by SA Conrad L. Trahern telling the following . . . [the reporter's] wife is the secretary to Congressman [name withheld]. [The newspaper reporter] stated that [name withheld] prior to marrying the Congressman, was . . . having an affair with a Negro . . . [and] also at one time carried on an affair with a House Post Office employee . . . and after marrying the Congressman, continued this association. During the Congressman's recent illness, [the Congressman] insisted that he have a male nurse and contacted the Indonesian Embassy to employ a man. . . . She endeavored to have an affair with this Indonesian who declined, stating that he is a foreigner and could be deported for misconduct.

SA Trahern, of course, was not a party to the conversation nor did he indicate any interest in the conversation of the participants.

On June 11, 1959, [name withheld], Office of the Sergeant of Arms, U.S. Senate, volunteered to SA Trahern that Senator [name withheld] is an alcoholic. He has recently been in Bethesda Naval Hospital from which he is brought when his vote is necessary on some important legislation, . . . [and] has appeared on the floor of the Senate on numerous occasions while intoxicated. . . .

■ **Letter, FBI Director J. Edgar Hoover to Acting SAC, Washington Thomas McAndrews, June 25, 1958**

Your letter of June 13, 1958, has been received, and I deeply appreciate your writing me.

It was certainly thoughtful of you to advise me of matters of current interest, and I am glad to have the benefit of this information.

■ **Letter, Washington SAC Leland Boardman to FBI Director
J. Edgar Hoover, August 8, 1958**
I thought you would be interested in the following information. . . . [An FBI source] advised SA Joseph I. Woods on August 7, 1958, that Senator [name withheld] prepares a personal check each month in the amount of $500, payable to [name withheld]. [The FBI's source] stated he had heard that [name withheld] is a "party girl" and that she may be living with Senator [name withheld] at the Shoreham Hotel, Washington, D.C.

Unless otherwise indicated, the foregoing material has been obtained from confidential technical sources [a wiretap or bug].

■ **Letter, Washington SAC Leland Boardman to FBI Director
J. Edgar Hoover, October 21, 1958**
There is set out below certain information which has come to the attention of this office during regular investigative activity.
WASHINGTON ACTIVITIES
. . . According to [name of source withheld] Senator [name withheld] who is married, has been frequently in the company of [name withheld] of the public relations staff of the Sheraton-Park Hotel. The relationship between the Senator and [this woman] appears to [the FBI's source] to be much more than casual. . . .

■ **Letter, Washington SAC James Gale to FBI Director J. Edgar Hoover, June 9, 1959**
On [date withheld] Special Agents of the Washington Field Office . . . [learned of activities of name withheld] "call girl," who operates in Washington, D.C. She numbers among her acquaintances persons of social prominence in Washington, D.C. Her reliability has not been determined.

She told the Special Agents that on [date withheld] she received a telephone call . . . [from] a member of the White House Staff . . . [who] asked her if she were available that evening to "entertain" one [name and title withheld] currently a guest of the White House. . . . She went to a suite at the Mayflower Hotel where she met [name withheld White House aide] who introduced her to [three name withheld individuals] . . . identified to her as members of the White House Staff. Later in the evening . . . she accompanied [name withheld] to his suite at the Mayflower, where she said she engaged in sexual relations with him, for which he paid her $150.00.

[Four-line paragraph withheld.]

It has been discreetly determined from reliable sources that there is a [name withheld] who is a [title withheld] at the White House. However no listing could be located for a [name withheld].

[Five-line paragraph withheld.]

She has had two dinner engagements alone with [name withheld White House aide] but denies sexual relations with him. During the second dinner date, [name withheld White House aide] asked her if she would be willing to entertain certain male White House guests on a discreet basis, since some of them could not be seen with her in public. She agreed, but would not include sexual relations, unless the person appealed to her. [Name withheld White House aide] told her this arrangement was satisfactory.

The informant said [name withheld White House aide] arranged for her to entertain White House guests [names and titles withheld].

ADDENDUM: FBI Liaison to the White House Orrin Bartlett, June 12, 1959

Pursuant to instructions, Liaison Agent Bartlett furnished the pertinent facts from this letter to Mr. James Hagerty, Press Secretary to the President [Dwight Eisenhower]. Mr. Hagerty advised that he appreciates the Director making this information available to him and that he will hold it in extreme confidence and will not attribute it to the Bureau if he finds it necessary to use in order to prevent further embarrassment to the White House. Mr. Hagerty said he wanted the Bureau to know that none of the persons mentioned by the informant were White House guests; further that if [name withheld White House aide] is doing these things, it is being done on his own and not as a White House task.

■ **Letter, Washington SAC James Gale to FBI Director J. Edgar Hoover, June 9, 1959**

You may be interested in the following information furnished by [an FBI source, whether the Washington police department or a wiretap concerning] a local prostitute . . . [who stated] that she had spent the afternoon of June 8, 1959, with Senator [name withheld] in his private office in the Senate. She also said she had sexual intercourse with the Senator during the afternoon "on the couch in the Senator's office."

You will recall [name withheld prostitute] previously associated with [name withheld senator] but this is the first occasion she has been with him in recent months.

■ **Personal Letter, FBI Director J. Edgar Hoover to Washington SAC James Gale, June 19, 1959**

I have received your note of June 9, 1959, and I want to thank you for bringing this informative data to my attention.

■ **Letter, Washington SAC James Gale to FBI Director J. Edgar Hoover, July 21, 1960**

I thought you would be interested in knowing that [a name withheld aide to] President Dwight D. Eisenhower . . . [was] seen in Rand's Nightclub, 1416 I Street, N.W., Washington, D.C., in a very intoxicated condition.

. . . [This White House aide] visited Rand's and . . . entered the club and became very boisterous and belligerent. He was asked to leave and refused. Thereafter, he was forcibly ejected . . . and he continued to be belligerent. . . . Metropolitan Police Department scout car appeared on the scene and inquired as to whether any assistance was needed. Informant advised that when the officers in the scout car saw who was causing the trouble, they conferred with the beatman and advised him of the identity and position of [name withheld who] was then driven to his home by the Metropolitan Police Department scout car. The informant was subsequently informed by the police that he should forget the entire incident. . . .

■ **Letter, Washington SAC James Gale to FBI Director J. Edgar Hoover, August 12, 1960**

For your information, on August 11, 1960, [name withheld] an admitted prostitute . . . became acquainted with the counselor of the company who occasionally arranged $100 prostitution dates for her with his friends. Among them she stated were Governor [name withheld] and United States Senator [name withheld]. . . . The counselor friend also arranged prostitution dates with United States Congressman [name withheld] according to [the prostitute].

About January, 1959, her counselor friend persuaded her to come to Washington, D.C., to work for [name withheld Congressman as a] clerk-typist. She worked in [name withheld Congressman's] office until May, 1959, and she stated that during that time the Congressman expected "my job to include taking care of him sexually." After quitting her job she practiced prostitution and [name withheld] was a customer of hers at a fee of $100.00 per date.

She made contacts with others on Capitol Hill . . . [including] United States Representative [name withheld], United States Representative [name withheld] and United States Representative [name withheld]. . . .

[She described name withheld Congressman] as a "weird one" in that he wanted her to perform unnatural sex acts with him. [Name withheld Congressman] took nude photographs [of the prostitute with] a Polaroid camera.

[Names and employees withheld of] both Washington, D.C. hotels, to steer $100 prostitution dates to her for which she gave them twenty per cent of her fees.

No investigation has been made concerning this information and the veracity or reliability of the source has not been established. [Name withheld prostitute] had no personal animosity toward the above-mentioned individuals and she was furnishing this information only to the Federal Bureau of Investigation on a confidential basis.

■ **Letter, Washington SAC Joseph Purvis to FBI Director J. Edgar Hoover, August 25, 1965**
On July 23, 1965, under the caption "Homosexuals in the Government," this office forwarded letterhead memorandum . . . concerning [name withheld] an employee of the Library of Congress; [name withheld] employee of the Central Intelligence Agency; and [name and title withheld]. [The FBI's informer] described himself to our Agents as a "male prostitute and thief." . . . At the time this information was furnished [the FBI's informer] declared that during the preceding two to two and a half years he had received a great deal of money, possibly in excess of $3,000, from a United States Senator for permitting the Senator to commit acts of oral sodomy on him. He declined to name the Senator. . . .
On August 19, 1965 [the FBI informer told] Special Agents Loren E. Beach and Harrold E. Charron, Jr., of this office, that [name withheld] was the Senator previously referred to by him. [FBI informer] first saw [name withheld senator] about twenty months ago . . . and, since that time over a period of about a year, had met him more than ten times at various locations in Washington. . . . [The FBI's informer said] his meetings with the Senator had always been arranged in conversations . . . [and] he had obtained in excess of $2,000 in cash from the Senator during their association. [The FBI's informer] had become fond of the Senator and during some of their meetings did not ask for money, although he had received as much as $460 from the Senator on one occasion. . . .
There has been no verification of the information furnished [by the FBI's informer]. It is not known whether any reliance whatever can be placed in the statements [of this informer]. I felt that having received this information I should advise you of it.

■ **Letter, FBI Director J. Edgar Hoover to Washington SAC Joseph Purvis, August 27, 1965**
I have received your letter of August 25th regarding information supplied to your office by [name withheld]. I appreciate your bringing this to my attention.

6: Members of Congress

BEGINNING INFORMALLY IN the 1940s, Hoover asked his aides for summary memoranda of relevant political and personal information already acquired by the FBI about members of Congress. This procedure was refined in the 1950s, and thereafter such memoranda were routinely prepared on all nonincumbent congressional candidates. These memoranda were maintained separate from the FBI's central records system in the Research Unit (later the Administrative Review Unit) under lock and key. FBI officials consulted these memoranda to assess the attitudes of member of Congress and to determine the FBI's relationship with them—and without risk of discovery. Because the memoranda were not files and were not incorporated in the FBI's central records system, Hoover could deny that the FBI maintained files (or dossiers) on members of Congress in its central records system.

The following examples document the type of information collected, the opportunities which allowed it to be used, and the range of Hoover's targets. While Hoover never directly blackmailed members of Congress, he subtly left the impression that he could. Former FBI assistant director William Sullivan has recounted how this was done: "The moment [Hoover] would get something on a Senator he would send one of the errand boys up and advise the Senator that we're in the course of an investigation and by chance happened to come up with this—we realized you'd want to know. . . . Well, Jesus, what does that tell the Senator? From that time on, the Senator's right in his pocket."

Not surprisingly, members of Congress were convinced that

*Hoover maintained files on them, despite his denials. The
powerful former chairman of the House Judiciary Committee,
Emanuel Celler, summed up these suspicions, attributing
Hoover's power to "the fact that he was the head of an agency
that in turn had tremendous power, power of surveillance,
power of control over the lives and destinies of every man in the
nation. He had a dossier on every member of Congress and
every member of the Senate....He had no right to have such
dossiers. But he had them, no question about it."*

*While Congressmen suspected that Hoover had information that
could ruin their careers, they hesitated to challenge him.
Hoover's power was also due to his helpfulness: he could help
to refute a highly damaging charge, or provide important
technical help. Over the years he forged a mutually beneficial
relationship with various chairmen of the House
Appropriations Committee, which had the power of the purse to
affect FBI operations. Hoover agreed to assign three FBI
agents to the committee's investigative staff. This arrangement
benefited both Hoover (ensuring a more favorable
consideration of FBI appropriation requests and, unknown to the
committee chairmen, providing Hoover with intelligence about
the plans of rival federal agencies) and the committee chairmen
(providing free access to experienced investigators).*

■ **Memo, FBI Supervisor Milton Jones to Assistant Director
Thomas Bishop, November 4, 1972, FBI 66-3286—Not
Recorded**
[Acting FBI Director L. Patrick] Gray has requested the infinite details
concerning our programs of collecting background information on Con-
gressional and gubernatorial candidates.
BACKGROUND:
An extensive search of Bufiles reveals nothing concerning these pro-
grams. . . .
Relying on the memory of employees who have been here since the late
1940s and early 1950s the following is the background of the Congression-
al program as best as can be recalled.
Early in the 1950s, added emphasis was placed on sending congratulato-
ry letters to successful Congressional candidates and to increased personal

contacts with Members of Congress. In conjunction with this some efforts were made to obtain biographical data on candidates and to determine what our relationship had been with them in the past. There apparently was no effort to compile this data in a central place.

About 1954 . . . a systematic review of data in Bufiles and available reference material was begun on Members of Congress. . . . Memos were not prepared in every instance but the data was summarized directly onto reference cards which [FBI assistant director Louis] Nichols about the same time, also apparently orally, instructed should be prepared on each Member of Congress so he and others dealing frequently with Congress would have readily available a summary of background data and pertinent information from Bufiles to refer to when it was necessary to contact the Members or when they received inquiries from them. . . .

During the early years of this program biographical data on newly elected members of Congress was gathered from whatever sources were available here in Washington but this proved unsatisfactory. SACs and ASACs then were requested to provide such data along with any information the field office might have in its files. These requests for several years were made orally during conferences and through other personal contacts with the Field Office officials. This also proved unsatisfactory so informal written requests were sent to the Field Offices for the background and summary of file information on major nonincumbent candidates. Data on incumbents has not been requested since we already knew them. Apparently, 1960 was the first year written instructions were used. . . .

Until this year the instructions cautioned that the matter was to be handled extremely discreetly and the information submitted on an informal basis [i.e., to ensure that it was not serialized and recorded in the FBI's central records system]. . . . In November, 1970, you . . . instructed, "Let's be even more circumspect next year—tell them to make no inquiries—get info only from records." Consequently, our instructions . . . directed—"Under *no* circumstances should you make outside inquiries such as checks of credit bureaus or newspaper morgues." . . . The instructions this year also specified the information was to be submitted "by routing slip, not letter." In the few instances where this was not complied with, the Field Office involved was told specifically to remove all copies of the material from its files and destroy it.

About 1959 we began the practice of submitting a memo on each newly elected Congressman and Senator incorporating the background information collected and a summary of data from Field Office and Bureau files. This was the only record ever kept on any information collected under this program. All data gathered on unsuccessful candidates was destroyed after the election. . . .

If a main file for general information, as contrasted to investigative type file, does not already exist in the Bureau on the new Member, this [summary] memo will become the basis for opening such a general file. This file then will become the repository for all future general information concerning the new Member. . . . If the Member becomes the subject of an investigation, either criminal or otherwise, a separate file on this matter is opened and records concerning the investigation will go into the investigative file, not the general file. . . .

HOW THE PROGRAM WORKED:

Following is a step-by-step account on how this program has worked. . . .

Each election year since 1960 routing slips have been sent to all Field Offices requesting background data and information from Field Office files on major nonincumbent candidates for Congress and for governor. . . .

Material has been received from the Field generally by routing slip or in sealed envelopes addressed to the Crime Research Division. On rare occasions some Field Offices have submitted the data in formal communications and in each instance these offices have been orally instructed to remove from their files all copies of the material, and the communications were treated here as informal ones with no record being made in Bureau files.

One clerical employee has been assigned to handle the election project each year. As data came in from the Field, she logged it in and then placed it in folders according to state and further broken down by Congressional districts. . . .

Early in September of election year this employee would request search slips from the Service Unit of the Files and Communications Division on each major nonincumbent candidate once she had collected sufficient biographical data to enable a reasonable check of Bureau indices. Where the search slip showed no record on the candidate in Bureau files this was attached to data received from the Field and held in the folder for use in dictating a memo should the candidate be elected.

If the search slip showed file references on the candidate, these files were requested and the references reviewed for information which should be included in the memo should the candidate win. Such information as the results of any prior investigations of the candidate, indications of criminal or subversive activities, indications of pro or anti law enforcement sentiments, prior contacts with FBI personnel, and positions on issues of interest to law enforcement would be summarized for inclusion in the memo. . . .

A reference card was then made up on the new Member. The first information on the card would be the biographical data included in the memo. Next would be a summary of any information contained in the memo which had come from Field Office or Bureau files. . . . Reference cards are filed alphabetically, divided by Members of the House of Representatives, Senators, and governors, the card on governors being maintained separately from Members of Congress. . . .

Reference cards are updated on a continuing basis . . . All information concerning Members of Congress from any source is supposed to be furnished to the Administrative Review Unit and tickler copies of all memoranda and correspondence prepared at Bureau headquarters to or related to Members of Congress are supposed to be designated for this Unit, and these items are reviewed for information to be added to the reference cards. Field offices periodically send to the Bureau information coming to their attention regarding Members of Congress, and this is reviewed for information which should be placed on the reference cards. No information is included on these reference cards unless it is supported by a document which has been designated to go into the official files of the Bureau. . . .

TYPE OF DATA RECEIVED AND HOW IT WAS SUBMITTED:

Most of the information which has been received on nonincumbent candidates has been of a routine biographical type, virtually all of which has come from two sources—campaign literature and news media articles. . . .

The type of information coming from Field Office files, if any, generally has related to some prior contacts office personnel have had with the candidate. On rare occasions, the Field has furnished information already in its files concerning allegations of criminal or corrupt practices, subversive activities, and immoral conduct. The vast majority of nonincumbent candidates have had no record in the Field Office files. The Field always has been instructed to submit material in this program informally. . . . Most of it has been received in this fashion. Some has been sent directly to the Crime Research Division in sealed envelopes. One or two offices this year, contrary to instructions, did forward the information to the Bureau by formal communication and each was promptly contacted telephonically and told to remove all reference to and copies of this material from Field Office files. . . .

We have not asked for data on incumbents since we already know them. The Field Offices from time to time, however, do submit to the Bureau in varying forms—letters, letterhead memoranda, airtels, teletypes—information which come to their attention concerning Members of Congress. This may include a contact the Member had with someone in the office, a speech he may have made in his home district wherein reference is made to the FBI, some allegations of possible criminal or subversive activity, or any number of other topics which the Field may consider of interest to the Bureau. All such information is supposed to be routed through the Administrative Review Unit for the information of its personnel and any action which it may deem necessary. Information of this type which might be pertinent to future dealings we may have with the Member will be summarized on the reference card maintained on him. . . .

THE FOLLOWING SUMMARY memorandum on Senator Henry Cabot Lodge, Jr., prepared in November 1946 following his reelection to the Senate, conveys the kind of information reported in FBI summary memoranda on members of Congress. What distinguishes the Lodge summary—and explains why Hoover maintained a copy in his secret office file—was the change in Lodge's political career in 1952. Defeated in his bid for reelection to the Senate that year by John Kennedy, Lodge did not retire from national politics. Instead, owing to his crucial support in achieving Dwight Eisenhower's nomination as the Republican presidential candidate, Lodge was rewarded with an appointment as U.S. ambassador to the United Nations.

Ironically, Eisenhower's requirement that all key executive appointees receive FBI security checks led FBI officials to investigate an allegation which they had earlier accepted without question—that Lodge was a homosexual. The resulting FBI investigation established that this allegation was unfounded—not surprisingly, given the nature of the source. Nonetheless, Hoover continued to maintain this misinformation in his office file, along with another allegation that Lodge "was having an affair with a woman" (the FBI has withheld the entire 1954 memo reporting this allegation and identifying its source).

Because the FBI's investigation established that the homosexual allegation was unfounded, Hoover did not report it to the Eisenhower White House in 1953. Nor was this allegation included in the 1960 summary memorandum which FBI officials prepared on Lodge when he was selected as Richard Nixon's vice-presidential running mate.

■ **Summary Memorandum Re Senator Henry Cabot Lodge, Jr., FBI Supervisor Milton Jones to FBI Assistant Director Louis Nichols, November 14, 1946**
There is set out below information in our files concerning [Lodge]. . . .
Attitude Toward The Bureau
Senator Lodge has corresponded rather frequently in a friendly tone with the Bureau since he entered the Senate. . . .
In October, 1937, Senator Lodge contacted the Director regarding the

possibility of designating an FBI man for a position of Chief of Police in a community in Massachusetts. The Director . . . [responded] that the personnel of the Bureau was so limited that he was unable to suggest an assignment of a Special Agent for this position. The names of three graduates of the National Academy, however, were submitted to Senator Lodge.

Addendum, 11-10-52, JTM [FBI supervisor John Mohr]: *mad; re Senator Henry Cabot Lodge, Jr. Information in Bureau Files:*

 . . . On October 26, 1947, the New York office reported in the Russian espionage case in which Jack Soble was the subject . . . that Julius Soble, a cousin of the subject, was the sponsor for the entrance of the whole Soble family into the United States through his contacts with [Massachusetts] Senators David Walsh and Henry C. Lodge. . . .

The April 4, 1950, edition of the Washington Post carried an article concerning Senator Lodge's disapproval of "public loyalty probes." Senator Lodge proposed that the best manner in which to conduct an inquiry into Communist infiltration of the State Department would be by "a twelve man, nonpartisan commission, a sort of American equivalent to a British 'Royal Commission.' "

Senator Lodge was also reported as saying that the "present method of hearing charges of Communism often smeared innocent persons and actually missed the really dangerous individuals and could actually protect the real Communist ring leaders." . . .

One [name withheld] was investigated by Army G-2 [military intelligence]. General Bolling of G-2 advised that one [name withheld] an employee at G-2 had been interrogated at great length . . . [and had] voluntarily furnished information regarding many individuals mentioned by and including [name withheld], a self admitted pervert, restricted his information to matters of perversion and according to Bolling, [name withheld's] testimony confirmed information previously obtained by CIC [Counterintelligence Corps].

In this regard [name withheld] advised an informant that Senator Henry Cabot Lodge was an alleged homosexual and . . . [that name withheld] was a social contact of [Secretary of State] Dean Acheson and an alleged Communist Party member.

[Nichols's handwritten insert: "Detailed memo 11/22/52 Reflects (name withheld) unreliable & charges vs Lodge unfounded"]

According to a G-2 report on July 28, 1950, it was ascertained from an informant that Senator Lodge was a frequent visitor to one [name withheld], an alleged homosexual and Communist Party member.

On November 10, 1950, the CIC reported that in all probability the aforementioned [name withheld] was actually [name withheld] a former page boy in the United States Senate. The CIC report stated "It is now believed that [name withheld] is the person with whom Senator Lodge is associated."

There was no further information of any kind in Bureau files substantiating these allegations. The Bureau did not institute any investigation in regard to these allegations. . . .

■ **Memo, FBI Assistant Director Alex Rosen to FBI Assistant Director D. Milton Ladd, December 17, 1952**

. . . To advise of certain derogatory information developed during the course of [security clearance] investigation of Henry Cabot Lodge, Jr. . . .

The records of the Massachusetts State Board of Probation . . . contain a record which shows that one Henry C. Lodge . . . was arrested in Roxbury District of Boston on October 28, 1922, charged with intoxication, but released without arraignment in court. The records of the Traffic Bureau, Metropolitan Police Department, Washington, D.C., indicate that on December 17, 1943, [Lodge] was ticketed for a parking violation and elected to forfeit $3.00.

[One paragraph withheld on national security grounds.]

. . . An investigation was conducted by the Department of the Army concerning one [name withheld] . . . [who] admitted to the Department of the Army that he was a homosexual and further admitted that many statements he had made . . . regarding his associations with high Government officials, were made for the purpose of impressing people. By his self-admission, many of his statements concerning the activities of Government employees were false, without foundation and were made to give him a feeling of importance. In addition to Lodge, among other prominent Government officials whom [name withheld] reportedly alleged were homosexuals were Franklin Delano Roosevelt, Dean Acheson, Harry Hopkins and Jesse Larson. . . . The current investigation of Lodge failed to disclose the slightest indication of any homosexuality on his part.

Recommendation

It is recommended that the information concerning the arrest of Lodge in 1922, the parking violation in 1943 [four lines withheld on personal privacy and sources and methods grounds] it is recommended that this information not be incorporated in the memorandum for [assistant to the president Sherman] Adams. Likewise, in view of the admissions of [name withheld] and in the absence of any indication of homosexuality of Lodge being disclosed during the current investigation, it is recommended that this information not be disseminated to Governor Adams. In the event you approve, there is attached hereto, a memorandum containing results of the investigation of Lodge which is being furnished to Governor Adams.

[Hoover's handwritten notation: "OK."]

■ **Summary Memorandum Re Henry Cabot Lodge, Jr., FBI
Supervisor Milton Jones to FBI Assistant Director Cartha
DeLoach, July 28, 1960**

The following is a summary of pertinent information in Bufiles concerning Lodge which has been prepared in anticipation of his nomination for the Vice Presidency at the Republican National Convention in
Chicago. . . .

We have had cordial relations with Lodge since 1937. In 1950, the press
carried an account of Lodge's disapproval of "public loyalty probes."
Lodge felt such probes often smeared innocent persons, missed the really
dangerous individuals, and could actually protect the real communist ring
leaders. . . .

In May, 1950, Lodge called on the Director to informally and confidentially discuss the matters which had developed in connection with the
review of State Department files by the Tydings Subcommittee. Lodge
informed the Director that in files he had reviewed at the White House,
there were cases which contained no recommendations and in many
instances there was no indication that leads had been followed. The
Director informed him that he had not seen the files and could not
speak authoritatively about them, and emphasized that it is not the FBI's
function to reach conclusions in FBI reports. Lodge appreciated the
position of the Bureau and said he had been confused about the files as a
whole. . . .

In December, 1952, at his request, we conducted a Special Inquiry–
White House investigation of Lodge in connection with his appointment by
President-elect Eisenhower as Ambassador to the United Nations. This
investigation was favorable, although it is noted that in 1922, at the age of
20 and while a student at Harvard, Lodge was arrested in Boston for
intoxication but was released without court arraignment. Records pertaining to this arrest were destroyed after 20 years and the details of this
matter were not available. . . .

■ **Memo, FBI Assistant Director D. J. Dalbey to FBI Associate
Director Clyde Tolson, March 10, 1971**

The Director's routing slip asked for my recommendation concerning the
material [concerning Senator George McGovern] appearing in a 3/9/71,
memorandum from [FBI supervisor Milton] Jones to [FBI assistant director
Thomas] Bishop, attached.

I recommend that this matter be dropped, for the following reasons:

1. Although McGovern can be expected to take an occasional potshot at
the Director, it seems to me that his present campaign based on the [Shaw]

case* is about ready to fade out. There used to be a saying in the
newspaper business . . . that no story can stay in the headlines more than 7
days. Public interest fades. I think McGovern's present sally is fading and I
would not want to do anything to fan the flames all over again at this time.
If he wants to be President, he'll have to run on something other than a
campaign against the Director.

2. There is no act that would get political sympathy for McGovern than
the belief of other politicians that the Director had used the power at his
disposal against McGovern. There is no gain here to justify the risk.

3. [Two and one-half lines withheld on grounds that information is
national security classified.]

4. [Twelve lines withheld on personal privacy grounds.]

Recommendation:
That no further action be taken concerning this information.

*THE ABILITY TO acquire and safely maintain derogatory information
about members of Congress invited use of the information,
especially if a member of Congress had the temerity to criticize
Hoover.*

■ **Summary Memorandum Re Senator George S. McGovern, FBI
Supervisor Milton Jones to FBI Assistant Director Thomas
Bishop, March 9, 1971**
 . . . The following summarizes all material concerning Senator George
Stanley McGovern as contained in Bureau files. . . .

[Twelve pages followed detailing McGovern's liberal political activities,
including opposition to the Vietnam War and support for civil rights and
civil liberties. The FBI also withheld one and one-half pages on personal
privacy grounds and one page on national security grounds.]

During October, 1970, it came to our attention that McGovern had sent a
questionnaire to numerous local and campus police chiefs relative to our
adding 1,000 Agents. . . . The thrust of this questionnaire was that the

*Hoover had fired FBI agent Jack Shaw upon learning that Shaw had written a
letter criticizing some of Hoover's decisions as FBI director. McGovern criticized
the Shaw dismissal and claimed to have received a letter from ten other FBI agents
expressing similar criticisms of Hoover.—Ed.

thousand Agents were being added so that we might become involved in police campus activities. The Director noted on one of these communications that "It looks as if McGovern is going all out in hopes of defeating the legislation." . . .

McGovern has taken upon himself to become involved in the matter of the resignation of former Special Agent John F. Shaw, Sr. . . . He has suggested an investigation of the matter and erroneously claimed that the Director refused to furnish information regarding this case to Senator [Edward] Kennedy although he furnished a detailed analysis of the matter to the press. (Actually the Director's letter which was published was sent prior to Shaw's filing suit and the Director's letter to Kennedy came after the suit was filed and after the Department had indicated the Bureau should not discuss this case further.) McGovern has continued his attack on the Director and on 3-1-71 released a statement critical of the Director, including an anonymous communication allegedly prepared by ten FBI Agents critical of the Bureau. McGovern also placed this anonymous letter in the Congressional Record.

A review of the personal records in the Director's Office failed to locate any additional pertinent material concerning McGovern.

■ **Personal Letter, SAC Memphis James Startzell to FBI Director J. Edgar Hoover, December 14, 1970**

The ridiculous nature of Congressman [William] Anderson's charges concerning your recent testimony before the House Sub-Committee on Appropriations [criticizing the Berrigan brothers and alleging that they were involved in a conspiracy to kidnap national security adviser Henry Kissinger] were most disturbing to the entire Memphis Office. So you can properly evaluate Anderson's creditability, I thought you would be interested in the following report on his personal habits and morality:

[One and one-half pages withheld on personal privacy grounds, but reports allegations that Anderson consorted with prostitutes.]

I thought you might like to know this background on Anderson.

■ **Letter, FBI Director J. Edgar Hoover to SAC Memphis James Startzell, December 16, 1970**

I received your letter of December 14th, with enclosures, and want you to know I very much appreciate your thoughtfulness in furnishing me this information concerning Congressman Anderson.

[Hoover's handwritten notation on bottom of his copy of this letter: "This shows what a whore-monger this old reprobate is!"]

■ **Personal Letter, FBI Director J. Edgar Hoover to Assistant to the President H. R. Haldeman, January 26, 1971**

As you are aware, some controversy has arisen as a result of this Bureau's investigation of the East Coast Conspiracy to Save Lives and a goodly portion of this has been as a result of comments made by Congressman William R. Anderson. . . .

[Four lines withheld on grounds of personal privacy and sources and methods of the FBI, but reports that Anderson consorted with prostitutes.] This Bureau has conducted no investigation regarding this as no Federal violation appears to be involved; however, it does tend to give some insight into the character of the man who, according to "The Washington Post," seems to enjoy quoting the Scriptures.

The information concerning Congressman Anderson's alleged extracurricular activities has also been furnished to the Attorney General [John Mitchell] and to the Vice President [Spiro Agnew].

■ **Strictly Confidential Memo, J. Edgar Hoover, March 23, 1942**

The attached photostatic papers [three letters] concerning [Senator] Claude E. Pepper were handed to me by Mr. Edmond Toland, Counsel for the Committee on Naval Affairs of the House of Representatives. They had been obtained by him in the course of an investigation conducted by that Committee. The attached document disclosed that certain credit was placed by Alexander Brest with the Brooks Brothers at New York City, permitting Senator Pepper to purchase haberdashery at that concern, to be paid for by Mr. Alexander Brest.

[Attached Document] According to the records of Brooks Brothers the shirt ($9.25) purchased by Senator Pepper on Mr. Brest's account was originally charged to the Senator's account but Mr. John Kertin of the Madison Avenue Store of this company was advised by the Senator that this charge should be made to Mr. Brest's account.

■ **Photocopy of Carbon Copy of Letter, Alexander Brest to Senator Claude Pepper, October 7, 1940**

When I wrote you this summer I was on my way to New York but we were awarded the contract at the Naval Air Base and for that reason the trip was postponed. I had intended while on my trip contacting Brooks Brothers. However, I have since written them and enclose herewith their letter to me which will take care of whatever purchases you may wish to make. . . .

■ **Photocopy of Letter, Senator Claude Pepper to Alexander Brest, October 11, 1940**

Many, many thanks for your kind letter of the 7th. I hope to be in New York early Saturday morning for a little while, and I hope I shall have an opportunity to take advantage of your very great kindness. . . .

■ **Photocopy of Carbon Copy of Letter, Alexander Brest to Senator Claude Pepper, December 10, 1940**

Sometime ago I wrote you about my brother and sister-in-law . . . and I should personally appreciate it if you could drop a personal note to the United States Consul at Jerusalem asking him to do what he can within his power to assist them in entering the United States. A letter from you to the Consul would guarantee that they would receive courteous and prompt treatment on any questions that they might wish to ask. . . .

P.S. Do not forget to see Brooks Brothers on your next visit to New York.

■ **Memo, FBI Director J. Edgar Hoover to FBI Assistant Directors Clyde Tolson, John Mohr, Thomas Bishop, and Nicholas Callahan, September 24, 1970, Tolson File**

I called Mr. Egil Krogh at the White House and told him the reason I was bothering him was the fact that I have been trying to do a little footwork around the Capitol to find out how our supplemental appropriation should be handled and get it through. . . . [I urged him] to get in touch with (John J.) Rooney who is chairman of our subcommittee. I said (Emanuel) Celler is very much angered by the crime bill because he was not consulted but [Appropriations Committee chairman George] Mahon is a very reasonable fellow and, in addition to that, I have a staff of agents who are assigned to the Appropriations Committee on the House side to conduct investigations for them, so he is very cordially inclined toward the Bureau for that assistance and would respond very readily, and Rooney is a Democrat but he is also cordially inclined toward the Bureau and has been over the years but it will make him happy to be consulted. . . .

■ **Memo, FBI Director J. Edgar Hoover to FBI Assistant Directors Clyde Tolson, John Mohr, Thomas Bishop, and Nicholas Callahan, September 30, 1970, Tolson File**

I called Mr. Egil Krogh . . . [and recommended that] in the future, when they have conferences like the one I attended at the White House last week, they should at least have present . . . the chairmen of the appropriations committees. I said Mahon is a very decent fellow and Senator (Richard B.) Russell is a very decent fellow; that whether or not Rooney should be invited, I don't know. . . .

I said we have with the appropriations committee, a staff of our own men who are assigned to the appropriations committee for three years and then they rotate, to carry on any investigations the chairmen may order in any of the government agencies. Mr. Krogh said this sort of cements good relations. I said yes, we have had excellent relations with the committee and, of course, I have always gotten along well with John Rooney, as well as the chairmen on back. . . .

7: "Subversive" Activities

BY STATUTE, THE FBI is the investigative division of the Department of Justice, with authority to look into violations of federal statutes. Under Hoover's direction, however, the Bureau was not fully accountable to the attorney general, nor were its investigative activities confined to accumulating evidence toward prosecution. These shifts in activities and accountability were a byproduct of the Bureau's investigations of "subversive" activities.

Hoover's obsessive concern with "subversives," defined so as to encompass the broad range of dissident political activities, marked the focus of FBI investigations after the 1930s and contributed to the emergence of a powerful, autonomous FBI. For example, the Bureau had 441 agents when Hoover became director in 1924, and the number declined to 391 in 1933. By 1936, however, the FBI had grown to approximately 600 agents (an expansion occasioned by the enactment between 1932 and 1934 of a series of laws criminalizing bank robbing, extortion, and kidnaping). And real growth occurred after 1936: to 898 in 1940, 4,886 in 1945, and 7,029 in 1952. The swelling of staff was not triggered by new federal laws or the Bureau's espionage and counterintelligence activities. Instead, the FBI focused on "subversive" activities—at first, during the 1930s and early 1940s, investigating "fascist and communist" activities; then, after 1945, focusing on "communist" activities.

The concern over communism did not mean that the FBI sought to prove Soviet direction and control over the U.S. Communist party and its affiliates. Rather, the FBI attempted to determine communist influence in a host of dissident political movements. *"Communist influence"* or *"communist infiltration"* provided the rationale for the FBI's surveillance efforts, most notably in four areas: the federal bureaucracy, trade unions, college campuses, and the civil rights movement.

The extent of the FBI's coverage of these activities makes it virtually impossible to convey the full scope of Hoover's obsession. For example, when the FBI initiated its investigation of the Southern Christian Leadership Conference in 1957, that investigation was case file number 438,794 in the Internal Security classification! What follows are representative documents which convey the scope and underlying political purpose of FBI "subversive" investigations as well as examples of Hoover's independence of any significant oversight.

The creation of federal employee loyalty programs, first on a temporary basis during World War II and then permanently under President Truman's executive order of March 1947, provided the cover for FBI investigations of "suspect" employees and applicants. In 1951, on his own authority, Hoover initiated a program to disseminate to governors and university officials information about the "subversive" background of college faculty. In 1968, again on his own authority, Hoover began COINTELPRO–New Left, a program "to harass, disrupt and discredit" New Left organizations and activists, including disseminating derogatory political and personal information to "reliable" reporters and influential citizens.

Hoover kept close tabs on the civil rights movement from the 1940s. His interest in the activities of Martin Luther King, Jr., was thus not atypical, except perhaps the desire to obtain compromising personal information. Exploiting the opening provided by Attorney General Robert Kennedy's interest in wiretapping King, and Kennedy's conditional approval of such a tap in October 1963, Hoover was able to expand FBI wiretapping activities. First he ignored Kennedy's stipulation of a follow-up review in thirty days; then he interpreted the original authorization as permitting FBI wiretapping and bugging of King's hotel rooms and temporary residences around the country.

Hoover's independence was challenged only by Attorneys General Nicholas Katzenbach and Ramsey Clark, both of whom instituted rules ensuring their prior review and reauthorization of wiretapping and bugging. These restrictions lasted only briefly; the election of Richard Nixon brought a return to the more permissive policies of earlier years.

■ **Personal and Confidential Memo, FBI Director J. Edgar Hoover to Attorney General Francis Biddle, September 1, 1942**

I am transmitting herewith . . . a revised report outlining the background, scope and results of the investigation orchestrated by the Bureau under the Congressional directive requiring it to investigate allegations of subversive activities on the part of Government employees. Having been advised [by the department] . . . that the report be submitted in anonymous form, that is, without the inclusion therein of the names of individuals or organizations which were subjects of the investigation, I have in accord with these instructions had this report prepared in a completely anonymous form.

The attached report does not set forth a comprehensive and complete picture of the Bureau's investigation of these cases. . . . The Bureau's complete four-volume report as submitted by me to you on July 16, 1942, is a more adequate presentation of the origin, policies and results of this project . . . [and sets] forth a complete resume of the background and handling of the cases referred to the Bureau with specific references to organizations included within the scope of the investigation. . . . In my opinion the report submitted to Congress should include the names of the organizations which were considered within the scope of the investigation, if not, the names of the individuals investigated.

Although the Department has ruled that a total of 47 organizations was subversive . . . the omission of the names of these organizations from the Bureau's report will enable these groups to continue their activities without any curtailment of their subversive efforts or intentions. . . . The inclusion in the report of the names of the organizations considered to be subversive would have a restricting effect upon the membership, policies and even the continued existence of the majority of these organizations. . . .

As to the naming in the report of specific individuals, . . . Congress would desire to have an indication of the nature of the cases investigated and the facts developed thereby. The omission of that section of the report . . . precludes Congress from obtaining this information. In addition, fairness and justice demands that the facts developed by the investigation of the Federal Bureau of Investigation . . . should be set forth since the names of many of these persons have been bandied around as charged with subversive activities, but the employing agencies have after receipt of the Bureau's report of these investigations in many in-stances advised the Federal Bureau of Investigation that the facts did not warrant administrative action on the part of the employing agency. This would afford vindication in those cases of accusations not resulting in administrative action, thereby preserving this basic principle of civil liberties. . . .

■ Do Not File Memo, FBI Assistant Director Edward Tamm to FBI Director, November 5, 1945, Nichols File

Attached hereto are several memoranda recommending discontinuance of technical surveillances [wiretaps] on CIO [Congress of Industrial Organization] units in which there is a strong element of Communist activity.* We have from time to time obtained some information from these technical surveillances which has constituted an "item of interest" in connection with memoranda which we have prepared, either upon our initiative or upon the request of an outside agency, for transmittal to the White House, the Attorney General, the Secretary of the Navy, and others. It is a fact, however, that in spite of our information about these Commu-nist activities in these units, in strikes, and in various other every-day occurrences, nothing whatsoever is done by the policy-making agencies of the Government about this Communist activity.

I think we should, consequently, evaluate this coverage, particularly since the termination of the war, upon the basis of a realistic approach predicated upon the fact that no affirmative action is taken upon the information which we furnish. . . . When these technical surveillances are evaluated upon the basis of the question, "What will anybody do about the information received from these technicals?", we might as well face the fact that our effort is practically wasted.

[FBI associate director Clyde Tolson's handwritten notation: "I agree 11/5." Hoover's handwritten notation: "I can't entirely agree. I do think there have been too many unproductive technicals installed but in these 3

*The FBI wiretapped at least six unions: the CIO maritime committee; the Food, Tobacco, Agricultural & Allied Workers of America (CIO); the International Longshoremen's and Warehousemen's Union; the National Maritime Union; the National Union of Marine Cooks & Stewards; and the United Public Workers of America (formerly the United Federal Workers of America). In addition, the FBI bugged meetings of the Congress of Industrial Organizations (CIO) council, the United Automobile Workers, the United Electrical Radio & Machine Workers of America, and the United Mine Workers.—Ed.

cases they are highly informative on an aspect of Communist activities of considerable importance."]

FOR REASONS OF "national security" and defense production, federal employees and labor unions commanded Hoover's interest; but no such rationale explains the FBI's monitoring of the political activities of university faculty. The following examples highlight the political criteria that governed FBI investigations of "subversive activities."

■ **Memo, FBI Assistant Director Hugh Clegg to FBI Associate Director Clyde Tolson, November 25, 1952**
[Name withheld but Illinois State Senator Paul Broyles] . . . advised as follows: . . .
Using blackmail and the threat of disclosing [Bradley University president David] Owen's [homosexual] tendencies, the Reds have infiltrated the [Bradley] university faculty until it today is in part suspected of being a portion of an espionage apparatus. Even narcotics violations are prevalent and the Narcotics Bureau has had some of the activity on the campus under their jurisdiction under surveillance. *The University Library is the headquarters of the Heroin dispensary. Even students are being corrupted. They can buy a "B" average for $50 or an "A" for $75. . . .* The Senator . . . *would appreciate the Bureau conducting an investigation within its jurisdiction concerning red infiltration and actual subversiveness and perhaps espionage. The blackmail angle may have involved interstate commerce but he has no information along this line. . . .*

■ **Airtel, FBI Director to SAC Springfield, December 2, 1952**
. . . [State Senator Paul Broyles] . . . suggested for additional leads that [names withheld Bradley University trustees] might be discreetly contacted. . . . You are instructed to discreetly interview these individuals without delay providing no information contained in your files which would preclude the interviews. The interviews should be conducted by

mature and experienced Agents and no additional investigation should be conducted without prior Bureau authority. . . .

■ **Memo, SAC Springfield to FBI Director, May 28, 1968**

[Names withheld Bradley University alumni] . . . are becoming increasingly concerned over the activities going on at Bradley University and the way the administration seems to be heading. On the basis of an exhaustive survey they have conducted, they have reached the conclusion independently that [university officials Heard and Kuchel] are responsible for hiring "Nuleft" liberal minded faculty members who are promoting liberal ideas and supporting the Students for a Democratic Society, recently formed on the Bradley campus. . . . Since Hurd's [sic] arrival, the following instructors and professors have been hired at Bradley who have continually espoused the "Nuleft" line and have supported, in statements and speeches, the Students for a Democratic Society, which was chartered at Bradley in 5-67. In addition, the majority of these newly hired faculty members have engaged in Anti Viet Nam War Demonstrations and have supported students engaging in protest marches directed against the administration on the Viet Nam war issues. These faculty members hired by Kuchel and Heard include the following: Dr. Ronald Simmons, Economic Department; Briant Lee, Assistant Professor Speech Department; L. Edgar Chapman, Assistant Professor English Department; Dr. Charles E. P. Simmons, Associate Professor History Department; Dr. Brenden Liddell, Associate Professor Philosophy Department; William R. Bellmont, Associate Professor Economics Department; James Ballone, Instructor History Department; Bernard Bray, Instructor Political Science Department; [five other faculty members' names and titles withheld]. . . .

All of the above group are extremely active in and have participated in Anti Viet Nam war support and are espousing "Nuleft" ideas and are avid supporters of SDS on the Bradley campus. Articles written and published by some of the above faculty members have followed the National SDS line as well as the "Communist" lines on such international issues as the Viet Nam war, "economic freedoms" and moral issues. Speeches made by these professors deal with "man and machine, alienation and existentialism and Viet Nam protests and draft registration alternatives."

[Five pages withheld on grounds of personal privacy and FBI sources and methods.]

■ **Memo, FBI Director J. Edgar Hoover to FBI Assistant Directors Clyde Tolson, Alan Belmont, Cartha DeLoach, and William Sullivan, January 28, 1965, Tolson File**

SAC Wesley G. Grapp, Los Angeles, returned my earlier call to him. I told Mr. Grapp that this situation [the free speech movement] at the University of California at Berkeley is, of course, infiltrated with a lot of communists, both in the student body and the faculty. I stated this afternoon [former CIA director] John McCone was over and . . . is a close personal friend of [name withheld member of the board of regents] who . . . recently had a conversation with Mr. McCone at which time he was disturbed about the situation at Berkeley and he says the Board of Regents has on it some substantial people like Mrs. Norman Chandler but there are two or three individuals who are inclined to be ultra liberal. I stated [this regent] is puzzled as to how he can handle the situation and is anxious to get a line on any persons who are communists or have communist associations either on the faculty or in the student body and then at a Board of Regents level handle it without disclosing his source.

I stated I had told Mr. McCone that I would have prepared and sent to him, Grapp, a memorandum in the next day or two of public source information on some of these individuals causing trouble at Berkeley.

[Tolson's handwritten insert: "done 1-29"]

I stated, of course, one of the principal factors is that [University of California] President [Clark] Kerr has not taken an active part in this but left it largely to a faculty committee. I stated the memorandum will be sent to him, Grapp, and I want him to then make an appointment to see [this regent] and give him the information, which is public source material but not to be disclosed to anyone as having emanated from the FBI. I stated we will see how that works out and if it looks all right and if his, Grapp's, reaction is that [this regent] is a safe individual to talk to, we may later give him some information which is not public source, but I did not want to do that now because I want to see what his, Grapp's reaction is of [this regent].

Mr. Grapp asked if I wanted to give the information forwarded to him to [this regent] orally or in writing. I told him that what we send in the next day or so can be given in writing because it will be public source and on plain paper and not identified with the FBI. . . . Mr. Grapp stated that from the local sense, the big problem is that [California] Governor Pat Brown and President Kerr do not have much backbone. I stated that apparently they had given in on everything these young punks causing the trouble have wanted and so told Mr. McCone that was my reaction and of the difficulties we had with President Kerr. . . .

EFFORTS TO CHALLENGE racial discrimination and segregation, even when championed by such respectable leaders as Eleanor

Roosevelt and Martin Luther King, Jr., triggered both FBI investigations and attempts to contain and disrupt these activities.

■ **Do Not File Memo, FBI Assistant Director D. Milton Ladd to FBI Director, September 11, 1942, FBI 62-116758**

As you know, the [FBI] Field [offices] is conducting a survey concerning foreign inspired agitation among the Negroes in this country. In conducting this survey, information was received by the Field concerning other causes of agitation other than those which are possibly foreign inspired. I wanted to bring to your attention rumors which the Savannah and Birmingham Offices have received concerning the formation of Eleanor or Eleanor Roosevelt Clubs among the Negroes in these respective Field Divisions.

The Savannah Field Division has received information relative to rumors of the existence of these clubs in Charleston, South Carolina; Sumter, South Carolina; and Savannah, Georgia. It is advised that in all of these cities evidence of unrest among the Negroes appears to be of considerable proportion. Such incidents as Negro maids allegedly demanding their own terms for working and at the same time stating they were members of an Eleanor Roosevelt Club are typical of the rumors reported to the Savannah Field Division. No substantiating information, however, has been received concerning these rumors. However, it is stated that complaints are received that the cause of agitation among the Negroes in this area is largely attributed to the encouragement given Negroes by Mrs. Roosevelt.

The Birmingham Field Division has received a report from the vicinity of Anniston, Alabama, to the effect that attempts in that area are being made to form Eleanor Clubs by a strange white man and a large Negro organizer traveling in an automobile. The unverified information indicates that only female domestics are desired for membership. The alleged slogan of the club is "A White Woman in the Kitchen by Christmas"; inferring that Negroes work only part of the day. Similar clubs are claimed to be in operation in other cities in Alabama.

In this connection the Birmingham Field Division has advised that Mrs. Roosevelt visited Tuskegee Institute at Tuskegee, Alabama, sometime in 1941, at which time she is stated to have made a talk commenting on the status of the Negro. During her visit, she is said to have refused to visit the white people in the vicinity and instead was entertained throughout her visit by Negroes. . . .

I wanted to bring this matter to your attention in view of its possible connection with the current unrest and dissatisfaction among the Negroes, especially in the aforementioned areas.

■ **Do Not File Memo, FBI Assistant Director D. Milton Ladd to FBI Assistant Director Edward Tamm, October 21, 1942, FBI 62-116758**

Attached hereto is a report [which] refers to the "Eleanor Clubs," advising that practically every negro knows of these Clubs and that they are places to patronize.

As you know, the Bureau has made many inquiries in an effort to obtain specific information concerning the existence of such Clubs, which inquiries have met with negative results. . . .

■ **Memo, FBI Assistant Director Louis Nichols to FBI Associate Director Clyde Tolson, October 19, 1955, FBI 61-3176-1076**

SAC Mumford called from Atlanta . . . [to report that on October 19, 1955, Georgia attorney general Eugene Cook] read prepared speech . . . in which he blasted the National Association for the Advancement of Colored People (NAACP). . . . In the speech Cook picked out individual officials of the NAACP and listed public source citations against them which is on the record with the House Committee on Un-American Activities. In conclusion he extemporaneously stated that it was his understanding that Director Hoover of FBI had indicated on one occasion that NAACP was not a Communist organization. He then added that . . . he had not meant to imply that the NAACP was a Communist organization, but that . . . officials of the NAACP have questionable backgrounds. . . . Mumford stated the wire services would probably carry this matter, consequently his call to the Bureau.

My memorandum to you today reflected that [name withheld SAC] had called from Memphis advising that the NAACP was apparently using to its advantage a letter which the Director wrote to [NAACP executive secretary] Walter White 4-14-47, which the NAACP is construing as an endorsement by the Director of the NAACP which may be what Cook had in mind. . . .

Walter White of the NAACP by letter 4-8-47, asked the Director to send a statement giving his opinion of the contribution to democracy of the work of the NAACP. The Director in reply by letter dated 4-14-47, wrote to White giving him permission to utilize the following statement in a pamphlet White proposed distributing:

"Equality, freedom, and tolerance are essential in a democratic government. The National Association for the Advancement of Colored People has done much to preserve these principles and to perpetuate the desires of our founding fathers."

This, apparently, is the letter [name withheld Memphis SAC] believes is being utilized by the NAACP to show it is not subversive.

[Hoover's handwritten notation: "Q. Note my letter was written nearly 9 years ago & when NAACP under Walter White was a well disciplined group. 2. Let me have general memo on NAACP."]

[Hoover's request was addressed by FBI assistant director Alan Belmont who prepared on October 21, 1955, a detailed memorandum about NAACP officials' "subversive" activities and associations in their challenge to racial discrimination and segregation.]

■ **Memo, FBI Assistant Director Courtney Evans to FBI Assistant Director Alan Belmont, July 16, 1963**

The AG [Attorney General Robert Kennedy] was contacted at his request late this afternoon. . . . The purpose of the AG's contact was . . . the possibility of effecting technical coverage on both [civil rights activist Clarence] Jones and Martin Luther King. I told the AG that I was not at all acquainted with Jones, but that, in so far as King was concerned, it was obvious from the reports that he was in a travel status practically all the time, and it was, therefore, doubtful that a technical surveillance on his office or home would be very productive. I also raised the question as to the repercussions if it should ever become known that such a surveillance had been put on King.

The AG said this did not concern him at all; that in view of the possible communist influence in the racial situation, he thought it advisable to have as complete coverage as possible. I told him, under the circumstances, that we would check into the matter to see if coverage was feasible and, if so, would submit an appropriate recommendation to him.

If you approve, we will have a preliminary survey made to see if technical coverage is feasible with full security.

[Hoover's handwritten notation at bottom: "1. Yes. 2. What do our files show on Jones?"]

■ **JUNE Memo, FBI Assistant Director F. J. Baumgardner to FBI Assistant Director William Sullivan, July 22, 1963**

. . . Pursuant to the Attorney General's request that consideration be given to placing a technical surveillance on King, our Atlanta Office was requested to conduct a survey to ascertain if such coverage is feasible and could be conducted with full security. Atlanta teletype 7/20/63 discloses that technical coverage on King is feasible and can be conducted with full security. . . .

In view of the Attorney General's request that our coverage be as complete as possible, it is felt that we should institute coverage not only on King's residence, but also on his office at the Southern Christian Leadership Conference.

Recommendation:

That the attached memorandum for the Attorney General go forward requesting authority to install a technical surveillance on King's residence, as well as his office at the Southern Christian Leadership Conference.

[Hoover's handwritten notation: "OK."]

[Reports captioned "JUNE" were not filed in the FBI's main case files. They were to be routed to the Special File Room ensuring that this information could not be publicly compromised. Wiretap and bugging requests, as well as reports from secretaries to prominent officials discussing these officials' activities, were to be captioned JUNE.]

■ **Memo, FBI Director J. Edgar Hoover to Attorney General Robert Kennedy, July 23, 1963**

. . . Pursuant to your request that in view of the possible communist influence in the racial situation consideration be given to placing a technical surveillance on King, it is requested that authority be granted to place a technical surveillance on King at his current residence or at any future address to which he may move. It is further requested that authority be granted to place a technical surveillance on the Southern Christian Leadership Conference of which King is President or at any future address to which it may be moved.

[Evans's handwritten notation: "A.G. (Attorney General) said *no.*"]

■ **JUNE Memo, FBI Assistant Director Courtney Evans to FBI Assistant Director Alan Belmont, July 25, 1963**

The Attorney General orally informed me today that he had been considering the request he made on July 16, 1963, for a technical surveillance on Martin Luther King at his home and office and was now of the opinion that this would be ill advised.

At the time the Attorney General initially asked for such a surveillance, he was told there was considerable doubt that the productivity of the surveillance would be worth the risk because King travels most of the time and that there might be serious repercussions should it ever become known the Government had instituted this coverage. These were the very thoughts that the Attorney General expressed today in withdrawing his request. . . .

■ **JUNE Memo, FBI Supervisor J. F. Bland to FBI Assistant Director William Sullivan, October 4, 1963**

Surveys have been made on the residence of Martin Luther King, Jr., in Atlanta, Georgia, and the headquarters of the Southern Christian Leadership Conference (SCLC) in New York City. These surveys indicate it is feasible to install technical surveillances on these places with full security. . . .

In view of the Attorney General's [earlier] request that our coverage be as complete as possible and because of the communist influence in the racial movement shown by activities of [civil rights activist and King adviser] Stanley Levison as well as King's connection with him, it is believed desirable to put all possible coverage on the racial leaders in order to obtain full information.

[Hoover's handwritten notation: "I hope you don't change your minds on this."]

Recommendation:

That the attached be sent to the Attorney General requesting authority to install technical surveillances on King's residence in Atlanta, Georgia, and the SCLC headquarters in New York City.

[Hoover's handwritten notation: "OK."]

■ **JUNE Memo, FBI Assistant Director Courtney Evans to FBI Director Alan Belmont, October 10, 1963**

The Attorney General . . . had before him our memorandum of October 7, 1963, requesting authority for technical surveillances on Martin Luther King at his residence at Atlanta and at the office of the Southern Christian Leadership Conference of which he is president, at New York City.

The Attorney General . . . recognized the importance of this coverage if substantial information is to be developed concerning the relationship between King and the Communist Party. He said there was no question in his mind as to the coverage in New York City but that he was worried about the security of an installation covering a residence in Atlanta, Georgia. He noted that the last thing we could afford to have would be a discovery of a wire tap on King's residence.

I pointed out to the Attorney General the fact that a residence was involved did not necessarily mean there was any added risk because of the technical nature of the telephone system. He was informed that the Bureau had had years of experience in this field and that we continually reviewed our procedures to insure that every measure possible to secure such installations was taken. It was nevertheless noted that of necessity we had to deal with established contacts in the telephone company to get the necessary leased lines, but once again we had procedures which minimized the risks to the nth degree.

After this discussion the Attorney General said he felt we should go ahead with the technical coverage on King on a trial basis, and to continue it if productive results were forthcoming. He said he was certain that all Bureau representatives involved would recognize the delicacy of this particular matter and would thus be even more cautious than ever in this assignment. He asked to be kept advised of any pertinent information developed regarding King's communist connections.

Our memorandum requesting authority for this surveillance was signed by the Attorney General. . . .

[Belmont's handwritten notation: "(Atlanta) SAC McMahon advised 10-21-63 re: authorization for tech (wiretap) on King."]

■ **JUNE Memo, FBI Supervisor J. F. Bland to FBI Assistant Director William Sullivan, October 18, 1963**

. . . A survey has now been conducted on the headquarters of the SCLC at Atlanta, Georgia, and this survey indicates it is feasible to install a technical surveillance on this place with full security. . . .

Recommendation:

That the attached be sent to the Attorney General requesting authority to install a technical surveillance on the headquarters of the SCLC in Atlanta.

[Hoover's handwritten notation: "O.K."]

■ **JUNE Memo, FBI Assistant Director Courtney Evans to FBI Assistant Director Alan Belmont, October 21, 1963**

The Attorney General spoke to me with reference to our memorandum of October 18, 1963, . . . [and] is apparently still vacillating in his position as to technical coverage on Martin Luther King and his organization, it being recalled that he had initially suggested such coverage and then changed his mind and felt it might be inadvisable.

The Attorney General said that he is still uncertain in his own mind about this coverage. I reminded him of our previous conversation wherein he was assured that all possible would be done to insure the security of this operation.

The Attorney General advised he was approving the October 18, 1963, memorandum but asked that this coverage [on the SCLC] and that on King's residence be evaluated at the end of 30 days in light of the results secured so that continuance of these surveillances could be determined at that time. This will be done. . . .

[Hoover did not comply with Kennedy's conditional requirement of a reevaluation in thirty days. Preoccupied with the assassination of his brother on November 22, 1963, the attorney general failed to request an evaluative report—nor did Hoover remind him of the condition. The King tap was rescinded when Attorney General Nicholas Katzenbach, Kennedy's successor, discovered its existence in 1965.]

■ **Letter, Frank Baruto to FBI Assistant Director William Sullivan, December 30, 1963**
Man-of-the Year now!!
(see enclosure) [*Time* magazine, January 31, 1964, issue, selecting Martin Luther King as Man of the Year]
Next, we'll have a Vice Presidential Candidate or Cabinet member on our hands! . . .

■ **JUNE Memo, FBI Assistant Direction F. J. Baumgardner to FBI Assistant Director William Sullivan, January 23, 1964**
. . . SAC [R. J.] Baker of Milwaukee Office [authorized to] survey, provided full security was assured, to determine the feasibility of installing microphone coverage to cover the activities of Martin Luther King, Jr., and his associates while in Milwaukee, Wisconsin. . . .
At 5 p.m., 1/22/64, ASAC J. Wallace LaPrade . . . advised me that with full security a survey had been completed [and] that the survey revealed the situation to be perfect from the standpoint of effecting the coverage desired and that they were ready to go ahead with the installation immediately.
Action:
Because *time is of the essence,* I gave LaPrade the requested authority for the installation, provided full security is assured. . . . I reiterated to LaPrade the absolute necessity for the exercise of utmost tact and discretion in handling all phases of this matter. Further, he is to advise us promptly when King takes over space at the Hotel and the surveillance is activated. . . .

■ **JUNE Memo, FBI Assistant Director William Sullivan to FBI Assistant Director Alan Belmont, January 27, 1964**

. . . Authority given to the Milwaukee Office for a microphone surveillance (misur) to cover the activities of Martin Luther King, Jr., and his associates while in Milwaukee, Wisconsin. . . . The misur was activated. . . .

[Milwaukee SAC] Baker also advised that the local police have taken a room close to the suite of rooms engaged by King so that protection might be afforded King. In view of this, it was the conjecture of Baker that the likelihood of King's going ahead with any [phrase withheld, but womanizing] plans is greatly minimized. I agree with this observation.

[Hoover's handwritten notation: "I don't share the conjecture. King is a 'tom cat' with obsessive degenerate sexual urges."]

Milwaukee is to keep the Bureau promptly advised of all developments and upon receipt of additional information you will be further informed.

■ **JUNE Memo, FBI Assistant Director William Sullivan to FBI Assistant Director Alan Belmont, January 28, 1964**

SAC Baker phoned . . . to advise that the misur [on King] was unproductive as there were no activities of interest developed. . . .

■ **JUNE Memo, FBI Assistant Director F. J. Baumgardner to FBI Assistant Director William Sullivan, July 7, 1964**

. . . The Atlanta Office requested authority to install 3 additional technical surveillances (tesurs) on the facilities of the Southern Christian Leadership Conference (SCLC). . . . for the purpose of providing additional coverage of the SCLC and its leader Dr. Martin Luther King, Jr. . . . With the addition of the 3 additional surveillances there would be in operation a total of 7 tesurs. The 3 additional surveillances are desirable to provide coverage of additional telephone service recently secured by the SCLC.

The SCLC and Martin Luther King, Jr., are subjects of intensified Bureau investigations inasmuch as it has been determined that communists and communist sympathizers exert a great deal of influence over this organization. The 4 surveillances already in operation have provided extremely valuable information regarding the activities of the SCLC and King, much of which is not available through any other source. The surveillances have been most valuable in uncovering the extensive communist infiltration and domination of both King and the SCLC. . . .

Since the Attorney General has already authorized technical coverage of the SCLC and King, additional authority is not necessary since this is merely an extension of current coverage brought about by additional telephone service within the SCLC.

Recommendations:

1. That the attached letter to the Atlanta Office he approved advising that additional coverage requested is authorized. . . .

[Hoover's handwritten notation: "OK."]

■ **Urgent JUNE Teletype, FBI Director to SAC New York, August 11, 1964**

. . . Providing full security assured, authority granted to install tesur [wiretap] on Martin Luther King, Jr., on his temporary residence [in New York while attending the Democratic National Convention]. . . . Sulet [submit letter] justification twenty days after installation in event King continues temporary residence at above address. . . .

Note:

King, his wife and children intend to stay in the [name withheld] apartment most of the remainder of August, 1964. . . . New York has advised that installation of tesur is feasible and security is assured. In October, 1963, we received the Attorney General's authority to place a tesur on King at his Atlanta, Georgia, residence or at any future address to which he may move. We previously extended such coverage to temporary residences of King [hotel rooms during King's trips around the country] and it is believed most desirable to do so in this instance in view of his association with communists and the very vital matters he is presently concerning himself with, such as the forthcoming Democratic National Convention; the Mississippi situation;* the matter of racial disorders and demonstrations in New York City; and, also, King intends to go abroad for a few days this month. We have been able to keep the White House and others very currently informed concerning King and these important matters. The recommended extension of coverage will enable us to continue to do so. . . .

---

*The "Mississippi situation" involved efforts of liberal Democrats to ensure the seating of the Mississippi Freedom Democratic party as the recognized delegation at the Democratic National Convention. President Johnson opposed this effort, fearing that it might precipitate defections from Southern Democrats. The FBI's electronic coverage of King provided valuable political intelligence which FBI officials reported to the White House.—Ed.

■ **Informal Memo, FBI Assistant Director William Sullivan to FBI Assistant Director Alan Belmont, December 2, 1964, FBI 100-106670-1024**

Informal memorandum 11/27/64 (attached) set forth a summary of data pertaining to highly sensitive coverage [bugging] afforded Martin Luther King, Jr., during 1964. The summary set out the various incidents covered and noted the number of reels of tape available, the approximate listening time and the extent to which transcripts are presently available.

[FBI associate director] Tolson noted "I think all should be transcribed" and the Director so instructed.

Pursuant to your instructions to get the maximum amount of material available transcribed, we propose doing the following. . . . We already have field-prepared transcripts . . . prepared by Agents on the scene [which] are sufficient to back up [some of] the tapes. . . .

In connection with . . . the Willard Hotel, Washington, D.C., incident, we have no transcripts but only an 8-page memorandum. We propose having transcripts prepared covering the 15 reels and approximately 17 hours listening time. In connection with . . . the Los Angeles, California, 7/8-9/64 incident, we have only 3 pages of transcript and inasmuch as there are 5 reels with approximately 7½ hours listening time we propose having a more complete transcript prepared. . . .

Addendum: FBI Assistant Director Cartha DeLoach, 12/10/64

I fully agree that this work should *eventually be done*, particularly if an additional controversy arises with King. I see no necessity, however, in this work being done at the present time inasmuch as the controversy [see following documents] has quieted down considerably and we are not in need of transcriptions right now. In view of the transcription already accomplished, and because of the above-mentioned reasons, I would recommend that we hold off doing this tremendous amount of work until there is an actual need.

[Hoover's handwritten notation: "I think it should be done *now* while it is fresh in the minds of the specially trained agents." DeLoach's handwritten notation, dated 2/23/65: "Done. We have prepared 321 pp of transcripts (231 pp. for [Willard Hotel incident] & 90 pp. for [Los Angeles incident])."]

[The transcriptions and summaries, based on the FBI's bugging of King's hotel rooms, were used to prepare the following anonymous letter. FBI officials did seek to share with selected reporters this information about King's sexual activities.]

■ **Anonymous letter (drafted by FBI) to Martin Luther King, Jr., undated but November 21, 1964**

In view of your low grade, I will not dignify your name with either a

Mr. or a Reverend or a Dr. And, your last name calls to mind only the type of King such as King Henry the VIII.

King, look into your heart. You know you are a complete fraud and a great liability to all of us Negroes. White people in this country have enough frauds of their own but I am sure they don't have one at this time that is anywhere near your equal. You are no clergyman and you know it. I repeat you are a colossal fraud and an evil, vicious one at that. You could not believe in God and act as you do. Clearly you don't believe in any personal moral principles.

King, like all frauds your end is approaching. You could have been our greatest leader. You, even at an early age have turned out to be not a leader but a dissolute, abnormal moral imbecile. We will now have to depend on our older leaders like [NAACP executive secretary Roy] Wilkins a man of character and thank God we have others like him. But you are done. Your "honorary" degrees, your Nobel Prize (what a grim farce) and other awards will not save you King, I repeat you are done.

No person can overcome facts, not even a fraud like yourself. Lend your ear to the enclosure. [Transcripts of intercepted conversations of King spliced to convey his involvements in illicit sexual activities] exposed on the record for all time. I repeat—no person can argue successfully against facts. You are finished. You will find on the record for all time [line withheld reference to illicit sexual activities] to your hideous abnormalities. [Phrase withheld] to pretend to be ministers of the Gospel. Satan could not do more. What incredible evilness. It is all there on the record, [five lines withheld, again referring to illicit sexual activities]. King you are done.

The American public, the church organizations that have been helping— Protestant, Catholic and Jews will know you for what you are—an evil, abnormal beast. So will others who have backed you. You are done.

King, there is only one thing left for you to do. You know what it is. You have just 34 days in which to do (this exact number has been selected for a specific reason, it has definite practical significance) [King was to be formally awarded the Nobel Peace Prize in thirty-four days]. You are done. There is but one way out for you. You better take it before your filthy, abnormal fraudulent self is bared to the nation.

■ **Memo, FBI Assistant Director Cartha DeLoach to FBI Assistant Director John Mohr, November 27, 1964, FBI 62-78270-16**
Roy Wilkins, Executive Secretary, National Association for the Advancement of Colored People, . . . stated that he had to fly down to Washington to see me immediately. . . .

Wilkins arrived at 4:00 p.m. He stated he was greatly concerned. He made reference to the Director's Loyola speech last Tuesday, 11/24/64, in which the Director made reference to "sexual degenerates" in pressure groups. Wilkins stated he personally knew about whom the Director was talking, although many other Negroes did not know. [Three and a half paragraphs withheld pertaining to the FBI's monitoring of King's political and personal activities.]

Wilkins stressed the fact that he was not seeing me as an emissary. He stated he had some influence on King but not much. He added that there were others within his movement who had greater influence and that perhaps together some pressure could be brought on King. Wilkins then added that he hoped that the FBI would not expose King before something could be done.

I interrupted Wilkins at this point. I told him that the Director, of course, did not have in mind the destruction of the civil rights movement as a whole. I told him the Director sympathized with the civil rights movement . . . [but] that we deeply and bitterly resented the lies and falsehoods told by King and that if King wanted war we certainly would give it to him. Wilkins shook his head and stated there was no doubt in his mind as to which side would lose if the FBI really came out with all of its ammunition against King. I told him the ammunition was plentiful and that while we were not responsible for the many rumors being initiated against King, we had heard of these rumors and were certainly in a position to substantiate them.

I told Wilkins that . . . he should know a few positive facts of life . . . [that] certain highly-placed informants of ours had tipped us off to absolutely reliable information that King had organized a bitter crusade against the Director and the FBI. I told Wilkins these long-standing and well placed informants had advised us that King had contacted people in various parts of the United States to get them to send telegrams to the President, the Attorney General, and the FBI asking for Mr. Hoover's retirement or resignation. I told Wilkins that King had also encouraged telegrams to be sent advising the FBI of laxness in the investigation of civil rights matters. I asked Wilkins how in the hell could he expect the FBI to believe his offers of friendship as a request for peace when King was at this time attempting to ruin us. . . .

Wilkins stated [King] was wrong in his criticism of the Director. He added that he was attempting to accomplish, in a mild manner, a division between the battle of the Director and King and any phases of the battle which would reflect upon the civil rights movement. . . .

Wilkins . . . will attempt to see King, along with other Negro leaders, and tell King he can't possibly win in any battle with FBI. . . . He stated he may not have any success in this regard, however, he is convinced that the FBI can easily ruin King overnight. [Two lines withheld referring to the FBI's derogatory personal information about King's sexual activities.] I told Wilkins this, of course, was up to him; however, I wanted to reiterate once again most strongly, that if King wanted war we were prepared to give it to him and let the chips fall where they may. Wilkins stated this would be more disasterous [sic], particularly to the Negro movement and that he hoped this would never come about. I told him that the monkey was on his back and that of the other Negro leaders. He stated he realized this. . . .

[Hoover's tough stand stemmed from concern for his job. He was to reach the mandatory retirement age of seventy on January 1, 1965, and his continued tenure as director was assured only because of an executive order issued by President Johnson in May 1964. King's criticisms had precipitated demands that Johnson rescind his order and effect Hoover's retirement the next month.]

■ **Memo, FBI Assistant Director Cartha DeLoach to FBI Assistant Director John Mohr, December 2, 1964, FBI 100-106670-634**

At Reverend King's request, the Director met with King; Reverend Ralph Abernathy, Secretary of the Southern Christian Leadership Conference (SCLC); Dr. Andrew Young, Executive Assistant to King; and Walter Fauntroy, SCLC representative here in Washington, at 3:35 p.m., 12-1-64, in the Director's Office. . . .

Reverend King spoke up. He stated it was vitally necessary to keep a working relationship with the FBI. He wanted to clear up any misunderstanding which might have occurred. He stated that some Negroes had told him that the FBI had been ineffective, however, he was inclined to discount such criticism. Reverend King asked that the Director please understand that any criticism of the Director and the FBI which had been attributed to King was either a misquote or an outright misrepresentation. . . . He stated that the only time he had ever criticized the FBI was because of instances in which Special Agents who had been given complaints in civil rights cases regarding brutality by police officers were seen the following day being friendly with those same police officers. . . .

Reverend King stated he personally appreciated the great work of the FBI which had been done in so many instances. He stated this was particularly true in Mississippi. . . . Reverend King denied that he had ever stated that Negroes should not report information to the FBI. He said he had actually encouraged such reporting . . . [and] would continue to strongly urge all of his people to work closely with the FBI.

Reverend King stated he has never made any personal attack upon Mr. Hoover. He stated he had merely tried to articulate the feelings of the Negroes in the South in order to keep a tradition of nonviolence rather than violence. . . .

Reverend King stated he has been, and still is, very concerned regarding the matter of communism in the civil rights movement. He stated he knew that the Director was very concerned because he bore the responsibility of security in the Nation. . . . He claimed that when he learns of the identity of a communist in his midst he immediately deals with the problem by removing this man. . . .

The Director interrupted King to state that the FBI had learned from long experience that the communists move in when trouble starts. The Director explained that communists thrive on chaos. The Director mentioned that his riot report [of 1964] to the President reflected the opportunistic efforts of communists. He then stated that communists have no interest in the future of the Negro race and that King, of all people, should be aware of this fact. The Director spoke briefly of communist attempts to infiltrate the labor movement.

The Director told King and his associates that the FBI shares the same despair which the Negroes suffer when Negro leaders refused to accept the deep responsibility they have in the civil rights movement. He stated that when Negroes are encouraged not to cooperate with the FBI this sometimes frustrates or delays successful solution of investigations. . . .

The Director told Reverend King that the FBI had put the "fear of God" in the Ku Klux Klan (KKK). . . . The Director then spoke of the terror in Mississippi backwoods and of the fact that sheriffs and deputy sheriffs participate in crimes of violence. . . . The Director added that the KKK constantly damns the FBI and that we have currently been classified as the "Federal Bureau of Integration" in Mississippi.

The Director told King that many cases, which have been brought about as a result of FBI investigation, must be tried in State Court. He spoke of the difficulty in obtaining a verdict of guilty in instances in which white juries are impaneled in cases involving white men. . . .

The Director made reference to Reverend King's allegation that the FBI deals or associates with law enforcement officers who have been involved in civil rights violations. He stated emphatically that "I'll be damned if the FBI has associated with any of these people nor will we be associated with them in the future." . . . He added that he made it a point, several years ago, to transfer northern Special Agents to southern offices. He stated that, for the most part, northern-born Agents are assigned civil rights cases in the South. The Director added that he feels that our Special Agents, regardless of where they are born, will investigate a case impartially and thoroughly. . . .

The Director explained that there is a great misunderstanding today among the general public and particularly the Negro race as to what the FBI can and cannot do in the way of investigations. The Director emphasized that the FBI cannot recommend prosecution . . . [but] merely investigates and then the Department of Justice determines whether prosecution be entertained or not. . . .

The Director told Reverend King and his associates that FBI representatives have held several thousand law enforcement conferences in which southern police officers have been educated as to civil rights legislation. . . . He added that this educational campaign will be continued and that it will eventually take hold. . . .

The Director told Reverend King he desired to give him some advice. He stated that one of the greatest things the Negro leaders could accomplish would be to encourage voting registration among their people. Another thing would be to educate their people in the skills so that they could compete in the open market. The Director mentioned several professions in which Negroes could easily learn skills. The Director also told King he wanted him to know that registrars in the South were now more careful in their actions. He stated that there were less attempts now to prevent Negroes from registering inasmuch as the FBI is watching such actions very carefully. The Director told Reverend King that the FBI was making progress in violations regarding discrimination in eating places. . . . The Director stated he personally was in favor of equality in eating places and in schools. He stated emphatically, however, he was not in favor of taking Negro children 10 or 12 miles across town simply because their parents wanted them to go to a school other than those in their specific neighborhood. . . .

The Director told King that he wanted to make it clear that the question is often raised as to whether the FBI will protect civil rights workers or Negroes. He stated that . . . the FBI does not have the authority nor the jurisdiction to protect anyone. He stated that when the Department of Justice desires that Negroes be protected this is the responsibility of U.S. Marshals. . . .

■ JUNE Memo, FBI Director J. Edgar Hoover to Attorney General Nicholas Katzenbach, December 1, 1965

This Bureau's investigation of the communist influence in racial matters has developed considerable information indicating the influence upon Martin Luther King, Jr., head of the Southern Christian Leadership Conference, by individuals with subversive backgrounds such as Stanley David Levison, Harry Wachtel, Bayard Rustin and others. From time to time, King meets with these individuals and coverage of these meetings by this Bureau results in the obtaining of evidence of the influences upon King and his organization in the civil rights movement. The coverage of these meetings also has developed information concerning King's involvement in the Vietnam situation. These meetings frequently take place in hotel rooms in New York City.

On November 29, 1965, information was obtained that King was to spend the night of November 29, 1965, at the Americana Hotel. . . . We also had information that King planned to meet with his advisors while in New York City, November 29, 30, 1965. Because of the importance of the meeting and the urgency of the situation, a microphone surveillance was effected November 29, 1965. . . . This surveillance involved trespass and was discontinued on November 30, 1965.

■ **Memo, Attorney General Nicholas Katzenbach to FBI Director J. Edgar Hoover, December 10, 1965**
Obviously these are particularly delicate surveillances and we should be very cautious in terms the non-FBI people who may from time to time necessarily be involved in some aspect of installation.

[This was one of three instances when the attorney general was advised that the FBI had already bugged King—despite Katzenbach's explicit requirement of March 1965 that all FBI microphone installations obtain his prior authorization. The two other instances, occurring in May and October 1965, similarly noted that the FBI had already installed and terminated bugs in King's hotel rooms in New York City.]

■ **JUNE Memo, FBI Assistant Director Charles Brennan to FBI Assistant Director William Sullivan, December 15, 1966**
This is to advise you of the microphone and wire tap coverage that we have afforded Martin Luther King, Jr., . . . [who] has been in close association with individuals having Communist Party backgrounds since his rise to prominence in the civil rights field. . . .
On October 10, 1963, Attorney General Robert F. Kennedy approved technical surveillances on King's current residence or at any further address to which he may move. He also approved the technical surveillance of the Southern Christian Leadership Conference New York City Office or any other address to which it may be moved.
A wire tap was installed on King's residence, . . . on November 8, 1963, and discontinued on April 30, 1965, when King moved from this address. . . .
From October 24, 1963, to January 24, 1964, and from July 7, 1964, to July 31, 1964, a wire tap was maintained on the Southern Christian Leadership Conference New York City Office. *In addition, on October 21, 1963, Attorney General Kennedy authorized a wire tap on the Southern Christian Leadership Conference Headquarters at Atlanta, Georgia, which was maintained from November 8, 1963, to June 21, 1966, when Attorney General Nicholas deB. Katzenbach ordered it discontinued. . . .*

In addition to the foregoing we maintained 16 microphones and 4 wire taps of a few days duration at various hotels and one temporary residence. These were installed because of the possibility of a meeting between King and his communist advisors. The 4 wire taps were installed under the original authority given by the Attorney General on 10/10/63 concerning King's residences.

Attorney General Katzenbach was specifically notified [after the fact] of three of these microphone installations. In each of these three instances the Attorney General was advised that a trespass was involved in the installation. . . .

■ **Memo, FBI Director J. Edgar Hoover to Attorney General Ramsey Clark, April 2, 1968**

By letter dated January 2, 1968, authority was requested to institute a telephone surveillance on the national headquarters of the Southern Christian Leadership Conference, 330 Auburn Avenue, N.E., Atlanta, Georgia, because its President, Martin Luther King, Jr., had publicly announced he would lead a massive civil disobedience in the nation's Capital in the Spring of 1968. At that time it was pointed out that these massive demonstrations could trigger riots.

By letter dated January 3, 1968, you declined authorization of this installation because, "There has not been an adequate demonstration of a direct threat to the national security."

In view of the recent developments in Memphis, Tennessee, where King led a march that ended in a riot, it is reasonable to assume the same thing could happen later this month when King brings his "Poor People's March" to Washington, D.C.

King, the day after the Memphis riot, was in conference with his principal adviser and long-time secret Communist Party member, Stanley Levison, concerning the events of the preceding day. King stated he was considering calling off the Washington march. Levison advised him to continue his plans for the Washington march.

Despite this violence in Memphis, Levison and King are continuing their plans for this massive civil disobedience to start the latter part of April, 1968, in Washington, D.C.

In view of the internal security aspect involved, authority is requested to install telephone surveillances of the Southern Christian Leadership Conference at its national headquarters, 1401 U Street, N.W., Washington, D.C., so that we can keep apprised of the strategy and plans of this group.

[Clark did not approve this wiretap request.]

HOOVER WAS NOT content merely to monitor "subversive"
activities. Concerned over the unwillingness of Presidents
Roosevelt and Truman to take "affirmative action" on
FBI reports of "communist activities" in the trade
union movement and in the federal bureaucracy, in February
1946 Hoover launched an "educational campaign" to
"influence public opinion" by leaking FBI information
to "available channels." These channels included
carefully screened reporters and members of Congress who
were willing to promote "the cause" of anticommunism.
The most dramatic of these educational initiatives involved
the FBI's covert assistance to the House Committee on
Un-American Activities (HUAC) in planning the highly
publicized hearings of 1947 into communist influence in the
film industry—an effort that involved the behind-the-scenes
assistance of actor Ronald Reagan. By the 1950s Hoover
had refined and radically expanded this educational
program, having developed a number of outlets for the
dissemination of FBI "educational" materials—on the
condition, once again, that the FBI's assistance would not be
disclosed.

■ **Memo, FBI Supervisor George Moore to FBI Assistant Director Charles Brennan, August 18, 1970, FBI 100-438794-2981**

This is to advise you of another scurrilous attack on the Director and the FBI by the SCLC [Southern Christian Leadership Conference], and to recommend a mass media item for approval.

At its Annual Convention in Atlanta, Georgia, 8/11–14/70, the SCLC adopted a resolution attacking the Director and the FBI for "their attacks on Martin Luther King, Jr. and their failure to meet their responsibilities such as protecting civil rights, stopping narcotics traffic and other organized crime." . . . The resolution was occasioned by an article in Time magazine which accused the Director, during his meeting with King on 12/1/64, of pressuring King to tone down his attacks against the FBI with tapes of King's immoral conduct. This article was false and King's three SCLC associates who accompanied him . . . all denied that the Director even mentioned King's immoral conduct. Now they turn around and allow a resolution to be passed which in effect accuses the Director of the same thing that they have already branded as a lie in the Time article.

Observations:

The history of this group indicates the deceitful accusations will continue. After expressing confidence in the Director and the FBI in civil rights cases and offering cooperation during the 12/1/64 meeting, King and this gang left the Director's office and immediately initiated an underhanded spurious campaign to malign the Director and the Bureau. Recently, Jesse Jackson, a SCLC national official, in utter disregard for denials by three of his associates that it occurred, launched a personal attack on the Director for threatening King with tapes about his conduct.

We have considered a strong letter to the SCLC on their false charges but feel a letter writing exchange would be useless with this group which would not recognize the truth if they saw it. . . .

If approved, Crime Records Division will furnish the attached to an appropriate media source.

[Hoover's handwritten notation: "OK."]

[FBI assistant director Thomas Bishop, head of the Crime Records Division, has a handwritten notation identifying the media source and the date disseminated which is too faint to be decipherable.]

Attached Blind Memo captioned "The Southern Christian Leadership Conference's Attack on J. Edgar Hoover"

Its most recent attack on Director J. Edgar Hoover and the FBI certainly does not depict the Southern Christian Leadership Conference as a responsible organization, a picture which the organization needs to overcome its financial dilemma. The latest attack was based on an article in Time magazine alleging that Mr. Hoover confronted Dr. Martin Luther King, Jr. with tapes about his immoral conduct and pressured Dr. King into toning down his criticism of Mr. Hoover and the FBI. Three of King's associates who accompanied Dr. King during his meeting with Mr. Hoover denied that Mr. Hoover even mentioned Dr. King's conduct during the meeting. Mr. Hoover characteristically said nothing. This should have laid to rest the situation once more.

Out in Chicago, Reverend Jesse Jackson, a national SCLC official . . . felt moved to comment. Ignoring the denials by his associates, . . . Reverend Jackson launched a bitter personal attack on Mr. Hoover, accusing him of trying to "whitemail" Dr. King. Then, the SCLC . . . in a resolution attacked Mr. Hoover and the FBI for "their attacks on Dr. King." To add further confusion to just what Mr. Hoover was accused of doing, the resolution noted that Dr. King's three associates . . . had said the published reports were "absolutely not true."

This confusing action by the SCLC must make the public wonder.

Surely they are trying to get all the mileage they can from the situation but it seems this time they have gone too far, and Mr. Hoover comes out looking better than ever for an awkward, contradictory, hypocritical attack by a bunch of preachers who should know better, if not as businessmen, then surely as preachers.

This is the kind of thing the civil rights movement can well do without. The shrieks of the extremists in the racial situation should be counterbalanced by responsibility and fairness. This type of attack is clearly counterproductive and, if the SCLC is to survive, must be halted and halted fast.

■ **Memo, FBI Associate Director Clyde Tolson to FBI Director, May 12, 1947, FBI 61-7582-1462**

SAC [Richard] Hood called from Los Angeles stating that he had a telephone call from Congressman [J. Parnell] Thomas [chairman of the House Committee on Un-American Activities] . . . that they were interested in finding out what we were doing with respect to the Communist picture in the movie industry and, of course, he wanted to advise Mr. Hood of what the Committee was doing concerning this subject. . . .

I told Mr. Hood to see Congressman Thomas this afternoon, to point out to him that the files of the Bureau are concentrated at Washington and only portions of the files are located in the various field divisions and these would not give a true picture of the situation. I told Mr. Hood to point out that he obviously could not appear before the Committee in open session [as Thomas had requested] because to do so would spotlight the things we are trying to do to keep in touch with the Communist situation. I told him to . . . explain to [Thomas] that we want to cooperate but that a public hearing would necessarily disclose confidential information and would make it more difficult for us to do our work. I told Mr. Hood that if Congressman Thomas insisted upon his appearance at a closed session, it would be satisfactory for him to appear, but that he should be very careful and discreet in answering any inquiries. I told him that we could not make available to the Subcommittee any confidential information from our files, that, of course, if any individuals in the motion picture industry had been the subject of publicity which is available to anyone, there would be no objection to pointing out such instances to members of the Committee. . . .

Mr. Hood will keep us closely advised as to the developments in this matter.

■ **Memo, FBI Assistant Director Louis Nichols to FBI Associate Director Clyde Tolson, May 13, 1947, FBI 61-7582-1465**

SAC Hood . . . saw Congressman J. Parnell Thomas. . . . Congressman

[John] McDowell and [committee counsel Robert] Stripling. The question
of Hood testifying before the Committee did not come up. The committee
was exceedingly friendly and Thomas emphasized the fact that the Committee was cooperating with the Bureau and the Bureau with the Committee, that the Committee had given the Bureau access to its files and was
appreciative of what the Bureau had been able to do to help. He pointed
out that at one time such a friendly relationship did not exist. . . . He
pointed out that they had [name withheld] in at 11 a.m. on Monday, May
12. He [name withheld, Hollywood personality] admitted attending only 1
Communist meeting; they knew nothing about him and could not question
him. [Thomas] wanted any information we could give them.

Stripling then furnished a list of nine names on whom Congressman
Thomas requested any information we had: [seven names were withheld on
claimed personal privacy grounds]. On the foregoing we have either main
files or numerous references in the Los Angeles Office. [Two names
withheld on personal privacy grounds.] We have no record on the last two.

Furthermore, Thomas stated they would like to have any data we can
furnish on the Communist infiltration of the motion picture industry which
would be helpful to decide whether they should put an investigator out
there for the next month or so and plan on holding open hearings in Los
Angeles on June 16th. They are interested in ascertaining the extent of
Communist infiltration, actual Communist activities; they understand, of
course, the confidential character of our files. They respect this and do not
want information the disclosure of which would in any way embarrass the
Bureau, but the Congressman felt there was background data to be
furnished which would not hurt the Bureau but which would further Mr.
Hoover's premise that the way to fight Communists was to expose them.

Hood and I discussed various possibilities such as furnishing the names
of known Anti-Communists who have some basis for knowledge of
Communist activities, the known Communist front groups and officers
concerning whom the Committee might investigate. I told Hood to prepare
summary memoranda on all these points and send in a teletype. . . .

[Hoover's handwritten notation: "Expedite. I want Hood to extend every
assistance to this Committee."]

■ **Urgent Teletype, FBI Director J. Edgar Hoover to Los Angeles
SAC Richard Hood, May 13, 1947, FBI 61-7582-1464**
Reurtel [re your teletype] May thirteen. . . . No objection to using this
information provided you are of the opinion that the disclosure of such data
will not in any way embarrass the Bureau. Re infiltration motion picture
industry approve memorandum listing individuals possessing information
relative infiltration. Your list should be divided in two parts, one listing
non-Communists and other listing those identified with Communist move-

ment. Re non-Communists, memorandum should state following persons may possess information of value re infiltration and would probably be cooperative and friendly witnesses. . . . Re Communists, memorandum should state following persons may possess information of value re infiltration but because of reported connections with CP or CPA may be hostile witnesses and uncooperative. . . . Upon furnishing information to Committee you should advise them that such material is furnished strictly for their confidential information and with the understanding that no circumstances will the source of this material ever be disclosed.

■ **Letter, Los Angeles SAC Richard Hood to FBI Director, May 14, 1947, FBI 61-7582-1468**
. . . Complying with Bureau instructions, memoranda were prepared and at 6:15 P.M. on May 13th, after I had personally talked to Congressman Thomas, [assistant SAC] Ellsworth and I delivered to Robert Stripling, Chief Investigator of the Committee, the originals of memoranda on the following individuals: Bert Brecht, Hanns Eisler, [seven other names withheld].

A memorandum was also delivered to Mr. Stripling Re: Communist Activities in Hollywood. . . .

Mr. Thomas and Mr. Stripling appeared to be very friendly and appreciative of this cooperation afforded them. . . .

Enclosure: *Re: Communist Activities in Hollywood*
It is believed that the following individuals are in a position to have information of value concerning the activities of the Communist Party in Hollywood. It is also believed that they would be cooperative and friendly witnesses. [The names of four individuals and background information on these four withheld.]

The following named persons may possess information of value regarding the infiltration of the Communist Party through the League of American Writers, but because of their reported connection with the Communist Party or Communist Political Association may be hostile witnesses and uncooperative: [the names of five individuals and background information on these five withheld]. . . . Another individual who is reportedly active in the League of American Writers is [name withheld], prominent writer in the movie colony, who probably would be uncooperative by reason of his reported membership in the Communist Party.

The following individuals would likely be in possession of information of value regarding the infiltration of the movie colony, but because of their reported connection with the Party may be hostile witnesses and uncooperative. . . .

[Seven names and further background information on these seven withheld.]

The Motion Picture Democratic Committee was formed in 1938 and it has been reported that this committee was highly successful in the Hollywood Section and acquired many famous personages as members, many of whom were not aware that the organization was infiltrated and cooperated with the American Peace Crusade which later became the American Peace Mobilization. The following prominent members of the Motion Picture Democratic Committee probably have information of value regarding the infiltration of the committee but because of their reported connection with the Communist Party may be hostile witnesses and uncooperative.

[Three names and background information on these three withheld.]

It is believed that [name withheld], previously mentioned, together with [two names withheld], the latter a writer and alleged member of the Communist Party who appeared as a witness before the Tenny Committee [a California legislative committee on un-American activities], are persons who have been prominent in the activities of such organizations as the Hollywood Writers Mobilization, the Hollywood Writers Congress and the Hollywood Chapter of the Independent Citizens Committee of the Arts, Sciences and Professions and more recently the Progressive Citizens Committee. Although these men probably possess valuable information regarding the infiltration tactics and extent of influence of the Communist Party in these groups, it is possible that they would be hostile witnesses and uncooperative by reason of their alleged connection with the Communist Party.

It is also reported that [name and title withheld] has spearheaded the activities of the Hollywood Anti-Fascist Refugee Committee, the Hollywood Anti-Nazi League and the American Peace Mobilization, but it may be that he would be a hostile witness. He has been reported as being a Communist Party member for several years.

The following named individuals, by reason of their position, may possess information of value regarding the Communist infiltration of their organizations and would probably be cooperative and friendly witnesses:

Ronald Reagan* and Robert Montgomery—both past presidents of the Screen Actors Guild.

*FBI officials in fact knew that Reagan could provide the desired information and would be cooperative. Recruited as a confidential informant for the FBI in 1943, Reagan had regularly briefed his FBI contact about the political activities of his Hollywood associates. On April 12, the month before chairman Thomas solicited the FBI's assistance, Reagan had reported that there were two cliques in the Screen Actors Guild that "follow the Communist Party line" on all policy questions and had further identified by name the actors and actresses who were members of each clique. Although Reagan did not "name names" during his public testimony before HUAC, he did provide these names during executive session testimony and concerted with HUAC staff counsel to conform his public testimony to the committee's expectations without violating the committee's agreement with the FBI.—Ed.

Emmett Lavery—president, Screen Writers Guild, who had previously testified before the Tenny Committee.

Upton Close—Radio Commentator and writer.

[One other name and background information withheld.]

The Actors Lab, 1455 North Laurel, is reportedly supported by various motion picture studios for the purpose of training their new stars. It has been alleged that this Lab is heavily infiltrated. The following individuals, by reason of their positions, may possess information of value regarding the infiltration but because of their reported connection with the Communist Party may be hostile witnesses:

[Two names and background information withheld.]

With respect to infiltration of the radio, the following individuals may possess information of value but may also prove to be hostile witnesses and uncooperative by reason of their reported connection with the Communist Party:

[Three names and background information withheld.]

The following are the reported Communist Party functionaries in the Los Angeles Area who may be in possession of information as to the extent of the Party's activities in Hollywood:

[Five names and background information withheld.]

RONALD REAGAN DID not confine his informing to fellow members of the Screen Actors Guild. Eager to ingratiate himself with the powerful FBI director, Reagan also volunteered information of personal interest to Hoover.

■ **Personal and Confidential Letter, SAC Los Angeles Richard Hood to FBI Director J. Edgar Hoover, February 22, 1945, Nichols File**

On the evening of February 16, 1945, the Los Angeles FBI Office Basketball Team played a game with the 18th AAF [army air force] Base Unit Team made up of men in the outfit formerly known as the First Motion Picture Unit, of which unit the motion picture actor Ronald Reagan is a member. . . .

Special Agent H. Rex Ellis . . . rode home with Reagan after the game and in the conversation Reagan asked Agent Ellis what former [Republican] presidential candidate Thomas E. Dewey had against John Edgar Hoover.

Reagan said that while he was not present personally, several of his friends were present during a private and "off the record" conversation with Dewey in Los Angeles while he was here on his [1944] campaign tour, at which time Dewey is supposed to have said that when he was elected President there would not be enough jails in the country to hold the people he was going to put into them, and that John Edgar Hoover of the FBI was going to be one of the first. Reagan went on to say that in a case of this kind he would certainly be inclined to side with Hoover.

No further discussion was had on this matter. . . . I am furnishing you the gist of this conversation for your information.

THE FBI'S ASSISTANCE to HUAC was not exceptional. By the 1950s, under Hoover's direction the FBI took a more active role in combating suspect political activities. In addition to collecting information, the Bureau also disseminated it to individuals and organizations who could act on it. Whether formally or informally, Hoover sought to shape public opinion and purge national institutions of "subversives."

■ **Urgent Airtel, FBI Director J. Edgar Hoover to SAC, Albany, February 18, 1953, FBI 62-88217-909**

Suairtel [submit airtel] setting forth the identity of faculty members presently employed at Bennington College, Bennington, Vermont; Harvard University, Cambridge, Massachusetts; and Sara Lawrence College, Bronxville, New York, who are included in the Security Index [an FBI index of individuals to be detained in the event of war or national emergency].
Note on Yellow [copy] only:

In connection with the memorandum of [FBI assistant director Louis] Nichols to [FBI associate director Clyde] Tolson dated February 11, 1953, concerning the request by [Senate Internal Security subcommittee counsel] Robert Morris for a "good case" at the above colleges for use in subsequent hearings [of the subcommittee] regarding Communist infiltration in education, the Director commented "Yes. Help if we can. H."

It is known that some faculty members of the above schools have been the subjects of security investigations by the Bureau and in some cases investigations are presently pending. A review of the Bureau's indices to determine the identity of all such individuals so that the best or most aggravated case could be determined is not feasible, as the Bureau's indices are not broken down in such a manner as to index each security subject's place of employment. It is believed that such information can more readily be secured from the interested field offices.

■ **Memo, FBI Executives' Conference to FBI Director, October 14, 1953, FBI 121-23278—Not Recorded**

The Executives' Conference . . . on October 14, 1953, considered current policy relative to furnishing information from Bureau files outside of the Executive Departments and made recommendations as to future procedures. . . .

(1) *Dissemination Under Program "Responsibilities of the FBI in the Internal Security Field"*

Under this program the Bureau volunteers information regarding subjects who are on the Security Index to the Governor of a state, or to a responsible local official, whoever is most appropriate under the circumstances, when the subject is employed in a public utility outside the vital facilities list (dissemination re vital facilities is made to Armed Forces), or in a public or semi-public organization. In each instance the Bureau specifically passes upon the information to be disseminated; the dissemination is oral; and the [FBI] field [office] is required to furnish a statement regarding the reliability and discretion of the individual to whom the information is to be given before authority is granted. . . .

The Executives' Conference unanimously felt that the advantage of disseminating information under this program outweighs the disadvantages and that the Bureau under this program is meeting a responsibility to the people of this country . . . [and] recommended that hereafter dissemination under this program should be made confidentially to the state governor, or in his absence or if reason exists why it should not be furnished to the governor, to another responsible state official recommended by the field office. [Hoover's handwritten insert: "I share this view."] If a good reason exists why the information cannot be given to the governor or state official, we can then consider as an exception furnishing the information to a reliable local official. This procedure would have the effect of keeping our dissemination on a high state level and restricting dissemination to 48 states, rather than to numerous local officials. [Hoover's handwritten insert: "It must be only when employed in a public utility & name is on our security list."] . . .

As a result of the conference on February 12, 1951, with representatives of the Governors' Conference, they were advised that if the governors desired information concerning an individual to be appointed to a state government office, the Bureau would furnish information to that governor in response to his request. . . .

The Executives' Conference unanimously recommended that we continue to accept such requests from governors and confine our name checks to requests re persons being considered for appointment to a state government position and that the material furnished should be public source material. [Hoover's handwritten insert: "I concur if limited to this source."] Each request will be considered on its merits and if a reason exists why the information should not be furnished, the request will, of course, not be honored.

(3) *Red Cross*

On January 14, 1943, Ugo Carusi, then Executive Assistant to the Attorney General, recommended to the Director that the FBI furnish to the American National Red Cross memoranda in response to their requests for name checks. We have made name checks for the Red Cross since that time, but do not furnish them the results of loyalty investigations. . . .

The Conference unanimously recommended that we continue to make name checks for the Red Cross. [Hoover's handwritten insert: "Do we limit to public source information?"]

(4) *Police Departments*

. . . Upon receipt of a specific request for information, a field office may furnish information of a public source nature relating to subversive matters by blind memorandum to proper representatives of local and state law enforcement agencies. The Bureau's identity as source must be kept confidential. . . .

The Executives' Conference recommended that we continue our policy, as set forth above, regarding Police Departments. [Hoover's handwritten insert: "OK but only public source information."] . . .

(7) *U.S. Courts*

We have received requests from time to time from Judges, including former Chief Justice Fred Vinson and Justice Tom Clark, for information from our files generally in connection with individuals they plan to employ in their offices. In such instances appropriate information has been furnished to these officials without obtaining Departmental approval.

Executives' Conference Recommendation:

The Executives' Conference unanimously recommended that we continue handling these requests as in the past. [Hoover's handwritten insert: "Is it limited to public source information?"] . . .

(9) *Other Individuals*

The general rule followed when requests are received for information from Bureau files from other individuals outside the Executive Branch of the Federal Government is to advise them that we are unable to assist in view of the confidential nature of FBI files and that we are not permitted to release such information except upon the expressed direction of the

Attorney General. All requests of this type are individually considered and information is furnished where the best interests of the Bureau would be served after approval is given by responsible Bureau officials. Among the individuals who have been furnished information are members of the new [Eisenhower] Administration who were furnished information from our files prior to the change in Administration, ex-President Herbert Hoover, a Commissioner of Municipal Civil Service Commission in New York City, and the Department of Welfare in New York City.

Executives' Conference Recommendation:

The Executives' Conference unanimously recommended that we continue our rule that the files of the Bureau are confidential and that any exceptions to this rule must be most carefully considered. [Hoover's handwritten insert: "Yes & no exceptions are to be made except upon my specific approval."]

(10) *Bar Associations*

From time to time the Bureau has extended assistance to Bar Associations in selected situations. . . . Inquiries have been received from time to time regarding applicants to the Bar and information has been furnished on a confidential basis. In addition, requests have been received regarding disbarment proceedings, such as the current case involving attorney Emanuel Bloch in NY [Bloch was the attorney for Julius and Ethel Rosenberg during their trial for atomic espionage].

Executives' Conference Recommendation: The Conference unanimously recommended that we stop furnishing information to the Bar Associations in view of the fact that . . . the National Conference of Bar Examiners in Denver may have been abusing our confidence by advising that we have been furnishing information. Relative to disbarment proceedings, the Conference felt that each instance should be considered on the merits of the case. For example, in the case of Emanuel Bloch, it is to the public interest that the Bureau furnish such information as is possible. [Hoover's handwritten insert: "OK."]

DISSEMINATION OF INFORMATION TO CONGRESSIONAL COMMITTEES:

Mr. Nichols presented to the Conference the matter of furnishing information to Congressional Committees. It was pointed out that we had furnished information to the following Congressional Committees: Joint Committee on Atomic Energy, Senate Appropriations Committee, Senate Armed Services Committee, Preparedness Subcommittee to the Senate Armed Services Committee, House Committee on Un-American Activities, Senate Judiciary Committee, House Judiciary Committee, Senate Committee on Labor and Public Welfare, Subcommittee on Labor Management Relations of the Senate Committee on Labor and Public Welfare, Senate Foreign Relations Committee—relations with Senator [Alexander] Wiley. We have furnished information to the Senate Permanent Investigating [sic,

Investigations] Committee (McCarthy) up until the late Summer when the Committee appointed former Special Agent [Frank] Carr as Staff Director. Since then no information has been furnished to this Committee.

It was further pointed out that there have been some isolated requests from other Committees and . . . that as a matter of present relations, the Senate Internal Security Committee ([chaired by William] Jenner) is the only Committee on which there is a continuing program of cooperation which was established by the Attorney General [J. Howard McGrath] personally on March 15, 1951. Following the advent of the new [Eisenhower] Administration, this relationship has been continued.

It was the unanimous recommendation . . . there be no change in relationship with the Internal Security Committee. (FBI Assistant Director Hugh) Clegg pointed out that considerable good has come to the Bureau from an amiable relationship with the Senate.

Those members of the Conference present also unanimously recommended that there be no change in the relations with the Senate and House Appropriations Committees and the Senate and House Judiciary Committees. Of course the cooperation extended the Joint Committee on Atomic Energy is pursuant to the law.

The Conference was unanimous, however, in recommending that requests from all other Committees be referred to the Department, which has been the traditional manner of responding to Congressional requests.

The Conference felt that the relationship with the Appropriations Committee was a little different inasmuch as the broad overall authority of the Appropriations Committees was different than that of any other Committee of Congress. The same reasoning was advanced with reference to the Judiciary Committee which has the overall supervision of the Department incomes. [Tolson's handwritten insert: "I think we should send memo to AG (Attorney General Herbert Brownell) and (Deputy Attorney General William) Rogers—advising of our present policy and requesting a definite statement of future policy." Hoover's handwritten insert: "I concur in Tolson's suggestion."] . . .

■ Informal Memo, FBI Assistant Director Cartha DeLoach to FBI Associate Director Clyde Tolson, July 10, 1967, FBI 100-106670— Not Recorded

With the Director's approval, I saw [President Johnson's aide] Marvin Watson . . . [who noted] that the same names were turning up each time with regard to civil rights matters as well as anti-Vietnam activities. Watson asked if we had noted this. I replied in the affirmative and stated that the Director had sent numerous communications to the White House reflecting this fact. . . .

Watson . . . then took me in to see the President. . . .

The President next asked if the FBI knew anything regarding the activities of [civil rights leaders Martin Luther] King, [Stokely] Carmichael and [Floyd] McKissick. . . . I told him the Director had constantly sent communications over to him regarding these individuals and the FBI kept abreast of all their activities. The President asked who was behind these people. I told him that Stanley Levinson [sic, Levison], a prominent member of the National Committee of the Communist Party, and Bayard Rustin were behind King, and that although McKissick and Carmichael had left wing individuals supporting them, they obviously were self-styled civil rights leaders who were seeking only to get as much money out of a troubled situation as possible. I told the President of the situation at the University of Wisconsin where Carmichael arrogantly demanded $1,800 prior to speaking and had raised hell simply because the students could only raise $1,300. I briefed the President generally regarding King and McKissick.

The President inquired as to whether the information concerning Carmichael and his speech making activities had been given to the press. I told him it had not. He asked that we give it to [syndicated columnist] Drew Pearson. I told him I doubted Pearson would print derogatory information concerning these characters. The President then stated that we should consider giving it to William White, the columnist, on an off-the-record basis. He stated that White was an old friend of his and would understand the circumstances. I told the President I would bring this to the Director's attention. . . .

The President turned once again to the subject of Carmichael and McKissick. . . . He asked if the FBI could have Chairman Ed Willis of the House Committee on Un-American Activities hold hearings concerning Carmichael and McKissick. I told him I thought it would be out of order for the FBI to make the request to Willis and . . . also that the President might like to consider the fact that the House Committee on Un-American Activities has little reputation at the present time and that hearings on McKissick and Carmichael might react to their advantage rather than hurting them.

The President then asked how such information could get out. I told him that handling such matters with newspapers was perhaps the best way, however, there obviously had been a reluctance on the part of some individuals to leak anything against King. (I, of course, meant the Attorney General [Ramsey Clark].) The President made no comment but stated that he hoped the anit-Vietnam activities of all these people could be watched most carefully. . . .

Action:

(1) If the Director approves, I will call Bill White and give him the above information concerning Stokely Carmichael.

[Hoover's handwritten notation: "Since President has ordered it I assume we have to do it but I dont like it."] . . .

■ **Informal Memo, FBI Supervisor Milton Jones to FBI Assistant Director Thomas Bishop, May 22, 1968**

Your attention is directed to the attached clipping from yesterday's "Washington Daily News" indicating that [Republican Senate Minority Leader] Hugh Scott . . . indicated he would introduce a bill to authorize the [minting of one million bronze medals commemorating Martin Luther King] and "a gold medal to be presented to Dr. King's widow." . . .

Over the years we have had very cordial relations with Senator Scott . . . [and he] has always been very friendly. In the recent past, he has been sympathetic to the Bureau's viewpoint in connection with the Safe Streets and Crime Control Bill now pending on the Hill.

Recommendation:

In view of Senator Scott's friendly and cooperative attitude over the years, it is recommended that [FBI assistant director Cartha] DeLoach brief him on a most confidential basis as to the background of Martin Luther King. Obviously, Scott has been "hoodwinked" as to King's true background.

[Scott was dissuaded, and his responsiveness led FBI officials to count on him again in 1970 when Congressman Peter Rodino introduced another bill to declare King's birthday a national holiday.]

■ **Memo, FBI Assistant Director George Moore to FBI Assistant Director William Sullivan, January 17, 1969**

It is recommended that the attached document regarding Martin Luther King, Jr., be furnished President-elect Nixon and the Attorney General designate [John Mitchell] after the inauguration, in view of the agitation by some individuals and groups that King's birthday be made a national holiday.

The Southern Christian Leadership Conference, formed by King, held demonstrations on January 15, 1969, King's birthday, to urge that that date be made a national holiday. According to press accounts, Reverend Ralph D. Abernathy and other prominent Negroes met with President-elect Nixon on January 13, 1969, and Abernathy then urged Nixon to make King's birthday a national holiday.

Attached document, briefed down to half the length of the last write-up of King's career, sets out the extensive communist influence on King and King's highly immoral personal behavior.

It is felt we should aim to have the attached document regarding King ready for delivery to President Nixon and the Attorney General on Thursday, January 23, 1969, in view of the inaugural events scheduled between now and that date. . . .

[Hoover's handwritten notation: "OK."]

■ **Top Secret Memo, FBI Director to Attorney General John Mitchell, January 23, 1969**

The Southern Christian Leadership Conference, founded by Martin Luther King, Jr., held demonstrations on January 15, 1969, King's birthday, urging that his birthday be made a national holiday. Reverend Ralph D. Abernathy, President of the Southern Christian Leadership Conference, has advocated national holiday status for King's birthday, according to press accounts.

In view of this, there is enclosed a document regarding the communist influence on King during his career and information regarding King's highly immoral personal behavior. For your information, a copy of this document is also being furnished to the President.

[The document recounted in detail examples of both "the extensive communist influence on King" and King's "highly immoral personal behavior," the latter derived from the FBI's extensive bugging of King's hotel rooms.]

PART TWO
INVESTIGATIVE TECHNIQUES

8: "Black Bag" Jobs

BEGINNING IN 1940, FBI agents broke into offices and private residences either to install microphones (bugs) or to photocopy papers (membership and subscription lists, financial records, correspondence). Hoover recognized the usefulness of this "clearly illegal" practice, yet he sought to ensure that FBI agents committing such break-ins would not be discovered. Thus in 1942 he devised the "Do Not File" system. Under this program, SACs had to request the director's authorization for any break-in and prepare a memorandum in which they spelled out the benefits of such potentially risky operations and the safeguards to be employed to preclude discovery. Captioned "Do Not File," these written requests were neither serialized nor indexed in the FBI's central records system. They could thus be safely destroyed.

In 1966, however, concerned that discovery of the FBI's illegal investigative techniques could result in his forced retirement as director, Hoover ordered break-ins stopped. He continued to receive requests from SACs for approval of break-ins, so in January 1967 he created another written record of his order banning such activities.

■ **JUNE Memo, [Name Deleted FBI Agent] to SAC New York, April 26, 1954, FBI 62-117166-131**
A survey of confidential anonymous investigations [break-ins] reveals that these investigation [sic] are handled in three phases: (1) the survey . . . (2) the actual assignment, and (3) processing information obtained on the assignment.

I. SURVEY

The survey entails file reviews and indice checks on occupants of the apartment or office involved. . . . In each case it is necessary to develop confidential sources at the apartment or building involved. In the average case this requires developing the superintendent and/or some other occupant of the building who is in proximity to the subject's apartment. Following the development of a source at the residence, the next problem is to set up a plant or cover apartment where photographic equipment can be operated and where possible movements of the subject can be physically observed. . . .

Once the cover apartment or plant has been established, it is necessary to conduct a physical surveillance prior to the actual assignment to determine the activities and movements of the subject and other occupants in the office or apartment in which he is located. . . .

II. ACTUAL ASSIGNMENT

Following the preliminary survey and the establishing of a plant and prior to the actual assignment itself, a conference is called to brief all agents assigned. Specific assignments are made and instructions given. In the average case, three to four agents are on the actual assignment. One of the men assigned, a supervisor, mans the handy-talkie, which is in direct contact with agents on surveillance covering the immediate apartment. Depending on the size of the assignment, two to three agents make the actual search. Two agents are assigned to the cover apartment; one agent is in charge of photographing material, the other agent assists in assuring that material to be photographed is not misplaced from its original location.

Depending on the building involved, the number of offices or apartments and the number of exits involved, additional agents are needed to assure the security of the agents on the assignment. It is also necessary to have the subject and the other occupants of the apartment or office located and under surveillance. The average number of agents assigned to surveillance in connection with the assignment is approximately eight to ten men.

III. PROCESSING INFORMATION RECEIVED

In the average assignment approximately 500 separate photographs or exposures are realized. These are developed by the office laboratory.

The first review of the material obtained is made by the two agents who conducted the initial file review for the assignment. The purpose of this first review is to check address and appointment books for any obvious "meets" or immediate leads requiring prompt action.

[One paragraph of six lines withheld on national security classified grounds.]

■ **Do Not File Memo, FBI Assistant Director William Sullivan to FBI Assistant Director Cartha DeLoach, July 19, 1966**

The following is set forth in regard to your request concerning what authority we have for "black bag" jobs and for the background of our policy and procedures in such matters.

We do not obtain authorization for "black bag" jobs from outside the Bureau. Such a technique involves trespass and is clearly illegal; therefore, it would be impossible to obtain any legal sanction for it. Despite this, "black bag" jobs have been used because they *represent an invaluable technique* in combating subversive activities of a clandestine nature aimed at undermining and destroying our nation.

The present procedure followed in the use of this technique calls for the Special Agent in Charge of a field office to make his request for the use of the technique to the appropriate Assistant Director. The Special Agent in Charge must completely justify the need for the use of the technique and at the same time assure that it can be safely used without any danger or embarrassment to the Bureau. The facts are incorporated in a memorandum which, in accordance with the Director's instructions, is sent to [FBI associate director Clyde] Tolson or to the Director for approval. Subsequently this memorandum is filed in the Assistant Director's office under a "Do Not File" procedure.

In the field the Special Agent in Charge prepares an informal memorandum showing he obtained Bureau authority and this memorandum is filed in his safe until the next inspection by Bureau Inspectors, at which time it is destroyed. . . .

We have used this technique on a highly selective basis, but with wide-range effectiveness, in our operations. We have several cases in the espionage field, for example, where through "black bag" jobs we determined that suspected illegal agents actually had concealed on their premises the equipment through which they carried out their clandestine operations.

Also through the use of this technique we have on numerous occasions been able to obtain material held highly secret and closely guarded by subversive groups and organizations which consisted of membership lists and mailing lists of these organizations.

This applies even to our investigation of the Ku Klux Klan. You may recall that recently through a "black bag" job we obtained the records in the possession of three high-ranking officials of a klan organization in Louisiana. These records gave us the complete membership and financial information concerning the klan's operation which we have been using most effectively to disrupt the organization and, in fact, to bring about its near disintegration.

It was through information obtained through our "black bag" operations that we obtained basic information used to compromise and to bring about the expulsion of William Albertson, the former Executive Secretary of the Communist Party New York District organization.

Through the same technique we have recently been receiving extremely valuable information concerning political developments in the Latin American field, and we also have been able to use it most effectively in a number of instances recently through which we have obtained information concerning growing [name of foreign country withheld] intelligence activities directed at this country.

In short, it is a very valuable weapon which we have used to combat the highly clandestine efforts of subversive elements seeking to undermine our Nation.

Recommendation:

For your information.

[Hoover's handwritten notation: "No more such techniques must be used."]

■ **Strictly Confidential Memo, FBI Director J. Edgar Hoover to FBI Assistant Directors Clyde Tolson and Cartha DeLoach, January 6, 1967**

I note that requests are still being made by Bureau officials for the use of "black bag" jobs techniques. I have previously indicated that I do not intend to approve any such requests in the future, and, consequently, no such recommendations should be submitted for approval of such matters. This practice, which includes also surreptitious entrances upon premises of any kind, will not meet with my approval in the future.

9: Electronic Surveillance

Hoover alone authorized break-ins, and without the prior knowledge and approval of his superiors, notably the attorney general but also the president. But these were not the only illegal investigative techniques employed by Hoover's FBI. FBI wiretapping and bugging activities differed in that the attorney general and the president had some (if intentionally limited) involvement.

In 1934, Congress banned wiretapping. Then, in 1937, and in a follow-up ruling of 1939, the Supreme Court (in Nardone v. U.S.*) ruled that this legislative ban applied to federal agents, including the FBI. Yet the FBI continued to wiretap. It did so, at first, because Justice Department officials concluded that the law prohibited only the interception* and *divulgence of conversations, and thus that intelligence (nonprosecutive) wiretapping was permissible. Then, in 1940, President Roosevelt secretly authorized FBI wiretapping in "national defense" investigations. Although Roosevelt's directive required the prior approval of the attorney general, a concern for secrecy led Attorney General Robert Jackson to decide not to maintain a record of approved wiretaps. Combined with a commitment to monitor German "espionage" and then communist "subversive" activities, this practice of the attorney general in effect granted Hoover a blank check in the use of wiretaps. This lasted until 1965 when Attorney General Nicholas Katzenbach ordered that written records be maintained of authorized FBI wiretaps and that all ongoing taps be regularly reauthorized by the attorney general.*

The roles of the attorney general and the president differed in

*the case of FBI bugging activities. Microphone surveillance
was not illegal but did require trespass for installation, which
entailed a Fourth Amendment violation. So when Hoover
decided to use bugs during "espionage" investigations in 1940,
he did not brief the attorney general or seek his approval.
Only in 1951, responding to potential prosecutive problems in
Smith Act cases, did Hoover formally brief the attorney
general on FBI bugging activities and seek his policy guidance.
Attorney General J. Howard McGrath decided that he could
not authorize this illegal practice, but he did not explicitly order
Hoover not to install bugs. Hoover continued on his own to
authorize FBI bugging while seeking to convince McGrath's
successors to revise this written (if secret) conclusion. Finally,
in 1954, Attorney General Herbert Brownell issued a broadly
worded secret directive authorizing FBI bugging. Rejecting
Hoover's recommendation that the attorney general approve each
bug on a case-by-case basis, Brownell preferred to grant
Hoover broad discretion in using this technique. This
unwillingness to monitor FBI bugging practices was continued
by Brownell's immediate successors, Republican Attorney General
William Rogers and Democratic Attorney General Robert
Kennedy. Not surprisingly, the FBI employed this technique
extensively, and the director unilaterally authorized the use of
bugs during criminal investigations. In August 1961 Hoover was
able to secure Kennedy's blind approval of future FBI
bugging. As in the case of wiretaps, this situation lasted until
1965 when Attorney General Katzenbach issued new rules
requiring his written authorization for all bugs and
reauthorization for ongoing bugs.
    Because Katzenbach's rules coincided with Hoover's concerns
over disclosure of the FBI's illegal activities, FBI wiretapping
and bugging were scaled down. These limitations proved
temporary, however. In 1968 Congress rescinded its 1934 ban
on wiretapping. Then, the election of Richard Nixon ironically
brought Hoover under pressure to increase FBI wiretapping
and bugging as well as to reinstitute break-ins and mail opening.*

■ **Memo, FBI Assistant Director Edward Tamm to FBI Director, December 22, 1937**

Pursuant to your instructions I conferred with [Assistant Attorney General Alexander] Holtzoff concerning the significance to the Bureau of the Supreme Court decision in the [Nardone] case . . . in which the court held that evidence obtained by wire tapping is not admissible in the trial of a case in Federal Court, with . . . the possibility of Bureau Agents being prosecuted for violating the penal provisions of the Federal Communications Act. . . .

Judge Holtzoff stated that . . . this decision *has been misinterpreted, particularly by the newspapers.* He points out that *Section 605* of the Federal Communications Act . . . *does not as a matter of fact prohibit the tapping of a telephone or telegraph wire. The statute prohibits the intercepting and divulging or publishing the existence,* contents substance, purport, effect or meaning *of such communications.* The statute . . . does not penalize the interception or divulgence, but . . . the intercepting *and* divulging or publishing, as a result of which *the interception* of telephone or telegraph messages by telephone tap or otherwise is not in itself a violation. . . . I pointed out to Judge Holtzoff that in our cases any man listening on a telephone would naturally report the results of his telephone surveillance . . . to the Bureau, and that this would probably constitute a legal [sic, illegal] divulgence and publication. Mr. Holtzoff stated that this might be true, but that . . . any prosecution . . . in a case of this kind could only be done with the approval of the Department [of Justice] in Washington and *that certainly the Department would not authorize any prosecution against its own employees in those cases* where the employees were proceeding in a course of official conduct authorized by the Director of the Bureau who must be depended upon by the Attorney General to use his best judgment in situations of this kind. . . .

Mr. Holtzoff stated that . . . the bulk of the telephone calls . . . are local and that he would not hesitate to inform the Bureau that it could place a telephone tap on any telephone at any time for the purpose of monitoring local calls. He pointed out that if interstate calls were received . . . of course, information so obtained could not be introduced in evidence, . . . [and] the Director could authorize a telephone tap at any time that he thought necessary, the tap to be placed, of course, for the purpose of intercepting anticipated local telephone calls and . . . that no telephone call of an interstate nature could be introduced in evidence, although the Bureau was at liberty to act in an investigative capacity upon any information which was developed over a telephone tap.

[Hoover's handwritten notation: "Please send letter to all SACs advising them same rule prevails as formerly—no phone taps without my approval & as previously we will not authorize any except in extraordinary case & then not to obtain evidence but only for collateral leads. 12/22/37." Tamm's handwritten notation: "Bulletin to all SACs prepared."]

■ **Strictly Confidential Memo—Return to Director as soon as noted—
FBI Director J. Edgar Hoover to FBI Assistant Directors Clyde
Tolson, Edward Tamm, and Hugh Clegg, May 28, 1940**

There is attached hereto a copy of a memorandum addressed to the
Attorney General by the President, and dated May 21, 1940. . . .

**Attachment: Memo, FBI Director J. Edgar Hoover for the Confidential
Files, May 28, 1940**

In regard to the attached memorandum of May 21, 1940, addressed to
the Attorney General by the President and marked "Confidential," you are
advised that in discussing this matter with the Attorney General, the
Attorney General decided that he would have no detailed record kept
concerning the cases in which wire-tapping would be utilized. It was
agreeable to him that I would maintain a memorandum book in my
immediate office, listing the time, places, and cases in which this procedure is to be utilized.

**Attachment: Confidential Memo, President Franklin D. Roosevelt to Attor-
ney General Robert Jackson, May 21, 1940**

I have agreed with the broad purpose of the Supreme Court decision
relating to wire-tapping in investigations. The Court is undoubtedly sound
both in regard to the use of evidence secured over tapped wires in the
prosecution of citizens in criminal cases; and is also right in its opinion that
under ordinary and normal circumstances wire-tapping should not be
carried on for the excellent reason that it is almost bound to lead to abuse
of civil rights.

However, I am convinced that the Supreme Court never intended any
dictum in the particular case which it decided to apply to grave matters
involving the defense of the nation.

It is, of course, well known that certain other nations have been engaged
in the organization of propaganda of so-called "fifth columns" in other
countries and in preparation for sabotage, as well as in actual sabotage.

It is too late to do anything about it after sabotage, assassinations and
"fifth column" activities are completed.

You are, therefore, authorized and directed in such cases as you may
approve, after investigation of the need in each case, to authorize the
necessary investigating agents that they are at liberty to secure information
by listening devices direct to the conversation or other communications of
persons suspected of subversive activities against the Government of the
United States, including suspected spies. You are requested furthermore to
limit these investigations so conducted to a minimum and to limit them
insofar as possible to aliens.

PRESIDENT ROOSEVELT AUTHORIZED FBI wiretapping only during "national defense" investigations and subject to the attorney general's approval. But Jackson's decision not to keep a record of authorized wiretaps or to require reauthorization after a period of time invited Hoover to expand wiretapping to include investigations of "subversive activities." Aware of the absence of explicit authority for this expansion, Hoover drafted a letter for Attorney General Tom Clark to send to President Truman. When quoting from Roosevelt's 1940 directive, however, Hoover dropped the final sentence. Truman, unwittingly, thought he was merely reaffirming the FBI's authority to wiretap "subversive activity."

■ **Letter, Attorney General Tom Clark to President Harry Truman, July 17, 1946**

Under date of May 21, 1940, President Franklin D. Roosevelt, in a memorandum addressed to Attorney General Jackson, stated: "You are therefore authorized and directed in such cases as you may approve, after investigation of the need in each case, to authorize the necessary investigating agents that they are at liberty to secure information by listening devices directed to the conversation or other communications of persons suspected of subversive activities against the Government of the United States, including suspected spies."

This directive was followed by Attorneys General Jackson and Biddle, and is being followed currently in this Department. I consider it appropriate, however, to bring the subject to your attention at this time.

It seems to me that in the present troubled period in international affairs, accompanied as it is by an increase in subversive activity here at home, it is as necessary as it was in 1940 to take the investigative measures referred to in President Roosevelt's memorandum. At the same time, the country is threatened by a very susbstantial increase in crime. While I am reluctant to suggest any use whatever of these special investigative measures in domestic cases, it seems to me imperative to use them in cases vitally affecting the domestic security, or where human life is in jeopardy.

As so modified, I believe the outstanding directive should be continued in force. If you concur in this policy, I should appreciate it if you would so indicate at the foot of this letter.

In my opinion, the measures proposed are within the authority of law, and I have in the files of the Department materials indicating to me that my two most recent predecessors as Attorney General would concur in this view.

[President Truman's handwritten notation: "I concur July 17, 1947."]

■ **Personal and Confidential Memo, FBI Director J. Edgar Hoover to Attorney General J. Howard McGrath, October 6, 1951**

Allegations made by defense attorneys relative to [wiretapping] by this Bureau in current prosecutions of Communist functionaries under the Smith Act of 1940* make it advisable . . . to review carefully our policies in that field with a view to insuring that sound practices are adhered to.

Use of wire tapping by this Bureau, as you know, has been carefully restricted to major crimes such as kidnaping, where the life and safety of a victim may be at stake, and to investigations essential to the national security involving such crimes as espionage and sabotage. Prior to utilizing this medium, specific approval has been secured in each instance from the Attorney General. It has been employed solely as an investigative technique and not for the purpose of procuring evidence to be used in prosecutions. . . . It is rapidly becoming the practice of defense attorneys in security-type cases to argue that the prosecution is predicated in part upon evidence obtained as a result of wire tapping. Such claims are accompanied by demands that all communications referring to relevant wire taps be made available for inspection. Manifestly, this Bureau cannot comply with these requests without disclosing a great mass of data, frequently relating to highly confidential matters, with the likelihood of compromising cases of vital importance to the protection of the United States.

Without legislation modifying the effect of Section 605 of the Communications Act of 1934, as interpreted by the courts, continued use of wire tapping in any form, however limited, raises these issues. This is true notwithstanding the fact that they are predicated upon Presidential authority and have the approval of responsible government officials. Allegations will be made that this Bureau is engaging in illegal practices. Officials authorizing wire tapping will be condemned for condoning these practices. FBI representatives may incur citations for contempt of court by declining to produce wire tap information and prosecutions may be dismissed if such information is not produced.

The FBI today has the gravest responsibility for protection of the national security of our country. To execute these responsibilities properly requires the employment of the entire resources of the FBI. Experience has demonstrated clearly that the use of wire tapping is a valuable and highly productive technique in intelligence coverage of matters relating to espionage, sabotage and related security fields. Wire tapping produces information which normally cannot be obtained through other channels.

In view of the issues continually arising from the use of wire tapping, even on the highly restrictive basis employed by this Bureau, I desire to be advised whether you consider that we should continue to employ this technique as at present, or discontinue it entirely.

*In *U.S.* v. *Flynn*, defense attorneys claimed that their clients' telephones had been tapped, resulting as well in the interception of conversations between defendants and their attorneys.—Ed.

As you are aware, this Bureau has also employed the use of microphone installation on a highly restrictive basis, chiefly to obtain intelligence information. The information obtained from microphones, as in the case of wire taps, is not admissible in evidence. In certain instances it has been possible to install microphones without trespass, . . . [and] the information obtained, of course, is treated as evidence and therefore is not regarded as purely intelligence information.

As you know, in a number of instances it has not been possible to install microphones without trespass. In such instances the information received therefrom is of an intelligence nature only. Here again, as in the use of wire taps, experience has shown us that intelligence information highly pertinent to the defense and welfare of this nation is derived through the use of microphones. . . . I would like to have a definite opinion from you as to whether, in view of the highly productive intelligence information gathered from these sources, we should continue to utilize this technique on the present highly restricted basis, or whether we should cease the use of microphone coverage entirely in view of the issues currently being raised.

■ **Personal and Confidential Memo, Attorney General J. Howard McGrath to FBI Director J. Edgar Hoover, February 26, 1952**

Reference is made to your [October 6, 1951] memorandum relative to wire tapping surveillances.

There is pending, as you know, before the Congress legislation that I have recommended which would permit wire tapping under appropriate safeguards and make evidence thus obtained admissible. [Congress did not enact this legislation.] As you state, the use of wire tapping is indispensable in intelligence coverage of matters relating to espionage, sabotage, and related security fields. Consequently, I do not intend to alter the existing policy that wire tapping surveillance should be used under the present highly restrictive basis and when specifically authorized by me.

The use of microphone surveillance which does not involve a trespass would seem to be permissible under the present state of the law. . . . Such surveillances as involve trespass are in the area of the Fourth Amendment, and evidence so obtained and from leads so obtained is inadmissible.

The records do not indicate that this question dealing with microphones has ever been presented before; therefore, please be advised that I cannot authorize the installation of a microphone *involving a trespass* under existing law.

It is requested when any case is referred to the Department in which telephone, microphone or other technical surveillances have been employed by the Bureau or other Federal Agencies (when known) that the Department be advised of the facts at the time the matter is first submitted.

■ **JUNE Memo, FBI Supervisor Alan Belmont to FBI Assistant Director D. Milton Ladd, March 14, 1952**

. . . The Attorney General in his memorandum of February 26, 1952, . . . stated that when any case is referred to the Department in which telephone, microphone or technical surveillances have been employed by the Bureau or other Federal Agencies (when known), the Department should be advised of the facts at the time the matter is first submitted.

In order to comply completely with this instruction an intolerable burden would be placed on the Bureau as it would be necessary to advise the Department in every case transmitted as the instruction is not restricted to cases being submitted for actual prosecution. . . .

To clarify this entire matter a discussion was held with [Assistant Attorney General] J. M. McInerney, on March 7, 1952. . . . Mr. McInerney agreed that it would be unnecessary and inadvisable to inform the Department in every instance where these devices have been used. . . . The Department need only be put on notice in those instances where the Department is seriously considering prosecution . . . [and] the Department will so notify the Bureau and, at the same time, request to be advised whether any of these devices have been used in conjunction with the case. . . .

■ **Memo, FBI Director J. Edgar Hoover for the Director's Files, June 9, 1952**

On June 6, 1952, I saw the [new] Attorney General [James McGranery] and . . . briefed him as to the procedure which the Bureau follows with reference to the installation of [wiretaps], pointing out to him that there were no surveillances of this type established without obtaining approval from him for the same and that we endeavored to confine requests for such authority to cases involving espionage, sabotage, kidnapping and a few major criminal cases. . . . The Attorney General stated that he approved of the procedure followed.

I then called his attention to the fact that the Department had, a few months ago, ruled that it could not approve the installation of any microphones where trespass was involved. I told the Attorney General that such installations had been utilized on a very limited basis by the FBI and only in cases which directly affected the internal security of the United States, wherein information could be obtained which would enable the FBI to take the necessary precautionary measures for internal security. I told the Attorney General that following this ruling by the Department, we discontinued some of the microphone installations which had been established, where it had been necessary to commit technical trespass. The Attorney General . . . thought it was entirely proper for installations of microphones to be made in any case where elements were at work against the security of the United States and he told me that in such instances where I felt that there was need to install microphones, even though trespass might be committed, that he would leave it to my judgment as to the steps to take. I told the Attorney General that this authority would only be used in extreme cases and only in cases involving the internal security of the United States.

[President Truman fired McGrath on April 3, 1952, nominating McGranery as his replacement. McGranery's nomination encountered opposition and he was finally confirmed on June 2, 1952.]

■ JUNE Memo, FBI Assistant Director Louis Nichols to FBI Associate Director Clyde Tolson, March 29, 1954

. . . I saw [Deputy Attorney General William] Rogers today. I advised him of the background of the memorandum from former Attorney General J. Howard McGrath dated February 26, 1952, limiting microphone surveillances only when trespasses are not involved. I further pointed out that the Department had given a rather narrow definition of trespassing . . . that this was not sufficient to give us the coverage that we felt was needed, and that for his strictly personal and confidential information, there had been a few instances wherein we had on our own utilized microphone surveillances, but that the Bureau felt we should have some backing of the [Justice] Department to utilize microphone surveillances where the intelligence to be gained was a necessary adjunct to security matters and important investigations, in instances when prosecution is not contemplated.

[One paragraph withheld on grounds that information involves personal privacy and is national security classified.]

Rogers stated that he agreed the Department's order should back the Bureau; and furthermore . . . that the Department's policy should be sufficiently general to cover all situations, and . . . whether or not it would be advisable to put into effect the system now followed in connection with wire tapping, namely to have the Attorney General approval. I told him that this, of course, would be a matter of Department policy, although . . . in a case such as this, that it might be possible for the Department to give an over-all policy to cover all needs. Rogers . . . agreed and asked that we think about how best this could be handled and . . . give him on an informal basis on plain paper a draft of what we needed. He will then use this as a means of talking to [Assistant Attorney General Warren] Olney and the Attorney General [Herbert Brownell] and try to get the matter adjusted.

I, frankly, can see nothing wrong with this type of approach.

■ Memo, FBI Assistant Director Leland Boardman to FBI Director, March 31, 1954

I talked to [Assistant Attorney General Warren] Olney on March 30,

1954, . . . relative to the Department backing our use of microphones in internal security cases. . . .

After considerable discussion it was agreed by Olney: (1) That microphone coverage is necessary in security cases in the national interest—(2) That any cases going to prosecution must be carefully evaluated if a microphone has been used—(3) That the Department will broaden its interpretation of what constitutes trespass in the installation of microphones, (4) That the Department would back the Bureau in the use of microphones in security cases, (5) That the Attorney General should furnish a memorandum to the Bureau covering points 1, 3 and 4 above.

To assist the Department in this respect, the Bureau will furnish an informal draft of a proposed memorandum covering these points from which the Attorney General's memorandum will be drafted.

Olney thought it would be desirable to parallel the present procedure in wire taps—that is—to present each proposed microphone to the Attorney General and get his specific authority, however he doubted that the Attorney General could authorize a microphone where trespass is clearly indicated. . . .

Frankly, we would not object to presenting each and every case to the Attorney General for his authority as we do in wire taps. This would enable the Bureau to say that no microphones are utilized without the Attorney General's authority. There are two possible drawbacks . . . First— that there are occasions when it is imperative that a microphone be installed immediately and there is a delay in getting the Attorney General's approval. Second—I doubt that the Attorney General will authorize microphones where the installation must be made by definite trespass, yet our responsibilities demand that a very limited number of such microphones be utilized.
ACTION

If you agree, we will prepare an informal draft to assist the Department in preparing the Attorney General's memorandum to the Bureau.

[Hoover's handwritten notation: "OK."]

■ **Memo, FBI Assistant Director Louis Nichols to FBI Associate Director Clyde Tolson, April 14, 1954**

. . . While talking to [Deputy Attorney General William] Rogers on other matters today, I gave him a copy of the draft of a memo [on microphone surveillance] dated April 1st. . . . Rogers did not think much, after further reflection, of the idea of having the Attorney General clear microphone surveillances on the ground that time was of the essence and he thought the Attorney General would be in a much better position to defend the Bureau in the event there should be a technical trespass if he had not heretofore approved it.

[Tolson's handwritten notation: "I think we would be in a better position

to submit requests to AG [attorney general] as we do wire taps 4-15."
Hoover's handwritten notation: "I agree."]

■ **Confidential Memo, Attorney General Herbert Brownell to FBI
Director, May 20, 1954**
The recent decision of the Supreme Court entitled *Irvine* v. *California*.
... makes appropriate a reappraisal of the use which may be made in the
future by the Federal Bureau of Investigation of microphone surveillance in
connection with matters relating to the internal security of the country.

It is clear that in some instances the use of microphone surveillance is
the only possible way of uncovering the activities of espionage agents,
possible saboteurs, and subversive persons. In such instances I am of the
opinion that the national interest requires that microphone surveillance be
utilized by the Federal Bureau of Investigation. This use need not be
limited to the development of evidence for prosecution. The FBI has an
intelligence function in connection with internal security matters equally as
important as the duty of developing evidence for presentation to the courts
and the national security requires that the FBI be able to use microphone
surveillance for the proper discharge of both of such functions. The
Department of Justice approves the use of microphone surveillance by the
FBI under these circumstances and for these purposes. . . .

It is quite clear that in the *Irvine* case the Justices . . . were outraged by
what they regarded as the indecency of installing a microphone in a
bedroom. . . . The Court's action is a clear indication of the need for
discretion and intelligent restraint by the FBI in all cases, including
internal security matters. Obviously, the installation of a microphone in a
bedroom or in some comparably intimate location should be avoided
wherever possible. It may appear, however, that important intelligence or
evidence relating to matters connected with the national security can only
be obtained by the installation of a microphone in such a location. . . .
Under such circumstances the installation is proper and is not prohibited by
the Supreme Court's decision in the *Irvine* case. . . .

The question of whether a trespass is actually involved and the second
question of the effect of such a trespass upon the admissibility in court of the
evidence thus obtained, must necessarily be resolved according to the
circumstances of each case. The Department . . . will review the circumstances
in each case in the light of the practical necessities of investigation and of the
national interest which must be protected. It is my opinion that the Department
should adopt that interpretation which will permit microphone coverage by
the FBI in a manner most conducive to our national interest. I recognize that
for the FBI to fulfill its important intelligence function, considerations of
internal security and the national safety are paramount and, therefore, may
compel the unrestricted use of this technique in the national interest.

■ **Memo, FBI Supervisor Alan Belmont to FBI Assistant**
Director Leland Boardman, May 21, 1954

The . . . memorandum from the Attorney General dated May 20, 1954, on microphone surveillance policy has been reviewed. . . . In this memorandum, the Attorney General is giving us the go ahead on microphones whether or not there is trespass at the same time suggesting that discretion be used in certain cases. We will continue to use microphones on a restricted basis and authority to install will be given to the field depending upon the merits of the cases and the need for coverage. Stress will be placed on the necessity to install microphones without trespass particularly where prosecution may be involved. However, where there is a definite need for coverage such as Communist Party underground and Soviet Intelligence matters careful consideration will be given to the facts in each case.

In criminal cases, care will be taken to restrict installation to only in important cases and in all installations authorizations for any microphone installation will only be approved by high Bureau officials. . . .

■ **JUNE Memo, FBI Assistant Director Alan Belmont to FBI**
Associate Director Clyde Tolson, July 2, 1959

. . . The Bureau is engaged in an intelligence effort in the criminal field, directed against top criminal leaders and organized crime. . . . The Bureau has a real need to develop intelligence in this area, and should be able to justify the use of microphones against top hoodlums on the basis of the threat to society from organized crime.

You inquired, however, if the Bureau should use microphones in criminal cases. . . .

The Bureau would be in a better position to be able to say that we utilize microphones in the same areas as delineated by the President and the Attorney General in the use of wire taps, namely security cases and cases involving jeopardy to human life. Frankly, . . . it would be a real pity if we were forced to restrict ourselves, because organized crime is a menace to society and we have too few weapons to combat it to give up the valuable technique of microphones. . . .

On March 30, 1954, [FBI assistant director Leland] Boardman and I talked to Assistant Attorney General Olney . . . regarding the use of microphones by the Bureau. The approach to Olney was made on the basis of security cases. As a result he agreed that it was necessary for the Bureau to use microphones. . . .

As a result of this discussion with Olney, he agreed that the AG should furnish a memorandum backing us in the use of microphones, including trespass where necessary. We did receive such a memorandum dated May 20, 1954 . . . [wherein] the AG clearly approves the use of microphone surveillances with or without trespass in security matters. Concerning criminal matters, the AG's letter states: "I recognize that for the FBI to fulfill its important intelligence function, considerations of internal security and the *national safety* are paramount and, therefore, may compel the unrestricted use of this technique in the national interest." . . .

The use of the terminology "national safety" was interpreted by the Bureau to include criminal cases, particularly as in the AG's letter he uses terminology such as the "need for discretion and intelligent restraint in the use of microphones by the FBI in all cases, including internal security matters." It appears, therefore, that the AG's letter, while primarily directed toward security matters as this was the basis on which the issue was raised with the Department, used terminology which was interpreted by the Bureau to apply to criminal cases as well. . . .

■ **JUNE Memo, FBI Executive Conference to FBI Associate Director Clyde Tolson, July 20, 1959**
On 7-20-59 the Executive Conference considered the question of seeking approval from the Attorney General (AG) [William Rogers] before instituting microphone surveillances. . . .

It was the belief of the Executive Conference that the language of the AG's 5-20-54 memorandum covered both Security and Criminal matters; that we are adequately protected by this opinion of the AG, supported by that of Mr. Rogers in his discussion of this matter with Mr. Nichols on 4-27-54. The Executive Conference unanimously agreed that as long as Mr. Rogers continues as AG this matter not be represented but that we proceed as in the past on the strength of the 5-20-54 memorandum.

[Attorney General Brownell's decision not to require his prior approval for all FBI microphone installations invited this 1959 decision to expand microphone use during criminal investigations—without briefing the attorney general and by simply reinterpreting the 1954 directive.]

ATTORNEY GENERAL ROBERT Kennedy's interest in intensifying the federal government's campaign against crime invited a further expansion of bugging, again without explicit authorization. Kennedy gave the FBI a blank check in August 1961 when he signed a leased-line arrangement with the New York Telephone Company.

■ **Memo, FBI Director to Deputy Attorney General Byron White, May 4, 1961**

In connection with the Attorney General's [Robert Kennedy] contemplated appearance before the Senate Subcommittee on Constitutional Rights [then considering wiretap legislation], our views on the use of microphone surveillances in FBI cases are set forth for your consideration. . . .

Our policy on the use of microphone surveillances is based upon a memorandum from former Attorney General Herbert Brownell dated May 20, 1954, in which he approved the use of microphone surveillances with or without trespass. In this memorandum Mr. Brownell said in part: "I recognize that for the FBI to fulfill its important intelligence function, considerations of internal security and the national safety are paramount and, therefore, may compel the unrestrictive use of this technique in the national interest."

In light of this policy, in the internal security field, we are utilizing microphone surveillances on a restricted basis even though trespass is necessary to assist in uncovering the activities of Soviet intelligence agents and Communist Party leaders. In the interests of national safety, microphone surveillances are also utilized on a restricted basis, even though trespass is necessary, in uncovering major criminal activities. We are using such coverage in connection with our investigations of the clandestine activities of top hoodlums and organized crime. From an intelligence standpoint, this investigative technique has profound results unobtainable through other means. The information so obtained is treated in the same manner as information obtained from wire taps, that is, not from the standpoint of evidentiary value but for intelligence purposes.

There is no Federal legislation at the present time pertaining to the use of microphone surveillances. The passage of any restrictive legislation in this field would be a definite loss to our investigative operations, both in the internal security field and in our fight against the criminal element. This is especially true in the case of organized crime where we have too few weapons at our command to give up the valuable technique of microphones. . . .

■ **Memo, FBI Assistant Director Courtney Evans to FBI Assistant Director Alan Belmont, July 6, 1961**

The Attorney General . . . raised, indirectly, the possibility of utilizing "electronic devices" similar to those being utilized in espionage cases in these organized crime investigations. This question was directed to me personally and since there were many attorneys present, I merely stated this had been afforded full consideration but that there were many problems in this regard. The Attorney General apparently took the hint as he dropped any further discussion of this topic. It would seem that information currently being furnished to the Attorney General in the "Newsweek" case may have brought this topic to the forefront in his mind. [Reacting to a *Newsweek* article about U.S. planning in Germany, President Kennedy demanded that the source of this leaked information be investigated. Attorney General Robert Kennedy, on June 27, 1961, ordered the FBI to investigate this matter. After establishing that the article had been written by Lloyd Norman, the FBI wiretapped the reporter's phone. Still, the Bureau was unable to determine whether Norman had obtained classified information or to locate the source of the suspected leak.]

In order to prevent any unwarranted requests being made by the Department for utilization of technical equipment, it is believed advisable to discuss this with the Attorney General. He is, of course, aware we do have some coverage of this type because of the nature of information that has been supplied to him, particularly in connection with the activities of leading hoodlums in Chicago. There is a serious question as to whether he has any comprehension as to the difference between a technical surveillance [wiretap] and a microphone surveillance. He should be aware of the strong objections to the utilization of any telephone taps and the limitations of microphone surveillances. Obviously, this is the field which should be closely controlled by the Bureau. If the Director approves, I will discuss this with the Attorney General personally so we can forestall any precipitous action by the Department.

[Hoover's handwritten notation: "Yes."]

■ **Memo, FBI Assistant Director Courtney Evans to FBI Assistant Director Alan Belmont, July 7, 1961**

In line with the Director's approval, the Attorney General was contacted. . . .

It was pointed out to the Attorney General that we had . . . [used] microphone surveillances in [organized crime] cases and while they represented an expensive investigative step, we were nevertheless utilizing them in all instances where this was technically feasible and where valuable information might be expected. . . . The Attorney General . . . recognized the reasons why telephone taps should be restricted to national-defense-type cases and he was pleased we had been using microphone surveillances where these objections do not apply whenever possible in organized crime matters.

The Attorney General . . . had approved several technical surveillances [wiretaps] in connection with security-type investigations since he took office, but . . . had not kept any record and didn't really know what he had approved and what surveillances were in operation. . . . For his own information he would like to see a list of the technical surveillances now in operation . . . this could be brought over to him personally and that he would look it over and immediately return it because he realized the importance of having these records maintained under the special security conditions which only the FBI had.

If the Director approves, we will have the list of technical surveillances prepared, delivered personally to the Attorney General and then returned to the Bureau's file.

[Hoover's handwritten notation: "OK."]

■ **Memo, FBI Assistant Director Courtney Evans to FBI Assistant Director Alan Belmont, August 17, 1961**

The Attorney General was contacted on the morning of August 17, 1961, with reference to the situation in New York City concerning the obtaining of leased lines from the telephone company for use in connection with microphone surveillances. The matter was discussed with the Attorney General and he was shown a specimen copy of the proposed letter [to New York telephone company executive] which would be used. The Attorney General approved the proposed procedure in this regard and personally signed the attached memorandum evidencing such approval.

Enclosure Letterhead Memo, August 17, 1961

In connection with the use of microphone surveillances it is frequently necessary to lease a special telephone line in order to monitor such a surveillance. These situations occur when it is impossible to locate a secure monitoring point in the immediate vicinity of the premises covered by the microphone. Even though a special telephone line is utilized, this activity in no way involves any interception of telephonic communications and is not a telephone tap.

In the New York City area the telephone company has over the years insisted that a letter be furnished to the telephone company on each occasion when a special telephone line is leased by the FBI. It is required that such a lease arrangement be with the approval of the Attorney General. In the past we have restricted the utilization of leased lines in New York City to situations involving telephone taps, all of which have been approved by the Attorney General.

We have not previously used leased lines in connection with microphone surveillances because of certain technical difficulties which existed in New York City. These technical difficulties have, however, now been overcome. If we are permitted to use leased telephone lines as an adjunct to our microphone surveillances, this type of coverage can be materially extended both in security and major criminal cases. Accordingly, your approval of our utilizing this leased line arrangement is requested. . . .

Approved: *Robert Kennedy* (signature)
Date: _____

■ **Administratively Confidential Memo, President Lyndon B. Johnson to Heads of Executive Departments and Agencies, June 30, 1965**

I am strongly opposed to the interception of telephone conversations as a general investigative technique. I recognize that mechanical and electronic devices may sometimes be essential in protecting our national security. Nevertheless, it is clear that indiscriminate use of these investigative devices to overhear telephone conversations, without the knowledge or consent of any of the persons involved, could result in serious abuses and invasions of privacy. In my view, the invasion of privacy of communications is a highly offensive practice which should be engaged in only where the national security is at stake. To avoid any misunderstanding on this subject in the Federal Government, I am establishing the following basic guidelines to be followed by all governmental agencies:

(1) No federal personnel is to intercept telephone conversations within the United States by any mechanical or electronic device, without the consent of one of the parties involved (except in connection with investigations related to the national security).

(2) No interception shall be undertaken or continued without first obtaining the approval of the Attorney General.

(3) All federal agencies shall immediately conform their practices and procedures to the provisions of this order.

Utilization of mechanical or electronic devices to overhear non-telephone conversations is an even more difficult problem, which raises substantial and unresolved questions of Constitutional interpretation. I desire that each agency conducting such investigations consult the Attorney General to ascertain whether the agency's practices are fully in accord with the law and with a decent regard for the rights of others. . . .

[In response, Attorney General Nicholas Katzenbach issued new orders governing FBI wiretapping and bugging: the attorney general's prior approval was required for all FBI wiretaps *and* bugs; the attorney general's reauthorization was required every six months to continue authorized taps and bugs; and the names of all individuals whose conversations were intercepted were to be recorded in a special electronic surveillance index.]

■ **Memo, FBI Director to Attorney General Nicholas Katzenbach, September 14, 1965**

In accordance with the wishes you have expressed during various recent conversations with me, . . . the Federal Bureau of Investigation has severely restricted and, in many instances, eliminated the use of special investigative techniques in carrying out our investigative work. This has been found necessary in view of the present atmosphere, brought about by the unrestrained and injudicious use of special investigative techniques by other agencies [notably the Internal Revenue Service] and departments, resulting in Congressional [notably the so-called Long subcommittee] and public alarm and opposition to any activity which could in any way be termed an invasion of privacy.

As a consequence, and at your request, we have discontinued completely the use of microphones. While we have traditionally restricted wire taps to internal security cases and an occasional investigation involving possible loss of life, such as kidnaping, I have further cut down on wire taps and I am not requesting authority for any additional wire taps. I have further refused to authorize any mail covers, trash covers, or the use of the polygraph in our cases. In addition, following your concern about the use of portable recorders, I have instructed that such recorders not be used by the FBI. I do not hold with the unrestrained use or the injudicious use of any of these techniques, and most certainly in the past this Bureau has been restrained in its application of such investigative techniques, with a tight central control of their use.

It is axiomatic that we can produce results in direct ratio to our ability to secure information. Traditionally we gather information through investigation, interviews, and through live informants and sources, and this we are continuing to do. However, in dealing with clandestine operations, such as in the internal security and espionage field, and in the field of organized crime, we long ago came to the realization that it was necessary to supplement our knowledge by other investigative techniques, such as wire taps, microphones, and others mentioned above. . . .

We have applied this classic pattern in our attack on the Communist Party and other subversive groups throughout the years, with the result that we have them in a constant state of confusion and we have been able to protect the internal security of the country through knowledge of their strategy and tactics. We have been applying the same aggressive, systematic program against Cosa Nostra and other elements of organized crime and, without question, we have been making good headway leading toward the ultimate destruction of such groups.

In dealing with the internal foes of this country, whether they be in the security or the criminal field, the maximum knowledge of them, individually and organizationally, gives the FBI the ability to formulate a line of attack, conserves manpower, and pinpoints our activities so that we get productive results. To the extent that our knowledge is reduced, to that extent our productiveness is reduced. . . .

With particular reference to the use of wire taps and microphones, . . . you are well aware that the selective and restrained use of these techniques has made it possible for the FBI to produce highly significant intelligence information to assist our makers of international policy, as well as to hold in check subversive elements within the country. Likewise the use of microphones in the field of organized crime has produced extremely valuable intelligence data.

I am extremely concerned about this situation because the heavy respon sibilities entrusted to this Bureau in the fields of internal security and organized crime are in no way abated, yet many of the tools by which we are able to produce the results expected of us in these admittedly complex and difficult fields are being taken away from us. . . .

■ **Memo, Attorney General Nicholas Katzenbach to FBI Director, January 27, 1966**
This refers to your memorandum . . . "as to the propriety of the utiliza-

tion of microphone coverage involving both use and nonuse of leased telephone lines in connection with investigations relating to security and/or criminal matters."

With respect to security matters, the guide lines and procedures governing the use of technical surveillance and electronic devices are covered by existing policy and directives.

With respect to criminal matters generally, microphone coverage may be accomplished by the tapping of a telephone line or installation of a listening device having no connection with both ends of a telephone conversation.

With respect to telephone wiretapping, Section 605 of the Federal Communications Act prohibits interception and divulgence of information obtained and also prohibits interception and use of the information obtained for the benefit of the tapper or another not entitled thereto. Obviously, evidence derived in such a manner cannot be divulged or used at trial. . . . The Department has taken the position that wiretapping without divulgence outside of the government agency does not violate Section 605. However, in view of the present composition of the Court and judicial expressions in collateral areas, it may well be that . . . [the court might rule differently] at this time.

Microphone coverage (not involving wiretapping) which is installed by unauthorized entry into protected premises is a violation of the Fourth Amendment, with the result that any information obtained by such means is barred from use as evidence. The decisions make clear that the violation continues as long as the coverage is maintained and that the means used to transmit the sounds picked up by a microphone, whether a wire, a spike or a leased line (as in your inquiry) are immaterial. . . .

Because your inquiry concerns "propriety" as well as legality . . . I am attaching a memorandum . . . [which] makes clear that certain techniques are illegal and therefore improper. On the other hand, it makes clear that electronic devices are permissible where constitutionally protected areas are not invaded; for instance, in the *Lopez* case, . . . a clear majority of the Court held that an agent or informant carrying a concealed tape recorder while talking to a subject commits no trespass, even though on the subject's premises. We cannot predict with any certainty what the Supreme Court would hold . . . [but] do not feel that the activities of Federal agents should necessarily be curtailed based on speculation as to possible court action. However, if words spoken within a man's home were picked up by an electronic device outside the home a closer question would be presented. The *Goldman* case, . . . held that there was no trespass in placing a contact microphone against the far side of a partition wall of a room occupied by the subject. . . . Yet, if the situation arises in the context of a [future] Supreme Court case, we must recognize that the Court might well find the technique both improper and illegal.

With respect to the invasion of Fourth Amendment rights, another difficult question is what constitutes a constitutionally protected area. The

Court . . . has been liberal in construing the scope of Fourth Amendment protection and . . . in addition to a house, an apartment, a hotel room, an office, a store, an automobile, and an occupied taxicab have been found to be protected areas. With respect to a public telephone booth, three Federal District Courts have held that such a booth is not a protected area, while two other District Courts have held that it is. . . .

With respect to criminal matters, two things are clear. . . . First, we should not make illegal use of electronic devices. Secondly, we should utilize such devices to the fullest extent within legal bounds. It is unfortunate that the evolving state of the law makes it difficult to provide specific instructions covering all situations. In the gray areas, we do suggest, however, that need and alternatives be carefully weighed.

If you would like a further opinion from the Department as to any specific matter not covered above, we should be pleased to furnish it.

KATZENBACH'S TIGHTER RULES were resented by Hoover and senior FBI officials who were accustomed to perfunctory oversight and rarely briefed their Justice Department superiors.

■ **JUNE Memo, FBI Assistant Director James Gale to FBI Assistant Director Cartha DeLoach, May 27, 1966**
Synopsis
The purpose of this memorandum is . . . what, if any, notice should be given to the Department concerning the extent of our microphone coverage.

A review of our microphone coverage from 1960 to the present revealed that the three investigative divisions operated a total of 738 such units during this period. . . .

The [Justice] Department and/or United States Attorneys were notified of 158 of these sources. . . .

We know that the Department completely lacks security, leaks confidential information to the press and has demonstrated a propensity for going forward and advising the courts wherever they have knowledge of the existence of microphone coverage regardless of whether or not this coverage had any bearing on the case under consideration.

The three investigative divisions concluded that to advise the Department at this time of our microphone coverage could result only in the

Department running to the courts with resultant adverse publicity to the Bureau which could give rise in the present climate to a demand for a Congressional inquiry of the Bureau. We know from experience that in taking this action, the Department would endeavor to convey to the public and to the courts that the Bureau's operations were without the sanction of the Department.

On the other hand, if we do not take action, where trial is imminent of a subject on whom microphone coverage has existed, we run the risks of similar adverse publicity and criticism from the courts and the Department for not having acquainted the prosecuting attorneys with the facts of our confidential coverage should such be revealed during the course of a trial.

We are on the horns of a dilemma which we propose to resolve by instructing our field offices to alert the prosecuting United States Attorney of the fact of our coverage in writing on those cases where prosecution is imminent. This procedure will . . . protect the Bureau from charges of failing to notify appropriate prosecuting authorities of information which could be of significance to them. . . . [Also] the impact of the notification will be dispersed in different areas of the country and will minimize the chances of unfavorable public and press reaction concerning our microphone coverage. The proposed course of action will protect the Bureau's interests and permit the present situation to cool down while still. accomplishing the desired notification to prosecuting authorities. . . .

If this recommendation is approved, each of the three [investigative] divisions will issue instructions for notification of the appropriate prosecuting official in those cases which they supervise where microphone coverage was present and where the case is set for trial in the near future.

[Hoover's handwritten notation: "OK."] . . .

General Consideration of the Problem

. . . In a majority of our microphone installations, trespass on the premises of the target is involved and revelations of the extent of our microphone coverage could well play into the hands of such groups as the Long Committee [a subcommittee of the Senate Judiciary Committee, chaired by Edward Long, which in 1965–1966 initiated hearings into surveillance practices and techniques of the federal intelligence agencies, including the FBI] and the vociferous elements speaking for constitutional guarantees against the invasion of privacy. Most disturbing to this element, ultimately, would be the revelation that the Bureau would become involved in burglary-type activity to effect an installation on the premises of a target.

To voluntarily disseminate to the Department the nature of our microphone coverage would place the Bureau in a position of having to rely on the internal security of the Department's operations. This we know, from past experience, is not possible. The Department in its zeal to be all things to all men in law enforcement, is frequently working in a direct relationship with such groups as the President's Crime Commission, special committees in Congress inquiring into matters of a criminal nature and with numerous local, state and Federal investigators seeking information which they feel they cannot obtain elsewhere. . . .

To make available to the Department, voluntarily, the extent of our use of this technique, could well serve as a further deterrent to an aggressive attitude looking toward prosecution. . . . In numerous of our top hoodlum cases, the Department has frequently found legal reasons or constitutional reasons in justification for their failure to initiate prosecution. . . . To provide the Department with information concerning microphone coverage could result in the Department possessing another crutch as an excuse for failure to prosecute. . . . The Department has successfully prosecuted 15 hoodlums of whom we are aware, but of whom the Department had no knowledge of our microphone coverage. It is seriously questioned whether the Department would have pursued these prosecutions if they had known of the existence of our coverage, even though no evidence utilized during the course of the trial was of a tainted nature. To elect to advise the Department at this time would probably result in the Department's desiring to petition the courts for reopening the matter. . . .

Proposed Course of Action

It is the consensus of opinion of the three investigative divisions involved that . . . we should take no action toward advising the Department at this time of the extent of our microphone coverage during the past six years. In arriving at this decision, we have taken into consideration the current adverse publicity stemming from the Black case, the real probability of leaks of such information from the Department to adverse liberal groups and the hostile press. We were also conscious that such leaks could be utilized to sponsor a Congressional inquiry of the Bureau with resultant further adverse publicity. . . .

This proposed course of action has the further value of permitting the current inflammed [sic] situation to cool down. If the lower courts in the Baker and Black cases rule in favor of the Government, as they should, a great deal of the present press interest will dissipate. At that time, the Bureau can re-evaluate its situation and determine whether any additional course of action is indicated. . . .

10: The Fred Black Case

In *averting critical* scrutiny of FBI wiretapping and bugging activities, owing to the unwillingness of attorneys general since Robert Jackson to monitor these activities, Hoover was encouraged to act on his own. Having devised reporting procedures to ensure secrecy, the once cautious director in time came to believe that he deserved the uncritical support and deference of the attorney general.

By the mid-1960s this system of tacit acquiescence, with its absence of specific authorization, ironically left Hoover vulnerable. A more liberal and assertive press and Congress began to question the legality of FBI electronic surveillance activities. At the same time, in the persons of Nicholas Katzenbach and Ramsey Clark, the insecure director (now past the mandatory retirement age of seventy) encountered attorneys general who were both less deferential and more demanding of their oversight prerogatives. The inevitable confrontation broke when the Fred Black case reached the Supreme Court.

A Washington, D.C., lobbyist convicted of income tax evasion, Black had been the target of an FBI bug because of his gambling associations and influence peddling. The bug was installed in February 1963 based on Hoover's unilateral authorization of December 1962. Then, when Black appealed his conviction to the Supreme Court, senior Justice Department officials, who had not known of the FBI's bugging of Black when they started prosecution, concluded that they had the legal responsibility to disclose this bugging to the Court. At the same time they claimed that the government's case against Black had not been based on information gained through this bug. A

*skeptical Court ordered the department to submit a brief
outlining the authority for the FBI's bugging of Black.*
Hoover and Katzenbach now became unwitting adversaries.
*Although Hoover alone had authorized this bug, he sought to
place the blame on Katzenbach's predecessor, Robert Kennedy.*
*Undaunted by Katzenbach's skepticism, the director adopted a
strategy which had always proved fruitful for him: exploiting his
contacts in Congress and at the White House. Here he
appealed to the shared anti-Kennedy biases of the Johnson White
House and of conservative senators, notably Edward Long
and James Eastland. The resulting standoff reflected the reality of
the relationship between the FBI director and the attorney
general: the attorney general, not the FBI director, resigned.
Katzenbach accepted an appointment as Under Secretary of
State. In the final denouement, the Supreme Court in November
1966 ruled the bug illegal and ordered a new trial for Black.
He was acquitted and eventually (in 1975) received more than
$900,000 in damages in compensation for the government's
(really the FBI's) violation of his privacy rights.*

■ **JUNE Memo, FBI Director to SAC, Washington, December 28,
1962**
. . . Based on your recommendations and provided complete security is
assured, authority granted to conduct surveys [of the office and residence
of Fred Black] at Suite 308, Riddell Building, Washington, D.C., and at
Suite 438–40 Sheraton-Carlton Hotel, Washington, D.C., and, if considered feasible, to install misurs [microphones] at one or both of these
locations. . . .

■ **Memo, FBI Director to Assistant Attorney General Mitchell
Rogovin, May 12, 1966**
. . . Concerning the Fred B. Black matter.
Inasmuch as the FBI is an investigative agency, we, of course, will defer
to the Department insofar as reaching a decision as to what information, if
any, should be volunteered to the Court . . . relative to the microphone
coverage on Black.
. . . To disclose our coverage on Black to the Court at this time would be
extremely poor timing. . . . Undoubtedly such a disclosure would result in
widespread publicity and would undoubtedly trigger a great deal of

unwarranted criticism against the Bureau and the Department. In the event there were any substantive violation of the defendant's rights as a result of microphone coverage or if the Government had taken advantage of this information in order to pursue its case against Fred Black, then we would certainly agree that it would be appropriate to advise the Court at this time. However, this is not the case. A review of our reports reflects that the conversations between Black and his attorney were not disseminated anywhere outside of the FBI and were absolutely of no pertinency insofar as the inquiry which we were making. . . .

■ **Memo, FBI Director to Attorney General Nicholas Katzenbach, May 20, 1966**
During [a recent] meeting [with Assistant Attorney General Mitchell Rogovin] the representative of this Bureau noted that [the proposed] petition [to the Supreme Court] was drawn in extremely broad fashion and unnecessarily volunteered information concerning highly confidential coverage [microphones] not only in Washington, D.C., but in two other cities. At the same time, Mr. Rogovin was informed that contrary to the statements set forth in the proposed petition Departmental attorneys did have knowledge of this coverage as far back as August 24, 1965.
. . . The earliest date of written notification to the Department occurred prior to the decision of the Court of Appeals, . . . on November 10, 1965. . . . In view of the above, it seems quite unnecessary to utilize language in the proposed petition to indicate that information concerning this coverage only recently came to the attention of the Tax Division. . . . It seems inconceivable that . . . the Department should now go out of its way to infer to the Supreme Court that knowledge of this confidential coverage had only been recently made available to the attorneys in the Tax Division of the Department. It appears from the foregoing that the attorneys in the Tax Division are attempting to make themselves look good with the Supreme Court at the expense of the FBI when they avoid mentioning that the Department had knowledge of our confidential coverage as early as August 24, 1965.

■ **Memo, FBI Assistant Director James Gale to FBI Assistant Director Cartha DeLoach, May 23, 1966**
. . . The Attorney General['s letter] to the Director dated 5/21/66, . . . states that as a result of a conversation with the Director he has substantially revised the proposed memorandum to the Supreme Court in this matter and would appreciate any comments the Director may have as to this revision. . . .
A review of this revised memorandum reveals that the Department has

eliminated . . . some of the more objectionable features which were present in the original draft. . . .

The Department has obviously determined to proceed with the filing of this memorandum with the Supreme Court. . . . The Attorney General has, however, made changes in the revised memorandum to accommodate the objections raised by the Director in the content of the original memorandum. Our position is and has been . . . that we see no need to file this memorandum at this time, but the Attorney General has apparently decided to proceed with this action despite our written and oral objections. . . .

■ **Memo, FBI Assistant Director James Gale to FBI Assistant Director Cartha DeLoach, May 23, 1966**

I contacted Senator Edward Long . . . [and] confidentially briefed him concerning the motion which the Department contemplates filing in [the Fred Black] case. . . .

I explained to Senator Long that . . . after the microphone was on for a short period of time it was determined that Black was not involved in anything in which we had an interest, and the microphone was immediately taken off.

Senator Long was further informed that, contrary to the impression which the Department is trying to give in the motion concerning the microphone coverage, the Department had complete knowledge of this microphone in August, 1965, and had ample opportunity to bring this to the attention of the Court of Appeals of the Supreme Court since that time.

Senator Long advised that he felt this was a most unfortunate development in that columnists like Drew Pearson, Fred Graham of the New York Times, and Dave Kraslow of the Los Angeles Times, together with liberals on his committee, and the anti-FBI groups, would again raise a hue and cry for the Long Committee to hold hearings on the FBI. He . . . has been able to get around this by claiming that the FBI only used these devices in organized crime and security cases. . . . He recognized this case on Black potentially involved organized crime, but it would be difficult to get this over to the public.

The Senator stated that as far as he knew this was the first time the government had admitted that the FBI had engaged in microphone surveillances. I informed the Senator that the government had previously admitted . . . that we had microphone surveillances . . . and triggered a demand for his committee to hold hearings in Las Vegas. I advised him that he very adroitly handled this situation and I felt there would be a possible hue and cry for several days regarding the current situation and then it would die down the same as it had before.

He stated this was probably right and he again reiterated that he had no desire to hurt the FBI or hold hearings on the FBI and he would figure out something with respect to handling his critics. . . . He was very appreciative

of the fact that he was briefed on this matter prior to the motion being filed
because otherwise some reporters could have really caught him off guard. . . .

■ **Memo, FBI Assistant Director James Gale to FBI Assistant
Director Cartha DeLoach, May 23, 1966**
 . . . Assistant Attorney General Rogovin . . . furnished the attached
memorandum which the Department proposes to file in the Supreme Court
today, and asked that it be reviewed by Bureau representatives. . . .

[Meeting with Katzenbach later] I informed the Attorney General that
footnote 4, page 4 of the revised memorandum was objectionable to the
Bureau in that it created an impression that the Bureau was acting entirely
without Departmental authority in the use of listening devices. It was
suggested that this footnote be eliminated from the new document filed
with the Supreme Court. He was specifically advised of the Director's
views in this regard and informed that the Bureau would very definitely
make it known publicly that Former Attorney General Robert Kennedy had
given general authorization for the use of microphones if this became
necessary because of any public misconception caused by this footnote.
Katzenbach was adamant that this footnote remain in the document and
stated he would not have included it in the proposed memorandum if he
had not desired it to be there. . . . He was willing to change the language
and suggested that instead of arguing about whether or not this footnote
should be placed in the document, that we should immediately draft
language which would avoid the objectionable features.

At this point I suggested . . . that he include the fact that there was
general Departmental authorization for the use of these devices. This statement would indicate to anyone reading it that the Bureau was acting with
Departmental authority and not acting on its own initiative with respect to
these devices. The Attorney General agreed to placing this statement in the
document and modified it to this extent "there was general Departmental
authorization of longstanding for the use of these devices." . . .

Pursuant to the Director's instructions, the Attorney General was advised that the Director still felt that the footnote was superfluous but that
we would have to defer to the Department. I advised him that the Director
hoped that this would not backfire wherein we would have to use the name
of former Attorney General Robert Kennedy as having given authority for the
use of microphones. The Attorney General indicated that Former Attorney
General Kennedy stated that he did not give such over-all authority but he
realized that the Bureau had certain documents which would raise a question
concerning this contention. I informed him that we certainly did. . . .

The Attorney General . . . felt the press would definitely want to know if
these practices still exist and ask questions along the lines of the information in the footnote. He . . . stated that if the Bureau desired, he would

eliminate instant footnote and have it answered by Departmental spokesmen when the press inquired. As the Director very quickly recognized, the Department would undoubtedly like to use this tactic so that [departmental press secretary] Rosenthal could conveniently omit that sentence about our having general Departmental authorization for the use of these devices in answering press inquiries.

Pursuant to the Director's instructions, the Attorney General was subsequently advised that we felt the statement should stand as it is on the record rather than by making reference to it orally to the press. . . .

ADDENDUM: At 6:55 p.m. Assistant Attorney General Rogovin . . . advised that the Department was going to substitute the following footnote for footnote number 4 in the petition for the Supreme Court . . . "Present Departmental policy which has been in effect since 1965 confines the use of listening devices such as those herein involved and also the interception of wire communications to the collection of intelligence affecting the national security. It also requires in each instance a specific authorization by the Attorney General. This policy superseded the broader authorization which had been in effect for a number of years."

I immediately objected to the revised footnote and stated that it materially differed from that which the Attorney General had previously agreed to in that it did not contain the fact that the *Department* had generally authorized the use of microphones. Rogovin then agreed to change the last sentence in the above quoted footnote to read "This policy superseded the broader Departmental authorization which had been in effect for a number of years." . . . This was an apparent attempt by the Department to throw us a real curve by attempting to slip through a revised footnote which would minimize or cause doubt as to the broad Departmental authorization of the use of electronic devices and create the impression that the Bureau was operating in this sphere without Departmental authorization. By inserting the word *Departmental*, . . . the impression that the Bureau was operating on its own initiative is not created.

[Hoover's handwritten notation: "Gale has handled this masterfully."]

■ **Memo, FBI Assistant Director James Gale to FBI Assistant Director Cartha DeLoach, May 24, 1966**
. . . Rogovin . . . advised that the AG [attorney general] had made a final decision to eliminate the footnote in question and to answer all press inquiries with "no comment," that this is a pending matter in court.

I advised him we very definitely would have preferred to have the footnote left in. He stated the AG realized this, but had made his decision. I informed Rogovin I hoped they would strictly follow this "no comment" procedure and that there would be no "leaks" to the press, which would definitely result in our taking appropriate steps to correct the record. . . .

I advised Rogovin if there was any confusion on the part of the press, the FBI very definitely was going to correct the record by giving detailed information as to our Departmental authority . . . and we have this authority from Attorney General Robert Kennedy well documented.

Rogovin inquired whether I was threatening him. I said I very definitely was not threatening him, but was merely making a statement of fact. . . .

It appears that Katzenbach and the Solicitor General, Thurgood Marshall, are trying to wiggle out of the AG's previous agreement concerning the footnote, and . . . we should be lining up our ammunition concerning Bobby Kennedy's authorization of microphones, for subsequent release to the press in the event the footnote is not put in writing and the Department attempts to double-cross us by putting out any ambiguous statements reflecting that we were installing these microphones on our own initiative. ACTION:

That the Special Investigative Division and the Crime Records Division coordinate and prepare for the Director's approval a statement concerning AG Kennedy's approval of microphone coverage, in the event it becomes necessary for us to use this because of a double-cross by the Department.

[Hoover's handwritten notation: "OK."]

■ **Memo, FBI Supervisor Milton Jones to FBI Assistant Director Robert Wick, May 24, 1966**

. . . Attached is a blank, undated statement by "an FBI spokesman" which clearly shows that Robert Kennedy, as Attorney General, had knowledge of and gave his approval to the FBI's use of electronic devices in crime and racketeering cases.

Recommendation:

That the attached blank, undated statement be approved and be returned to your (Mr. Wick's) office for possible future use. Specific approval [from the director] will be needed *at the time it is given out*.

■ **Letter, FBI Director J. Edgar Hoover to Special Assistant to the President Marvin Watson, May 27, 1966**

I am enclosing herewith a copy of a memorandum . . . which I have sent to the Attorney General today and which . . . I thought I should bring to your attention for the information of the President.

It pertains to the action which the Attorney General recently took in having filed with the Supreme Court an unusual memorandum concerning the use of microphones by the FBI in 1963 in the hotel room of Fred B. Black, Jr. . . .

In several discussions with the Attorney General I pointed out that the memorandum as originally drafted by the Department was not accurate as to the facts stated and that the use of these microphones in 1963 was in line with general Departmental approval by the Attorney General of microphone use in cases involving organized crime.

The Attorney General insisted that he had discussed this matter with former Attorney General Kennedy, who denied emphatically that he knew or had approved that the FBI might use microphones in its investigations in the field of organized crime. I stated to the Attorney General that former Attorney General Kennedy was either lying or had a very convenient lack of memory and supported my statement by . . . certain memoranda in which former Attorney General Kennedy had specifically approved the general procedure for the use of microphones in the Bureau's campaign against organized crime. This apparently did not convince the Attorney General of the true facts because in the memorandum filed . . . with the Supreme Court, he does not include a statement which he had assured me would be included that the actions of the FBI in these microphone installations was in line with a previously approved Departmental policy. If he had used that statement, it would have been a correct one, but he preferred to use the assurances of former Attorney General Kennedy that he, Kennedy, knew nothing about the use of microphones by the FBI, which is . . . absolutely untrue.

Of course the press, as a result of the memorandum filed by the Attorney General with the Supreme Court, has taken up the hue and cry that the FBI without the knowledge of any Department official had indulged in the use of microphones in its investigative work. . . .

It was in order to have a written record established that I sent the memorandum to the Attorney General today repeating and including as exhibits the evidence supporting my contention that the memorandum filed with the Supreme Court was misleading and inaccurate.

I thought that you should have before you the above information and enclosure and that probably the President might want to look it over in the event he is questioned at any time concerning this matter.

■ **Memo, Attorney General Nicholas Katzenbach to FBI Director, May 31, 1966**
I am writing in response to your memorandum. . . .

I think it would be helpful . . . to give you my understanding of the general background of the matter and what I conceive to be the basic problems involved.

You are, of course, rightly concerned with the problem of authorization for the use of microphone surveillance involving trespass in criminal matters. But the question of authorization was not and is not itself relevant to the legal problems which arose in the *Black* case and which may arise in other cases.

Under existing law, any information obtained as a result of microphone coverage installed through trespass . . . is inadmissible in court. Consequently, information or leads obtained by this means can not be used for purposes of prosecution. Moreover, if such coverage results in an invasion of . . . the attorney-client privilege—prosecution cannot properly be maintained—without informing the court—irrespective of the use of information derived from the microphone. . . .

Our review of the *Black* case satisfied us that the evidence was not tainted and that the accidental invasion of the attorney-client privilege was so insignificant that it in no way affected the fairness of the trial. Nonetheless, . . . I believe that there was an inescapable duty imposed upon the Department to disclose the facts to the courts for them to make the judgment as to fairness, irrespective of the embarrassment that could thereby be caused to the Department. While I recognize that a contrary view . . . had some support in some past decisions, both I and my principal advisers felt that we were under a duty to disclose, as officers of the court, the fact of the inadvertent invasion of the attorney-client privilege.

I regret the embarrassment that this disclosure . . . has caused all of us, but I greatly appreciate your willingness to defer to the views of the Department as to our legal obligations in the circumstances.

With respect to "authorization," I have never doubted the good faith or integrity of the Bureau. The eliminated footnote . . . was an effort to express this publicly, and was based on the following understanding of the facts:

1. The use of microphone surveillances (including those involving wiretaps) was discussed by the Bureau with Attorney General [William] Rogers in 1958 and he expressly authorized the use of such devices in organized crime and national security investigations at the discretion of the FBI. . . . He felt it unnecessary for the Attorney General specifically to authorize each such instance (contrary to the practice in wiretaps) and . . . did not wish himself or other attorneys in the Department to be informed of the existence of such devices. These devices were to be used strictly for the purposes of intelligence and not for the purposes of prosecution. (My understanding of these facts is based on conversations with you and other Bureau personnel, and if I am incorrect, I would appreciate being informed as to the true facts.) . . .

2. Former Attorney General Kennedy has stated to me that he was not aware of his predecessor's authorization; that he did not in fact know that such surveillances were undertaken in circumstances involving trespass; and that he did not "authorize" the use of microphone surveillance *involving trespass*, either generally or in specific instances.

3. The thrust of your memorandum and its attachments is . . . that Mr.

Kennedy did in fact know of the existence of such devices, on occasions encouraged their use, and thus "authorized" them.

4. There is no need for me to pass judgment on the extent of Mr. Kennedy's actual knowledge as to Bureau practices. How fully Mr. Kennedy was advised and what he understood Bureau practice to be does not fully appear from the documents themselves and necessarily depends upon inference and conclusion. One reader might be fully satisfied as to his knowledge and approval; another might inquire as to why the Bureau never explicitly informed him as to its practices and never sought his express approval; a third might point to ambiguities within the documents themselves and conclude that there was a failure of communication on both sides with resultant misunderstanding. . . .

Whatever the differences between you and Senator Kennedy concerning precisely what he did or did not authorize, . . . a public dispute at this time on the question could not possibly serve any good purpose. This is particularly true . . . in circumstances where it would be difficult for us to comment fully on matters in litigation. The deletion from the memorandum filed with the Supreme Court of a reference to the fact that the Bureau was authorized was aimed precisely at avoiding a public airing of differences . . . where comment would be inappropriate. . . .

■ **Memo, FBI Director to Attorney General Nicholas Katzenbach, June 3, 1966**

This will acknowledge your memorandum. . . .

You contend that the question of authorization for the Bureau's use of microphones is not relevant to the legal problems which arose in the Black case. It is, however, highly relevant in the light of the publicity arising from the filing of the memorandum with the Supreme Court. News media have made it relevant by press accounts conveying the impression that the Bureau utilized microphones without authorization. The documents which I transmitted to you . . . clearly indicate to me that there could be no possible doubt but that the Bureau was operating in this field with the authorization of former Attorney General Robert F. Kennedy. . . .

■ **Letter, FBI Director J. Edgar Hoover to Special Assistant to the President Marvin Watson, June 7, 1966**

. . . I am enclosing herewith a copy of the Attorney General's reply to me dated May 31, 1966, together with my reply to him dated June 3, 1966.

I personally deplore that this situation has arisen and has degenerated into an effort upon the part of the Attorney General to absolve former

Attorney General Kennedy from the responsibility of having knowledge of and having given authorization for the use of wire taps and microphones with trespass. It has been presented by him in such manner that the FBI has been operating in this manner without the authorization and specific approval of the Attorney General of the United States. . . .

I do not object, of course, to being held responsible for any procedures or decisions which I make, but I do vigorously object to a complete ignoring of facts which show that the actions of the Federal Bureau of Investigation regarding microphone coverage during the period encompassing the Black situation were taken with the over-all general approval of Attorney General Kennedy and our use of microphones was certainly known to him. According to Attorney General Katzenbach, he has taken the verbal assurance of former Attorney General Kennedy that he did not know of any of these matters whereas the written record clearly proves to the contrary.

■ **Letter, *St. Louis Globe-Democrat* Washington Bureau Chief Ed O'Brien to FBI Supervisor Robert Wick, June 3, 1966**

Here's my story on the Black case. [My secretary] Miss Martino will mail on Monday a clip from the paper.

I am grateful for your help.

■ **Informal Memo, FBI Supervisor Robert Wick to FBI Assistant Director Cartha DeLoach, June 6, 1966**

Attached is a column by Edward J. Mowery, Pulitzer Prize winner, setting the record straight concerning the FBI's use of a microphone in the Black Case. . . .

Mowery's column is distributed by General Features Corporation in New York to many of its clients and thus far, says Mowery, 14 papers use it throughout the United States with a minimum circulation of 2½ million daily.

O'Brien's column is particularly hard hitting and completely lays the blame on the [Justice] Department.

Other columns of the same nature will begin appearing this week by other writers and you will be advised.

■ **Informal Memo, FBI Assistant Director Cartha DeLoach to FBI Associate Director Clyde Tolson, June 6, 1966**

Mildred Stegall, President Johnson's personal secretary . . . told me in strict confidence on Saturday, June 4, 1966, that the President was quite disturbed over the situation in the "Black Case." She explained that the President had read the Director's letter to the Attorney General in connection with this matter. The President is chiefly concerned over the fact the Attorney General appears to be "fronting" for others, namely, Bobby Kennedy. . . .

Marvin Watson has asked me to have lunch with him today at 12:30 p.m. With the Director's permission, I intend to go into this matter to some extent. . . .

■ **Informal Memo, FBI Assistant Director Cartha DeLoach to FBI Associate Director Clyde Tolson, June 6, 1966**

As the Director is aware, I had lunch with Marvin Watson today at the White House . . . [and] showed him the Director's letter to the Attorney General dated June 3, 1966, in the Black case. He read it very thoroughly and then reread it. After he finished reading it a second time, he turned to me and said, "Great!" He next stated that this was a very hardhitting memorandum and one which the Attorney General completely deserved. He stated this was the only way to put Katzenbach in his place.

We had a brief talk concerning [Deputy Attorney General] Ramsey Clark. Watson shares the Director's opinion that Clark is somewhat infiltrated. Watson told me that he had tried a number of times to make Ramsey Clark understand the fact that the Kennedys were poison. He stated that Clark feels to the contrary, i.e., that there is nothing wrong with the Kennedys. Watson explained that the President Lyndon Johnson feels that Clark is thoroughly loyal and is a "Johnson man," however, the fact remains that Clark has failed to find anything wrong with Bobby Kennedy. On occasions he has defended Kennedy. . . .

■ **Memo, Deputy Attorney General Ramsey Clark to FBI Director J. Edgar Hoover, June 13, 1966**

. . . The Supreme Court has asked the Government to file a response in *Fred B. Black, Jr.* v. *United States*. This response is to include, but not necessarily limited to, the following:

(1) the kind of apparatus used by the Government;

(2) the person or persons who authorized its installation;

(3) the statute or Executive Order relied upon;

(4) the date or dates of installation;

(5) whether there is in existence a recording of conversations heard;

(6) when the information concerning *Fred B. Black, Jr.* came into the hands of any attorney for the Government, and to which ones, as well as what use was made of the information in the case against *Black*. . . .

It is requested that the Bureau official designated by you to cooperate in the preparation of our reply contact Mr. Rogovin.

■ **Memo, FBI Director to Attorney General Nicholas Katzenbach, June 14, 1966**

. . . With respect to the order issued by the United States Supreme Court . . . I am submitting the following information with the request that it be used in conjunction with the Solicitor General's response to the Court.

(1) The listening device involved in this situation consisted of a tubular microphone installed from an adjoining room into the common wall to monitor conversations. . . .

(2) The installation of the microphone in this matter was made with general Departmental authorization under former Attorney General Robert F. Kennedy for use of this investigative technique. . . .

(3) Regarding the FBI's authority for the use of listening devices, former President Franklin D. Roosevelt, in a memorandum to the Attorney General dated May 21, 1940, expressed his recognition of the need for the Government's use of wire tapping . . . [and] empowered the Attorney General to authorize . . . [wiretaps] in investigations involving subversive activities against the Government of the United States. . . .

By letter of May 20, 1954, . . . former Attorney General Herbert Brownell . . . noted that . . . the national interest requires that microphone surveillances be utilized by the FBI. In emphasizing that the FBI has an intelligence function equally as important as the duty of developing evidence for presentation to the courts, he expressed his recognition that . . . the Department should adopt the interpretation which will permit microphone coverage by the FBI in a manner most conducive to our national interest. He also recognized that for the FBI to fulfill its important intelligence function, considerations of internal security and the national safety are paramount and, therefore, may compel the unrestricted use of this technique in the national interest.

Subsequently then Deputy Attorney General Rogers . . . informed the Bureau that it was unnecessary for the Attorney General to authorize each instance of microphone use. . . . This policy was continued during Mr. Kennedy's tenure as Attorney General and was unchanged until the Spring of 1965 when under your administration of the Department of Justice, microphone installations were specifically and individually authorized by you. . . .

(4) The microphone installation was effected at 3:00 p.m., February 7, 1963, and monitoring of this device commenced at 3:00 p.m., February 8, 1963. The microphone installation and the monitoring thereof were discontinued on April 25, 1963. . . .

(6) By letter dated August 24, 1965, the FBI advised the Attorney General that there was a microphone on the office of Fred Black in a Washington, D.C., hotel from February 7, 1963, to April 25, 1963. . . .

The written transcripts were reviewed during September and October, 1965, by Departmental Attorneys . . . [and] were again reviewed on April 29, 1966. . . . Departmental Attorneys should have detected that certain of

these conversations involved interchanges between petitioner and his lawyer during the September-October 1965, review.

On June 2, 1966, former Assistant Director Courtney A. Evans advised
that . . . he had often briefed Mr. Kennedy concerning the Black investigation. Mr. Evans said that on one occasion he furnished Mr. Kennedy
information which only could have come from a microphone . . . [and]
Kennedy could well have inferred the usage of microphones as a result of
this information furnished to him by Mr. Evans.

Any use of the information made available to the Department is of
course not known to this Bureau.

I would appreciate seeing the final draft in this matter before it is filed
with the Supreme Court.

■ **Informal Memo, FBI Assistant Director Cartha DeLoach to FBI
Associate Director Clyde Tolson, June 15, 1966**
. . . [On June 12] Watson stated that he had just returned from the
President's office where they had discussed [the Black case]. The President
asked Watson to call over and state that "Edgar Hoover should get a good
lawyer from amongst his group of men and should furnish the Attorney
General a good, strong memorandum laying on the line the fact that Bobby
Kennedy was responsible for the usage of the microphone in the Black
case." Watson stated the President also had suggested that the Director
insist that the Attorney General should let him see the final draft which
was to be sent to the Supreme Court from the Department. Watson
continued that if the Attorney General slants the facts in this matter the
President may have to step into the controversy. He asked that this be kept
on a strictly confidential basis. . . .

Mildred Stegall, who handles all personal matters for the President, told
me at 9:30 a.m. this morning that she had . . . told the President that "this
Black situation is certainly a mess." The President replied, "I'm glad it
happened. This puts the finger on Bobby Kennedy where it belongs. Edgar
certainly has the goods on Bobby."

■ **Informal Memo, FBI Assistant Director Cartha DeLoach to
FBI Associate Director Clyde Tolson, June 22, 1966**
Senator Edward Long called . . . [having] just returned from the bill
signing ceremony at the White House. . . . He referred to our conversation
last night wherein he had told me he was sending a letter to the Attorney
General putting him on notice that the Attorney General's reply to the
Supreme Court concerning the microphone in the Black case had better be
absolutely truthful and factual or else hearings would be held.

Senator Long . . . saw the Attorney General also at the White House this
morning. He . . . called the Attorney General over to one side and told him
he was very interested in the microphone in the Black case and that, as a
matter of fact, he was sending the Attorney General a letter concerning this
matter. He . . . told the Attorney General that unless the Department's
reply to the Supreme Court was handled in a proper manner . . . it might
be necessary to call both the Director and the Attorney General for public
hearings. Senator Long told me that the Attorney General . . . stated, "Oh
my God, not that! Let's don't bring all this stuff out." Senator Long replied
that he would take no action until he saw the Attorney General's reply to
the Supreme Court. The Attorney General then walked away very rapidly.

Senator Long . . . got quite a chuckle out of the above action. . . . He of
course had no intention of calling the Director or the Attorney General,
however, he felt that his conversation this morning and his letter would
certainly put the "fear of God" in the Attorney General. He . . . would
follow this matter closely.

■ **Letter, Senator Edward Long to Attorney General Nicholas
Katzenbach, June 22, 1966**

It is with a great deal of interest that members of [the Senate judiciary
subcommittee on administrative practice and procedure], my staff and I
have been watching the proceedings with respect to the use of microphones
and eavesdropping equipment by the Department of Justice in matters now
before the Supreme Court, as well as in other cases. It is only natural that
the various articles by the Washington Post have been of considerable
interest to us. There would seem to be the strong possibility such articles
have been inspired by one side or the other in this particular issue.

We have been especially interested in the announcement to the Supreme
Court by the Solicitor General and also the various requests made by the
Supreme Court with respect to such announcement.

We are very deeply concerned about the information which has been
revealed concerning these matters. It is hoped that no deliberate attempt
will be made for anyone to shield or defend any parties in this controversy
and that "the chips fall where they may." As Chairman of the Administrative Practice and Procedure Subcommittee which is investigating eavesdropping and invasion of privacy by federal agencies, we are, of course,
concerned in seeing that responsibility for such actions is properly fixed.

At this time, we have not definitely set any hearings in regard to the
Justice Department but will certainly be interested in the reply of your
Department to the Supreme Court in regard to the questions raised
concerning various wiretapping activities. No doubt we will want to
schedule hearings at some later date so that the Congress may have
perhaps further details in the matter than might be filed with the Supreme
Court.

Will look forward to visiting with you about the hearing at some later date.

■ **Letter, Attorney General Nicholas deB. Katzenbach to Senator Edward Long, June 23, 1966**
Thank you for your letter concerning the use of microphones and eavesdropping equipment. I would, of course, be pleased to discuss the matter with you at any mutually convenient time.

■ **Informal Memo, FBI Assistant Director Cartha DeLoach to FBI Associate Director Clyde Tolson, June 24, 1966**
Marvin Watson called . . . and stated he had been talking with the President, who told Watson to get word to the Director that the Director might desire to bring "the facts" concerning Robert F. Kennedy's authorization of wire tapping [sic] before a Congressional Committee. The President told Watson to have the Director thinking of someone like [House Appropriations subcommittee chairman] John Rooney, or perhaps another committee.

I told Watson the Director would, of course, consider this matter and would be grateful for the President's interest. Watson stated the President was most anxious to see that the Director not get hurt in connection with this matter. He wants to put Kennedy in his place.

The President obviously wants to get these facts out, inasmuch as Kennedy will be seriously injured, as far as the left wing is concerned, if such facts become known. At the same time, . . . there are far better ways of getting these facts out than through the medium of a Congressional Committee.

■ **Informal Memo, FBI Assistant Director Cartha DeLoach to FBI Associate Director Clyde Tolson, June 30, 1966**
Bobby Kennedy, AG Katzenbach, and the Department have thus far strongly attempted to make the FBI the scapegoat in the current issue regarding the usage of microphones in criminal matters. Aside from getting out the truth concerning Katzenbach and Kennedy attempting to protect their own skirts and for that reason condemning the FBI, we need to convince the American public of the absolute justification of the FBI's role in protecting the security of the country through the medium of gaining intelligence by usage of microphones in cases involving those organized crime barons who deal in narcotics, white slavery, obscene literature, murder, shylocking, and general activities which not only undermine the security of the country, but absolutely destroy the moral concept of our government.

[Name withheld, Mutual Radio commentator] is a great supporter of the FBI, his background is clean, we have used him before in confidential matters involving the press, and he can be used again. . . .

Considering the above, it is recommended that I call [name withheld] and ask him in strict confidence, to have his agency next week ask these questions of the general public:

1. Do you believe that the FBI should be entitled to use wiretaps and listening devices (microphones) to protect the internal security of the United States?

2. Do you agree that the FBI, after securing authorization from the chief legal officer of the United States—the Attorney General—as has always been the practice, should be allowed to use microphones in obtaining intelligence concerning those individuals who are committing murder, dealing in heavy traffic involving narcotics, white slavery, and general organized crime activities?

3. Do you think that the FBI, from your knowledge of its activities over the years, has operated in a generally satisfactory manner in handling its jurisdiction in the past?

While this, of course, is a gamble, I think it can be very carefully handled. If the results are unfavorable, the results of the poll will, of course, be buried and forgotten. If favorable, we will see to it that not only the 422 Mutual radio stations carry the matter, but also the wire services and newspapers throughout the country.

[Hoover's handwritten notation: "Handled with (writing faint but apparently Henleigh) 7/1/66—he will do—."]

■ **Memo, FBI Assistant Director Cartha DeLoach to FBI Associate Director Clyde Tolson, July 6, 1966**
. . . I went over to Deputy Attorney General Clark's office. . . . He told me Attorney General Katzenbach . . . had delegated to him the problem of getting the answer to the Supreme Court worked out. . . .

Clark told me that the Attorney General had talked with former Attorney General Brownell, . . . [and] with former Attorney General William P. Rogers. According to Clark, both Brownell and Rogers stated that they had never authorized the usage of microphones outside of the internal security area and that they were completely unaware of trespass being involved in the usage of any microphones. . . . Both Brownell and Rogers had advised Katzenbach that the Director's language, as proposed in the brief to the Supreme Court, was completely unsatisfactory. . . . According to Clark, Brownell and Rogers would agree with the statement ". . . the FBI consistently interpreted and understood our decisions to apply to major crimes."

Clark told me that Brownell's and Rogers' refusals to go along with the Director's suggested language put a different light on the matter. . . . Attorney General Katzenbach did not wish to issue any statement which a former Attorney General might later refute. I told Clark it was surprising that Brownell and Rogers had refused to agree with our suggested language, particularly in view of the specific phraseology in Brownell's memorandum to the Director dated May 20, 1954. . . .

Clark told me that Katzenbach . . . had talked to former Assistant Director Evans . . . [who] appeared to be quite vague about any conversations he had with former Attorney General Kennedy concerning the Black case. I told Clark there was no question about Evans having admitted . . . that he had frequently briefed Kennedy regarding this case and, furthermore, Evans had freely admitted that Kennedy would have inferred that information he was being furnished had come from a microphone. . . .

Clark asked me if I thought it might be a good idea to have all memoranda concerning this entire issue sent over to the Department, including those dictated by Evans. I asked Clark if he had ever played poker. I told him a good poker player usually conceals his hand until absolutely necessary to expose it. He laughed and stated apparently the FBI had considerable memoranda dictated by Evans. I told him this was true. . . .

In concluding our conversation, I told Clark that the decision would be made relative to contacting Brownell and Rogers and that I would be back in touch with him. . . .

■ **Informal Memo, FBI Assistant Director Cartha DeLoach to FBI Associate Director Clyde Tolson, July 8, 1966**

Pursuant to the Director's instructions, I saw Deputy Attorney General Ramsey Clark. . . .

Clark was advised that . . . I had seen former Attorney General William P. Rogers . . . [and] that Rogers had advised me that Attorney General Katzenbach had distinctly told him that the FBI over the years had no authorization for usage of microphones other than former Attorney General Brownell's memorandum of 5/20/54. I stated it had been necessary to correct the record. . . . I enumerated for Clark the specific documents shown Rogers to prove this point . . . that Rogers had been very resentful of the misleading information given him by Katzenbach and that undoubtedly Katzenbach would be hearing from Rogers within the near future. Clark replied . . . that, as a matter of fact, Rogers had an appointment with Katzenbach as of Monday, 7/11/66. . . .

At this point, Clark's telephone buzzer sounded and . . . it was apparent that he was talking to Attorney General Katzenbach. After some prolonged conversation, Clark hung up the phone and . . . stated "You obviously did a good day's work yesterday. The 'ancient history' will undoubtedly be removed from the brief." From his demeanor it seemed quite apparent that Rogers had called Katzenbach in some anger and had laid the law down to him.

We then got back on the subject of the brief. I told Clark that Katzenbach had stated that . . . Evans had been "vague" relative to the personal briefings he had given Kennedy in 1963 on the Black case. I stated that Mr. Gale and I had once again patiently interviewed Evans on 7/5/66 and that Evans had again confirmed, without hesitation and without "vagueness," the fact that he had frequently briefed Kennedy concerning the Black case . . . that Evans had additionally once again stated that during one briefing he had given Kennedy information that could only have come from a microphone and Kennedy could well have inferred that this information did come from a microphone. I told Clark that if there was any doubt in his mind concerning Evans' confirmation of the facts he should not hesitate to call Evans down to his office as of that moment while Mr. Gale and I were present so that we could question him face to face. Clark replied there was no doubt in his mind and therefore no necessity of doing this.

I told Clark that all we desired in this entire matter was the truth . . . that the Department should realize that the FBI was not going to be made the "goat" in this case . . . that we were perfectly willing to lay the evidence before Senator Ed Long's committee and thereafter stand on the record. Clark made no reply, but I am certain he got the point.

We then reexamined the brief['s current language]. . . .

We next came to the crux of the problem, i.e., the phraseology . . . which we insisted read . . . "No information obtained by means of the listening device, other than that verbally given to the Attorney General on a frequent basis during the course of the Black investigation. . . ." Clark stated that Katzenbach would never go for this language. We told him that this was the truth and . . . that he might desire to bring Evans down on a face-to-face basis. He again stated this would not be necessary. . . . Whether or not the Attorney General had been briefed was a factual question and that on the one side there would be Evans making certain contentions which Kennedy would unquestionably deny. . . . This would simply mean one man's word against the other and would place the Supreme Court in quite a dilemma. We told Clark that it would place the Supreme Court in even more of a dilemma if the truth was not told. Clark then suggested the phraseology, "No information obtained by means of the listening device, other than that verbally given to a Departmental official on a frequent basis during the course of the Black investigation. . . ." In other words, Clark suggested substituting "Departmental official" rather than pinpointing Bobby Kennedy. We told him that this proposal represented very definite problems and that, while we would consider the matter, we still felt that in order to escape future ramifications, i.e., such as questions being asked by the Supreme Court, the true facts should be set forth. He indicated that our entire conversation was tentative and would necessarily have to be cleared by Katzenbach. . . .

Action:

Clark fully understands that it is now the responsibility of the Department to prepare a new draft and send it over to the FBI. . . .

Pursuant to the Director's instructions, upon receipt of the new draft we will examine it most carefully and then prepare in writing our reply as to the draft.

The Director's instructions concerning specific identification of Bobby Kennedy on Page 3, . . . will be adhered to.

■ **Memo, FBI Assistant Director Cartha DeLoach to FBI Associate Director Clyde Tolson, July 12, 1966**

Pursuant to the Director's instructions, I . . . told Clark that the Director was very definitely outraged over the claim that Katzenbach has made to former AG Bill Rogers that the FBI's sole authority for the usage of microphones stemmed from the Brownell memorandum of 5/20/54. Clark was told that, in view of this, the FBI must necessarily protect itself; consequently, we were insisting that necessary exhibits of proof of authorization be included as attachments to the Supreme Court brief. . . .

I also mentioned to Clark that . . . the Director was most anxious for Senator Long to initiate inquiries concerning this matter . . . that the FBI had nothing to fear, yet would have considerable evidence to present in behalf of this case . . . that Katzenbach and Kennedy should realize that all we wanted was simply to have the facts spelled out in the form of truth.

Clark . . . was trying to be a good "soldier" and work things out; however, Katzenbach, Kennedy, Bill Rogers, and the FBI all had different ideas. I told him that might be true; however, our ideas were on a sound basis and we had proof to back them up.

Clark's phone rang at that time and he later told me it was Katzenbach calling him to advise that Kennedy had been shown the proposed brief and "had blown up." Clark did not know what Katzenbach was going to do about that situation. . . .

■ **Memo, Attorney General Nicholas Katzenbach to FBI Director, July 13, 1966**

I am transmitting herewith a copy of the supplemental memorandum which will be filed today in the *Black* case. . . .

In your memorandum to me of July 12, 1966, you suggested that the following sentence . . . be deleted: "There is, however, no specific statute or executive order expressly authorizing the installation of a listening device such as that involved in this case."

. . . Without some such language the specific request by the Court . . . for information concerning "the statute or Executive Order relied upon" would be inadequately answered. Consequently, a reference to the lack of reliance upon a specific statute or Executive Order is included in the memorandum. However, the language does not use the word "authority" or "authorization."

The previous draft contained the following sentence . . . "No information obtained by means of the listening device, other than that incorporated in the above-mentioned reports and memoranda, was communicated to attorneys of the Department of Justice until August 1965."

In your memorandum of July 12, you suggested that the following language be incorporated in the sentence after the word "memoranda": "and that verbally given the then Attorney General when he was briefed by an FBI representative during the course of the Black investigation." You make that suggestion "In view of the fact that former Assistant Director Courtney A. Evans advised that he had often briefed former Attorney General Kennedy concerning the Black investigation, that on one occasion he furnished Mr. Kennedy information which could only have come from a microphone and that Attorney General Kennedy could well have inferred that this information did come from a microphone. . . ."

Since there is no indication that Mr. Evans ever told Mr. Kennedy anything not contained in the memorandum or reports, I see no reason to adopt this suggestion and the sentence has been deleted.

Finally, you suggested that copies of designated internal Departmental and Bureau memoranda and a letter from Assistant Attorney General Herbert J. Miller, Jr., to Senator Sam J. Ervin, Jr., be attached to the document to be filed in the Supreme Court in order that the Court be given "an accurate picture of the authorization insofar as the FBI's usage of microphones is concerned." Unfortunately, the memorandum would not . . . provide the Court with a fully accurate picture. This could not be done without at least supplying the Court with copies of Attorney General McGrath's memorandum of February 26, 1952, as amended on March 25, 1952, and Attorney General Brownell's memorandum of May 20, 1954, and, perhaps, Department Order 263-62 of March 13, 1962, and your memorandum to Attorney General Kennedy of March 19, 1962, concerning that order. . . . Even the addition of these documents would give an incomplete and possibly distorted picture without a further extremely detailed explanation. Moreover, unless compelled to do so in a legal or legislative proceeding, I would have very strong objections to volunteering internal department and FBI memoranda. . . .

In order to meet our deadline, I will require your written or oral comments by 3:00 P.M. today.
Attachment

■ **Letter, FBI Director J. Edgar Hoover to Special Assistant to the President Marvin Watson, July 13, 1966**
I thought the President would be interested in the events leading up to the contemplated filing in the Supreme Court today of the proposed supplemental memorandum. . . .

At approximately 1:45 p.m., July 13, 1966, Deputy Attorney General Ramsey Clark telephonically contacted this Bureau and advised that the final draft of the proposed supplemental memorandum . . . would be available for review shortly after 2:00 p.m. . . . The final draft of this supplemental memorandum was picked up in Mr. Clark's office. At that time, Mr. Clark pointed out that the final draft contained several changes from the previous drafts submitted for the consideration of this Bureau over the past several weeks, and contained changes from that submitted for our review on the night of July 11, 1966. Mr. Clark . . . asked that this Bureau analyze the final draft and provide . . . its views . . . by 3:00 p.m., July 13, 1966.

Following a hasty review of the proposed final document . . . Clark was telephonically furnished the following information.

Mr. Clark was told that inasmuch as the final draft omitted any mention of the fact that a former Bureau representative had frequently briefed former Attorney General Robert Kennedy on the Black investigation, and on one occasion had provided him with information which could only have come from a microphone and which Mr. Kennedy could well have inferred came only from a microphone, this Bureau could not acquiesce in the filing of this document.

It was pointed out . . . that in two letters to the Attorney General dated July 12, 1966, it was strongly recommended that the briefing of former Attorney General Kennedy, referred to above, should be included in the final document filed in the Supreme Court . . . [and] that certain documents proving this Bureau's authorization to utilize microphones in criminal matters should be attached as exhibits to the proposed supplemental memorandum for the benefit of the Supreme Court, and that the Department had not seen fit to do this in the final draft. . . .

Mr. Clark was also told that the time limitation imposed on this Bureau to review this final document was insufficient to prepare a proper analysis for the Department's consideration.

Accordingly, Mr. Clark was informed that in the light of the omissions of material considered by this Bureau to be most pertinent, that it would not be possible to endorse the document which the Department of Justice contemplated filing. Mr. Clark was also informed that this Bureau preferred to stand on the recommendations furnished the Attorney General in the two letters of July 12, 1966, copies of which are enclosed for your information.

■ **Memo, FBI Supervisor Milton Jones to FBI Assistant Director Robert Wick, July 14, 1966**
Attached is a proposed statement which (1) quotes a portion of the supplemental memorandum in the Fred B. Black case which the Justice Department filed before the Supreme Court yesterday and (2) clearly states that the FBI has documentary evidence that the Department had knowledge of and granted authority for our use of electronic listening devices.

This proposed statement has been prepared for possible issuance in the event former Attorney General Robert F. Kennedy makes a public denial that he authorized the use of microphones in criminal-type cases. This

statement can be issued in the Director's name or by "an FBI spokesman."
Recommendation:
The attached brief statement is for possible use in setting the record straight with regard to the FBI's authority to use electronic listening devices.

Enclosure Draft Press Release
As stated by the Department of Justice in the supplemental memorandum which it filed with the Supreme Court on July 13, 1966, in the Fred B. Black, Jr., case, ". . . the Director of the Federal Bureau of Investigation was given authority to approve the installation of devices such as that in question for intelligence (and not evidentiary) purposes when required in the interest of internal security or national safety, including organized crime, kidnappings and matters wherein human life might be at stake. Acting on the basis of the aforementioned Departmental authorization, the Director approved installation of the device involved in the instant case."
The above facts speak for themselves. There are, of course, numbers of signed documents and memoranda which fully support the FBI's position.

■ **Memo, FBI Assistant Director James Gale to FBI Assistant Director Cartha DeLoach, August 19, 1966**
In connection with the August 17, 1961, memorandum by which Attorney General Robert F. Kennedy approved the action of leasing telephone lines in New York City in microphone surveillances in both security and major criminal cases, the Director has asked three questions . . . :
1. Is the August 17, 1961, memorandum classified?
2. If so, who classified it?
3. If classified, who can declassify it?
In answer to the above questions, the memorandum was classified "Top Secret" by Assistant Director Courtney A. Evans. . . .
Classification of documents is covered by Executive Order 10501, as amended, and provides . . . that [this document] can be declassified by the agency making the original classification, requiring that notification is given to other agencies receiving copies of the classified document. In the FBI, the Director, Assistants to the Director and other specially designated personnel are authorized to declassify documents.
With reference to the particular document in question here the established practice in documents of this nature the original and one copy would be taken to the Attorney General's Office, his approval noted on the original by signature and the original returned for retention in the Bureau's files. The original of this particular document is in the Bureau's files and, quite likely, a carbon was left with Attorney General Kennedy by Assistant Director Evans.
The copy left with Attorney General Kennedy was in connection with

his then official capacity. Also, the present Attorney General [Katzenbach] was furnished a copy of the memorandum . . . [on] May 26, 1966. . . . A copy was also sent to the White House . . . [on] May 27, 1966. . . .
Action:
None. This memorandum has been prepared in answer to the Director's inquiry. . . .
[DeLoach's handwritten notation: "There appears to be no problem regarding declassification." Hoover's handwritten notation: "I am not so certain knowing of Katzenbach's effort to protect Kennedy. Proceed & get it declassified."]

■ **Memo, FBI Assistant Director James Gale to FBI Assistant Director Cartha DeLoach, August 25, 1966**
The purpose of this memorandum is to record the declassification of the memorandum dated August 17, 1961, prepared by former Assistant Director Courtney A. Evans to obtain the approval of former Attorney General Robert F. Kennedy for the leasing of telephone lines in New York City to be used in microphone surveillances. The memorandum dated August 17, 1961, was classified "Top Secret." . . .
(1) It is recommended that the memorandum dated August 17, 1961, prepared by former Assistant Director Evans be declassified. [Hoover's handwritten notation: "Yes."]
(2) It is further recommended that Mr. DeLoach orally advise Mr. Marvin Watson at the White House and Mr. Harold F. Reis in the Attorney General's office on his next regular contact with these individuals that this document has been declassified. Following this notification, this action *will be reduced to writing to make it a matter of record*. [DeLoach's handwritten notation: "Believed advisable so that we can be prepared to defend ourselves." Tolson's handwritten notation: "I think not 9-13." Hoover's handwritten notation: "No." DeLoach's handwritten notation: "Director on 8/26, per Mr. Tolson, stated no action should be taken."]
[In December 1966, working through Republican Congressman H. R. Gross, Hoover successfully publicized his claim that Kennedy had authorized FBI microphone surveillances. In a letter to the congressman, the director wrote, "Your impression that the FBI engaged in the usage of wiretaps and microphones only upon the authority of the Attorney General of the United States is absolutely correct." Hoover thereupon cited Kennedy's authorization as confirmed in his signing of the August 17, 1961, telephone lease line letter, having listened "to the results of microphone surveillances" in "different metropolitan areas," and Assistant Attorney General Herbert Miller's 1961 letter to Senator Sam Ervin reporting that the FBI currently had sixty-seven microphones in operation.]

PART THREE
THE USES OF THE FBI

11: The Presidency and FBI Authority

HOOVER WAS NOT *troubled by questions of legality as long as he could be assured that FBI activities were conducted without risk of discovery. Do Not File procedures could successfully immunize break-ins from discovery in part because they were used sparingly and with great caution. But such records procedures could scarcely safeguard the FBI's massive investigations of "subversive activities." With the advent of the Cold War, American conservatives (and many liberals) were no longer concerned about the absence of legal authority for the FBI's intrusive monitoring of the American left. Indeed, many conservatives demanded such investigations and accused the Truman administration of hamstringing the FBI. Regardless, FBI investigations of "subversive" activities predated this changed political climate. Given Hoover's cautious bureaucratic style, they were predicated on presidential authorization.*

Franklin Roosevelt's interest in possible foreign direction of the American fascist and communist movements led him to the ambitious FBI director. FDR concluded that he would be a dutiful servant. Roosevelt found Hoover's willing helpfulness doubly attractive: because the director wished to avoid legislative authorization for such "counterespionage" investigations, fearing that leading congressmen would revive memories of the post–World War I Red Scare, he agreed to conduct them in secret.

Eventually this resort to secret FBI investigations opened a Pandora's box. Halfhearted efforts to rein in FBI "subversive" investigations were successfully rebuffed by Hoover who, at the same time, jealously guarded the FBI's "internal security" monopoly from would-be interlopers.

*Hoover's monitoring of dissident activists and organizations
received a second boost with the start of a permanent federal
employee loyalty program ordered by President Truman in March
1947. The required security clearances provided additional
justification for FBI investigations of the political affiliations
of employees and prospective employees. Confirming the shift
in American conservatism toward tolerance of investigations into
political and personal activities, and attuned to the
anticommunist fervor of the time, the newly elected Eisenhower
administration extended the security clearance requirement to
include cabinet appointees. No American and no dissident
organization was theoretically immune from FBI scrutiny.*

*The FBI's resourcefulness and assurances of secrecy invariably
led presidents to turn to Hoover for other tasks, having faith
in his abilities to acquire useful information without risk of
disclosing their interests. This extended even to the arena of
foreign intelligence, despite the fact that this responsibility had
been assigned to the CIA upon the creation of that agency in 1947.*

■ **Confidential Memo, FBI Director J. Edgar Hoover, August 24,
1936**
This morning, in accordance with the request of the President [Franklin
Roosevelt] . . . I called at the White House . . . [to discuss] the question
of subversive activities in the United States, particularly Fascism and Communism. [Roosevelt] had previously received the memorandum which I
had prepared covering my conversation with General Smedley Butler and
the effort of Father [Charles] Coughlin to have General Butler head an
expedition to Mexico. I informed the President concerning certain recent
developments in the Communist activities in the country, particularly the
efforts of the [Harry] Bridges organization [the Longshoremen's Union] in
San Francisco and their progressive control of the shipping on the Pacific
Coast, the Gulf Coast and their recent expansion to shipping operations on
the Atlantic Coast. I told him that while their contract will expire on
September 30, 1936, they are endeavoring to have it temporarily extended
until April 1, 1937, in order to conform to the same date that the United
Mine Workers' contract expires, which organization is headed by John L.
Lewis. I told him that the Bridges organization was practically controlled
by Communists and that the Communists had now decided to make very
definite plans to get control of the Lewis organization.
I called his attention to the activities of the Newspaper Guild headed by

Heywood Broun, which has strong Communist leanings, and which has been responsible for putting out of operation the Seattle Post Intelligencer. I told him that my information was that the Communists had planned to get control of these three groups and by doing so they would be able at any time to paralyze the country in that they could stop all shipping in and out through the Bridges organization; stop the operation of industry through the Mining Union of Lewis; and stop publication of any newspapers of the country through the Newspaper Guild.

I also related to him the activities which have recently occurred within Governmental service inspired by Communists, particularly in some of the Departments and in the National Labor Relations Board.

I likewise informed him that I had received information to the effect that the Communist Internationale in Moscow has recently issued instructions for all Communists in the United States to vote for President Roosevelt for reelection and against Governor [Alf] Landon because of the fact that Governor Landon is opposed to class warfare.

The President stated that he had been considerably concerned about the movements of the Communists and of Fascism in the United States and that while the Secret Service of the Treasury Department had assured him that they had informants in every Communist group, he believed that if that was true it was solely for the purpose of getting any information upon plots upon his life, whereas what he was interested in was obtaining a broad picture of the general movement and its activities as may affect the economic and political life of the country as a whole. I told him that there is at the present time no governmental organization which is getting any so-called "general intelligence information" upon this subject. I told him that the appropriation of the Federal Bureau of Investigation contains a provision that it might investigate any matters referred to it by the Department of State and that if the State Department should ask for us to conduct such an investigation we could do so under our present authority in the appropriation already granted. He stated that he is reluctant to have a formal request come through the State Department because of the many leaks therein, but that what he would do would be to put a *handwritten memorandum of his own in his safe in the White House, stating he had instructed the Secretary of State to request this information* to be obtained by the Department of Justice. He stated he would have the Secretary of State at the White House . . . [so that] an oral request could be made of me by the Secretary of State for investigation so as to avoid any possibility of any leak.

He suggested that I endeavor to coordinate any investigation along similar lines which might be made by the Military or Naval Intelligence Services. . . .

■ **Confidential Memo, FBI Director J. Edgar Hoover, August 25, 1936**

Today, in line with the request of the President, I called at the White House at 1:45 p.m., and present at the conference were the President, the Secretary of State [Cordell Hull] and myself. The President related to the Secretary of State his concern relative to Communist activities in this country, as well as Fascist activities. He stated that he was very desirous of having a survey made of these conditions and informed the Secretary of State that this survey could be made by the Department of Justice if the Secretary of State requested the Department to conduct the inquiry. . . . The President pointed out that both of these movements were international in scope and that Communism particularly was directed from Moscow, and that there had been certain indications that [Constantine] Oumansky, attached to the Russian Soviet Embassy, was a leading figure in some of the activities in this country, so consequently, it was a matter which fell within the scope of foreign affairs over which the State Department would have a right to request an inquiry to be made.

The Secretary of State inquired if a request should be made in writing. The President indicated that it *should not* be since he desired the matter to be handled quite confidentially and that it would be sufficient that the President, the Secretary of State and I should be the ones aware of this request.

The Secretary of State asked that the investigation be made and then made several suggestions—one, relative to the making of a protest, either formally or informally, to the Russian Government relative to its interference with affairs in this country. . . . The President asked that I speak to the Attorney General, upon his return to the city, about this matter, and he suggested to the Secretary of State that he talk over the technique to be followed in this particular aspect, with the Attorney General.

■ **Strictly Confidential Memo, FBI Director J. Edgar Hoover to FBI Assistant Director Edward Tamm, September 10, 1936**

In talking with the Attorney General [Homer Cummings] today concerning the radical situation, I informed him of the conference which I had with the President on September 1, 1936,* at which time the Secretary of State [Cordell Hull] was present, and at which time the Secretary of State, at the President's suggestion, requested of me, the representative of the Department of Justice, to have investigation made of the subversive

*The conference was held not on September 1 but on August 25, 1936. Why Hoover misinformed Cummings of the date of this meeting is unclear.—Ed.

activities in this country, including communism and fascism. . . . The Attorney General verbally directed me to proceed with this investigation and to coordinate, as the President suggested, information upon these matters in the possession of the Military Intelligence Division, the Naval Intelligence Division, and the State Department. This, therefore, is the authority upon which to proceed in the conduct of this investigation, which should, of course, be handled in a most discreet and confidential manner.

■ **Confidential Memo, FBI Director J. Edgar Hoover, November 7, 1938**

On Tuesday evening November 1, 1938 . . . [Hoover contacted presidential secretary Steve] Early . . . and he stated that the President was desirous of [a conference on] November 2nd. He said he did not know the purpose of the conference. . . .

[At this conference] the President advised me that he had that day communicated with the Director of the Budget, Mr. Bell, and instructed him to include in the Appropriation estimates $50,000 for Military Intelligence, $50,000 for Naval Intelligence and $150,000 for the Federal Bureau of Investigation to handle counter-espionage activities. He stated that he had approved the plan which I had prepared . . . except that he had not been able to grant the entire amount of money indicated as necessary for each of the three agencies. . . .

[In October 1938 Roosevelt had directed Attorney General Cummings "to inquire into the so-called espionage situation" and to report whether "additional appropriation for domestic intelligence" was needed. Cummings advised Roosevelt that a "well defined system was functioning," involving MID, ONI, and the FBI. He recommended increased appropriations of $35,000 each for MID and ONI and $300,000 for the FBI. Cummings counseled against seeking "additional legislation to accomplish" the expanded counterespionage program, emphasizing that "the matter should be handled in strictest confidence." His recommendations merely reiterated Hoover's own warning that "in considering the steps to be taken for the expansion of the present structure of intelligence work, it is believed imperative that it be proceeded with, with the utmost degree of secrecy in order to avoid criticism of objections which might be raised to such an expansion by either ill-informed persons or individuals having some ulterior motive." Hoover had further opposed seeking special legislative authority as this "would draw attention to the fact that it was proposed to develop a special counter-espionage drive of any great magnitude."]

■ **Press Release, FBI Director J. Edgar Hoover to All Law Enforcement Officials, September 6, 1939**

For your information, the following formal statement was today issued by the President of the United States:

"The Attorney General has been requested by me to instruct the Federal Bureau of Investigation of the Department of Justice to take charge of investigative work in matters relating to espionage, sabotage, and violations of neutrality regulations.

"This task must be conducted in a comprehensive and effective manner on a national basis, and all information must be carefully sifted out and correlated in order to avoid confusion and irresponsibility.

"To this end I request all police officers, sheriffs, and all other law enforcement officers in the United States promptly to turn over to the nearest representative of the Federal Bureau of Investigation any information obtained by them relating to espionage, counterespionage, sabotage, subversive activities and violations of the neutrality laws."

I am bringing this statement to your attention in order that if you have not already been advised of the President's desires in the handling of cases of the type above enumerated, you may be informed concerning the Federal Government's program. I am confident that you will cooperate in this matter by immediately notifying the nearest representative of the Federal Bureau of Investigation of any information received relating to cases in the above classifications.

HOOVER'S OBJECTIVES WERE more ambitious than those responsibilities noted in Roosevelt's 1936 authorization. He sought to monitor "subversive activities," so he was quick to challenge the limitations set forth by Attorney General Jackson in 1941.

■ **Memo, Attorney General Robert Jackson to All Departmental and Agency Heads, undated but ca. April 1941**

A good deal of misunderstanding has resulted from the effort of the Federal Bureau of Investigation to cooperate with other departments of the government and it is found necessary to regularize this cooperation by the adoption of some rules so that each situation will not have to be considered by the Attorney General. I am enclosing [proposed] rules. . . . Most of them are self-explanatory but I would be glad to amplify our reasons for any of them and to receive any reaction which you have as to any adverse effect of the work of your department.

We have been in frequent receipt of requests for investigations from subordinates in departments. We are presented with the initial problem of whether to check up on the subordinate, or whether to go ahead and run the risk of learning later that the investigation was unauthorized. Rule 2 is designed to escape this risk and to fix the responsibility for the commencement of investigations.

We have been subjected to embarrassment and prejudice from the use that has been made by some departments of reports. It has occurred that learning from reports the sources of information employees of other departments have endeavored to obtain additional information by contacting the sources. Much of the information obtained is given in confidence and some sources of information have been closed to us through the action thus taken. These reports are often confidential, particularly as to sources, and we have found that they have been passed in some departments to many hands and their confidential character has been lost. There has been a tendency in utilizing the information furnished by the Federal Bureau of Investigation to attribute the action taken to the Federal Bureau of Investigation in such cases such as severance from the service even though the Bureau had no advice in such action. . . .

The Federal Bureau of Investigation is the subject of frequent attack as a Gestapo or an Ogpu. These attacks, if believed by a large number of people, are disastrous to its work and its standing in court when we seek conviction in its cases. It cannot be used except for the investigation of crimes and subversive activities which amount to overt acts rather than matters of opinion.

In the field of labor relations, the Federal Bureau of Investigation is not trained or equipped to form judgments in labor controversies even if that were a proper activity or action. On the other hand it must have, in dealing with definitely subversive activities, the cooperation of labor groups. It cannot undertake the type of investigation which has been condemned legislatively when used by private employers. . . .

The intervention of the Federal Bureau of Investigation in a strike is apt to be a highly provocative feature and to prolong labor disagreements. It should only be undertaken in cases where the Office of Production Management, the Department of Labor, and the department for whom goods are being produced concur. When undertaken reports or information should never be made available to private employers or to rival unions. The investigation of labor relations in our opinion is an important, but a wholly separate line of investigation requiring special qualifications and we believe should be in the main preceded by the departments awarding the contracts as they have the only means of control of the employers without which the handling of labor relations is one-sided.

I believe the other proposed rules are self-explanatory.

If you see any reason why any of these rules will unduly prejudice your work, I shall be glad to have an expression of your views.

[Proposed] Rules for Inter-Departmental Use of Federal Bureau of Investigation Facilities

Except upon special direction of the President or the Attorney General, the use of the facilities of the Federal Bureau of Investigation shall be subject to the following rules.

1. The Federal Bureau of Investigation's activities shall be confined to investigating and do not extend to policing, patroling, or guarding either persons or property.

2. Investigation shall be undertaken for departments, other than the Department of Justice, only on the written request of the head of the Department or Agency, or of one specially designated for that purpose by the head of such department or agency.

3. Reports of investigation shall be furnished only to the person designated by the head of the department or agency as the custodian thereof. They shall not leave the custody of such person or of the head of the Department. Departmental action taken on the basis of information contained in FBI reports shall not be attributed to the FBI and no department or employee thereof shall contact sources of information mentioned in said report in reference thereto.

4. The subject matter of investigations which the FBI has authorized to undertake do not extend beyond charges of suspicion or crime, or of definite subversive activity which does not consist of views or expressions of opinion, but of overt acts of incriminating relationships.

5. Charges of communism or subversive activity in connection with activities in labor relations shall be investigated only with the knowledge and approval of the Department of Labor, the Office of Production Management, and the department for which supplies are being produced. It will not be undertaken except in connection with defense production. No matter which would constitute a matter of labor relations in a dispute between employer and employee will be investigated and no reports shall be made available to rival unions or to employees. . . .

8. Departmental personnel will be investigated only at the request of the heads of the departments or agencies affected and will not be undertaken as to qualifications or desirability of the employee but will be related only to activities of a criminal or subversive nature.

The Federal Bureau of Investigation will report only its information as to matters of fact and will make no recommendation as to severance from service and any action taken thereof shall not be attributed to the Federal Bureau of Investigation.

■ **Memo, FBI Director J. Edgar Hoover to Attorney General Robert Jackson, April 1, 1941**

I have reviewed the suggested "Rules for Inter-Departmental Use of Federal Bureau of Investigation Facilities" . . . and desire to offer the following comments and suggested revisions. . . . I am convinced from the Bureau's study of the causes of the collapse of France that this catastrophe was brought about by the impotency of the French Government in failing to be alert to or aware of the growth and influence of the subversive groups in the labor field. I, of course, have no controversy with bona fide organized labor but . . . Nazi and Communist agents have deliberately endeavored to attach their tentacles to the labor groups, in Great Britain, the United States, Mexico, and in many countries of South America. Recognizing the tremendous force for evil that may be exercised through domination of the labor organizations, the agents of the totalitarian powers have attached themselves to legitimate labor like barnacles attach themselves to a ship. It is consequently highly important that the Federal Bureau of Investigation be unhampered in its authority to conduct investigations into situations involving potential danger to the Government of the United States.

I fully realize that the Bureau in initiating and carrying on investigations in this field must follow a very careful course . . . and that undoubtedly some sources will accuse the Bureau of illegal activities as a result of the conducting of investigations in this field. I believe, however, that we must have the courage to face the yelping of these alleged Liberals who are vociferous in their condemnation of any legitimate effort to enforce the existing laws of the United States.

You will recall that last year in accord with the instructions of the President the Bureau initiated a program [the Custodial Detention Index] of establishing and maintaining a list of persons whose activities were considered so dangerous as to justify consideration of their detention in the event of a national emergency. I explained this program to a Congressional Committee and following the resultant publicity the Bureau was the subject of vitriolic criticism by a handful of pseudo-liberals who cry "Gestapo" upon the slightest provocation. I must point out, however, that if the Bureau had not compiled such a list and maintained it in an up-to-date fashion, we would be in a pitiful position today in view of the forthcoming crisis in our international relations.

I feel frankly that the hue and cry of a small group of pseudo-liberals, who are either affiliated with Communist Front organizations or out-and-out Communists, that the Bureau is a "Gestapo" should give us little concern as long as we know that we are functioning in a legal, legitimate, ethical and honorable manner. . . . It is a mistake to give such undue heed to the cry of these pseudo-liberals as to result in any circumscribing or circumventing of the legitimate work of the Federal Bureau of Investigation. As you know, no one is more intensely interested in maintaining the civil rights of our American people. . . . I feel consequently that my views about the current situation may be considered in the light of a number of years' experience in meeting and coping with law enforcement problems on a national basis and meeting them with legal, ethical and honorable tactics.

I have gone to some length to outline my views concerning the legitimate field of activity of the Federal Bureau of Investigation during the current emergency because I believe that certain of the restrictions placed upon the Federal Bureau of Investigation in these proposed rules and regulations would burden the Bureau down with administrative regulations of such a cumbersome nature as to make ineffective any work that the Bureau might attempt to do. I, of course, do not desire that the services of Agents of the Federal Bureau of Investigation be utilized in the investigation of situations which involve solely labor disputes or other bona fide disturbances of the normal employer-employee relationship. I do not believe, however, that any regulation should be established and promulgated which would preclude or circumvent the Bureau from promptly investigating situations in which there is a real potential element of subversive activity, which is the real motivating factor behind a tie-up of an industry engaged in carrying out an essential part of the National Defense program. I feel most strongly that it is essential no regulations be undertaken which would in any way hamper or hamstring the Federal Bureau of Investigation in meeting the obvious menace and danger to the internal security of this Nation presented by the present activities of foreign agents in labor union fields. . . . The Bureau has not at any time initiated an investigation of any labor situation as such. I am confident that the intelligence and good judgment of the Special Agents in Charge and supervisory staff of the Bureau . . . may be depended upon to note and refer to the Department any case in which there is involved any question of Departmental policy with reference to the participation of the Department in a labor controversy. . . .

There is one particular regulation which I am desirous of commenting upon generally at this point. It is the provision which would preclude the Federal Bureau of Investigation from conducting any investigation of Communism or subversive activities which have connection with activities in labor situations without the approval of the Department of Labor, the Office of Production Management, and the Department for which supplies are being produced. If this regulation were adopted, it would practically nullify any investigative action of Communists or subversive activities. It is a basic premise, well established over a period of years, that Communists and most subversive activities are always attached to labor situations. Communism in particular has grown out of the labor situation in the world and the Communist leaders and agitators always aim to attach themselves to and bore from within legitimate labor organizations. Therefore, it is a practical impossibility to divorce Communism from labor situations. Consequently, it would mean that the FBI would be conducting no investigations into Communism or other subversive activities until it had obtained the approval of three other Governmental agencies. . . . Time is frequently of the essence in investigations into matters of this character. If certain facts on prima facie cases must be considered and approved by the Department of Labor, the Office of Production Management, and the Department of Government for which the supplies are being produced, I think it can be readily seen that days and weeks, and even months, may elapse before an investigation is approved and authorized. By that time [the contemplated investigation] will inevitably have leaked out through so many sources . . . that when finally the FBI would be authorized to make the investigation, information, records and leads which would have been available in the original stages of the situation will have been destroyed or completely covered up, and any such investigation would then be nothing but an idle gesture.

Another aspect of this whole matter which I do not believe was considered in the rough draft of the proposed regulations, is the difference between "investigative" activity and "intelligence" activity. . . . Investigative activity, such as is conducted when there is a specific violation of a Criminal Statute involved, always presupposes an overt act and is proceeded upon with the very definite intention of developing facts and information that will enable prosecution under such legislation. Intelligence activity is predicated upon an entirely different premise. Much of the activity indulged in by the Communists and subversive elements does not, in its original stage, involve an overt act or a violation of a specific statute. These subversive groups direct their attention to the dissemination of propaganda and to the boring from within processes, much of which is not a violation of a Federal Statute at the time it is indulged in, but which may become a very definite violation of law in the event of the declaration of war or of the declaration of a national emergency. Consequently, it is imperative, if the internal security of this country is to be maintained, that the FBI be in a position to have available in its files information concerning the activities of individuals and organizations of a subversive character. The gathering of such information is a progressive matter, and cannot be initiated upon a specific case, nor would it be logical or practical for such matters to be approved in each instance by the Department of Labor, the Office of Production Management and the Department of the Government for which supplies may be produced. You will recall that last year one of the very things which the Communists endeavored to do in the so-called "Norris Smear"* was to prevent this Bureau from collecting information upon subversive elements in this country and maintaining a national defense index. The wisdom of the President in 1939 in ordering that this Bureau gather such information has now been more than justified. Had we refrained from gathering such information or had it been discontinued last year when the hue and cry of the Communists was raised, this Bureau would not be in a position today to furnish to the Department the names of individuals who should be considered for either internment or prosecution in the event of the declaration of a complete national emergency. None of these persons today had violated a specific Federal law now in force and effect, but many of them will come within the category for internment or prosecution as a result of regulations and laws which may be enacted in the event of a declaration of war. To wait until then to gather such information or to conduct such investigations would be suicidal.

Therefore, I very strongly feel that the most careful consideration should be given to any regulation which will compel the Federal Bureau of Investigation to discontinue or to materially circumscribe its intelligence work and the progressive gathering of information concerning Communists and subversive groups, irrespective of what field of activity in which they may be involved, because to adopt such a regulation will make utterly impotent the work of the FBI in subversive fields.

I desire to . . . offer you a suggested revision . . . to these proposed rules:

"1. The Federal Bureau of Investigation's activities shall be confined to investigating and do not extend to policing, patroling, or guarding either persons or property."

I am dubious of the wisdom of going on record as indicating that the Federal Bureau of Investigation shall be confined to investigating activities primarily because the Bureau is specifically authorized and obligated under the terms of its Appropriation Act to carry on a variety of operations which are not actually investigative. . . . I am fearful that if the Department permits any rules and regulations to restrict the operations of the Federal Bureau of Investigation solely to investigative activities, some issue may be taken with the Department concerning aspects of the Bureau's work which have been specifically authorized by Congress. I propose consequently that this provision be revised to read as follows:

"The duty of the Federal Bureau of Investigation is to conduct investigations of violations of specified Federal Statutes, to collect evidence in cases in which the United States is or may be a party in interest and to perform

*Senator George Norris had criticized the FBI's conduct in the arrest of recruiters for the Spanish Loyalist cause, and had demanded an investigation of the FBI. —Ed.

certain other duties specifically established by law. The services of the Federal Bureau of Investigation may not be utilized for the purpose of patroling or protecting private property or the guarding of private citizens except as otherwise specifically provided by law or by existing regulations of the Department of Justice."

"2. Investigation shall be undertaken for departments, other than the Department of Justice, only on the written request of the head of the Department or agency, or of one specially designated for that purpose by the head of such Department or agency."

Under the provisions of the Bureau's Appropriation Act the Bureau is obligated to conduct investigations of official matters under the control of the Department of State. Over a period of many years the Bureau has been accustomed to initiate investigations in which the State Department is interested without the formality of a written request from the Secretary. In connection with its Internal Security operations the Bureau is in constant contact not only with the Military and Naval Intelligence Units but also with other Governmental Departments. Through the liaison thus maintained the Bureau is constantly obtaining data and information which result in the initiation of investigations by the Bureau in which other Governmental Departments may be interested and for the most part these investigations are initiated without the formality of a written request. . . .

I am also apprehensive that the promulgation of such a rule by you would result in the initiation of investigations by the heads of various branches of the executive agencies of the Government which would be primarily within the investigative jurisdiction of the Federal Bureau of Investigation but in which the head of the Department would be reluctant to make a written request for an investigation. In this type of case I am fearful that rather than formally request an investigation, Departmental heads would utilize the personnel of their own departments to initiate investigations which should properly be handled by the Federal Bureau of Investigation. . . . I offer, consequently, the following suggested revision in this regulation:

"No investigation shall be undertaken by the Federal Bureau of Investigation at the request of any Governmental agency or department except upon the written request of the head of that Department or agency unless other provisions are specifically established by policy or by established procedure of the Department of Justice."

"3. Reports of investigation shall be furnished only to the person designated by the head of the department or agency as the custodian thereof. They shall not leave the custody of such person or of the head of the department. Departmental action taken on the basis of information contained in FBI reports shall not be attributed to the FBI and no department or employee thereof shall contact sources of information mentioned in said reports in reference thereto."

I am exceedingly anxious, of course, to insure and maintain the confidential category of the FBI reports, but in order to insure the practical operation of this regulation I suggest that a proviso be set forth therein requiring that no department or employee thereof shall contact sources of information mentioned in investigative reports without the specific authorization of the Federal Bureau of Investigation. I suggest, therefore, that this provision be revised to read as follows: .

"All Governmental Departments and agencies are cautioned to treat the contents of reports of the Federal Bureau of Investigation which are furnished to those departments and agencies as being in a highly confidential classification. The Department of Justice will furnish reports of investigations conducted by the Federal Bureau of Investigation only to the heads of Governmental departments or agencies or to a representative specifically designated by the head of a Department or agency to receive such reports. Federal Bureau of Investigation reports shall not leave the custody of the head of the Department or the person entrusted therewith. Departmental action taken on the basis of information contained in Federal Bureau of Investigation reports shall not be described as being predicated upon the Federal Bureau of Investigation reports. On those occasions when it is essential that a source of information mentioned in the Federal Bureau of Investigation reports be contacted by a representative of a Governmental Department or agency, this shall not be done without the authorization of the Federal Bureau of Investigation."

"4. The subject matter of investigations which the FBI has authorized to undertake do not extend beyond charges of suspicion of crime, or of definite subversive activity which does not consist of views or expressions of opinion, but of overt acts of incriminating relationships."

. . . I believe that the provisions of my suggested regulation No. 1 describe the jurisdiction of the Bureau in such a manner as to make this paragraph unnecessary.

"5. Charges of communism or subversive activity in connection with activities in labor relations shall be investigated only with the knowledge and approval of the Department of Labor, the Office of Production Management, and the department for which supplies are being produced. It will not be undertaken except in connection with defense production. No matter which would constitute a matter of labor relations in a dispute between employer and employee will be investigated and no reports shall be made available to rival unions or to employers." . . .

I am apprehensive that this rule as it is presently worded will completely prohibit the Bureau from investigating the activities of communists and other subverters who are active in labor circles. I believe that if it is desired to place some limitation upon the responsibility of the Federal Bureau of Investigation . . . the regulation should be clearly and concisely worded in such a manner that it will be applicable only to labor disputes and will not preclude or circumscribe the conducting of investigation into the activities of communists and subverters whose operations are inimical to the national defense and who may be incidentally associated with or active in the labor field. For these reasons I suggest the following revision of this paragraph:

"The Federal Bureau of Investigation will not conduct any investigation of bona fide labor disputes without appropriate notification to the Department of Labor and the Office of Production Management. Investigation of labor disputes will not be undertaken in any instance without the specific authorization of the Attorney General. Investigative reports prepared by the Federal Bureau of Investigation in cases investigated in this field will not under any circumstances be made available to any private person or organization, including unions, employers or employees." . . .

"8. Departmental personnel will be investigated only at the request of the heads of the departments or agencies affected and will not be undertaken as to qualifications or desirability of the employee, but will be related only to activities of a criminal or subversive nature.

"The Federal Bureau of Investigation will report only its information as to matters of fact and will make no recommendation as to severance from service and any action taken therefrom shall not be attributed to the Federal Bureau of Investigation."

Here, again, I do not believe that the Federal Bureau of Investigation should be restricted by a Departmental regulation from initiating an investigation into charges of subversive activity on the part of a Government employee. It is conceivable that information will be received from time to time concerning subversive activities on the part of Government employees which should not be brought to the attention of the head of the Department involved, at least until some investigation has been conducted. I believe, consequently, that the Department should avoid circumscribing the right of the Federal Bureau of Investigation to conduct investigation of this type of case. It is suggested, consequently, that this paragraph be revised to provide:

"Heads of governmental departments or agencies receiving information concerning subversive activities on the part of personnel of their Departments or agencies are urged to bring this information promptly to the attention of the Federal Bureau of Investigation for appropriate investigation." . . .

■ **Memo, Attorney General Robert Jackson to FBI Director J. Edgar Hoover, April 4, 1941**

I think I have failed to make clear what I was trying to accomplish in the [Rules for Inter-Departmental Use of the FBI]. I had no thought to restrict

or alter in any manner the internal operation of the F.B.I. or the Department of Justice, or its *right* to proceed in all the fields in which it has been
operating.

It was my thought that we might be able to erect a barrier against
demands by other Departments that we proceed into fields in which they
wanted to use us to pull their own chestnuts out of the fire. I see no
difference of opinion between us as to the scope of your intelligence work
and responsibility, but it seems to me that such work should be solely
under the direction of this Department and not at the service of outside
agencies who have no responsibility in the matter. . . .

*On april 24, 1965, a group of dissident junior officers
in the Dominican Republic launched a coup to overthrow the
military government and restore President Juan Bosch to power
(Bosch's government had itself been overthrown by this military
junta the previous year). Concerned about the leftist cast of
the restored Bosch government and its military supporters, on
April 28 President Johnson sent in American troops,
ostensibly to protect the American embassy and evacuate foreign
nationals. Through news reports it soon became clear that the
U.S. intervention was designed to aid the military government
against the coup. The Johnson administration then shifted its
stated rationale for introducing U.S. troops, claiming that the
coup's leaders had lost control to Castroites. To confirm this
contention, U.S. Ambassador to the Dominican Republic William
Bennett released a list of names of these alleged Castroites,
a list prepared by CIA Director William Raborn in conjunction
with FBI Director Hoover. Examining the list, the press
successfully refuted the claims. Many of the named individuals
had not been in the Dominican Republic while other names
were duplicated—collapsing the number from the original list of
fifty-six. President Johnson retained an interest in monitoring
political developments in the Dominican Republic and to achieve
this purpose turned not to the CIA but to the FBI.*

■ **Memo, FBI Director J. Edgar Hoover to FBI Assistant Directors Clyde Tolson, Alan Belmont, Cartha DeLoach, and William Sullivan, May 20, 1965, Tolson File**

President Lyndon B. Johnson called. He asked if I was going to send [name withheld] to Santo Domingo as Legal Attache. [Line withheld on national security grounds.]

The President stated he told them last night he wanted this done and they said they normally do it themselves, but he said he wanted this as an aid to the Embassy.* The President . . . thought the quicker [name withheld FBI legal attache] was there, the better even though there is no agreement yet so he can see "who's who" and "what's what." . . .

The President stated he would take care of jurisdiction and he would like to have [name withheld] on the next plane and to send whatever I need with him.

■ **Memo, FBI Director J. Edgar Hoover to FBI Assistant Directors Clyde Tolson, William Sullivan, John Mohr, Thomas Bishop, Charles Brennan, and Nicholas Callahan, November 20, 1970, Tolson File**

Secretary of State William P. Rogers called. He stated he was calling, after a discussion with the President [Nixon], about the Bureau's liaison offices abroad, and, of course, he thought it was a good idea [to expand the number]. . . . I said I thought it would help in getting additional information.

Mr. Rogers asked if Richard Helms, Director, Central Intelligence Agency (CIA), knew about it, and I told him he did not and I did not believe the President was desirous for him to know. I said that in September the President made the suggestion to me as he wanted better intelligence. Mr. Rogers said he, the President, mentioned it to him and it was his idea and noboby else's. I said when the President handed it to H. R. Haldeman he told him to take it up with him, Rogers, and only him, so I assume he did not notify the CIA and certainly we have not. . . .

---

*Name withheld led a group of fourteen FBI agents dispatched to the Dominican Republic to investigate the backgrounds of prospective members of the provisional government which the administration sought to install, until elections were held, and also to monitor the political situation. The president later asked Hoover to "take the evidence coming in and prepare in writing the strongest case [you] can to prove [communist domination] when and if we have to." Hoover agreed to "have this done."—Ed.

■ **Memo, FBI Assistant Director W. Mark Felt to FBI Associate Director Clyde Tolson, June 10, 1971**

. . . [FBI assistant director William Sullivan opposes] expansion of our foreign liaison program and suggested that some of current liaison offices could be closed. . . . Director requested [FBI assistant director D. J.] Dalbey for his views . . . [who] strongly recommended expansion (1) because of White House request, [one line withheld on national security grounds] because of his personal experiences in foreign liaison during World War II when the Bureau was praised by high Government officials for accomplishments. . . .

Since 1/1/71 a record has been maintained of items of interest disseminated to the [Nixon] White House. . . . My review reflects so far this year over 200 items have been furnished to the White House. The Director has received several warm letters of appreciation from Dr. Kissinger. . . . But in reviewing samples of dissemination to the White House I find, much of the information relates to political, economic and social areas. While much of this information is picked up in conversations, newspapers and various sources, Bureau personnel are probably far more qualified than State Department personnel to put things in the proper perspective and to sense relative importance.

In view of specific request of the White House, continued highly favorable comments of Dr. Kissinger, and because we are producing a substantial volume of valuable political information, I feel we should go forward with the expansion program. . . .

[Tolson's handwritten notation: "I agree." Hoover's handwritten notation: "1. I shall further discuss this with Dr. Kissinger. Meanwhile *no positive action* should be taken with any expansion abroad. 2. I would like to have from Sullivan the list of foreign liaison offices he would recommend be closed *now*."]

■ **Memo, FBI Supervisor W. R. Wannall to FBI Assistant Director W. Mark Felt, July 28, 1971**

. . . In the past year, while I have been directly associated with the foreign liaison program, I have had the opportunity to meet a number of high-level officials of foreign police and security agencies who have called at the Bureau. Without exception, they have been highly complimentary of the Bureau and the Director's administration of it. By having Agents located strategically in foreign countries, we are able to convey a true picture of the Bureau's jurisdiction and efficiency. The men who man our foreign posts obviously are quite attentive in discharging their responsibilities in this regard. They are also fostering a spirit of cooperation in the law enforcement area by seeking and securing cooperation of the organizations abroad. . . .

Another area in which our men abroad render valuable service not only to the Bureau but to the Government as a whole regards the travels of dignitaries. Whenever the President, Vice President or high-level U.S. official, as well as friends of the Bureau, go to areas where we have Legal Attache (Legat) posts, our men have performed outstanding services not only in providing information relating to security of these individuals but in assisting them in connection with many complex problems which arise during foreign travel. . . .

Without question, officials on the highest level in our Government [including the president and national security adviser Kissinger] recognize the value of having FBI personnel in selected areas. . . .

■ Memo, FBI Assistant Director J. K. Ponder to FBI Associate Director Clyde Tolson, September 14, 1971
. . . Recommendations:
1. That we retain our 17 existing Legal Attache Offices. [Hoover's handwritten notation: "Yes."]
2. That we reopen the Resident Agency at Hermosillo, Mexico. . . . [Hoover's handwritten notation: "Yes."]
3. That the Director . . . recommend expansion of foreign operations by reopening Manila, Rio de Janeiro and Santo Domingo; and opening Canberra, Kuala Lumpur and New Delhi. Also, that we are ready to do this whenever [President Nixon] so directs and arrangements can be perfected with the State Department. [Hoover's handwritten notation: "I shall discuss matter with Dr. K(issinger)."]
4. That upon receipt of White House approval of this proposal, the State Department be requested to authorize an increase in FBI personnel on foreign assignment from the present 88 to 100 and that other necessary arrangements be handled with State Department to open the new offices. [Hoover's handwritten notation: "After Dr. K. has considered it."]

■ Letter, FBI Director J. Edgar Hoover to President Richard Nixon, September 20, 1971
In confirmation of our discussion this morning, I am proceeding to make the necessary arrangements for the opening of additional liaison offices at Manila, Philippines; Rio de Janeiro, Brazil; Santo Domingo, Dominican

Republic; Canberra, Australia; Kuala Lumpur, Malaysia; and New Delhi, India. . . .

I have today asked the Secretary of State to secure the necessary clearances, both for the increase in our personnel ceiling and for the opening of the new posts. I will inform you promptly when this has been accomplished.

12: Political Uses of the FBI

*WHILE SECRET PRESIDENTIAL directives provided the ostensible
authority for FBI investigations and wiretapping of
"subversive activities," neither President Franklin Roosevelt, who
issued the first such directives, nor his successors defined the
precise meaning of this nebulous phrase. No president or attorney
general seriously attempted to confine FBI investigations to
agents of foreign powers. Instead, presidents welcomed the
latitude afforded by secret, broadly worded directives,
perceiving Hoover's FBI as a useful political tool. Beginning
with Roosevelt (though his predecessor, Herbert Hoover, had
occasionally solicited Hoover's assistance) and extending through
Richard Nixon, presidents came to rely on Hoover's FBI as the
intelligence arm of the White House. And Hoover invariably
complied with politically motivated requests—as long as they
were not crassly partisan.*

*Hoover's services ranged from volunteering information which
allowed presidents to avoid political scandal or
embarrassment, to help in rebutting press or congressional
criticism, to intelligence about the plans and strategies of
the administration's political adversaries, and even—though this
was clearly exceptional—to help candidates in securing the
presidential nomination of their party (in the case of Thomas
E. Dewey in 1948 and Hubert Humphrey in 1968). Perhaps
the most sensitive of these operations was Hoover's willingness
to service President Nixon's November 1970 request for
derogatory information on members of the Washington press
corps. In fact, even before the request Hoover had
accumulated the kind of noncriminal but derogatory information*

*that Nixon wanted. This information served no legitimate
law-enforcement purpose but enabled the person who had it to
influence public opinion and advance special political
objectives.*

■ **Memo, FBI Assistant Director Edward Tamm to FBI Director,
July 2, 1940, Nichols File**
I called upon [Assistant Secretary of State Adolf] Berle on . . . July
2, 1940. He advised me that the President had requested him to ask you to
conduct an investigation. . . . The President received word from Marcus
[sic, Marquis] Childs, a newspaper reporter, that while [former Republican
President] Herbert Hoover and his former Secretary, Larry Ritchey [sic,
Richey] were attending the Republican National Convention in Philadelphia they addressed certain cablegrams to former Premier [Pierre] Laval of
France . . . to obtain some statement from Laval indicating that President
Roosevelt had made definite commitments to send men to France to fight
for France in the present war. The President desired that you determine
what messages, if any, were sent by Mr. Hoover and Mr. Ritchey and what
replies were received.
Mr. Berle stated that the President felt that the politics and political
activities of Mr. Hoover and Mr. Ritchey were their private business but
that when they injected themselves into international entree of this type the
matter became so related to the operation of the Federal Government that it
was subject to official inquiry. . . .
Upon your statement that since the President had instructed that this
matter be investigated, you would, of course, be required to investigate it,
I contacted [FBI assistant director P. E.] Foxworth in New York City,
. . . and requested that he initiate appropriate inquiries to determine the
facts in this situation. . . .

■ **Memo, FBI Assistant Director Edward Tamm to FBI Director,
July 10, 1940, Nichols File**
. . . A check [re Herbert Hoover matter] has been completed by the
New York office which has failed to disclose any such messages were sent.
I called Mr. Berle and so advised him.
[While Great Britain and France went to war with Germany in Septem-
ber 1939 after the German invasion of Poland, the United States remained
neutral. Roosevelt identified with the European democracies, but he soon
encountered opposition from isolationists in his own administration and
among Republicans in Congress. Unwilling to risk his chances for reelec-

tion by challenging isolationist sentiment, FDR was concerned that the Republicans would exploit the foreign policy issue in the 1940 presidential campaign. Despite these concerns, the president on May 22, 1940, had ordered the sale of World War I military equipment to the British and French and had allowed French pilots to train in the United States. This policy of encouragement and covert assistance suffered a crushing blow when the French, on June 22, sought an armistice with Germany.]

■ **Confidential Do Not File Memo, FBI Director J. Edgar Hoover, January 30, 1941**
. . . I told the President that in regard to the matter which he told me about last fall concerning the letters which Vice President [Henry] Wallace had written to Nicholas K. Roerich and Francis R. Grant [Roerich's secretary], which the President had said last fall were being shown to certain parties in New York, which might be used to the detriment of Mr. Wallace and the President, I had been able to obtain a set of these letters, together with the proposed [Republican National Committee] press release which had been drafted at the time but which had not been issued, together with the code symbols used in these letters and written in [Wallace's] own handwriting, and in which some of these symbols refer most disparagingly to the President. I gave to the President this material which he hurriedly examined and laid aside for further examination. . . .

[Henry Wallace had an interest in mysticism and the occult. In 1933 he had begun corresponding about such matters with Roerich and Grant, in part out of interest in Roerich's eccentric plans for world peace. Wallace eventually broke with Roerich, but in 1940 White House aide Harry Hopkins learned—and so informed presidential aide Sam Rosenman—that the treasurer of the Republican National Committee had secured copies of this correspondence. White House fears that the Republicans might exploit these letters in the campaign intensified when a *Pittsburgh Post Gazette* reporter asked Wallace about the authenticity of these letters. Wallace denied them. The Republicans' press release was not issued, and Wendell Willkie, the Republican presidential candidate, never raised the matter during the campaign, some say because he was warned that should he do so the Democrats would publicize his own extramarital affair.]

IN THE AFTERMATH *of the Watergate affair during the Nixon administration, a more skeptical press and Congress began to explore the relationship between presidents and the federal intelligence community, notably the FBI. They found that presidents since Franklin Roosevelt had used the FBI's resources for political purposes. At the same time these inquiries seemed to document the uniqueness of Nixon's uses of the FBI and his almost paranoiac suspicions—documented by his request for FBI wiretaps of his appointees to the National Security Council and White House staffs. In fact, Nixon was not the first president to suspect the political loyalty of his closest aides. That dubious honor belongs to Harry Truman.*

When Truman assumed the presidency upon Franklin Roosevelt's death on April 12, 1945, he not only succeeded a popular president who had dominated national politics since 1933; he also confronted problems stemming from his own selection as vice president. In 1944 Roosevelt had decided to placate the Democrats' conservative wing by dropping incumbent Vice President Henry Wallace. He selected Missouri Senator Harry Truman as a compromise candidate. Roosevelt's decision was unpopular among liberal Democrats, many of whom continued to hold important positions in the executive branch, the Congress, and the Democratic National Committee. When FDR died, the liberals feared that Truman would overturn the Roosevelt agenda. Both to sustain their own influence and to shape national policy, influential liberals sought to limit Truman's initiatives, in part by carefully timed leaks to the media. Truman, clearly overwhelmed, found it difficult to impose his own authority.

For his own bureaucratic interests, FBI Director Hoover sought to curry favor with Truman. On April 23, just eleven days after Roosevelt's death, he submitted a report to the White House detailing some of the political activities of these disgruntled liberals. Acknowledging Hoover's report on behalf of the president, presidential aide Harry Vaughan responded that Truman had read it "with much interest" and felt that "future communications along that line would be of considerable interest whenever in your opinion they are necessary."

In time the White House went well beyond this solicitation of further FBI reports. It requested that the FBI "secure all information possible on White House employees . . . and intercepts of their phone conversations would be of extreme value." Within two weeks, Hoover had identified Edward Prichard as especially disloyal. Prichard was an aide to Truman's close political adviser Fred Vinson, who directed the Office of Mobilization and Reconversion and whom Truman later promoted to Secretary of the Treasury and then to the Supreme Court. On May 8 Hoover authorized a tap on Prichard's phone. This wiretap provided invaluable political intelligence but, more dramatically, precipitated White House requests that the FBI wiretap syndicated columnist Drew Pearson and Thomas Corcoran, a former Roosevelt aide and influential Washington attorney.

Hoover did not authorize a tap on Pearson (that was too risky), but he did authorize a tap on Corcoran. Installed on June 8, the Corcoran tap produced considerable political intelligence for the Truman White House. Corcoran had extensive contacts within the liberal wing of the Democratic National Committee, the Congress (notably Lyndon Johnson, Claude Pepper, and Lister Hill), and the executive branch (Harold Ickes, but also Attorney General Tom Clark). The Corcoran tap further provided advance information on the proposed commentary of influential national columnists Drew Pearson, Irving Brant, and Ernest Cuneo, and on the political plans of influential national figures, as, for example, Supreme Court Justice William Douglas.

Ostensibly the Corcoran and Prichard wiretaps had been installed to identify the sources of leaks of classified information. Because neither tap uncovered such information, and because Hoover alone had authorized their installation (and had thereby contravened Roosevelt's May 1940 directive calling for prior approval by the attorney general), the White House was uncomfortable. In order to continue the Corcoran tap (Prichard left government service in October 1945), the president asked Attorney General Tom Clark for formal approval to tap Corcoran in November 1945. This tap continued until April 16, 1947, by which time it ceased to provide information of any value, Corcoran having correctly suspected that his office and resident phones were tapped. Then, in April 1948, having been alerted to the efforts of liberal Democrats to deny

*his nomination or influence his vice-presidential choice, Truman
asked that the tap on Corcoran be reinstalled. During the
course of these taps, the FBI forwarded some five thousand pages
of wiretap summaries to the Truman White House under
carefully controlled procedures to ensure against discovery of
both the FBI's wiretap and its political assistance.*

■ **Memo, FBI Assistant Director D. Milton Ladd to FBI Director,
May 23, 1945**
[FBI inspector Myron] Gurnea has had prepared the attached
transcripts of telephone conversations between [Edward] Prichard and
[Supreme Court] Justice [Felix] Frankfurter and between Prichard and
[syndicated columnist] Drew Pearson which it is thought you may desire to
personally discuss and furnish to [White House aide Edward] McKim. You
may also desire to discuss the [John] Maragon matter* with McKim on this
same occasion.
[Hoover's handwritten notation: "I sent copies to McKim 5/29/45."]

■ **Transcript, Telephone Conversation, Edward Prichard to
Supreme Court Justice Felix Frankfurter, May 8, 1945, 9:35 PM**
. . . Frankfurter: . . . We thought the text of what [Truman] said [an-
nouncing the end of the war in Europe] was good, appropriate, fitting . . .
whoever wrote it. . . . Who did do it? Col. [Harry] Vaughan?
Prichard: No. . . .
Frankfurter: You?
Prichard: Yeah. . . .
Frankfurter: Well, I thought it was very good. . . . How did you come to
get that assignment? That's very good. . . . Wait a minute (apparently
listening to aside). Madge (phonetic) [Frankfurter's wife] thinks you've got
it all cut out for you, that you must be the Charlie McCarthy [the dummy
of ventriloquist Edgar Bergen] of this administration. . . .
Prichard: The Edgar Bergan [sic]!
Frankfurter: The Edgar Bergan. You mean to say that we've got a Charlie
McCarthy? . . . How'd you get it. Who gave you that assignment? . . .

*Maragon was a passenger agent for the Baltimore and Ohio Railroad who helped
secure tickets and reservations for senators and congressmen and who ran other
errands in order to curry favor with prominent Washingtonians. Maragon had
developed a close relationship with President Truman's military aide, General
Harry Vaughan, and sought to exploit this relationship by representing himself as
an intimate friend of Vaughan.—Ed.

Prichard: [Secretary of the Treasury] Fred [Vinson].

Frankfurter: Oh, really? Why was it given to him?

Prichard: I don't know.

Frankfurter: By direct command of the commander?

Prichard: Yeah. . . .

Prichard: Did you hear about [Assistant Secretary of State] Nelson Rockefeller coming back and going up to the Appropriations Committee and telling them that they had to take Argentina in [to the United Nations] to form an anti-Soviet block and that Argentina was the most anti-Soviet country and they had to have them in? . . . And this meant they had to put an end to the influence of Lombardo Toledano (Vincente Lombardo Toledano, Mexican Labor leader and Head of the Confederation of Latin-American Workers. Lombardo Toledano was a close associate of the late Soviet Ambassador to Mexico, Constantine Oumansky, and contacts Earl Browder, President of the Communist Political Association whenever he visits the United States.) and asked for $2,000,000 to be used in propaganda down there, $2,000,000 extra. Let's see what was the other thing he said?

Frankfurter: Are you sure about that? For heavens sake!

Prichard: Yes.

Frankfurter: I'm almost persuaded to have you tell that to Drew. (Drew Pearson)

Prichard: I think that's been done, or will be. . . .

Frankfurter: . . . I saw Dave today. [White House aide] Dave Niles. They are very nice and want him to hang around, and I told him not to.

Prichard: I told him not to a week ago. Absolutely foolish to stay.

Frankfurter: I told him you fix the date. Don't wait to be accepted. . . . Dave told me all sorts of things he's been telling about various people, [Edward] McKim and— . . . Dave is rather full of what he heard was a mistreatment of [Postmaster General] Frank Walker. [Truman announced Walker's resignation on June 30—the first Roosevelt cabinet officer he replaced.]

Prichard: It wasn't very good treatment.

Frankfurter: Isn't he one of the 'itty' (phonetic) boys?

Prichard: Well, I guess it was closeness to the Boss [President Roosevelt] that made him 'itty'. . . .

■ **Transcript, Telephone Conversation, Syndicated Columnist Drew Pearson to Edward Prichard, May 13, 1945, 10:30 AM**

    . . . Pearson: Say, I see Leo (Leo Crowley) and the boys gave them the business [a reference to the abrupt cutting off of lend-lease assistance to the Soviet Union]. . . .

Prichard: No they didn't.

Pearson: Did you see the announcement?

Prichard: What did the announcement say?

Pearson: The announcement said all Lend Lease to those not participating in the war with Japan was out.

Prichard: Well the memorandum that was approved said just the opposite.

Pearson: It did?

Prichard: Yeah.

Pearson: Well, what's the explanation?

Prichard: I don't know. . . .

Pearson: Well, that could, I mean Leo couldn't have been giving them the double cross.

Prichard: Well, now I know what the memorandum was that was approved over there the other afternoon; that it should continue.

Pearson: Uh, well, I don't doubt your word. I just wonder what, uh, what the tactics are, what. . . .

Prichard: Uh, furthermore, the Predecessor (Franklin Delano Roosevelt) assured the Head Man (Josef Stalin) at the Last Meeting [at Yalta] that—the Predecessor of the present Chief— . . . it would be continued.

Pearson: Before he left you mean.

Prichard: Well, before he passed away.

Pearson: Oh. Oh. Uhuh.

Prichard: Assured Uncle Joe that it would be continued. . . .

Pearson: . . . Did you see this [Assistant Secretary of State] Joe Grew statement about Trieste?

Prichard: No, what did he say?

Pearson: He . . . [stated] that the Allies were going to keep Trieste for the time being in spite of Mr. Tito. Well, that wouldn't have been so significant had it not been for the fact that Tito had just issued a statement that there would be very serious consequences—very serious and unpleasant consequences if New Zealand troops remained in Trieste and that knowing Joe Grew, there was no question but that was aimed right at the present difficulty—this present note.

Prichard: Uhuh.

Pearson: Did you hear any more about that? You didn't know anything about the note at all, I know, but that note that I told you about.

Prichard: [British Foreign Minister Anthony] Eden's here in town.

Pearson: Oh, is he? I heard on the radio he was on his way.

Prichard: Got in last night, but what happened I don't know.

Pearson: Yeah, well that. I hear also that [Secretary of State Edward] Stettinius is going to come back to talk to Truman. I got a wire from San Francisco this morning that Truman is coming back here this next week or Stettinius, to confer with Truman.

Prichard: I think that's probably right.

Pearson: To confer on Trusteeships and regional arrangements. They're going to put the Trustee matter and solve it later on. They're not going to solve it in San Francisco.

Prichard: Uhuh. . . .

Prichard: I think you ought to blast, uh, Leo (Leo Crowley) a little bit on this shutting off Lend Lease and I think you ought to blast a little bit of this reparations business on this soft reparations policy [toward Germany].

Pearson: What is that? You mean about the labor?

Prichard: Uhuh. . . . I think you ought to blast them on this Lend Lease thing.

Pearson: Well, when it comes with playing in with the Chief, [Crowley's] a cautious guy. Now when he comes out and makes an official statement it (garbled) on him. I can't think that he's doing that on his own. Now look, confidentially, I talked to Leo yesterday morning. He told me that he didn't want to say anything about it; that he was going to. That it was in a state of flux. . . . That it was much better that nothing be said and that the only thing that could be said was that the President had the whole matter under advisement. He suggested that I say that on the radio.

Prichard: Uhuh.

Pearson: The whole thing would have to be considered. Now I haven't talked to him since then, but during the course of the afternoon he gave out this statement—some hours after I talked with him.

Prichard: Uhuh.

Pearson: Without. The only thing I can figure out maybe something happened in the interim.

Prichard: I don't know. He never saw the President yesterday.

Pearson: Well, maybe he talked to him on the phone. I don't know. He of course, I know how he feels about this whole thing, but.

Prichard: Naw, he's a horse's ass now don't you fool yourself on that.

Pearson: Oh, I know he is on these things.

Prichard: These and all the others. I mean, uh.

Pearson: But, uh, he's also a cautious one.

Prichard: That's right. . . .

Pearson: Hell, he stuck his neck right out—100% out. That's the only thing that I can't conceive that he'd do on his own.

Prichard: Uhuh. Well, I don't know a thing more about it except what was proved at that meeting the other afternoon.

Pearson: That was to continue.

Prichard: That's right.

Pearson: I heard that Russian troops were being switched over to the Siberian front.

Prichard: Well I don't know a thing about that. . . .

Pearson: Oscar [Cox] out on the West Coast says that Lend Lease will continue to Russia off the record and must give them a chance to regroup their forces and get a breathing spell.

Prichard: Uhuh. Well, he obviously doesn't know.

Pearson: Well, I shouldn't think so. Well, he says, he also says the meeting at the White House with Crowley and Truman reaffirmed this.

Prichard: Uhuh.

Pearson: So apparently he knows something.

Prichard: Yeah, well he got that from somebody. I know where he got that, but, uh, and I don't think the person that told him knows. I mean I think I know about that meeting, but I don't think he knows anything that's happened since.

Pearson: Well these be parlous times. . . .

■ **Strictly Personal and Confidential Memo, FBI Inspector Myron Gurnea to FBI Director, June 2, 1945, Nichols File**

[White House aide Edward] McKim . . . opened the conversation by stating: "First of all, I want to personally compliment the Director and the Bureau for the hell-of-a-swell job you fellows did" [on the White House staff report]. He stated, "Both the President and I were particularly impressed with the report and . . . I want to convey to Mr. Hoover my personal gratitude."

He then went on to state: "Now, with respect to that other thing (the technical [wiretap] log [on Prichard]), that is unbelievable." He stated that after receiving it he was so amazed that he was "afraid to show it to the President until they were on the boat and out in the river." He remarked, "That is treasonable."

I inquired of McKim as to the President's reaction. He stated that upon reading the technical log the President commented that in some ways it was comical (meaning that a Justice [Frankfurter] would engage in such juvenile conversations), whereas with reference to the major portion of it he stated that it is "the damnedest thing I have read." McKim then advised, "Incidentally, for your confidential information, we are taking corrective steps." I was not, of course, in a position to inquire of him what measures were anticipated.

With further reference to the [White House security survey] report he . . . stated that he observed that there was nothing radical in the administrative recommendations but that they appeared sound and provided for a general tightening up in the administration of the White House. He stated, "Just as soon as we can get to it we will go into it (the reorganization plans) thoroughly." Referring to the technical log he stated, "We want to keep that tap on." I explained to him that the technical was not on the Justice's line but on Prichard's. He stated that . . . they (he and the

President) desired that it be continued. He requested that he be advised currently as to any conversations such as the one of reference.

He continued by stating, "We want to know of any other sources that Drew Pearson has, and I want a tap put on his telephone." He also advised that Thomas Corcoran has also been engaged in questionable activities, and that he wanted a technical placed on his telephone line. . . .

■ **Index Card, White House Security Survey (1945)**

This folder contains 400 pages of documents dated between July 31, 1945 and August 13, 1945. The contents are described as follows: ". . . Entire folder deals with Bureau investigation into 'leaks' to the press concerning telegrams from Harry Hopkins to the White House dealing with Hopkins-Stalin conversations in 1945. Drew Pearson was one person to whom 'leaks' were reportedly furnished. Some items '*TOP SECRET.*' "

[The FBI has withheld in entirety the contents of this folder on national security grounds. Other FBI documents, reprinted following, provide insights into the scope and underlying political purposes of this so-called security survey which went beyond the leaks to Pearson concerning Hopkins's mission to Moscow in 1945.]

■ **Memo, FBI Assistant Director D. Milton Ladd to FBI Director, June 5, 1950, Nichols File**

. . . You will recall that in 1945, while we were conducting a survey of the White House, . . . [FBI assistant director Gordon] Nease . . . was requested to secure all information possible on White House employees and it was suggested by Mr. Vardaman [Commodore James K. Vardaman, naval aide to the president] that intercepts of the phone conversations of those employees would be of extreme value. Vardaman said if it became known that we were investigating these people, it would be incumbent upon both the President and him to deny that any such investigation had been ordered. . . .

■ **Memo, FBI Assistant Director Louis Nichols to FBI Associate Director Clyde Tolson, June 13, 1950, Nichols File**

On June 2, 1945, [FBI inspector Myron] Gurnea . . . [reported] that it was his very distinct impression that when Mr. McKim conveyed to him the request to make the investigation and install the technical [on Corcoran and Pearson] that it was something he had discussed with the President;

however, McKim did not say this. It was Gurnea's recollection that following this memorandum he saw the Director personally and the Director specifically instructed that there should be no technical on Drew Pearson but pursuant to the White House request there was installed a technical on Thomas Corcoran; that there appeared to be ample justification for this.

Gurnea further stated that at the time of his conversation with McKim nothing was said in any way, shape or form as to the consequences should this technical ever become known. It was understood that it was to be highly confidential.

I talked to [FBI assistant director Gordon] Nease . . . [who] delivered some of the stuff to [White House aide James] Vardaman although most of it went to [White House aide Harry] Vaughn [sic, Vaughan]. He recalls that on one occasion Vaughn stated that if the technical should ever become known it would be our baby and that Vaughn would deny any knowledge.

■ **Transcript, Telephone Conversation, Thomas Corcoran to Senator Lister Hill, June 9, 1945, 9:45 P.M.**

. . . Hill: Well, now listen, that's all right to talk about the past; but what are you going to do about the present and the future.

Corcoran: Well, what you ought to be able to do is pick this [liberal] crowd up and put them together; but they've got to begin to play the ball a little. And the only way you're going to get them to play ball is to have them meet and agree on a course of action and have them move.

Hill: Have you got a course of action that will get them to move?

Corcoran: Well, I think if you got them all sitting around the table I think you could evolve one. . . .

Hill: Well, the truth is though, Tommy, you and Hal Ickes knocked Henry Wallace out of that box [referring to developments at the 1944 Democratic National Convention when Wallace was denied renomination as Roosevelt's vice president, leading to Truman's nomination].

Corcoran: No, we didn't. Harold Ickes worked as hard for Henry Wallace as anyone did.

Hill: Oh no, I know what I'm talking about. He did after he got to Chicago, but he sure as hell didn't beforehand. . . . You all helped to knock him out.

Corcoran: No, we didn't. We recognized the situation when we saw it and nobody else did.

Hill: Maybe so.

Corcoran: That's true. . . .

Hill: . . . Well, listen, Tommy, outside of little [Postmaster General]

Robert E. [Hannegan] from St. Louis, Mo., who else is on that soccer team [of Truman insiders]?

Corcoran: [Senate secretary] Les Biffle (Phon.) is the most important.

Hill: He's on that team, eh.

Corcoran: Really on it too.

Hill: Tell me, how did he get such a hold on him.

Corcoran: Oh, just relationships. . . . Guess he was nice.

Hill: Well, he furnished the toddy's in the afternoon, didn't he?

Corcoran: Yeah . . . well Les is the unofficial secretary.

Hill: That's just what he is exactly.

Corcoran: That's right.

Hill: Well, is that just 'Auld Lang Syne' or not, must be something more than that.

Corcoran: No, it's personal friendship, it's trust, confidence.

Hill: Trust, Confidence; Truman's really got confidence in him.

Corcoran: That's right. . . . Well, I think you ought to get these fellows together this week.

Hill: Let me ask you this question, Tommy; Is there anybody . . . in the Senate that's really got an influence on that fellow [Truman]?

Corcoran: Oh yes, [Carl] Hatch has, a great deal.

Hill: You really think Carl Hatch has? More than the man they got in there now?

Corcoran: Some.

Hill: [Alben] Barkley got any?

Corcoran: No, because his people said some awful nasty things about Truman at the convention, that bright son-in-law of his. . . .

Hill: And Truman knew that because he's been told it a thousand times, and is reminded of it every day. . . . That's an unfortunate thing. You can't imagine what a hell of a job [Senate Majority Leader] that Alben Barkley has. The old President didn't given him his confidence, and now this fellow doesn't give him his confidence. It's a hell of a commentary, god-damn if it ain't. Well, sometimes I don't know.

Corcoran: Well, if you want to put this crowd together, you can have my house this week.

Hill: Well, who do you suggest, Tommy?

Corcoran: Well, there's you, Hugo [Black], and Claude [Pepper], and maybe Josh [Lee]. I guess [Theodore] Green is too uninterested, isn't he?

Hill: You know, he's a wonderful fellow, but a peculiar fellow. . . . Who else do you suggest?

Corcoran: I don't know. The very fact that it is so hard to name them shows you how difficult it is, shows to what low estate we have fallen. . . . Let me get in touch with you tomorrow. . . . Barkley is another one.

Hill: Of course he is.

Corcoran: And Bob LaFollette I think. . . .

Hill: . . . Well, Tom, make up that list see, and then do this, make up your mind what the program ought to be.

Corcoran: Yes. . . .

■ **Strictly Confidential Memo, FBI Director J. Edgar Hoover, November 15, 1945**

Last evening, the Attorney General [Tom Clark] called me to his office and stated that he had just . . . talked with the President concerning the activities of Thomas G. Corcoran. He stated the President was particularly concerned about the activities of Corcoran and his associates and was desirous of a very thorough investigation being made so that steps might be taken, if possible, to see that such activities did not interfere with the proper administration of the government.

The Attorney General stated that, therefore, he wanted me to look into these activities and see what, if any, of them might constitute a violation of law. He authorized the placing of a technical surveillance [wiretap] upon Corcoran and authorized the investigation of any leads developing therefrom that might tend to establish facts concerning the activities of this individual and any of those persons associated with him in connection with the operations of government.

[Attorney General Clark was unaware that the FBI had been wiretapping Corcoran since June 8, 1945, at the request of the president and with the understanding that "nothing was said in any way, shape or form as to the consequences should this (wiretap) ever become known. . . . If it should ever become known it would be our (the FBI's) baby and that (White House aide Harry Vaughan) would deny any knowledge."

From the original Corcoran tap, the president had learned of Corcoran's extensive contacts in the executive branch, the Democratic National Committee, and the Congress, and his use of these contacts to advance his own business interests. Accordingly, the president decided to shift responsibility for this tap to the attorney general with the further purpose of containing Corcoran's business activities. Seemingly unrecognized was the Supreme Court's ruling on wiretapping: any information obtained through a wiretap on Corcoran could not be used to prosecute him, and if it produced information which led to a legal investigation, the case would be ordered dismissed.]

■ **Do Not File Memo, FBI Assistant Director Gordon Nease to FBI Director, September 25, 1946**

I called on [White House aide Harry] Vaughn [sic, Vaughan] this morning in connection with the C.O. [Thomas Corcoran wiretap] summary in which the conversation of [Anthony] Panuch of the State Department is set forth. He was very appreciative of this information and again went into quite a tirade against Corcoran and his activities. He stated he thought he might suggest to [Treasury Secretary] John Snyder that he conduct a very complete investigation concerning Corcoran's income tax return since he (Vaughn) feels that undoubtedly Corcoran did not declare his full income. . . .

General Vaughn apparently furnishes information simply as a matter of interest to you. He stated that in connection with the assignment of these two [FBI] Agents to War Assets Administration the President was particularly eager that they remain there for the time being since the mere fact that two FBI Agents were assigned in their capacity gave prestige to the organization and built up more confidence in the eyes of the public. He stated further that besides being President of the United States, President Truman is a member of the Democratic Party and that if anything should blow up in the War Assets Administration now it might not only affect the elections six months [sic, weeks] from now but also in 1948, and that very naturally he wished to do all in his power to prevent anything from cropping up within the War Assets Administration which, to say the least, is a headache. . . . This gave me opportunity to explain to Vaughn the fact that we were in need of the services of these men but that, of course, you desire to comply entirely with the President's wishes in the matter. I pointed out to him that our appropriations had been reduced; that work and delinquency was piling up; and that we were badly in need of our top personnel at this time for which reason you had been extremely eager to get these men back. . . . He remarked that the President was very appreciative of your cooperation in the matter and that he was sure that these men would be released as soon as the President felt they were no longer necessary in their present capacity. . . .

I think Vaughn's conversation this morning gave me an excellent opportunity to present to him some of the problems the Bureau is facing in connection with the reduced appropriations and reduced personnel, et cetera.

■ **Memo, FBI Assistant Director D. Milton Ladd to FBI Director, April 14, 1948, FBI 62-63007-31**
Harry Vaughan, Military Aide to the President inquired . . . if the Bureau could reinstitute its technical coverage on Thomas Corcoran. Vaughan stated that Corcoran was again becoming very active and has caused considerable embarrassment to the White House, and further that he had been attempting through associates to influence Presidential appointments. . . .

He further stated that . . . if it could be done without too much expense and trouble, he would like to have the coverage put into effect immediately. . . .

■ **Office of the FBI Director Memo, Helen Gandy [Administrative Assistant to FBI Director], April 22, 1948, FBI 62-63007-30**

I contacted Harry Vaughan today and advised him that we would reinstitute the technical on Corcoran. He emphasized the fact that he did not want it done if it was going to involve any expense or difficulty. I assured him that you were very happy to assist them in this regard and at the same time tactfully emphasized that absolute confidence and secrecy in connection with the matter was desired. Vaughan indicated he was appreciative of your consideration in this regard and stated that if it was not productive it should be discontinued within a month.

[The FBI installed the requested wiretap on Corcoran on April 28, 1948, on the phones of his unlisted residence and the seven extensions of his office. These wiretaps were discontinued on May 21, 1948, at Vaughan's request.]

■ **Transcript and Summary, Robert Berger to Thomas Corcoran, May 5, 1948, 10:40 PM**

Bob asked what Tom observed of the political front and Tom said he didn't know as he's only been [in Washington, D.C.] 24 hours. Bob said, "Lots of things are happening and lots of things for our old friend, W.O.D. (William O. Douglas) [a reference to a movement to draft Douglas for the Democratic vice-presidential nomination] and I'd like to stop in and see you about it." Tom said . . . "I don't want to get involved in that—I don't—no, I want to keep out of it—I ain't in politics this year."

Berger: Well, the Democrats are having a lot of fun.

Corcoran: Yeah. I feel sorry for them. It's always a pity to see a great Empire break up. . . . I understand [Truman aide] George Allen is gonna take Gael Sullivan's place [as treasurer of the Democratic National Committee].

Berger: Well, that's what I hear and I don't know; the claim is no. I don't know. He'd be a good hand shaker and what have you; they've got me in the fire there again as to possible usage, whatever they do or don't I don't know, but they asked for a profile on me that they didn't have. . . .

■ **Do Not File Memo, FBI Assistant Director D. Milton Ladd to FBI Director, May 10, 1948**

The following conversation has been omitted from the finished summary [submitted by the FBI to the Truman White House] for May 8, 1948: 1:00 PM (Alliston) Cragg to Tom Corcoran. The [omitted] conversation is as follows:

. . . Cragg: Why, Tom, I got to thinking about the order of your calls tomorrow; that is, (William O.?) Douglas, Gael (Sullivan)—

Corcoran: Now wait a minute. Whew! Watch this telephone; it's—it's loaded! . . . This is a tapped phone; there's a record on this phone. . . . I'll call you over some other phone later in the afternoon, huh?

Cragg: Uh—

Corcoran: Where can I call you?

Cragg: Righto. I'll be at the hotel all afternoon.

Corcoran: All right. . . .

[The decision of FBI officials to withhold this conversation in which Corcoran acknowledged that his phone was tapped was motivated by their desire to continue this tap. They feared that had the White House been advised of Corcoran's suspicions, the tap would have been terminated. A wiser Cragg, conversing later with Corcoran over the phone, was careful in what he said about the attempt of liberal Democrats to draft Douglas for the vice presidency. Alerted to this effort through the Corcoran tap, Truman recognized the political advantages of the move. In the week before the convention, he telephoned Douglas and offered him the vice presidency. Douglas asked for time to consider the offer, then declined, saying he did not believe the Supreme Court should be a stepping stone to political office.

In a memorandum he wrote about these developments, Truman revealed the extent to which information from the Corcoran tap influenced his decisions. Douglas, he wrote, "belongs to that crowd of Tommy Corcoran, Harold Ickes, Claude Pepper crackpots whose word is worth less than Jimmy Roosevelt's. I hope he has a more honorable political outlook. No professional liberal is intellectually honest. That's a real indictment—but true as the Ten Commandments. Professional liberals aren't familiar with the Ten Commandments or the Sermon on the Mount."]

LOCKED IN A *close primary contest with Minnesota Governor*
Harold Stassen for the Republican presidential nomination in
1948, New York Governor Thomas E. Dewey faced a crucial
primary in Oregon. He was scheduled to debate Stassen on a
national radio program on the question whether to enact
legislation to outlaw the Communist party. Dewey turned to
FBI Director Hoover for assistance.

Aware that Dewey might dismiss him as FBI director if he
won the presidency, Hoover willingly complied, hoping
thereby to curry favor and undercut Dewey's suspected
antipathy toward him. Then, after Dewey's nomination as the
Republican standard bearer, Hoover ordered FBI agents to
prepare position papers criticizing the Truman administration's
internal security procedures (these were later issued as
Republican campaign literature) as well as providing
derogatory information about the president (focusing on Truman's
earlier relationship with Kansas City "boss" Thomas
Pendergast).

■ **Memo, FBI Director J. Edgar Hoover to FBI Assistant Directors**
  Clyde Tolson and Louis Nichols, April 27, 1948, 11:56 A.M.
Governor Dewey called me this morning and stated that he was terribly
concerned about Harold Stassen's movement to outlaw the Communist
Party. . . . Governor Dewey stated he was going out to Oregon and had
been thinking that he would rather be defeated and be right and therefore
he had decided to go all out for killing this movement of Stassen's. He is
thinking of making a series of speeches and wanted my views on outlawing
the Communist party. He wondered if there was a possibility that the
Supreme Court would declare it [proposed legislation to outlaw the
Communist party] unconstitutional and I told him that with the complexion
of the Supreme Court being as it is now there was every possibility. I
commented that if this were done we would be making martyrs of them all.
Governor Dewey then asked me what I thought about requiring them
[Communist members] to register and I told him I thought it had definite
possibilities, however, I felt the people really needed a will to enforce the
laws rather than new laws. He wanted to know under what laws some of
the aliens were being deported and I told him this came under the regular
Immigration and Naturalization laws. I told him that by requiring these

people to register there should also be a tightening up on the laws and there should be imposed in that law certain additional penalties which I thought the House was considering at the present time. I commented that I thought this was just brought out in the last few days. I told Governor Dewey that I would have an analysis of this Bill [Mundt-Nixon] made for him and would send it to him right away at Albany, by airmail. I also advised him that I would send him a copy of my speech given before the Committee on Un-American Activities of the House of Representatives and a copy of my article appearing in Newsweek.

With regard to outlawing the Communist Party I advised Governor Dewey that Canada had done this very thing and the Communist Party there immediately changed its name and started operating under another name. . . . I told him that I was not so afraid that they would go underground as we had excellent contacts but that I was looking at it from the over-all picture and felt it would be most impractical to outlaw it. Governor Dewey asked me whether I had ever made the statement that I was afraid of having it outlawed because of the investigative point of view and I told him I had never made such a statement . . . [and] just as soon as you outlaw these people they start great gatherings for collection of funds, supposedly for the defense of those members of their party who needed it but that this money was not always used for that purpose.

I also told Governor Dewey very confidentially that I saw in the paper this morning that Senator [Homer] Ferguson last night . . . made a statement that he thought there should be a test case made as to the legality of the Communist Party. I advised Dewey that there was contemplation [by the Justice Department] of bringing to the Grand Jury the problem of the legality of the Communist Party and bringing it under the Smith Act which provides for the prosecution of members of an organization advocating the overthrow of the Government by force and violence. [That month the Justice Department sought the indictment of the twelve leaders of the U.S. Communist party under the Smith Act, and sealed indictments were handed down on June 22. They were not unsealed until after the Democratic National Convention.] I explained that this is an enforcement of our current laws and that I thought it would be a far sounder approach than outlawing the Party.

Governor Dewey commented that he had heard there were about 3,000 Communists in this country representing Russia. I told him that we had had various figures but I thought it would be a little lower, perhaps 2,000. However, I stated that the menace of a subversive movement could never be judged by its number but by its intensity and fanaticism and in addition to these Communists there were all the fellow travellers. . . . I told him the fact that there were such a small group was misleading as they had groups dedicated to boring from within by getting into important positions and carrying on propaganda. I advised him that it was most important that we have a strong intelligence service but that there cannot be a so-called division between domestic and foreign intelligence because Communism is international.

Governor Dewey stated that he was leaving for Oregon very shortly and therefore would like to have the material as soon as possible. I told him I would see that it was flown to him so he would get it tomorrow morning. In addition to the other material I stated I would send I also told him I would include material on the [name withheld] matter. I told him I would underscore the pertinent portions of my two speeches. [FBI assistant director Louis] Nichols has already been advised to handle this matter.

■ **Confidential Memo, FBI Director J. Edgar Hoover to FBI Assistant Directors Clyde Tolson and Louis Nichols, April 27, 1948, 2:45 P.M.**

I called Governor Dewey . . . and advised him I was sending Mr. Louis B. Nichols, an Assistant Director, to see him. He was advised the material was all ready and Mr. Nichols would be there any time tomorrow morning convenient for him. Governor Dewey said he would be very glad to see Mr. Nichols at 10:00 tomorrow morning. . . . I commented that if he had any questions to ask Mr. Nichols would be most happy to answer them or to help him in any way. Governor Dewey was very pleased with this and stated that he would have a draft of his speech by that time and would be glad to have Mr. Nichols go over it. . . .

HOOVER PROVIDED A variety of personal services to Lyndon Johnson dating from his tenure as senator and continuing into his vice presidency and presidency. In this case Hoover's usefulness proved crucial to his continued tenure as FBI director. Having reached the mandatory retirement age of seventy on January 1, 1965, Hoover was able to continue in his job only because on May 8, 1964, Johnson issued an executive order waiving the mandatory retirement requirement. The recipient of Hoover's willing assistance—including the dispatching of a

*special FBI squad to monitor political developments at the
1964 Democratic National Convention and provide advance
intelligence—Johnson had come to appreciate the value of
having Hoover as FBI director.*

■ **Memo, FBI Assistant Director Gordon Nease to FBI Associate
Director Clyde Tolson, April 4, 1958**

At 10:50 a.m. today, George Reedy, Secretary of the Senate Democratic Policy Committee . . . [reported that] Senator Lyndon B. Johnson
has been attacked in a Mimeographed, undated letter being widely circulated in Texas. . . . The Mimeograph sheet, in effect, charges Senator
Johnson with the delay in our missile program . . . [and that this] fact
should be remembered when the Senator runs for re-election again [in
1960].

Reedy said the Senator wanted a copy of the letter . . . brought to the
FBI's attention as a possible violation of Federal law. . . .

Reedy also asked whether we might have anything in FBI files on [name
withheld author of this letter]. We told [Reedy] we would be of whatever
help we could. Reedy's secretary, . . . brought the attached letter to my
office this morning at which time she was told we had no identifiable
references on [name withheld author]. She was told that with respect to the
letter itself we would get in touch with [Reedy] per his request, upon his
return to the office, Tuesday, April 8, 1958.

OBSERVATION: Senator Johnson's term expires in 1961, and there may
be a question as to whether he is an avowed candidate at this time. Also
there is some question whether the signing of a fictitious name on the
material described would constitute a violation.

RECOMMENDATIONS:

(1) That this memorandum and attachment be referred to the Investigative Division so that the matter may be referred to the [Justice] Department
on Monday, 4-7-58 for an opinion. [This was done by letter to Assistant
Attorney General White on April 7, 1958.]

(2) That Mr. Reedy be advised by my office that we have referred the
[name withheld] letter to the Civil Rights Division of the Department of
Justice to determine whether a violation within our jurisdiction exists.
Reedy will also be told we have no identifiable information on [name
withheld].

(3) That upon receipt of a determination respecting this matter by the
Department, Reedy be so advised by my office.

[Hoover's handwritten notation: "Yes."]

■ **Memo, FBI Director J. Edgar Hoover to FBI Assistant Directors Clyde Tolson, Alan Belmont, John Mohr, Alex Rosen, Courtney Evans, and Cartha DeLoach, June 13, 1962**

While talking to Vice President Lyndon Johnson, he mentioned that he gets about ten or twelve rumors a day and finds out they all tie in with the Governor's race in Texas, and he mentioned specifically one that CBS had a girl doing research for a reporter, Roger Mudd (phonetic) of CBS, and this girl had . . . a tape which purported to be an interview between a newspaper man and [Billie Sol] Estes' partner in which Estes' partner said Mrs. Lyndon Johnson lent $5,000,000 to Estes, and a lot of stories. The Vice President . . . complained to CBS for circulating this and not giving them a chance to answer. The Vice President stated that Frank Stanton of CBS . . . sent the girl back and this employee of Estes' said he had never been interviewed, had never heard of it and he had access to Estes' books and it was not true, so they went back to the weekly editor who played the tape for them.

The Vice President wondered if the Bureau could talk to the editor of the weekly newspaper in Pecos, Texas . . . that there are two people connected with the operation of the paper, one is named [name withheld] and the Vice President forgets the name of the other, but those two men are reputed to run the paper which Dr. Dunn owns, but the people with that paper have played this tape to the girl representing CBS. I stated I would get started on it right away.

The Vice President stated he did not know what to do on these things except to call [FBI assistant director Cartha] DeLoach, and I told him that was the thing to do, so the Vice President . . . would have his assistant, Walter Jenkins, get in touch with Mr. DeLoach in such instances.

■ **Memo, FBI Assistant Director Cartha DeLoach to FBI Assistant Director John Mohr, June 22, 1962**

Walter Jenkins, Executive Assistant to the Vice President, called me . . . [and] stated that the Vice President was extremely disturbed over an editorial which had appeared in the July, 1962, issue of "Farm and Ranch Magazine" . . . [and] asked that I get in touch with George Reedy in the Vice President's office who would arrange to send the editorial to us immediately.

Upon talking with Reedy the Vice President interrupted him and stated he wanted to talk with me. The Vice President told me he was very angry at the false allegations made in this editorial and would deeply appreciate the Director having FBI Agents interview the editor of this magazine, Mr. Tom Anderson, to ascertain if Anderson had any basis for making such false allegations. I told the Vice President I knew the Director would want this done immediately. He expressed appreciation.

The Vice President called me back . . . to state that one of the allegations in the editorial reflected that he met . . . [Billie Sol] Estes, on April 28, 1962, at the Midland, Texas, Airport after having arrived there in a Government plane. The Vice President stated that . . . the records of Secret Service reflected that on April 28, 1962, he had lunch with the President and [British] Prime Minister [Harold] McMillan [sic, Macmillan] at the White House. Following the lunch, he returned to his office and . . . that evening he accompanied the President to the British Embassy for a reception. On April 29, 1962, and the following day, he was in Washington in his office. The Vice President . . . had never been to the Midland, Texas, Airport.

The Vice President . . . could clearly state for the record that neither he nor any member of his family, or any of his relatives as far as that was concerned, had ever had any connection whatsoever with Billie Sol Estes; however, the scurrilous allegations kept cropping up. The Vice President indicated apparently the editor of "Farm and Ranch Magazine" had sent this editorial, [approximately one line withheld on grounds of personal privacy and sources and methods of the FBI] to Anderson Clayton, who has a worldwide [commodities] concern and who might be passing out these scurrilous allegations without any basis in fact.

The Vice President reiterated that he would appreciate the above-named editor of "Farm and Ranch Magazine" being interviewed for information which he might possess concerning allegations that the Vice President or Mrs. Johnson had any connection with Estes and dissemination that might have been made by this editor through Anderson Clayton or others in connection with these scurrilous allegations. . . .

ACTION:

It is suggested that this memorandum be forwarded to the General Investigative Division for appropriate action. Upon receipt of the information, I will advise the Vice President's office of the results of the interviews.

[Hoover's handwritten notation: "OK." Unidentified FBI official's handwritten notation: "Tel[ephone] to Memphis 6/22/62." DeLoach's handwritten notation of 6/22 (withheld on personal privacy grounds).]

■ **Memo, FBI Director J. Edgar Hoover to FBI Assistant Directors Tolson, Belmont, Mohr, Conrad, DeLoach, Evans, Rosen, and Sullivan, November 29, 1963**

. . . The President [Lyndon Johnson] asked if I have a bulletproof car and I told him I most certainly have. . . . I stated I think the President ought to have a bulletproof car; . . . that all assassinations have been with guns; and for that reason I think very definitely the President ought to always ride in a bulletproof car; that it certainly would prevent anything like this [the Kennedy assassination] ever happening again; but that I do not mean a sniper could not snipe him from a window if he were exposed.

The President asked if I meant on his ranch he should be in a bulletproof car. I said I would think so; that the little car we rode around in when I was at the ranch should be bulletproofed; that it ought to be done very quietly. . . .

The President then asked if I think all the entrances should be guarded. I replied by all means, that he had almost to be in the capacity of a so-called prisoner because without that security anything could be done. I told him lots of phone calls had been received over the last four or five days about threats to his life. . . .

The President then stated he is going to take every precaution he can; that he wants to talk to me; and asked if I would put down my thoughts. He stated I was more than head of the FBI—I was his brother and personal friend; that he knew I did not want anything to happen to his family; that he has more confidence in me than anybody in town; that he would not embroil me in a jurisdictional dispute; but that he did want my thoughts on the [appointment of the membership of the Warren Commission to investigate the assassination of President Kennedy and on the results of the FBI's investigation] to advocate as his own opinion.

I stated I would be glad to do this for him and that I would do anything I can. The President expressed his appreciation.

■ **Personal and Confidential Letter, FBI Director J. Edgar Hoover to SAC San Antonio J. Myers Cole, December 26, 1963**

I wanted to . . . advise you that in conversation with the President he anticipated that he may from time to time use the facilities of our Austin Resident Agency Office when he visits the LBJ Ranch near Johnson City. I know steps have already been taken to acquire space and furniture should the President desire to use any of our facilities at Austin.

I want you to make sure that our personnel at Austin are properly qualified in personality and ability so that any contacts the President may have with them will result in a favorable reaction. The President holds the FBI in very high esteem and I do not want him to gain any different impression through any contact with our personnel throughout the country. . . .

Therefore, it is imperative that you see that our facilities are at all times in proper condition and, should the President see fit to use them or call upon our Austin Office for any services, that they are immediately made available.

■ **Informal Memo, FBI Assistant Director Cartha DeLoach to FBI Director Hoover, January 20, 1964**

[White House aide] Walter Jenkins called me . . . [and] referred to the [congressional] testimony of Don Reynolds of the Don Reynolds Associates, Inc., organization. This is the insurance company which holds the $200,000 policy on President Johnson. . . . [Former Johnson aide and Senate secretary] Bobby Baker arranged for Reynolds to contact Jenkins and handle the insurance. Following the establishment of the $200,000 insurance policy, Reynolds was supposedly contacted by a representative of the LBJ Enterprises, Inc., and told that he should arrange for advertising through Lady Bird Johnson's radio stations in Texas. Reynolds did this. Jenkins said . . . this was a perfectly legitimate deal and that Lady Bird Johnson's representatives were contacting quite a number of people in connection with soliciting advertising for the radio stations. . . .

Reynolds has also testified that Jenkins personally contacted one A. G. Young in 1957. Young is the head of the Mid-Atlantic Steel Corporation which manufactures pots and pans and sells them throughout the United States. . . . Jenkins denied that he has ever contacted Mr. Young. . . .

Jenkins . . . would appreciate very much the FBI interviewing Young to ascertain what knowledge he has of the Bobby Baker case [recently indicted for tax evasion and fraud for income received through his influence peddling] and, specifically, asking him whether or not he was contacted by Jenkins in 1957 or any other time relative to procuring advertising or doing favors for Baker or any one else.

Jenkins is probably correct in his assumption that he never contacted Mr. Young. I have always noted that he takes shorthand regarding any call he receives or any personal contact that is made with him. He keeps meticulous records and, of course, has had considerable experience in administration.

We, of course, have a legitimate reason for contacting Young in that his name has been bandied around by the Subcommittee in connection with the Bobby Baker case. We are conducting a full scale investigation concerning this case. We, therefore, have a right to contact people who might have information concerning this specific matter. On the other hand, the Republican members of the Subcommittee could claim that we are conducting an investigation to vindicate Jenkins and the President.

Bureau files reflect no connection of Mr. Young with the Bobby Baker case.

While Jenkins' request is somewhat irregular, it appears obvious that he has discussed this matter with the President and that the President is in accord with our making contact with Young. If you have no objections, we will have two experienced Agents interview Young [Hoover's handwritten insert: "Yes"], or I can handle it personally if you so desire in connection with asking him only if he has any information concerning possible violations committed by Baker but specifically if he recalls any contact made with him by Jenkins in 1957 or any other time.

HOOVER ALSO MOVED *quickly to exploit Lyndon Johnson's concerns about Robert Kennedy as a potential presidential rival. Both as vice president and president, Johnson had met with personal hostility from Kennedy loyalists on the White House staff and in the Democratic National Committee. As president he suspected the loyalty of Kennedy holdovers and their relationship with Robert Kennedy who resigned as attorney general in the spring of 1964 to seek election as U.S. senator from New York.*

■ **Informal Memo, FBI Assistant Director Cartha DeLoach to FBI Director Hoover, January 15, 1964**
[White House aide] Walter Jenkins told me last night at the White House that he was seriously concerned about the continued employment of Paul Corbin at Democratic National Committee Headquarters. He indicated that the President had also expressed some concern about Corbin. Jenkins told me that Corbin was strictly Bobby Kennedy's boy and that Kennedy had been protecting him all along. He further indicated, as a matter of strict confidence, that the President was not yet quite ready to take on Bobby, however, Corbin would definitely be eased out in the near future when the time was ripe. . . .
[Hoover's handwritten notation: "Have we furnished Jenkins a memo on Corbin?" DeLoach's handwritten notation: "Yes 1/15/64—Director verbally advised 1/15."]
[Jenkins's interest in Corbin had been triggered by news stories that Corbin had been in New Hampshire earlier that month to promote a slate endorsing Robert Kennedy for the Democratic vice-presidential nomination. Corbin's appointment to the Democratic National Committee staff in 1961 had been engineered by Robert Kennedy, the attorney general and President Kennedy's campaign manager in the 1960 presidential campaign. Kennedy's endorsement of Corbin stemmed from the important role this

political operative had played in both the 1960 primaries and final election in developing support for his brother's candidacy.]

■ **Letter, Minneapolis SAC Richard Held to FBI Director J. Edgar Hoover, February 10, 1964**

United States Attorney Miles Lord of Minneapolis has always been a very good friend of the FBI, and an ardent admirer of you. Late Friday afternoon, February 7, 1964, he dropped in to see me, and . . . stated that during a recent trip to Washington, he had occasion to visit, both socially and officially, with a group of individuals in the Justice Department whom he described as the "Kennedy crowd." Lord stated that these individuals openly discussed how they were doing everything they could to stir up the "Bobby Baker mess" [the former Senate secretary and aide to Lyndon Johnson who was the subject of criminal inquiry because of his business activities], with the avowed purpose of trying to embarrass the President in every way possible. He added that certain individuals in the group had inferred that they hoped to create a situation whereby the President would be forced to pick the Attorney General, Robert Kennedy, as his running mate in order to assure his re-election.

He further stated that they were supposed to have remarked that prior to the assassination of President Kennedy, they had intended to use the Baker issue as a means of freezing Mr. Johnson out as Vice President.

At the first opportunity I pointed out to Lord that . . . I didn't see where I, or the FBI, entered into the picture. He stated that he fully realized that the activities of this group amounted to nothing more than "dirty politics," but that he had heard something else he felt I should know.

He claimed that this same group openly criticized you and the FBI, and indicated that they would like to break up the excellent relationship that exists between you and President Johnson. Lord was either reluctant, or not able, to elaborate on just what it was that these individuals were critical about. As to actual identities of the members of the group, all he would say was that it was "that wide-eyed bunch around the Attorney General." He did say that he had heard nothing that would directly connect the Attorney General with the reported plans of this group, but that inasmuch as they were all close to the Attorney General, he felt that they could possibly be repeating or expressing his views. . . .

Lord has been acquainted with Senator Hubert Humphrey for many years, both socially and politically, and is indebted to him for his present position. He is intensely loyal to the Senator, and actually one of his staunchest supporters so that it is entirely possible that he is merely repeating something that he picked up in the Senator's Office during his visit to Washington. Also, in view of Senator Humphrey's acknowledged interest himself in the possibility of becoming Vice President, it could be that this has slanted Lord's feelings and remarks. In either event, he did seem quite upset over what he claimed to have picked up.

At first I was prone to dismiss the entire matter from my mind as it just didn't seem possible that any group or faction could be in a position to do the things that Lord claimed. However, in view of the alleged remarks about you and the Bureau, I felt I should pass them on to you, as vague as they are.

[Hoover's handwritten notation: "I believe the President is alert to this."]

■ **Informal Memo, FBI Assistant Director Cartha DeLoach to FBI Director Hoover, March 6, 1964**
For the past two weeks Ed Guthman of the Department has attempted to arrange a luncheon date with me. . . .

Our conversation at lunch [today] proceeded casually until Guthman stated he had a serious question to ask. He . . . then asked if I knew the answer to why the relationship between the Department of Justice and the FBI, specifically the Attorney General's office and your office, had "cooled" considerably since November, 1963, following the assassination. I told Guthman that I had noted no difference, perhaps it was because the Attorney General had spent a great deal of time out of his office and therefore had not been in touch with us as much as usual. . . .

Guthman told me that a number of individuals close to the Attorney General felt that the President's body had not even become cold before you started circumventing the Attorney General and dealing directly with the President. He stated that these individuals felt that this was wrong and hurt the relationship between the Attorney General and you. I told Guthman that I had heard there was some "petty jealousy" on this subject; however, these individuals, whoever they may be, should realize the President for 19 years was an across-the-street neighbor of yours, had had you down to his ranch in Texas, and had been a close personal friend.

Guthman stated there was more to the basis for his question than merely friendship between you and the President. He advised that you and I had furnished either files or memoranda of a derogatory nature, concerning White House employees close to the Attorney General, to the President. Guthman indicated that his information was that we had voluntarily done this in order to get the Attorney General's "friends" removed from office. . . . He then advised that the United States Attorney from Minneapolis, Miles Lord, . . . allegedly had overheard several of the Attorney General's closest aides conspiring to embarrass President Johnson by "blowing up" the Bobby Baker case. Guthman continued that Lord also allegedly had overheard these same aides making derogatory remarks concerning you and the FBI. Guthman added that when Lord returned to Minneapolis he told either our SAC or an Agent of the Minneapolis Office of these alleged remarks. Guthman stated that you then prepared a letter to the President concerning this matter. Guthman summed up his remarks by stating that the "close aides" to the Attorney General apparently felt that there was a campaign on in the FBI to embarrass the Attorney General by "carrying tales" to the President. . . .

I told Guthman that if we had any desire to issue a "campaign" against the Attorney General or him, we would come to them direct. I told him also that quite naturally the FBI has good liaison with the White House and that any time the President asked for information from FBI files it is our responsibility to furnish such information. I further told Guthman that obviously petty jealousy and envy might rear its ugly head and bring on ill-advised gossip from small people; however, he should know that there was no "campaign" to destroy the Attorney General's image with the President.

I told Guthman I wanted him to know that to my knowledge you had never prepared a letter to the President concerning any incident involving the United States Attorney in Minneapolis. I asked Guthman where he learned such gossip. He replied that apparently the Attorney General had gotten this information from a source either at the White House or somewhere else. I asked Guthman if the President or one of his aides had personally brought this to the Department's attention. He replied that he didn't know this to be true but stated that the Attorney General had picked up this information from a rather substantial source. I asked Guthman if he would be willing to produce this "substantial source" so that we could question him about this rumor as well as any other rumors. Guthman stated he could not. I told him he had mentioned these allegations, therefore, he should be willing to prove them by putting up or shutting up. . . .

Obviously there has been a bad leak either in the White House or at FBI Headquarters. With your permission, I showed Jenkins, and he showed the President, the letter from the SAC in Minneapolis, quoting United States Attorney Miles Lord concerning the statements he had obviously heard while at the Department of Justice derogatory to President Johnson and you. Jenkins told me that the President was shocked over this matter. The second allegation specifically concerns the two memoranda we furnished the President regarding Paul Corbin and Carmine Bellino, after which both men were fired. These memoranda were specifically furnished at the direction of the President. Jenkins told me later on in confidence, as I reported to you in blind memoranda, that the Attorney General was extremely shaken by the dismissals of Corbin and Bellino. He obviously expected to use these men in the campaign for the Vice Presidency. He became so mad with the President that he walked out of the President's office. He also told Ken O'Donnell, who sided with the President, that he would never speak to him again.

I recommend that I inform Jenkins in strict confidence that these matters have been brought to our attention and that obviously there is a "leak" somewhere. You may desire to mention this to the President on Monday at the time of your luncheon with him.

■ **Informal Memo, FBI Assistant Director Cartha DeLoach to FBI Director Hoover, March 9, 1964**

Pursuant to your instructions, there are attached the cover memoranda and the yellows [carbon copies] of the summary memoranda we did for the White House on Pierre Salinger and Carmine Bellino. We apparently did not do cover memoranda for [other Kennedy holdovers] [William] Wieland, [Richard] Goodwin and Corbin. . . .

You may be interested in knowing that Jenkins told me late on Saturday night, 3-7-64, that he and the President had concluded that [White House aide Kenneth] O'Donnell was the "leak" of information from the White House. He stated that both he and the President were deeply hurt about this matter but that obviously O'Donnell had more loyalty to the Attorney General [Robert Kennedy] than he had to the President.

■ **Informal Memo, FBI Assistant Director Cartha DeLoach to FBI Assistant Director John Mohr, March 20, 1964**

. . . Last night, 3-19-64, at the conclusion of our conversation [Guthman] asked me if the FBI had received any further knowledge as to the manner in which the President became cognizant of comments by U.S. Attorney Miles Lord. . . .

Instead of answering Guthman's questions, I asked him what the source of his information had been. He told me he did not know the source. I told him if he had no better facts than this it seemed useless to carry on this matter any further. Guthman then told me that if allegations had been made against him he would certainly confirm or deny the allegations. I told Guthman that one doesn't make allegations without having some facts and it appeared that he had none at all. I told him when and if he did uncover a source we could discuss the matter further. . . .

[FBI assistant director Courtney] Evans, additionally, has been "needled" a couple of times by Deputy Attorney General Nicholas DeB. Katzenbach. This was on the occasion of chance meetings in the corridor of the Justice Building. Katzenbach's remarks as to possible disclosure to the White House of information indicating a possible dispute between the

Attorney General and the President were of a "fishing" nature and these were dismissed when Evans indicated no knowledge as to what he was talking about. . . .

It would appear that these probing contacts, both by Katzenbach and Guthman, must be predicated upon some inquiry from the Attorney General himself. Obviously neither Guthman, Katzenbach or the Attorney General Robert F. Kennedy desire to reveal Ken O'Donnell as their source of information at the White House. They know that to confirm our suspicion in this regard would mean that the President would have proof that O'Donnell has not been loyal to him; consequently, it is believed that this matter will not be carried to any great length in the future. . . .

[Hoover's handwritten notation: "1. If Guthman, Katzenbach or anyone else brings this up again they should be told I have instructed that if they seek any information to take it up with me as I am fed up on the malicious lies & calumnies they have circulated."]

■ **Informal Memo, FBI Assistant Director Cartha DeLoach to FBI Director, November 18, 1964, FBI 77-51387—Not Recorded**
. . . The President stated that he had previously talked with the Director about the fact that the Department of Justice was re-employing a number of individuals who had worked on the Bobby Kennedy [senatorial] campaign. The President asked how many of this number had been re-employed. I told him I knew of only a few; however, a discreet check would be made. He asked if there had been as many as three or as many as seven. I told him I did not know; however, I would advise him after a check had been made. He stated he would like to know as soon as possible. . . . He stated that the re-employment of these people could prove very embarrassing to the Administration and that after he gets the facts from the FBI he plans to raise hell with [Attorney General Nicholas] Katzenbach regarding this matter. . . .

(2) We should attempt to find out discreetly the names of the individuals being re-employed in the Department of Justice after these same individuals had worked in the political campaign in New York for Bobby Kennedy. I will pass this information to [White House aides William] Moyers or [Jack] Valenti verbally so that nothing will be written in this regard.

[Hoover's handwritten notation: "Yes."]

■ **Memo, FBI Assistant Director Cartha DeLoach to FBI Associate Director Clyde Tolson, January 17, 1967**
Request for name checks by President
[White House aide] Marvin Watson . . . referred to the Director's memo-

randum to the President setting forth the fact that the FBI, in the [Bobby] Baker case, had refused a request from the Department of Justice to utilize a recording device in Los Angeles. Watson stated that, inasmuch as Narcotics had later handled this matter for the Department of Justice, the President had demanded that Secretary [Henry] Fowler of Treasury give him a summary memorandum concerning this matter. Watson stated the President was quite exercised about the fact that the FBI had properly refused, only to have Treasury go ahead and honor the request of the Department.

Watson, while not handing me the memorandum to read, did point out several names in the rather lengthy memorandum that Secretary Fowler had sent the President. . . .

Watson told me that the President wanted a complete rundown on the listed names. He stated these checks should be made as discreetly as possible and that we should specifically point out whether any of these individuals were close to Bobby Kennedy. *The President does not want any record made of this request.** He wants the memoranda in question to be blind memoranda. He desires that they be as thorough as possible and wants this done on an expeditious basis. . . .

These memoranda will be prepared on an expeditious basis and submitted to the Director for consideration.

THE OUTBREAK OF racial unrest in American cities in the summer of 1964 deeply worried President Johnson, for they occurred during a presidential campaign against the conservative Republican candidate, Senator Barry Goldwater. Goldwater was both an ardent anticommunist and an opponent of civil rights legislation. Johnson thus feared that Goldwater might exploit the riots politically by charging a nation-wide subversive conspiracy. To neutralize this issue, the president turned to Hoover for assistance—not only to prepare a report but, given Hoover's anticommunist credentials, to rebut any conspiracy charges.

---

*Not only did DeLoach create this record of Watson's request, but FBI associate director Tolson directed Hoover's administrative assistant, Helen Gandy, on January 27, 1967, to "keep this in (Hoover's) Official Confidential files."—Ed.

■ **Do Not File Memo, FBI Assistant Director Alan Belmont to FBI Assistant Director William Sullivan, September 8, 1964**

At 2:20 p.m. today, the Director . . . talked to [former New York Republican governor] Tom Dewey in New York. The President has asked Mr. Dewey to make recommendations as to what can be done to stop the riots and violence throughout the country.

The Director conveyed to Mr. Dewey that we are having surveys made of each of the riots that have occurred and at Mr. Dewey's request the Director agreed to send him copies of these surveys. . . . Mr. Dewey wants a picture of each of the riots with the de facto causes, etc., and he would like this information broken down as to what is hearsay and what are actual facts. . . .

The Director said we should also send to Mr. Dewey a memorandum with any suggestions we have relative to the stopping of riots. . . .

Mr. Dewey indicated he would suggest that the President, in the next few days, come out with a statement that he deplores acts of violence that have occurred in various parts of the country by various groups and that while this is primarily a local problem, to be handled by local law enforcement agencies and local authorities; nevertheless, the Federal Government is studying the situation from the standpoint of possible legislation or suggestions that could be offered.

Mr. Dewey contemplates recommending that the President set up a committee of three men to come up with some recommendations for the next Congress. Mr. Dewey had in mind anti-Communist individuals, at least two of whom would be attorneys and who would have practical knowledge of the problems. Dewey strongly suggested that the Director be one of the committee and solicited suggestions as to the other two. . . . [He] suggested that at least one of the committee should be a sound liberal. . . . Director said to give him a list of these men, together with summaries on them which could be sent to Mr. Dewey. . . .

■ **Memo, FBI Director J. Edgar Hoover to FBI Assistant Directors Clyde Tolson, Alan Belmont, Alex Rosen, William Sullivan, and Cartha DeLoach, September 9, 1964, 5:25 P.M.**

President Lyndon B. Johnson called and stated that . . . at his press conference today, he had stated that he was going to ask for a complete compilation of FBI reports . . . in connection with these disturbances around the country that we make available to suitable police officers and mayors for information concerning the problems and that he was going to ask me to compile this for him and see if there is any consistent pattern and what action this might indicate is justified. He stated he was asked if this included legislation and he had stated that he would not exclude it but we would have to see what the reports showed. He stated he was further asked if the reports showed any members of the Communist Party were involved and he stated he did not want to discuss that. I told the President I thought this was a good statement and that this would be handled.

■ **Informal Memo, FBI Assistant Director Cartha DeLoach to FBI Director J. Edgar Hoover, September 9, 1964**
. . . [White House aide Walter] Jenkins told me that he had received the Director's memorandum regarding the Director's visit with former Governor Thomas E. Dewey and the Director's memorandum regarding possible solutions to the various riots that have taken place in a number of cities. Jenkins stated he had shown both of these memoranda to the President and that the President was very grateful for the excellent suggestions given therein.

The President told Jenkins that he would like to have us consider the possibilities of holding a conference of law enforcement officials, or civic officials, in Washington. At this conference the President would make an appearance following which the Director would speak to the group later followed by prominent individuals of the judiciary or law enforcement background. . . . The President wanted the FBI to "mastermind" the project although the FBI could be kept in the background. . . .

Jenkins mentioned in confidence that the President, of course, desires to issue a number of press releases which will convince the American public that the Johnson Administration is actually attempting to do something about the many riots going on. . . .

It is suggested that this matter be given consideration and that a memorandum be prepared outlining the possibilities of such a conference. . . . [Hoover's handwritten insert: "Yes. Do so at once." DeLoach's handwritten notation: "Done. Letter to Walter W. Jenkins at the White House 9/11/64."] As indicated above, the President is toying with many possibilities which will give him favorable publicity inasmuch as he considers the various riots to have lost him votes. Jenkins described the riots as the "Achilles' heel" of the Johnson Administration. . . .

■ **Memo, FBI Director J. Edgar Hoover to FBI Assistant Directors Clyde Tolson, Alan Belmont, Alex Rosen, William Sullivan, and Cartha DeLoach, September 16, 1964, 11:35 AM**
While talking to Honorable Walter W. Jenkins, Special Assistant to

the President, I [reported that former Governor Dewey] will probably have a draft soon; that he wanted some additional information which has been sent to him and he . . . [would] try to work it into a readable form in layman's language in case the President wants to release it as it is.

I told Mr. Jenkins that the Governor does not want to sign his name on it and has suggested it be a report from me to the President so if it is released, it would give no indication that Mr. Dewey had anything to do with it and I think Mr. Dewey had that understanding with the President. I stated the Governor wants to remain entirely anonymous because he said if it became known there would probably be allegations he is switching parties, which is not the case.

I continued that the Governor is then going to send the draft to me just as soon as he finishes, . . . and I will go over it and consult with the Governor so as to get his concurrence and then I will send it to him, Jenkins. . . . I stated we are trying to make a deadline of the end of this week or the first part of next week. . . .

■ Memo, FBI Assistant Director Cartha DeLoach to FBI Assistant Director John Mohr, September 25, 1964

I showed the Director's revised report on rioting to [White House aide] Billy Moyers. . . . I went over the report page by page with Moyers and showed him the corrections that had been made. . . .

While talking with Moyers, I told him that although the President had stated last night that he desired that the Director issue this report, it seemed to me that this point might be reconsidered inasmuch as the report was a submission to the President by the Director. I told Moyers also that the FBI, as a matter of policy, did not issue press releases inasmuch as this was a responsibility of the Department of Justice. Moyers stated he definitely understood the Director's viewpoints, however, that he had discussed this matter further with the President and the President definitely wanted the report to be issued under the Director's name.

I immediately returned to the Bureau and . . . discussed the matter telephonically with the Director.

Mr. Moyers was contacted at approximately 5:30 p.m. and told that inasmuch as the FBI did not issue press releases that he might desire to inform Acting Attorney General Katzenbach that the President desired that the FBI report be released as revised and that the FBI would turn over a sufficient number of copies of this report to the Department to be given to the press at 2:00 p.m. tomorrow, 9-26-64. Moyers stated he would handle this with Katzenbach immediately and would ask Katzenbach to call the Director in this regard.

[Hoover's handwritten insert: "I never received any call from Katzenbach."]

We will furnish the Office of Special Information in the Department a sufficient number of copies of the revised report so that they can give this report to the press in accordance with White House desires.

■ Memo, FBI Director J. Edgar Hoover to FBI Assistant Directors Clyde Tolson, Alan Belmont, Cartha DeLoach, and William Sullivan, June 4, 1965

This morning while I was at the White House discussing a number of matters with the President, he mentioned to me his great concern about leaks that had occurred and [cited] the attached article, "Russ Bombers Reported in Hanoi," which appeared in the Chicago Daily News of June 3rd and written by Peter Lisagor, the Washington Bureau Chief of the Chicago Daily News, was most disturbing. He said this information was known only to Secretaries [Dean] Rusk and [Robert] McNamara, Under Secretary of State [Thomas] Mann, and to the Joint Chiefs of Staff. He asked me whether we could very discreetly endeavor to find out how this information was leaked to the Chicago Daily News and from what source. There is considerable suspicion upon the part of Under Secretary of State Mann, as well as the President, that [name withheld] may be the one leaking such information which causes the Administration embarrassment.

I would like to have Mr. DeLoach most discreetly endeavor to ascertain through his confidential contacts the source of this particular article. It is most important that it be handled promptly, as the President is desirous of reaching a final conclusion for action to be taken in this matter.

■ Informal Memo, FBI Assistant Director Cartha DeLoach to FBI Assistant Director John Mohr, June 4, 1965

Pursuant to instructions, I have ascertained the following information regarding the article entitled "Russ Bombers Reported in Hanoi." . . .

The information was first obtained by Marguerite Higgins who was formerly employed by the New York Herald Tribune. Miss Higgins is widely known around Washington. Her reputation is spotty. The newspaper men refer to her as "mattress-back Maggie." . . .

Miss Higgins is very close to Peter Lisagor. They have been friends for a long period of time. My source [reporter Jeremiah O'Leary] feels that Miss Higgins obtained this information from her husband [retired Lieutenant General William E. Hall], who has high-ranking connections in the Air Force and among the Joint Chiefs of Staff. She then, instead of using it in one of her columns, gave it to her close friend, Lisagor, who used it in the category of a fast-breaking news story. . . .

■ **Informal Memo, FBI Assistant Director Cartha DeLoach to FBI
Associate Director Clyde Tolson, June 17, 1965**

The Director instructed that I keep in mind the fact that the [Washington] "Evening Star" has published a number of articles and cartoons which could be considered critical of the President. The President is well aware of this fact and at a recent meeting with the Director questioned what might be behind such criticism.

I have discussed this matter on a very discreet basis with at least five officials of the "Evening Star," including the editor, Newbold Noyes. None of these sources, of course, were advised why I was interested in such a matter.

[Reporter Jeremiah O'Leary] has made a careful tally of the articles both pro and con concerning the President and the Administration. He finds that the favorable articles far outweigh the critical ones. He admits, however, that the "Bobby Baker case" brought on a considerable number of articles which critically mentioned the President and Walter Jenkins. O'Leary and Noyes both point out that the "Evening Star" has always been a slightly right of center newspaper in editorial policy. It has always been strongly Republican in political philosophy. In the early days of the 1964 campaign Noyes met with Governor Scranton of Pennsylvania and pledged support to Governor Scranton in the race for the Presidential nomination in the Republican Party. When Barry Goldwater won this nomination, the "Evening Star" decided to "faintly" support President Johnson.

Old-timers at the "Star" feel that President Johnson's similarity to former President Franklin Roosevelt, in his humanitarian thinking, has brought on some bitterness. The "Star" is basically against big government and give-away type programs of big government.

In summary, there appears to be no one individual or individuals who have given instructions that the "Star" must be critical of the President and the current Administration. The "Star" . . . does not hesitate to take a slap at the President if the situation presents itself. . . .

It might be desirable to suggest to the President that he talk to Newbold Noyes occasionally in an effort to build up friendship in that direction. Noyes is not the smartest person in the world and can be led around by the nose if the President pays the slightest bit of attention to him. The Director may recall that the President also recently indicated that he had learned that Bobby Kennedy had bought considerable stock in the "Star." We found through careful checking that this just was not correct.

■ **Memo, FBI Director J. Edgar Hoover for Official Confidential Files, February 25, 1966**

Assistant to the Director DeLoach . . . stated that Honorable Marvin Watson said that the President feels [Peter] Lisagor is tearing him apart and getting information from someplace and thought we ought to put a surveillance on him to find out what he is doing and where he is getting his information. Mr. DeLoach told him we could not do that; if it were found out it would bring considerable discredit not only on the FBI, but the President himself. The White House understands this and Mr. DeLoach indicated that it was felt that Lisagor is tearing the President apart and even though we sent over a name check on Lisagor and that was what was asked for, it is not what they want as they want something substantive.

Mr. DeLoach stated we have given them everything we have and he thought what we ought to do is to stand pat for a few days and not make any positive emphasis on investigating Lisagor. I told Mr. DeLoach that I thought this was the thing to do and to just indicate we have various lines out to get a line on Lisagor and let it hang on that point.

■ **Informal Memo, FBI Assistant Director Cartha DeLoach to FBI Associate Director Clyde Tolson, March 1, 1966**

Marvin Watson . . . [referred] to two previous communications sent to the White House over the Director's signature. These communications concerned a request for information from Watson regarding Senator Stephen Young (D.—Ohio) and Senator William Fulbright (D.—Arkansas), Chairman of the Senate Foreign Relations Committee.

Watson stated that he and the President wanted to make certain that the FBI understood that when requests were made by the President, Watson, or Mrs. Mildred Stegall, concerning matters of extreme secrecy, the FBI should not respond in writing by formal memorandum. Watson stated that what the President actually wanted was a blind-type memorandum which bore no government watermarks or no letterhead signifying the source of the memorandum.

I told Watson that I felt certain the Director would honor this request, however, I wondered if he had fully thought out all the ramifications of this matter. . . . I told him there would be instances in which both the White House and the FBI would necessarily want to point to the record regarding certain matters. . . . I told Watson that I felt certain Mrs. Stegall and the White House could be trusted to keep letterhead-type memoranda in a secure place, and that no one else at the White House would see such material. I mentioned that the Director long ago had given me specific instructions to keep all matters pertaining to the President in a certain file which is not available to all [FBI] personnel.

Watson stated he readily recognized the merits of my argument; however, the President had ruled otherwise and he did not want to bring the matter up with the President again. . . .

In order to handle this matter in accordance with the President's and Watson's instructions, I recommend that in the future, in those cases involving extremely confidential matters, we prepare the usual formal cover letter, over the Director's signature, but attach a blind memorandum which will contain the pertinent subject matter. The letter over the Director's signature will not reveal the specific subject matter, but will merely indicate that a memorandum is attached. We will, of course, in our records here at the seat of government indicate on the yellow [carbon copy] of the Director's letter the subject matter in the blind memorandum. This will give us a record for future reference purposes.

The above procedure will be carried out if the Director approves.

[Hoover's handwritten notation: "O.K."]

■ **Memo, FBI to Senate Select Committee on Intelligence Activities, January 31, 1975, Hearings, Vol. 6, p. 720**

. . . On February 19, 1966, Marvin Watson called from the White House advising the President wanted the FBI to cover Senate Foreign Relations Committee television presentation with a view toward determining whether Senator Fulbright and the other Senators were receiving information from Communists. . . .

By letter dated February 24, 1966, Marvin Watson was advised "In response to your request . . . is enclosed a memorandum which sets out the Communist Party line concerning some of the issues raised during the Senate Foreign Relations Committee hearings on U.S. policy on Vietnam."

In this memorandum . . . parallels are drawn between the television presentation and documented Communist Party publications or statements of Communist leaders.

■ **Informal Memo, FBI Assistant Director Cartha DeLoach to FBI Associate Director Clyde Tolson, March 7, 1966**

Pursuant to instructions, I saw [Minority Leader] Senator [Everett] Dirksen . . . [who] was advised that it would be appreciated if our entire conversation could be maintained in strict confidence. He agreed to this.

I told Senator Dirksen that I was seeing him at the specific request of the President to the FBI. [Four lines withheld on national security grounds.]

Senator Dirksen was advised that [four paragraphs withheld on national security grounds, but refers to information concerning Senators J. William Fulbright and Wayne Morse]. . . .

Senator Dirksen mentioned that he was not aware of all the entanglements involving Senators Fulbright and Morse; however, he felt that both men were deeply involved and very much obligated to communist interests. He stated the information he had been furnished by me, if known to the American public, could obviously ruin Senator Morse. . . .

Senator Dirksen mentioned that Senator Fulbright had now initiated hearings concerning Red China. He stated that obviously Fulbright had been instructed to do this by certain contacts.

Senator Dirksen asked if the information furnished above would be given to any other senators. I told him that [Republican] Senator [Bourke] Hickenlooper was to be advised [and was on March 8]; however, this was the only additional person who would receive this information. . . .

If the Director has no objections, I will advise Marvin Watson verbally of the above facts.

[Hoover's handwritten notation: "O.K. but after doing so prepare memo of action taken."]

CONCERNED THAT CIVIL *rights activists might provoke demonstrations and force the seating of the Mississippi Freedom Democratic party at the 1964 Democratic convention, President Johnson sought to limit the potential damage to his candidacy in the Deep South states. He went to Hoover who responded by dispatching a thirty-man squad, headed by FBI assistant director Cartha DeLoach, to Atlantic City. The FBI provided the president with intelligence about the plans and activities of the civil rights community and their supporters at the convention.*

■ **Memo, FBI Assistant Director Cartha DeLoach to FBI Assistant Director John Mohr, August 29, 1964, Senate Select Committee on Intelligence Activities Hearings, Vol. 6, pp. 495-502**

In connection with the assignment of the special [FBI] squad to [the Democratic National Convention in] Atlantic City, New Jersey, 8/22-23/64 at the direction of the President, I wish to report the successful completion of this assignment. By means of informant coverage, by use of various confidential techniques [wiretaps and bugs], by infiltration of key groups through use of undercover agents, and through utilization of agents using appropriate cover as reporters, we were able to keep the White House fully apprised of all major developments during the Convention's course.

For example, through informant coverage and by controlling the situation, we were able to prevent a potentially explosive stall-in and sit-in demonstration planned by [two civil rights organizations]. By counseling [White House aides] Jenkins, Carter, and Moyers, we convinced them that they must make major changes in controlling admissions into the Convention Hall and thereby preclude infiltration of the illegal Mississippi Freedom Democratic Party (MFDP) delegates. Through our counterintelligence efforts, Jenkins, et al., were able to advise the President in advance regarding major plans of the MFDP delegates. The White House considered this of prime importance.

Through our highly confidential coverage [wiretaps] of Martin Luther King [and name withheld] together with similar coverage we established on the headquarters of CORE-SNCC, we were in a position to advise the White House in advance of all plans made by these two sources in an effort to disrupt the orderly progress of the Convention. This coverage was highly effective. . . .

During our Convention coverage, we disseminated 44 pages of intelligence data to Walter Jenkins. . . . Additionally, I kept Jenkins and Moyers constantly advised by telephone of minute by minute developments. This enabled them to make spot decisions and to adjust Convention plans to meet potential problems before serious trouble developed. . . .

Prior to the squad's departure for Atlantic City, we secured all available pertinent background information on dissident groups and their leaders who were expected to be present. In addition, we took blind memoranda with us which were prepared and approved prior to our departure. This proved most helpful. On Wednesday morning, Mr. Jenkins urgently requested background information on [name withheld]. . . . The White House also requested a blind memorandum on [names withheld]. Within 15 minutes of the request, the desired blind memoranda were furnished to Jenkins. He was highly pleased and said this was of vital importance to their operation. . . .

[Hoover's handwritten notation: "DeLoach should receive a meritorious award."]

■ **Personal Letter, FBI Assistant Director Cartha DeLoach to Special Assistant to the President William Moyers, September 10, 1964, Lyndon Baines Johnson Library**
Thank you for your very thoughtful and generous note concerning our

operation in Atlantic City. Please be assured that it was a pleasure and privilege to be able to be of assistance to the President, and all the boys that were with me felt honored in being selected for the assignment.

I think everything worked out well, and I'm certainly glad that we were able to come through with vital tidbits from time to time which were of assistance to you and Walter [Jenkins]. You know you have only to call on us when a similar situation arises. . . .

GROWING POPULAR DISMAY over the Vietnam War resulted in a direct challenge to President Johnson's renomination in 1968, led by liberal Democratic senators Eugene McCarthy and Robert Kennedy. After Johnson's dramatic disavowal in March that he would neither seek nor accept the nomination, Vice President Hubert Humphrey announced his candidacy. As the administration candidate, Humphrey benefited from the support of moderate and conservative Democrats but was bitterly opposed by antiwar activists. Briefed by the president on the FBI's helpful assistance at the 1964 Democratic National Convention in Atlantic City, candidate Humphrey contacted Hoover through an aide to request similar FBI assistance at the 1968 convention in Chicago.

■ **Memo, FBI Director J. Edgar Hoover to FBI Assistant Directors Clyde Tolson, Cartha DeLoach, Thomas Bishop, and William Sullivan, August 15, 1968, 10:09 a.m., Tolson File**
Mr. William Connell, Executive Assistant to the Vice President . . . stated what he had called about was that he had talked to the Vice President about the [FBI] team I sent into the [Democratic National] convention area in 1964 that was so helpful. He stated he was hoping perhaps I might be able to do the same thing for the Vice President out in Chicago and have my men directly in contact with him (Connell).

I advised Mr. Connell that I had already initiated that [having been briefed by DeLoach who took Connell's call in the absence of the director] and that he will be supplied by Special Agent in Charge Marlin Johnson in Chicago; that any kind of assistance he wants to just let Mr. Johnson know and he will take care of it. . . .

10:13 a.m.

I called SAC Marlin Johnson in Chicago and told him I had just talked to Mr. William Connell, Executive Assistant to the Vice President, and what he wanted done was an operation similar to what we did down at Atlantic City at the last Democratic Convention when Mr. Johnson was running for renomination. I explained that he would like to have us furnish the same type of information and be in contact with him, Connell, on any so-called intelligence we might get. I stated I told Mr. Connell we would do that and that SAC Johnson would be in contact with Connell and anything he wanted to let Johnson know. I told Mr. Johnson we were not going to get into anything political but anything of extreme action or violence contemplated we want to let Connell know.

Mr. Johnson stated he would get in touch with Mr. Connell promptly . . . [as] we have what he believes is excellent coverage of that area and he believes we will be in a position to furnish Mr. Connell, the Secret Service and local authorities intelligence concerning the kooks coming in from outside and the troublemakers there. . . .

■ **Memo, FBI Assistant Director Cartha DeLoach to FBI Associate Director Clyde Tolson, August 22, 1968, Senate Select Committee on Intelligence Activities Hearings, Vol. 6, p. 760**

John Criswell, National Treasurer, Democratic Party, called this afternoon to indicate that he had had dinner with Marvin Watson, the Postmaster General, last night, and Watson had informed him of the great service performed by the FBI [for President Johnson] during the [1964] Democratic Convention in Atlantic City, New Jersey. Criswell wanted to know if the same services could be performed this time in Chicago. He also asked if I could personally go out and take charge, as was the case in Atlantic City.

I told Criswell that Bill Connell, Executive Assistant to the Vice President, had already called regarding this matter, and had personally discussed the entire matter with the Director. I stated the Director had made complete arrangements to have a topflight group of experienced agents, under the supervision of the Special Agent in Charge of the Chicago Office, handle the assignment. I told Criswell I felt certain these men would do an excellent job and the Vice President's office would be kept fully advised at all times of need-to-know information. . . .

*HOOVER'S EAGERNESS TO stay on as FBI director led him to perform
a series of political services for the Nixon White House.*

■ **Memo, FBI Director J. Edgar Hoover to FBI Assistant Directors
Clyde Tolson, Cartha DeLoach, and James Gale, November 25,
1968, Tolson File**
Mr. Henry R. McPhee of President-elect Richard M. Nixon's staff . . .
[will serve on] the transition operation for Mr. Nixon and is working with
H. R. Haldeman and Harry Fleming (phonetic), and one thing he appar-
ently will have the entire responsibility for is personnel security and this
means investigations by my fabulous agency. . . .
I said under the Eisenhower Administration, before he came in as
President and while he was President-elect, he sent for me to go to New
York to see him as I had asked for an appointment because one person
appointed but not checked [Arthur Vandenberg, Jr.] was to be a White
House aide and had a bad record as a homosexual and he was the son of
a prominent Senator and when I told the President-elect about it, he was
astounded. I told him that this showed the wisdom of getting these
people checked so they can find any black shadow in the picture before
they make a public announcement, to call and ask for a check to be made
of them. I said this took away the idea they were being checked for
security by asking it themselves and it relieved the President of that
responsibility. . . .
Mr. McPhee said it was his understanding that [Nixon] wants to have
everybody checked. I stated I thought that was good because you may have
a conflict of interest or individuals who have members of the family who
may be involved in trouble with the Government . . . so if you check all of
them, you are pretty safe from having anything break on you as we have so
many coyotes like Drew Pearson around and I think it is a safety
precaution. Mr. McPhee . . . commented that they really did that toward
the end of the Eisenhower Administration and he thought they had a good
system with no backfire and I said none after being saved from the one
[Vandenberg] I spoke to the President-elect [Eisenhower] about and pre-
vented what would have been an embarrassing situation. . . . [I pointed
out] when President Johnson came in he brought in Walter Jenkins and he
later had a bad scandal as [Jenkins] was arrested here in Washington [in
1964 on a homosexual charge] and had not been checked by anybody, but
Johnson vouched for him, but it goes to show how one can burn his
fingers. . . .

■ **Memo, FBI Supervisor T. J. Smith to FBI Assistant Director Edward Miller, February 2, 1973, Senate Select Committee on Intelligence Activities Hearings, Vol. 6, pp. 643–644**

The FBI Intelligence Letter for the President was instituted in November, 1969, pursuant to then FBI Director J. Edgar Hoover's instructions to keep the President [Richard Nixon] fully informed of significant intelligence developments within the purview of the Bureau's security responsibilities. Dissemination was restricted to the President, the Attorney General [John Mitchell], and later, the Vice President [Spiro Agnew].

By letter dated November 26, 1969, all FBI field offices were advised to flag information obtained in our investigations important enough for the President's interest with the code word "INLET." This was to include:

. . . (6) Items with an unusual twist or concerning prominent personalities which may be of special interest to the President or the Attorney General.

■ **Memo, FBI Director J. Edgar Hoover to FBI Assistant Directors Clyde Tolson, Cartha DeLoach, William Sullivan, and Thomas Bishop, May 9, 1969, House Impeachment Hearings, Book VII, Part 1, p. 142**

Dr. Henry Kissinger, National Security Adviser to the President, . . . advised that there is a story on the front page of the New York Times by William Beecher which is extraordinarily damaging and uses secret information. Dr. Kissinger said they wondered whether I could make a major effort to find out where that came from. I said I would. Dr. Kissinger said . . . to put whatever resources I need to find who did this. I said I would take care of this right away. Dr. Kissinger said to do it discreetly, of course, but they would like to know where it came from because it is very damaging and potentially very dangerous. I commented it is this kind of thing that gives us headaches of where they came from; that if we can find the source one time and make an example it would put a stop to it. Dr. Kissinger agreed and said that is what they propose to do.

[Hoover's handwritten notation: "What do you suggest?"]

[Beecher's article reported that the administration had authorized the bombing of Cambodia—an activity which the Nixon administration had sought to conceal by false reports to Vietnam-based reporters and to the Congress.]

■ **Memo, FBI Director J. Edgar Hoover to FBI Assistant Directors Clyde Tolson, Cartha DeLoach, William Sullivan, and Thomas Bishop, May 9, 1969, House Impeachment Hearings, Book VII, Part 1, pp. 143–145**

I called Dr. Henry A. Kissinger . . . [and] told him I had some information which I thought he ought to know about so as to bring him up to date.

[Six paragraphs reporting on Beecher and three National Security Council officials suspected of being the source of the leaked information. Hoover detailed these officials' suspect political associations, most notably that they "express a very definite Kennedy philosophy," were "arrogant Harvard-type Kennedy men" or "a part of the Harvard clique, and, of course, of the Kennedy era."]

I said that is as far as we have gotten so far. Dr. Kissinger said he appreciated this very much and he hoped I would follow it up as far as we can take it and they will destroy whoever did this if we can find him, no matter where he is.

I told Dr. Kissinger I wanted him to know the developments and he said he appreciated it very much and they will certainly keep looking into it at their end. I told him we would keep after it and he said they were counting on whatever we can find out.

■ **Memo, FBI Director J. Edgar Hoover to Attorney General John Mitchell, May 12, 1969, House Impeachment Hearings, Book VII, Part 1, pp. 192–193**

On May 10, 1969, Colonel Alexander M. Haig, who is assigned to Dr. Henry A. Kissinger's staff, . . . [requested] on the highest authority which involves a matter of most grave and serious consequence to our national security. He stressed that it is so sensitive it demands handling on a need-to-know basis with no record maintained. He requested that a telephone surveillance be placed on the following [two National Security Council staff] individuals to determine if a serious security problem exists:

. . . This Bureau is in a position to conduct the necessary telephone surveillances requested by Colonel Haig.

Approved *John N. Mitchell* (signature)

Date *5/12/69*

[As part of this "leak" investigation, the FBI eventually wiretapped seventeen individuals—three White House aides, seven National Security Council staff, Beecher, *New York Times* reporter Hedrick Smith, *London Times* reporter Henry Brandon, CBS correspondent Marvin Kalb, and three State and Defense Department officials. The Nixon White House asked Hoover not to maintain records of these taps, fearing the political consequences in the event of discovery. Hoover nonetheless created such records—under a do-not-file procedure and secured in FBI assistant director William Sullivan's office separate from other FBI wiretap records. Because this operation also produced valuable political intelligence about the plans of the White House's Democratic adversaries, Hoover's retention of such records suggested that he might use them to preserve his position as director.]

■ **Memo, FBI Director J. Edgar Hoover to FBI Assistant Directors Clyde Tolson, Cartha DeLoach, James Gale, Alex Rosen, William Sullivan, and Thomas Bishop, April 23, 1969, Tolson File**
The President [Richard Nixon] called and said he was sitting there thinking about a few things. . . .

I said the problem of the draft is a serious one and, of course, the Supreme Court says the police cannot arrest a person and take his fingerprints because if they do, they are violating the Constitution. I said that is an unheard of thing . . . [the] kind of thing we are getting, not only at the local level but at the Federal court level, which makes me at times almost be despondent whether anything can be done. The President said it is going to take at least four years or more to get the courts changed. I said I thought he was going to have the opportunity to make progress on the Supreme Court as there will be four vacancies. The President seemed surprised and asked if there were four. I said I understand the fellow from New York, and the President said [John] Harlan, and I said, yes, . . . and, of course, [Earl] Warren will be going off and [Hugo] Black's health is getting worse. The President commented that Black is 80 and I said he was 82. I said [William] Douglas, of course, is crazy and is not in too good health. I said that makes Harlan, Douglas, Black, and Warren.

The President said there is one other thing as he understands *Life* is coming out with an expose of [Supreme Court Justice] Abe Fortas. I said they have a story by Bill Lambert and the President said that I knew about it then. I said it is a very strong story as they went to see Fortas to see what answer he was going to make, if any, in order to protect themselves from libel. I said Lambert was formerly [phrase withheld] and did a fine job exposing [name withheld] so if he has the facts, and I understand he does, it ought to do something. The President asked why a man like Fortas, who does not need the money, would do such a silly thing. I said he has not only done that, but I showed Assistant Attorney General Will Wilson the other day an article which was in the paper about three months ago and had pictures of Fortas, [two names withheld, circuit judges] and three or four prominent people who bought a building in Arlington County which was rented to the Government through the General Services Administration (GSA). I said while that is not a violation of law, it is a tax dodge because they can claim depreciation. . . . I said there are many buildings in Arlington County which are being rented by the Government through the GSA. I said the thing I have been checking into is to find out what pressure, if any, has been brought to bear on GSA by Fortas or anybody in his behalf to get these buildings rented to the Government. I said if there is any indication, it is a conflict of interest and I am hoping to dig something up. The President said [Fortas] ought to be off of there [the Supreme Court]. I said I did not know him except by reputation until the Walter Jenkins case* came up in that he and Clark Clifford tried to suppress the story here in Washington. I said the President [Lyndon Johnson] thought it was a frameup and called me to make an investigation which we did. . . .

[Lambert's article appeared in the May 4, 1969, issue of *Life*. It disclosed that Fortas had received a $20,000 check from the Wolfson Foundation, and raised questions about Fortas's relationship with this recently convicted industrialist. Lambert's article precipitated demands for Fortas's impeachment, and the beleaguered justice resigned on May 15, 1969.]

■ **Memo, FBI Director J. Edgar Hoover to FBI Assistant Directors Clyde Tolson, Cartha DeLoach, and James Gale, July 1, 1969**
The Attorney General [John Mitchell] called. He stated the President is considering the appointment to the Supreme Court of Judge Clement [sic] Haynesworth [sic], Chief Judge of the Fourth Circuit, and he wondered, to fill the requirements of the Judiciary Committee, if we could make a quiet check to the extent that we find it necessary so they could have that in the record when and if he decides to make the announcement. I said I would be glad to. The Attorney General asked that it be done as quietly as possible.

I told the Attorney General I would have our Agent in Charge there give me a rundown on his ability and standing without making any outside inquiries. The Attorney General said that would be excellent.

*Jenkins, an aide to President Johnson, was arrested on a "morals charge" (homosexuality) in August 1964. Fortas, a private attorney at the time, interceded with the FBI, in Johnson's behalf, to contain this matter, the president fearing its potentially adverse impact in the presidential campaign. Furthermore, Johnson had asked Hoover to check the personal background of Republican presidential nominee Barry Goldwater's Senate staff aides for any derogatory information. Hoover did not advise Nixon of this request. Nor did he report how FBI officials had, in 1966, sought to exploit their earlier assistance to Fortas to convince the Supreme Court justice to intercede in Hoover's behalf in his conflict with Attorney General Nicholas Katzenbach.—Ed.

■ **Memo, FBI Director to Attorney General John Mitchell, July 1, 1969**

Our Special Agent in Charge, in Columbia, South Carolina, Mr. Roland Trent, is acquainted with Judge Haynsworth. He advises that Judge Haynsworth is generally regarded as the foremost jurist in the area, is considered very conservative, and is well disposed toward law enforcement. He is definitely in favor of law and order. Mr. Trent advised that Judge Haynsworth has a slight lisp but is considered to have a brilliant mind.

He knew of no derogatory information concerning the Judge.

[Fortas's resignation provided an opening for Nixon to appoint a conservative Southerner to the Court. Sharing the president's ideological orientation, Hoover did not delve deeply into Haynsworth's record on the federal bench. Questions about Haynsworth's civil rights and labor decisions eventually led the Senate, on November 21, 1969, to reject his nomination by a vote of 55 to 45.]

■ **Memo, FBI Director J. Edgar Hoover to FBI Assistant Directors Clyde Tolson, Cartha DeLoach, James Gale, and Thomas Bishop, January 19, 1970, Tolson File**

Attorney General John N. Mitchell called. He advised that the President has pretty well decided that before the day is out, he is going to announce the nomination of Judge [G. Harrold] Carswell for the spot on the Supreme Court. I commented that he is a good man. The Attorney General said he thought they had been around him pretty well and with his age, he should have a long tenure with the right kind of approach on the Supreme Court.

The Attorney General said he knew we had checked him out extensively in connection with his designation to the Circuit Court last June and he wondered if, as in the past so the President can make the presentation, before too late in the afternoon, he, the Attorney General, might have the same kind of communication from us on Judge Carswell as on the other nominees. I told the Attorney General I would take care of it right away.

I instructed Mr. Gale to prepare this right away.

[Senate rejection of the Haynsworth nomination led Nixon to seek confirmation of another Southern conservative. While Hoover was willing to accommodate this presidential request, Carswell's nomination was also rejected by the Senate on April 8, 1970, by a vote of 51 to 45.]

■ **Memo, FBI Director J. Edgar Hoover to FBI Assistant Directors Clyde Tolson, Cartha DeLoach, Alex Rosen, and Thomas Bishop, June 5, 1970, Tolson File**

The President called. . . .

I said I have been strongly in favor of capital punishment and the President said he was with me. . . . I said the court has several cases involving capital punishment and I would imagine the court is going to be 5-4. The President said, "To knock it out completely?" I told him I would not be surprised unless we can get another vacancy to be filled by a real man. The President said if we get one, we will do it.

I said we have the same problem in obscenity; the current court will not declare obscene even that which is raw obscenity. . . . I said cases have gone up before from Customs or the Post Office Department of the Inspectors sending money and buying material themselves and the Court frowns on this as entrapment. I said these things we had were for sale in stores or being brought down to Washington from New York and I am urging prompt trial in the District Court and then it can be appealed to the Supreme Court. The President said to tell the people in Justice to get some publicity out on that; that the country is sick of that crap they see in the newsstands. The President said he is no prude, but "my God," this stuff they are doing now—that's what is getting kids on dope and everything else. The President continued that (Justice) [William] Douglas had an article in one of those magazines [*Evergreen*]. I said he did—a magazine that is pornographic. I said the attitude of (Justices) Douglas and [Hugo] Black is they won't look at a pornographic motion picture like "I Am Curious—Yellow." The President asked if he had [Republican congressman] Jerry Ford call me, would I fill him in on this; that he is a good man. I told him I would. . . .

The President said if I could stir up this thing on capital punishment and obscenity, he is for it and if I see they are not doing something, to let him know, as he is going to ride herd on these.

[House Minority Leader Ford, on April 15, 1970, reacting to the defeats of the Haynsworth and Carswell nominations, had introduced a resolution calling for Douglas's impeachment. Questioning Douglas's fitness to continue serving on the Court, Ford cited in particular the publication of an article by Douglas in *Evergreen Review*, a journal which Ford characterized as erotic. In fact, Douglas had not written an article for this magazine; rather the magazine had run an excerpt from Douglas's recently published book, *Points of Rebellion*. Ford's impeachment effort, however, went nowhere, and was dismissed as partisan opposition to Douglas's judicial philosophy. Nixon's attempt to solicit Hoover's assistance proved equally unavailing as the director lacked any information that could sustain impeachment.]

■ **Memo, FBI Director J. Edgar Hoover to FBI Assistant Directors Clyde Tolson, William Sullivan, Thomas Bishop, Charles Brennan, and Alex Rosen, November 25, 1970, 4:32 PM, Tolson File**

Honorable H. R. Haldeman, Assistant to the President, called. He stated the President wanted him to ask, and he would imagine I would have it pretty much at hand so there would be no specific investigation, for a run down on the homosexuals known and suspected in the Washington press corps. I said I thought we have some of that material. Mr. Haldeman mentioned [name withheld] and some of the others rumored generally to be and also whether we had any other stuff; that he, the President, has an interest in what, if anything else, we know.

I told Mr. Haldeman I would get after that right away and we ought to be able to send it over certainly not later than Friday.

[FBI assistant director Richard Beaver's handwritten notation: "I advised [FBI assistant directors William] Sullivan and [Thomas] Bishop All have copies [of above memo] 5:20 pm 11/25." FBI assistant director Thomas Bishop's handwritten notation: "Letter to H. R. Haldeman 11/27/70."]

■ **Memo, FBI Director J. Edgar Hoover to FBI Assistant Directors Clyde Tolson, Cartha DeLoach, William Sullivan, and Thomas Bishop, April 20, 1970, Tolson File**

Honorable Kent Crane, Assistant to the Vice President [Spiro Agnew], called. He said . . . I had sent to them over the past year some very interesting and alarming statistics where I have totaled things like the number of attacks on police, the number of disturbances in schools, bombings, et cetera, and he, Crane, was just telling the Vice President about that and that it has gotten to the point where everybody takes bombings, et cetera, so routinely that you find them on page fifteen of the New York Times. . . . Mr. Crane said that what the Vice President and he were talking about was whether it would be useful to make a speech that here, these people are not fooling around and it is time we took cognizance of the fact and here are some statistics. . . .

I told him I would get started on it and see if we can't prepare it. . . . I will initiate it immediately and try to get a memorandum to him. Mr. Crane said they are facing three big speeches in the South where he thought this would be well received. I told him I would try to get the material together and send it to him. . . . Mr. Crane said that any thoughts as to how to present this would be most helpful because he knew I could

put it in context much better than anyone else. I told him I would be glad
to prepare it. . . .

■ **Memo, FBI Director J. Edgar Hoover to FBI Assistant Directors
Clyde Tolson, Cartha DeLoach, William Sullivan, and Thomas
Bishop, April 21, 1970, 11:25 AM, Tolson File**
Vice President Spiro Agnew . . . was putting together some comments
on the student thing and [said] that he had been looking over some of the
reaction to his previous speeches around the country. He stated he wondered if the Bureau had a collection of incidents that had happened such as
at Cambridge and at Harvard where the administrations had yielded to the
student demands. He stated it would be a great help if we could make this
available to him. . . .
Mr. Agnew said that he was working on two speeches for next
week and would appreciate receiving any material regarding the schools
yielding to the students. I stated that I would send the information
over. . . .

■ **Memo, FBI Director J. Edgar Hoover to FBI Assistant Directors
Clyde Tolson, Cartha DeLoach, Alex Rosen, William Sullivan,
and Thomas Bishop, May 14, 1970, Tolson File**
Honorable Kent Crane . . . [stated] that the Vice President, as I well
know from my conversations with him, is very impressed with the material
he received from the Bureau and as I know, he is under fire at the moment.
I commented that I hope he keeps to the line and keeps hitting. Mr. Crane
said I was on his wave length with that.
Mr. Crane said what the Vice President would like to have is material
that he can look over before he goes on a program in summary form and if
they start calling him on it, he wants to be able to let them have it. Mr.
Crane said he has received tremendous material from the Bureau, but he
has too much to review and he would like to have it in a briefing form
book where he can have something on the Panthers and other violence-
prone groups and he would like to have something on the campus unrest;
and he would like to have total damages, injuries, and especially graphic
incidents that could be used as examples, which Governor Ronald Reagan
has done a beautiful job with. . . . He continued that he would like to have
some information on the organization, finances, and philosophy of these
radical groups, and he wants to be able to emphasize it is a minority that is
involved and the others following along blindly. . . .

I told Mr. Crane I thought we could be of some help on that and I would start getting it in summary form. I said I know we sent a great deal of material in great detail every day on these things and it gets voluminous and I would start getting it summarized down so it can be reviewed more or less quickly and get the real "guts" of the material stated.

Mr. Crane said he thought we might, if I thought it useful, consider the possibility of having it up-dated every couple of months, as he thought it would be useful. I said we could do it and I would be happy to have it done and to bring it up to date so he can have readily at hand things he can talk about. . . .

■ **Memo, FBI Director J. Edgar Hoover to FBI Assistant Directors Clyde Tolson, Cartha DeLoach, Alex Rosen, William Sullivan, and Thomas Bishop, May 18, 1970, Tolson File**

Vice President Spiro Agnew called . . . to see whether I could be of some assistance. He said he was really concerned about the continuing inflammatory pronouncements of [SCLC president] Ralph Abernathy. I commented that he is one of the worst. The Vice President said he had seen some of the background material on him and he knows what that is, but it is beyond the pale as far as executive use is concerned. He said in view of [the race riots] in Augusta and other places, it is important to have the information that revolved around this; the involvement of these people, what information we have, whether fleeing from looting or what is going on. He asked if there is any information available.

I told him we are working on these at the present time. . . .

The Vice President said what he wants to be able to do is bring out some facts the media conveniently overlooked. I said they never give the things that are done constructively, many times by students, to try to prevent this, but they emphasize all the things these jerks are doing.

The Vice President said he saw a picture about Augusta showing some of the Negroes jumping out of store windows with loot and booty and fleeing and you never hear anything about that. He said whatever I can give him that can ameliorate some of the impact; that he understands some of these things are wrong and we are probably going to find some of the shootings showed too much force, but none the less, the people have to understand the very thrust of the newspaper articles is that a bunch of police shot down six Negroes and what happened before—why did they shoot at them—not just because they felt like killing people. I said they were severely provoked at Kent [State] and we will finish Augusta, Atlanta, and Jackson, this week. . . .

The Vice President said he thought he was going to have to start destroying Abernathy's credentials so anything I can give him would be appreciated. I told him I would be glad to. I said I was the only one who spoke out against Martin Luther King and I got hell, but I did not give a damn because it is more like bouquets than brickbats from some people. The Vice President said we can't let demagogues become martyrs and heroes. I said I had briefed the [House] Appropriations Committee about his (King's) background and it has been effective recently because they have been trying to make a national holiday of his birthday, and many of the congressmen who know the facts are opposing it. I said I did not put it on the record, but I told the Appropriations Committee [two lines of derogatory information on King withheld on personal privacy grounds] in turn, briefed some of their colleagues, but I will see that he, the Vice President, gets the details even before we finish the report.

The Vice President said he would like to be thoroughly conversant with all of that because if the crisis comes where we need to throw it, he will. I told him I would get it over in the next 24 to 48 hours as to the highlights. The Vice President thanked me.

■ **Memo, FBI Director J. Edgar Hoover to FBI Assistant Directors Clyde Tolson, Cartha DeLoach, Thomas Bishop, James Gale, Alex Rosen, and William Sullivan, June 4, 1970, Tolson File**

After the ceremonies at the White House this morning . . . [the president] asked the Attorney General and myself to come into his private office.

The President stated that in a recent check or poll which they had made, crime was the number one item of concern of the citizens of the country. . . .

The President stated that Congress had failed to enact one piece of legislation which had been recommended and suggested by the Administration on the matter of crime and that he was considering asking the Vice President to make some speeches placing the responsibility directly on Congress for its failure to function in this field.

The President asked my opinion on this, and I told him I thought it was an excellent idea. . . . The President stated that there seemed to be no one in either house of Congress who was pressing vigorously for the enactment of the crime legislation which he had recommended. . . .

I stated that unless real progress was made against organized crime in this country, it was reasonable to expect that the opposition party would lay the blame on the present administration and it was for this reason I felt that

Vice President Agnew should take a particularly strong position against Congress for inaction in this field. . . .

The President asked me to supply the Vice President with any material which the latter could use in speeches on organized crime, and I told him that I would. . . .

13: Senator Joseph McCarthy

An obscure junior senator from Wisconsin, Joseph McCarthy catapulted to national prominence in February 1950 by claiming to have evidence of "known Communists in the State Department." He was immediately confronted with a Democratic challenge to confirm this charge, resulting in the creation of a special Senate committee, the so-called Tydings Committee after its chairman Millard Tydings. Throughout his anticommunist campaign, McCarthy relied on assistance from the FBI. He received carefully camouflaged leaks of FBI information as well as information provided him by conservative reporters and congressmen who had acquired it from sources in the FBI.

McCarthy's reelection in 1952, combined with Republican successes in gaining control of Congress and the presidency, enhanced McCarthy's stature and influence. He became chairman of the Senate Government Affairs Committee and its permanent investigations subcommittee, positions which enabled him to advance the cause of anticommunism.

At first Hoover extended the level of FBI assistance in this shared cause, from selected leaks to an increased volume of information as well as personal counsel on political strategy and the appointment of better-qualified staff members. This assistance even extended to McCarthy's effort to torpedo President Eisenhower's nomination of Charles Bohlen as U.S. ambassador to the Soviet Union. With direct access to Hoover, McCarthy sought the director's help in obtaining derogatory personal information about Bohlen's character and sexual orientation.

In time, however, McCarthy's irresponsibility (he had a
penchant for making extreme charges without developing
credible information to substantiate them), but more important his
tendency to compromise the secret character of the FBI's
assistance, led Hoover in July 1953 to cut off aid to McCarthy.
Hoover did so only when McCarthy's appointment of FBI
supervisor Frank Carr to his staff had created the appearance of
a McCarthy "pipeline" to the FBI.

■ **Memo, SAC Washington Guy Hottel to FBI Director,**
September 19, 1950, FBI 121-41668-28

Former FBI Special Agent Don Surine, who is now employed as an investigator by U.S. Senator Joseph R. McCarthy, . . . [requested] "a copy of the Bureau's summary report on [Owen] Lattimore." . . . Surine indicated that in the past, he had been able to secure some information from the New York Office of ONI [Office of Naval Intelligence]. He stated that he needed such a report inasmuch as Senator McCarthy, in the future, would not make any further allegations without being able to support such allegations by an investigative report. He said that if he could get the report, he could attribute the information contained therein to another government investigative agency, explaining that "this is what happened in the Posniak Case." . . .

Surine said that if he had the Lattimore summary report, it would be handled in the same fashion as was done in the Posniak Case, explaining that he would insert the information appearing in the Bureau report in the form of a summary of information appearing in the CSC [Civil Service Commission] investigative files, thus making it appear that his office had secured a CSC file rather than a Bureau file. In this way, Surine said he would not be violating any laws inasmuch as the CSC summary report would not be a bona fide report of a government agency and thus a theft of government property case, as such could not be proved. He also believed that a theft of government property with respect to the information contained in the report could not be proved inasmuch as the information would be completely paraphrased making it impossible for any observer to determine that the information was actually taken from a Bureau report. . . .

[On February 21, 1950, Senator McCarthy had cited eighty-one cases of "known communists in the State Department," a charge that resulted in the establishment of a special Senate committee, chaired by Millard Tydings, to determine the validity of his charges. After completing its investigation, the Tydings Committee issued a report dismissing McCarthy's charges as unfounded. Responding in a Senate speech, McCarthy characterized the Tydings report as a "whitewash" and further claimed that the files which the committee had consulted to reach its conclusions had been "raped." To support this latter allegation, McCarthy cited the case of Edward Posniak, one of the eighty-one cases, and from a classified Civil Service Commission report he quoted information not included in the Tydings report on Posniak.

President Truman's 1948 executive order prohibited the release of any loyalty report to the Congress without the president's explicit authorization, so McCarthy could not have lawfully acquired the report on Posniak. Attorney General J. Howard McGrath therefore directed the FBI to initiate a criminal investigation to determine how McCarthy had acquired this "stolen property." McGrath's request placed the FBI in a bind and led Hoover and other FBI officials to be extra-cautious in processing further McCarthy requests for FBI assistance. The above memo describes the subterfuge by which FBI officials leaked information to McCarthy's staff.]

■ **Memo, FBI Assistant Director D. Milton Ladd to Director, October 5, 1950, FBI 121-41668—Not Recorded**

(1) To advise you that when Don Surine told us if we gave him a copy of the summary report on Lattimore, it would be handled in the same manner as was done in the Posniak case, he was undoubtedly unthinkingly referring to the document distributed by Senator McCarthy on July 25, 1950, which purported to be a Civil Service Commission summary of the investigation of Edward Posniak.

(2) To suggest we do not interview Surine concerning the above [as part of the investigation demanded by Attorney General McGrath as to how McCarthy had acquired a copy of the loyalty report on Posniak].

. . . You will recall on September 15, 1950, Surine . . . volunteered if he had the Lattimore summary report it would be handled in the same fashion as was done in the Posniak case. You noted, "Just what does he mean by this?"

You will recall that Senator McCarthy on July 25, 1950, made a statement on the floor of the Senate concerning "Mr. X" in the State Department, who was subsequently identified as Edward Posniak, subject to a full field loyalty investigation by the Bureau. In making his statement, Senator McCarthy distributed copies of a document which purported to be a Civil Service Commission summary of the investigation of Posniak. On July 25, 1950, the Attorney General asked us to conduct an investigation to determine the source from which Senator McCarthy obtained his document. The investigation disclosed that Senator McCarthy's document is apparently not an authentic copy of any document prepared by the CSC, the State Department or the Loyalty Review Board, according to representatives of these three Agencies. In addition, the document distributed by Senator McCarthy contains inaccuracies, and it was prepared in such a way as to indicate it could not have been prepared as a CSC summary of the investigation of Posniak. In addition, you will recall that on March 23, 1950, the [FBI's] Baltimore Office advised us that Surine had advised an Agent of that office that Senator McCarthy was going to expose Edward Posniak, a State Department employee. At that time, Surine had in his possession a memorandum, apparently from Senator McCarthy's office, which included quoted material, apparently from Bureau investigative reports. The possibility exists that the document which Senator McCarthy used on July 25, 1950, is the same document which Surine had in his possession on March 20, 1950, and the possibility further exists that this is the document that Surine was referring to on September 15, 1950, as noted above. It would further appear from the above that Surine was not thinking when he said what he did on September 15, 1950.

At the suggestion of the Attorney General, I interviewed Senator McCarthy on August 4, 1950, as to the source of the document which accompanied his press release regarding Edward Posniak. Senator McCarthy refused to disclose his source, and he further said he had instructed the employees in his office not to disclose the source of any of his material, since he felt it his duty to protect his sources.

In view of the above, it is respectfully suggested that we do not interview Surine concerning his statement given to us on September 15, 1950. . . .

■ **Memo, SAC Washington Guy Hottel to FBI Director, November 28, 1952, FBI 94-37708-76X**

During a recent interview . . . Senator McCarthy indicated he anticipated closer cooperation with and more extended use of the FBI and its facilities following the beginning of the new Congress [the Republicans had won a sweeping victory in the 1952 elections, winning the presidency and control of both houses of Congress]. He said he realized that in the past it was not always to ones advantage to be seen talking to or associating with McCarthy, but that he felt all this would be changed now with his re-election and the new Congress.

Senator McCarthy . . . [plans] to confer with the Director in the not too distant future relative to obtaining suggestions for prospective investigative personnel for his investigative committee.

The above is being furnished for your information.

■ **Memo, FBI Director J. Edgar Hoover to FBI Associate Director Clyde Tolson, December 1, 1952, FBI 94-37708-77**

On November 28, 1952, Senator Joseph McCarthy called and stated he would become Chairman of the Senate Committee Investigating Government Operations and Expenditures. He stated he would be in need of a good staff and asked that I give some thought to recommending to him a number of competent investigators that he might consider for appointment to this staff. I would like to have this given prompt attention.

■ **Memo, FBI Director J. Edgar Hoover to FBI Associate Director Clyde Tolson, January 13, 1953, FBI 94-37708-79X**

Yesterday afternoon, Senator Joseph McCarthy called to see me. The Senator stated that he wanted me to feel free at any time to contact him whenever I saw any activity of any member of his staff on the new committees of which he will be chairman, which I did not feel was in the best interests of good administration.

The Senator discussed generally the over-all plans which he has for carrying on the work of his committee and will, no doubt, be in contact with us from time to time.

■ **Memo, FBI Assistant Director D. Milton Ladd to FBI Director, February 24, 1953, FBI 94-37708-81**

At 4:40 P.M. on February 24, 1953, Senator Joe McCarthy . . . [reported] that about two years ago in Honolulu [McCarthy's administrative assistant] Jean Kerr fell in an unlighted hallway and broke her hip and . . . the man who owned the premises is [name withheld] a wealthy man. . . .

Senator McCarthy said that he is endeavoring to locate [name withheld] in order that he may be served with process in connection with this accident prior to the running of the three-year Statute of Limitations. He said that [name withheld] is not evading process as he was fully covered by insurance.

Senator McCarthy wondered if our Detroit Office would be so kind as to ascertain the whereabouts of [name withheld] and advise the Senator so that he could be appropriately served. I told the Senator we would see what we could do on this.

Recommendation:

It is recommended that I call Detroit and have them discreetly ascertain where [name withheld] is at this time and advise the Bureau in order that Senator McCarthy may be informed.

[Hoover's handwritten notation: "O.K."]

■ **Memo, FBI Director J. Edgar Hoover to FBI Assistant Directors Clyde Tolson, D. Milton Ladd, and Louis Nichols, March 18, 1953**

Senator Joseph McCarthy called with reference to the [Charles Bohlen] appointment [as U.S. ambassador to the Soviet Union]. . . . He stated he was quite concerned regarding this entire picture as there was practically no change [in State Department loyalty procedures] and everything was running about the same as it was a year ago. Senator McCarthy wondered whether I could tell him in complete confidence just how bad [Bohlen] actually was. I told him this, of course, was very hard to evaluate; that we made the investigation and that the request for the investigation was not received by us until after [Bohlen] was named for the appointment. [One and one-half lines withheld on personal privacy grounds.]

[Three and one-half lines withheld on personal privacy grounds] I commented that I guessed it all depended on the viewpoint and how you looked at a thing of that kind; that quite a number of reputable persons spoke very highly of [Bohlen] and there were some people who had very detrimental things to say about him. Senator McCarthy asked whether I thought he was a homosexual and I told him I did not know; that that was a very hard thing to prove and the only way you could prove it was either by admission or by arrest and forfeiture of collateral. I stated this had not occurred in his case at all as far as we know, but it is a fact, and I believed very well known, that he is associating with individuals of that type . . . and certainly normally a person did not associate with individuals of that type.* I stated he has been a very close buddy of [Charles Thayer]** for many years and he is a well-known homosexual. The Senator was advised that we had no evidence to show any overt act, but he, [Bohlen], had certainly used very bad judgment in associating with homosexuals. The Senator stated this was a matter that he was almost precluded from discussing on the Floor [of the Senate]; that it was so easy to accuse a

*During its investigation, the FBI focused on Bohlen's sexual orientation. Indeed, syndicated columnist Drew Pearson reported that when FBI agents interviewed him, they asked whether Bohlen "was a homo and then quoted me [Pearson] as once having said he was."—Ed.

**Thayer was Bohlen's brother-in-law, at the time consul general in Munich. The evidence consisted of anonymous letters claiming that Thayer was a homosexual. McCarthy acquired these letters and threatened to subpoena Thayer to appear before the permanent investigations subcommittee. Rather than submit to a public hearing on his morals, Thayer resigned.—Ed.

person of such acts but difficult to prove. I agreed and stated that it was often a charge used by persons who wanted to smear someone. . . .

The Senator referred again to [Bohlen's nomination] and stated he was going to make a talk on the Floor concerning [Bohlen] and he wondered if I had any public source information such as from the Daily Worker which he could use. I told him that we had investigated [Bohlen] from the security and morals angle and that frankly most of the material we got was from the State Department. I indicated we did not go into the analysis of political speeches, and so forth, as that was supposed to be handled by the State Department.

■ **Memo, FBI Assistant Director Louis Nichols to FBI Associate Director Clyde Tolson, June 24, 1953, FBI 94-37708—Not Recorded**

. . . [Senator McCarthy] thinks he has now made a lot of progress in building up the Committee Staff, that he is easing [Francis] Flanagan out and, in fact, is getting some Texas oil men to get up a job for Flanagan to get him out of the Committee completely.

He stated that he will make J. B. Matthews the Staff Director, that Matthews is very experienced, has a dominant personality and will be able to control the situation so far as the Committee is concerned, and he knows this will be highly pleasing to the Director.

It [sic] told the Senator that, quite frankly, while we had never expressed ourselved [sic] publicly, it was difficult for us to forget some of the activities of Mr. Matthews during the days of the Dies Committee [in the late 1930s when Matthews was counsel to that committee] when we were fighting with our backs to the wall, and further there had been instances wherein we had contacted Matthews and shortly thereafter seen items in the papers.

McCarthy was very much taken back by this and stated he had been led to believe by [three names withheld] that Matthews was very close to the Bureau and the Bureau held Matthews in high regard.

I told the Senator that we had never expressed ourselves on that point, that naturally we would subordinate our feelings on those fighting Communism but that he, McCarthy, should be cautious about Matthews issuing press releases. . . .

McCarthy said that he certainly was sorry to get this reaction and that he would be very cautious.

I do know that [name withheld] is very close to Matthews and Matthews, in fact, has been a bulwark for the anti-Communist writers in New York City. I think that we should give Matthews a chance and when he does take over as Staff Director, I think we should keep our guard up but at the same time, see if he has changed his ways.

[Hoover's handwritten notation: "Let me see what we have on Matthews first."]

[The Matthews appointment did not work out, but not because his interest in publicity threatened to compromise the FBI's covert assistance to McCarthy. The publication of an article by Matthews in the right-wing *American Mercury*, about communist influence among Protestant clergy, appeared almost concurrent with the announcement of his appointment as staff director and provoked a firestorm of criticism—heightened by McCarthy's Catholicism and his prominent support by Catholic church leaders. McCarthy was forced to seek Matthews's resignation. To resolve his recurring staff problem, McCarthy considered appointing an FBI supervisor, Frank Carr, as his new staff director.]

■ Memo, FBI Director J. Edgar Hoover to FBI Assistant Directors Clyde Tolson and Louis Nichols, July 14, 1953

Yesterday Miss Jean Kerr, formerly secretary [and currently administrative assistant] to Senator [Joseph] McCarthy, called to see me and stated that her visit was to be considered as confidential and that the Senator did not know that she was coming to see me. . . .

Miss Kerr . . . was considerably concerned about the situation existent in the Senator's Committee, growing out of the recent Matthews incident, and that she understood that there was a Special Agent by the name of Francis P. Carr attached to our New York Office that the Senator would appoint as Chief of Staff if I would agree to it but that I had not seen fit to accede to the request. She wanted to know whether I wouldn't reconsider this matter and either agree to the appointment of Special Agent Carr or suggest someone else who is either in the Bureau or has been in the Bureau who could be appointed to this position.

I told Miss Kerr . . . there was some misunderstanding as to my position in this matter. I stated it was not up to me to concur or not concur as to whom Senator McCarthy appointed as Chief of Staff of his Committee. I stated it was a fact that Senator McCarthy and Mr. Roy Cohn, counsel for the Committee, had been in contact with the Bureau and had inquired about the availability of Mr. Carr . . . [and] that Mr. Cohn had directly contacted Mr. Carr about this appointment. . . . I stated that the Senator and Mr. Cohn had been informed that I would not ask Mr. Carr to take the position as Chief of Staff of the McCarthy Committee and that I would neither approve nor disapprove if he took such a position, but it had been pointed out to the Senator that the appointment of an Agent now in the service and engaged upon work dealing with subversive activities would, no doubt, be seized upon by critics of the Senator and of the FBI as a deliberate effort to effect a direct "pipe line" into the FBI and that it would make it necessary for the Bureau to be far more circumspect in all of its dealings with the McCarthy Committee should Mr. Carr be appointed.

Miss Kerr . . . could see this aspect . . . and inquired as to whether I would in any way indicate publicly that I disapproved of the Carr appointment should it be made. I told Miss Kerr that I would neither indicate approval nor disapproval of whatever Mr. Carr did should he resign from the Bureau.

She . . . was concerned that the Senator might make a very sudden decision as to the appointment for this position and she feared that he would either appoint Mr. [Robert] Kennedy . . . or assign [subcommittee general counsel Francis] Flanagan . . . to the position of Director of the Staff. She . . . believed that either of these designations would be unfortunate. I told her that I did not know anything about Mr. Kennedy but that I was pretty well familiar with . . . Flanagan and that certainly this Bureau could have no dealings with him, irrespective of what position he might hold.

She . . . hoped that the Senator might delay taking final action upon this matter and that I might give some thought to suggesting some name or names to the Senator as to what he should do or as to whom he should appoint.

She inquired . . . what I thought of Bob Lee who is now with the Appropriations Committee of the House. I told her that Mr. Lee had had a very good record in the Bureau and I believe he had been out of the Bureau long enough so as not to have anyone attach to any such appointment the same suspicion that would attach to an Agent now in the employ of the Bureau. I told her that the only ex-Agent I knew . . . without commitments in the immediate future was former Special Agent Robert Collier . . . but I did not believe he would be available for several months and I doubted whether he would be interested in the position now vacant with the McCarthy Committee.

■ **Informal Memo, FBI Assistant Director Louis Nichols to FBI Associate Director Clyde Tolson, July 23, 1953, Nichols File**
. . . [Senator McCarthy] is going to try to get [Deputy Attorney General] William Rogers to make available to the [Government Operations] Committee [which McCarthy chaired] instances wherein [Truman's Assistant Attorney General] James McInerney failed to initiate prosecutive action against subversives. He stated that no doubt there were numerous cases which McInerney squelched and that by investigating these cases, he would not be investigating anyone connected with the Eisenhower administration. I told McCarthy that I doubted if he could possibly expect to have any success inasmuch as his close associate [committee counsel] Francis Flanagan was very close to Mr. McInerney and likewise was close to Rogers. McCarthy then stated he had talked the matter over with [Vice

President Richard] Nixon and Nixon thought it was a good idea. I then inquired if Flanagan was not also very close to Nixon. McCarthy stated they, of course, did know each other.

2. The Senator commented . . . that he now feels good over having former Special Agent Frank Carr on the staff and that he was very glad the Director finally approved Carr's coming with the staff. I inquired of the Senator if I understood him correctly, that it was his view that the Director had approved Carr's coming on the staff. The Senator stated that this was his understanding, that he had deliberately not contacted the Director as he wanted to be in the position of saying that he had not been in touch with the Director but that he had been led to believe the Director had approved Carr from comments from [his staff aides] Jeannie Kerr and Roy Cohn, in fact the Senator stated he had Jean Kerr see the Director as he wanted to avoid the position of talking to the Director.

[Hoover's handwritten insert: "No. I told Jean Kerr & Cohn I was opposed to it."]

I told the Senator I happened to be very familiar with the Director's position on Carr and the Director's position had never wavered from that which I had personally conveyed to him some weeks ago, namely, that we would not give Carr a leave of absence, we would not release him, we would not ask him to go to the Committee, we would not approve his going with the Committee, that obviously if Carr resigned and wanted to go with the Committee this was his business. I further told the Senator that I knew this was the position the Director had taken with Jeannie as well as Roy Cohn, that in essence the Director's position was that he would neither approve nor disapprove, that the Director had stated out of deference to him, the Senator, he would not make any public protest. . . .

I further told the Senator I expected the next time he saw the Director, the Director would literally and figuratively "give him hell."

I told the Senator that the appointment of Carr was bad because it now placed a tight restriction upon the Bureau, that we would have to lean over backwards because if at any time the Committee came up with something having an FBI angle, the charge would be made that Carr was a pipeline and that it would have been so much better to have had an outsider. The Senator stated he understands this, that he hopes the Director will not be too angry.

I am wondering if it would not throw a little more consternation in the ranks if I would take Roy Cohn to task for telling the Senator the Director had approved Carr's going with the Committee.

[Tolson's handwritten insert: "I see no need to do this." Hoover's handwritten insert: "I agree with Tolson. Cohn will just doubletalk & fast."]

3. In the course of the conversation I told the Senator that we were worried for fear that the cause had suffered and that there was a very definite reaction setting in against Congressional Committees and he would

be smart to get off on some other subject. The Senator stated he agreed, that he wanted to wind up the Voice of America situation, he had some good information on the effect that our stockpiling program was bad on American mines, namely, that we have been buying metals from foreign countries and have closed down our mines with the result that our mines are flooded, have not been kept up and are becoming worthless. . . .

4. In discussing information the Committee had on the smuggling of guns to Latin America, . . . I told the Senator I had to ask him directly for the information as we had previously asked Cohn, Cohn's secretary had referred the matter to Flanagan, Flanagan in turn had told us we could come down and review what information he had. I told the Senator quite frankly that we would not embarrass any Agent of this service by sending him to that "SOB" Flanagan to secure anything. The Senator personally got the file and gave it to me.

The Senator then stated that Flanagan was out of the way and was completely off in a corner and that he was arranging to get Flanagan the job as counsel for a shipping company in which Clint Murchison owns an interest . . . [having] adopted the practice with the staff of trying to take care of each staff member as a means of building loyalty. I told the Senator he was shadow boxing, that certainly Flanagan was not loyal to him and that he ran the risk of having Flanagan alienate his chief financial support [Texas oil millionaire Clint Murchison]. I don't know how much effect this had on the Senator.

■ **Memo, FBI Executives' Conference to FBI Director, October 14, 1953, FBI 121-23278—Not Recorded**

The FBI Executives' Conference . . . considered current policy relative to furnishing information from Bureau files outside of the Executive Departments and made recommendations as to future procedures. As the problem covers a wide area, it is broken down, as set forth below, under separate captions. . . .

DISSEMINATION OF INFORMATION TO CONGRESSIONAL COMMIT-TEES:

. . . We have furnished information to the Senate Permanent Investi-gating [sic, Investigations] Committee (McCarthy) up until the late Sum-mer [1953] when the Committee appointed [Former FBI supervisor] Frank Carr as Staff Director. Since then no information has been furnished to this Committee. . . .

14: Political Intelligence

UNDER HOOVER'S DIRECTORSHIP, the FBI's resources were greatly expanded, both in numbers of agents and in the use of illegal investigative techniques. Hoover also developed a nation-wide system of willing sources—reporters and conservative activists and organizations, such as the American Legion. These resources enabled him to monitor not only "subversive" activities within the body politic but, more important, political developments within the federal government, the candidacies of prominent liberal politicians, and, more disturbing, the personnel, orientation, and decisions of the U.S. Supreme Court.

Exploiting this intelligence purposefully but with great care to preclude discovery, the FBI director sought to purge the federal bureaucracy of suspect radicals and liberals through the Federal Employee Loyalty Program. And he closely monitored policy decisions and personnel changes within the federal bureaucracy and the Supreme Court as well as the electoral strategy and personal background of prominent politicians. Hoover's purposes were both to safeguard the FBI's bureaucratic interests and to acquire advance information of specific decisions and personnel likely to affect the national interest—as Hoover defined it. Virtually no information, whether rumor or hard evidence, escaped the FBI director's attention.

■ **Memo, FBI Assistant Director Louis Nichols to FBI Associate Director Clyde Tolson, May 23, 1957, FBI 62-27585-61X**
[Name withheld] called. He was just wondering if any consideration had ever been given to running a check on the law clerks of the justices on

both the Circuit Court of Appeals and the Supreme Court. He stated he was bringing this up because he had been told there is a ring of left-wing law clerks who have pretty well established a hierarchy in certain instances.

He then related that [four lines withheld, but names withheld law clerks and that Nichols's name withheld source] has been told that this whole crowd is a group of left-wingers.

He further related that, when Judge [Sherman] Minton was confirmed on the Supreme Court, Senator [Pat] McCarran had reviewed all of his opinions as a circuit court judge. They were sound and solid; but as soon as he went on the Supreme Court and started having the succession of law clerks, his opinions "stunk."

[Name withheld] thought it might be a good idea for someone to get a discreet line on the law clerks of [name withheld Supreme Court Justice] and a few of the other judges as it might disclose revealing information. I told him, of course, that this was not a matter in which we could take part as it would be improper for the Bureau to launch an investigation; however, if in any inquiries he made there were any indications of subversive activities, we would certainly like to know about it.

■ **Memo, FBI Supervisor Alan Belmont to FBI Assistant Director Leland Boardman, May 29, 1957, FBI 62-27585-61x1**
Memorandum from Mr. Nichols to Mr. Tolson May 23, 1957, set forth information received from [name withheld] stating that a group of left-wing law clerks was established with justices on the Supreme Court and the Circuit Court of Appeals.

A review of Bureau files has been made on the names of the law clerks specifically mentioned by [name withheld]. No information could be located identifiable with [two of the named clerks]. A separate memorandum is being prepared on [the third named clerk].

The following is a summary of information located in the Bureau files concerning [this third clerk, which the FBI withheld on personal privacy and sources and methods grounds].
Recommendations:
. . . 2. That attached airtel to Washington Field Office requesting it to discreetly ascertain identities of newly appointed law clerks to [name withheld Supreme Court justice] be approved.
[Hoover's handwritten notation: "OK."]
Action:
This is for information and to advise that Bureau files are being reviewed on other law clerks for justices of the Supreme Court and the Circuit Court of Appeals in the District of Columbia. . . .

■ **Memo, FBI Supervisor J. F. Bland to FBI Supervisor Alan Belmont, June 5, 1957, FBI 62-27585—Not Recorded**

. . . [Re allegation] that a group of left-wing law clerks was established with justices on the Supreme Court and the Circuit Court of Appeals. One of those named was [name withheld] who was described as a former law clerk to [name withheld Supreme Court justice].

[The FBI has withheld three pages of derogatory personal and political information on this former Supreme Court clerk.]

Action:

Refer [above information concerning this former clerk] to Mr. Nichols . . .

[Tolson's handwritten notation of June 7, 1957: "I think we should discreetly ascertain whether (this former law clerk) is presently employed in any branch of the Government service." Hoover's handwritten notation: "Yes."]

■ **Memo, FBI Assistant Director Louis Nichols to FBI Associate Director Clyde Tolson, October 8, 1957, FBI 62-27585-91**

I am attaching a list of 1957 employees of the Supreme Court by each individual Justice, by the Clerk's Office, by the Marshal's Office, and by other miscellaneous offices of the Court.

■ **Airtel, Director to SAC Washington, October 9, 1957, FBI 62-27585—Not Recorded**

. . . You are requested to ascertain, in a most discreet manner, the identities and available background of all newly appointed law clerks to [name withheld Supreme Court justice].

The above should be handled promptly. . . .

■ **Informal Memo, FBI Assistant Director Cartha DeLoach to FBI Associate Director Clyde Tolson, September 12, 1966**

A reliable source has advised that the Supreme Court, in its opening session, October, 1966, plans to call Solicitor General Thurgood Marshall and really "put him on the griddle" in connection with the answers he has given the Supreme Court in the case involving Fred Black.* The Court apparently did not like Marshall's first presentation inasmuch as there were too many "loopholes" and failure on his part to mention specific information. This of course was the presentation in which Marshall admitted the usage of a microphone in the Black case.

The Supreme Court also did not like Marshall's . . . [brief stating] ". . . the FBI had general authorization from the Department for the usage of such devices . . ." Members of the Court apparently feel that again Solicitor General Marshall failed to be specific in his answers. For the most part, the Court thinks that Marshall is being evasive and is failing to put some individuals on the spot.

It appears that Justices [Abe] Fortas and [Tom] Clark are leading the fight to get all aspects of the truth concerning this matter. The above-mentioned source indicated that undoubtedly their actions represented a very carefully conceived campaign in which Bobby Kennedy's actions and the encouragement of the usage of microphones and other electronic devices would necessarily be forced out in the open. Justices [Byron] White and [William] Douglas seem satisfied, however, their hand is being forced by the majority of the other Justices.

I was further advised that the Court plans to issue a "sweeping statement" against the usage of electronic devices . . . [and] that there undoubtedly would be numerous additional questions asked regarding the role the [Justice] Department played in the handling of this entire situation. It was indicated that all Justices, with the exception of Douglas and White, are quite angry over the handling they have received from Attorney General [Nicholas] Katzenbach.

It was, of course, understood that the above-mentioned information was given in strict confidence. We are in good shape to answer questions. We have two separate, thoroughly prepared briefs on the history of the usage of wiretaps and microphones by the FBI since 1908. These are being constantly kept up to date.

[DeLoach's source apparently was Supreme Court Justice Abe Fortas. Either Fortas relayed this information about the Court's deliberations directly to DeLoach or DeLoach learned of Fortas's account indirectly from his contacts in the Johnson White House.]

■ **Informal Memo, FBI Assistant Director Cartha DeLoach to FBI Associate Director Clyde Tolson, June 14, 1966**
Justice Abe Fortas returned my call of midday, 6/13/66, late last

*For information about this case and about Hoover's attempt to place responsibility for the bugging with former attorney general Robert Kennedy, see Chapter 10, The Fred Black Case.—Ed.

night. I told him that I wanted to see him about a matter which he might consider bordered on a violation of judicial ethics. He was told that I had been able to discuss matters in confidence with him on several other occasions, i.e., the [Walter] Jenkins case, [name withheld's, but one of President Johnson's daughters] boyfriend, and other items which Mr. Hoover had me handle with him, and that I therefore felt that he wouldn't mind if this matter was brought to his attention.

The [Fred] Black case was then brought up and he was told that although he had disqualified himself, he might not desire to discuss this matter. Justice Fortas replied that he would be glad to not only discuss this matter but any other matter with me on a confidential basis at any time. . . .

I gave him a complete rundown on the exchange of correspondence that the Director had had with [Attorney General] Nicholas deB. Katzenbach. He was told specifically of Katzenbach's evasive tactics in attempting to defend Bobby Kennedy. I then mentioned the Black case and told him that while the Director planned to furnish the Attorney General specific, honest, hardhitting answers to the Supreme Court's questions, we nevertheless knew that Katzenbach would throw our answers out the window and present his own slanted version to the Supreme Court. Justice Fortas agreed.

Justice Fortas stated that the entire matter boiled down to a continuing fight for the Presidency. He stated that Kennedy was of course out to capture that segment of voters which in the past had belonged to Vice President [Hubert] Humphrey. He mentioned that Kennedy, to a certain extent, had succeeded in capturing this left-wing group. He added that of course if facts, as possessed by the FBI, concerning Kennedy's approval of wiretapping were made known to the general public that it would serve to completely destroy Kennedy.

Justice Fortas spoke of the Black case. He stated that after Solicitor General Thurgood Marshall had ineptly and inadequately presented the matter of electronic devices to the Supreme Court, the Supreme Court had held a confidential meeting among themselves. . . . At the meeting it was decided among the Justices that rather than remand the Black case to a lower court, the Supreme Court would set itself up as a tribunal to gather further information concerning the usage of electronic devices and afterwards make a decision. The Justices, with the exception of Byron White, felt that if the case were immediately remanded to a lower court Attorney General Katzenbach would, in order to win the case, pick his own Judge and thereby attain victory. Justice Fortas stated that some of the Justices in the Supreme Court were somewhat belligerent in their attitude toward Kennedy and Katzenbach. He stated these men would not be "pushed around" regardless of the politics involved.

Justice Fortas stated that the problem at hand was to determine how the FBI's irrefutable evidence exposing Kennedy and the [Justice] Department in their clear-cut authorization for usage of microphones could be gotten to the Supreme Court and to the people. I showed him at this point several memoranda taken from the file. . . . He stated that there was no doubt in his mind but what the FBI acted in a complete, above-board and honest manner at the specific urging of Kennedy and the Department. He then stated that he fully recognized that Katzenbach would only slant any reply the FBI gave him in answer to questions posed by the Supreme Court.

After some deliberation, Justice Fortas stated that he thought the best thing to do would be for him to slip in the back door and see the President. He stated he would tell the President all of the above facts. As an aside, Justice Fortas asked me if the President had been aware of the exchange of correspondence pertaining to the Director and the Attorney General. I replied that the Director in all fairness and in order to protect the FBI, had definitely advised [White House aide Marvin] Watson and the President. The Justice replied that this was good, however, he felt that the President would want to know his opinion as a result of seeing it from the Supreme Court.

He then stated that his plan of action would serve to protect the President and the FBI and could spell "back seat" for Katzenbach and Kennedy. He mentioned that he would recommend to the President that the President should immediately call Katzenbach in his office and tell him that he was very greatly concerned about this entire matter and that, in order for honesty and justice to prevail, an arbitrator should be set up who would listen to all of the evidence and then furnish a complete report to the Supreme Court. Justice Fortas added that naturally the arbitrator would be someone whom the President could trust to furnish the absolute true facts.

He stated the next problem would be to find this particular man. He said he had in mind somebody like Ken Royall, former Secretary of the Army. He asked me what I thought of him. I told him I naturally had heard Mr. Royal's [sic] name, however, Mr. Hoover would have far better judgment on this matter than I would. He next stated that perhaps someone like Ross Malone, former President of the American Bar Association, would be good in this regard. I told him that we had enjoyed very favorable relations with Mr. Malone. Justice Fortas then mentioned that there was an immediate past President of the American Bar Association from the State of Virginia. I told him he probably was thinking of Lewis Powell. He stated this was correct. He asked me what I thought of Powell. I told him that Mr. Powell had generally concurred with Mr. Hoover's beliefs concerning crime, however, on occasions he had been somewhat naive and a little weak. . . .

Justice Fortas told me that . . . he was going to Jacksonville, Florida, today; however, he would try to talk to the President prior to his departure—if not, he would discuss this matter with the President Thursday morning, 6/16/66. I told him that time was growing short inasmuch as the Supreme Court wanted an answer almost immediately. He stated this was true and that, as a matter of fact, once the arbitrator was appointed all of his facts would have to be gathered and furnished to the Supreme Court within two weeks. He stated he thought this could be done.

Justice Fortas told me that he wanted to mention another subject. He stated that he had already taken steps to disqualify himself in the Hoffa case. He mentioned that the Black, [Bobby] Baker and Hoffa cases would be continuing cases which would go on for many years. He asked me if I knew of any irregularities on the part of Bobby Kennedy in connection with the Hoffa case. I replied in the affirmative, stating that Kennedy on one occasion had specifically asked an FBI representative to place a microphone on an attorney by the name of Haggerty . . . [and] that the FBI had not wanted to do this. Justice Fortas replied that he had felt that such might be the case and that under the circumstances he would sit with the rest of the Supreme Court on the Hoffa case and would make certain that Kennedy was exposed. He stated that he felt that the Supreme Court would definitely confirm the decision of the lower court in the Hoffa case. He mentioned that this opinion had been expressed to him by the other Justices. . . .

Justice Fortas next made reference to the decision handed down by the Supreme Court yesterday in connection with confessions. He stated that he sincerely hoped that the Director and the personnel of the FBI would pay close attention to the conclusion by Chief Justice [Earl] Warren wherein the Chief Justice clearly implied that the FBI was a model agency for all law enforcement to follow. Justice Fortas told me that he wanted the Director to know that following Thurgood Marshall's inept and stupid presentation to the Supreme Court regarding the general matter of confessions, he, Justice Fortas, had been instrumental in instructing Thurgood Marshall to specifically return to the Department and ascertain exactly how the FBI handled the matters of questioning of subjects, arraignment of subjects, confessions, etc. He stated that Marshall therefore, as a result of such action, had found it necessary to submit such procedures to the Supreme Court. He stated on this basis, Chief Justice Warren had no alternative but to pat the FBI on the back. . . .

At the conclusion of our discussion, the Justice reiterated once again the action he planned to take with the establishment of an "arbitrator." He stated that I should keep in touch with him on a confidential basis regarding this matter. He also stated that I should not hesitate in the future to get in touch with him concerning any problems in which the FBI's interest should be protected. He reminded me that the President had great faith in the Director and the FBI and that in many instances we undoubtedly found ourselves in a position where we could not protect ourselves. . . .
Action:
    . . . (2) If the Director agrees, I will advise Justice Fortas that the

Director is of the opinion that Ross Malone would probably be the best man to serve as an "arbitrator."

[Hoover's handwritten notation: "OK. Certainly Royal would be impossible. I had enough of him when he was counsel for the saboteurs & later when as Secretary of War [sic, Army] he was instrumental in throwing us out of SIS [Special Intelligence Service] & setting up CIA. As to the practicality of an 'arbitrator' I have some doubts. It can be another 'Warren Commission' & end in a fiasco."]

▣ Memo, FBI Director J. Edgar Hoover for Personal Files, June 14, 1966

Assistant to the Director DeLoach . . . [reported on his meeting with Fortas and] stated he outlined to the Justice the entire Black matter and told him what it is necessary for us to do is to protect the Bureau and gave the Justice the background of the exchange of correspondence and how Attorney General Katzenbach tried to blacken our name. . . . [Hoover then summarized the essence of DeLoach's memo on his meeting with Fortas.]

I told Mr. DeLoach I would, of course, be strongly inclined toward Ross Malone as I thought he would be a better man if they are going to name an arbitrator, although I did not see how they could work that around to supercede the Attorney General and the Solicitor General. I stated this means the whole thing then goes over to the fall term because an arbitrator will have to hold hearings and get our report. . . .

I told Mr. DeLoach that I thought if they felt it can be done by appointing an arbitrator, that's all right, that I knew the Department will not send up what we send over as they will distort and twist it. . . .

Mr. DeLoach stated there was one other angle; that Fortas referred to the Hoffa case and said he had disqualified himself insofar as the Hoffa case was concerned but he might get back in and asked DeLoach if he knew anything about electronic devices there and DeLoach said he did and that Kennedy had asked us to put one on Haggerty, the attorney in the case and Fortas was amazed and commented that now DeLoach had told him, he was going to qualify himself in that case again. I commented that they also had some man wired up who was dealing with Hoffa from New Orleans; that they put out orders to wire him up so there could be a recording of that although I did not know if it went through or whether he saw Hoffa or not, but I did know of the lawyer incident and that is damning itself. . . .

Mr. DeLoach commented he thought this meeting with Fortas was well worth it. I stated as it turned out, it was; that I was dubious as I don't know Fortas well myself, but I thought he would try to weasel out on the grounds it was improper for him as a member of the Court to even discuss the matter and then, of course, nothing could have been obtained, but he apparently is a more honest man than I gave him credit for. DeLoach stated that it boils down to the fact that he has to defend the President. . . .

■ **Informal Memo, FBI Assistant Director Cartha DeLoach to FBI Associate Director Clyde Tolson, June 21, 1966**

. . . [Fortas] told me in strict confidence that considerable progress had been made regarding the establishment of a three-man committee on wire tapping and electronic devices. I interrupted to ask him what had become of the single "arbitrator" idea originally proposed. He stated the President felt a three-man committee would be far better than one man.

Fortas told me that the President had decided to appoint Ross Malone, Lewis Powell, and Thurmond Arnold. Fortas stated he knew we did not care too much about Arnold; however, Arnold had been his former law partner and he not only would talk to him but would assure us that he would "handle him." He stated that if Arnold did not want the appointment the President was considering Whitney North Seymour. . . . Fortas asked that I check these matters with the Director and call him back as soon as possible inasmuch as he had to report to the President.

Fortas further told me that he had personally drafted the announcement that the President would make with respect to the establishment of this committee. He said it was more or less in the form of a general announcement which concerned "private usage" and pointed the finger at industrial espionage. He said he preferred to handle the announcement in this way inasmuch as both he and the President were anxious that no criticism should be made or intimated concerning the FBI.

After discussing the matter telephonically with the Director, I called Justice Fortas back and told him that, while the Director would defer to the President's desires, the Director did feel that Arnold would be a better man than Seymour. Fortas agreed and stated he would so advise the President.

At 1:30 today Watson's secretary called and asked that I come to Watson's office at 2:30 p.m. today. . . . [Watson] showed me a copy of a draft in connection with the above-mentioned committee. He asked that I examine this draft at once and give him an opinion. I told Watson it would be far better if I could bring the draft back to FBI headquarters and show it to the Director. Watson stated the President did not want the draft to leave the White House and he would prefer the matter not to be discussed over the telephone. He stated I could discuss the matter later with the Director upon returning to FBI headquarters. The draft ran thusly:

"The President has appointed a committee of three distinguished lawyers to report to him concerning the use within the United States of wire tapping and electronic espionage devices and to recommend such measures as they may conclude to be necessary and appropriate.

"The members of the committee are Thurmond Arnold, . . . Lewis S. Powell, Jr., . . . and Ross L. Malone, . . .

"The Committee has been requested to study available information with respect to the use of these devices by private persons and organizations for industrial espionage and other purposes, and their use by Federal agencies and officers within the United States. It is anticipated that the recommendations of the committee may lead to government-wide regulations applicable to all agencies, as well as to proposals for legislation.

"It is and has always been my conviction," continued the announcement, "that while special problems exist in certain areas, such as those affecting the national security, the use of espionage devices can lead to abuses which cannot be reconciled with a free society. Recent disclosures have indicated that there may be widespread use of such devices by private persons and organizations. This would raise problems of law enforcement and might suggest the need for legislation, and although I have heretofore admonished the agencies of the Federal Government with respect to the use of such devices, I believe that a complete, objective report, covering all agencies and officers of the Federal Government within the United States, will serve an important purpose.

"I have instructed all Federal agencies to cooperate with the committee that I am appointing and to furnish it with complete factual information, as well as with their suggestions. I have asked the committee to submit its report and recommendation to me on or before November 1, 1966."

I told Watson . . . I would like to suggest that, in the first paragraph, the reference to "electronic espionage devices" be changed to merely "electronic devices" or "electronic listening devices." I mentioned that usage of the word espionage implied jurisdiction by the FBI and perhaps unintentionally pointed the finger at our work. I stated also that the usage of phraseology such as "electronic espionage devices" implied usage of such devices in espionage cases alone, while microphones had definitely been used in organized crime cases and those involving kidnaping and extortion. I stated the same thing applied to the words "espionage devices" later on in the announcement, which should be changed to merely "listening devices," inasmuch as such phraseology again implied blame of the FBI.

Watson agreed . . . [and] called the President, who was up in his living quarters at the time. He told the President of my objections. . . . The President then told Watson to put me on the phone.

I explained to the President why I made such objections. . . . [He] then put Justice Fortas on the phone. I explained to Justice Fortas and Justice Fortas agreed thoroughly and stated the objectionable phraseology would be removed. I told Justice Fortas that I would appreciate the opportunity of acquainting Mr. Hoover with such phraseology. He asked that I do so and call him back if the Director had any further objections.

I returned immediately to FBI headquarters and acquainted both you and the Director with the above facts. The Director indicated he had no further objections and Justice Fortas was accordingly advised. . . .

■ **Informal Memo, FBI Assistant Director Cartha DeLoach to FBI Associate Director Clyde Tolson, June 23, 1966**

Marvin Watson called . . . to advise in confidence that the President had decided for the time being not to appoint a 3-man committee to study the subject of wiretapping and usage of electronic devices. Watson stated that the President had changed his mind in favor of other consideration. He did not elaborate on this statement.

You and the Director were both advised immediately of this information.

Justice Fortas called . . . [and] regretted the President's decision inasmuch as he felt this is the thing to do. I told him I hoped that this meant that certain people [Attorney General Katzenbach] were leaving the Government and therefore there would be no need for such action. He caught on to what I was talking about and stated he certainly hoped so too. He added that the man in question was certainly of no benefit to the President. . . .

[Katzenbach officially resigned as attorney general to accept an appointment as under secretary of state, and in later congressional testimony admitted that his conflict with Hoover over the Black case had made him "dramatically aware of the lengths to which the Bureau would go in trying to justify its authority. My correspondence with Mr. Hoover at that time unavoidably became a bitter one, and it persuaded me that I could no longer effectively serve as Attorney General because of Mr. Hoover's obvious resentment toward me."]

OVER THE YEARS, Hoover's FBI cultivated a variety of Washington sources for information. The gleanings may not have borne on the FBI's law-enforcement responsibilities, but they allowed Hoover to stay current with political developments in the nation's capital.

■ **Memo, FBI Assistant Director Edward Tamm to FBI Assistant Director Gordon Nease, January 5, 1946**
. . . Special Agent William H. Porzer is presently engaged on an undercover assignment at the Mayflower Hotel. . . . His responsibility is to work his way into the social and official strata to endeavor to develop information about irregularities, fraud and fixes in surplus property and also in frauds against the government and other matters in which the Bureau is interested. This assignment has been under way for about two weeks and up to the present time Porzer has devoted most of his time to making contacts.* He is telling everyone, including Bureau personnel whom he meets accidentally, that he has resigned from the Bureau. . . . He reports by telephone every morning and I arranged for him to dictate reports of developments by coming surreptitiously to my office. After he gets established in an undercover capacity this practice will become increasingly risky and I think we will have to arrange to have a male stenographer call upon him, probably at his hotel room, to take dictation. . . .

■ **Do Not File Memo, FBI Assistant Director Gordon Nease to FBI Director, January 9, 1946**
A confidential source [William Porzer] advised that Miss Mary McDonnell, secretary to Bob Lynch, formerly of the State Department, has advised that there is much discord between [Postmaster General] Bob Hannegan and Secretary [of State James] Byrnes because Byrnes is attempting to take complete leadership in the Democratic Party. Hanne gan and [White House aide] George Allen are now teaming up against Byrnes.
   The original point of issue between Byrnes and Hannegan was when Byrnes announced the Adele [sic, Adlai] Stevenson appointment direct rather than advise Hannegan so that appropriate officials in Chicago, Illinois, could be questioned as to their pleasure in the matter. . . .

*Porzer's contacts included five State Department officials (including assistant secretaries of state Spruille Braden and Patrick Hurley); Assistant Attorney General A. Gus Vanech; nine secretaries to prominent officials (including the secretaries to Solicitor General J. Howard McGrath, White House aide George Allen, a U.S. senator, and U.N. ambassador Edward Stettinius); two U.S. ambassadors (Francis Corrigan, Venezuela, and Joseph McGurk, Dominican Republic); two Commerce Department officials (Joseph Carroll, director of compliance, War Surplus Administration, and his assistant, Leo Laughlin); two White House aides; a Reconstruction Finance Corporation official; a Federal Trade Commission official; a War Department official; three War Production Board officials; four prominent businessmen; an Associated Press reporter; a friend of syndicated columnist Drew Pearson; a congressman; a federal judge; and numerous Washington socialites.—Ed.

The State Department employees are said to dislike Byrnes very much and are not cooperating with him.

John Paul Fitch who . . . was formerly with FEA [Foreign Economic Administration] and the State Department has advised [Porzer] that Wilson Wyatt of New Orleans who is now hooked up in some way with [head of the office of War Mobilization and Reconversion and Truman confidante] John Snyder, will be appointed head of the new National Housing Administration. Fitch will go with him. . . .

■ **Do Not File Memo, FBI Assistant Director Gordon Nease to FBI Director, January 10, 1946**

Our under cover man [William Porzer] called this morning and advised that he had . . . [met] the Ambassador from the Dominican Republic, who spoke very highly of our representatives in South America. He also renewed acquaintance with Hayden Raynor, the Economic Political Advisor to James Dunn of the State Department, who brought up the question of SIS [Special Intelligence Service, the specially created FBI intelligence section assigned by President Roosevelt to conduct intelligence operations in South America during World War II], stating he had seen numerous letters from Ambassadors protesting the recall of our men and when asked the reason for the recall, Raynor stated he supposed it was due to appropriations and partly due to the proposed intelligence set-up in the State Department.

[Porzer] stated that there appears to be some friction in the State Department resulting from the functions of the RFC [Reconstruction Finance Corporation] and the FEA [Foreign Economic Administration] being taken to the State Department; that Sewell Young appears to be the leader of the opposition, feeling that the work taken over from these two agencies should be under one head in the State Department.

He had nothing further to report.

■ **Do Not File Memo, FBI Supervisor R. W. Wall to FBI Assistant Director D. Milton Ladd, December 24, 1947**

Colonel C. W. Clarke of the Intelligence Division of the Army suggested that Special Agent S. W. Reynolds of the Liaison Section review two reports received through Colonel Clarke's most secret source regarding the Palestine situation. These reports both emanated from the French Embassy in Washington and were addressed to London. They indicate that such individuals as *Henry Morganthau* [sic], *Felix Frankfurter, Sol Bloom, Rabbi Stephen Wise* and *Bernard Baruch* all contacted the French Ambassador advising that France should vote positively in the Palestine affair. The reports indicate that these individuals are influential and have spoken of their devotion to the Franco-American cause.

Colonel Clarke confidentially advised Mr. Reynolds that he has learned that the Zionist groups spent millions in procuring an affirmative vote on the Palestine question. Colonel Clarke also advised confidentially that he had learned that *Robert Nathan* recently visited Washington, at which time he is alleged to have made it clear that the Jewish hierarchy expected the [Truman] Administration to furnish arms and equipment to the Jewish cause in Palestine or else the Administration could expect no support from the Jewish groups in 1948 elections.

It should be noted that Colonel Clarke advised Mr. Reynolds of the above information in extreme confidence.

■ **Memo, FBI Supervisor Christopher Seyfarth to FBI Assistant Director Louis Nichols, February 26, 1953**

I wish to call to your attention the fine cooperation that I am receiving from [Department of Justice employee Mrs. Donlan] in connection with official work concerning the FBI and the Department of Justice. . . .

At the present time it is very difficult to secure a Department of Justice file due to security measures. On numerous occasions I receive requests from FBI officials and supervisors to try and secure a Department of Justice file without the Department knowing that the FBI is interested. I immediately contact Mrs. Donlan and she gets the file in her name, places same in envelope, calls me on the telephone, hands me the envelope, and in this way I am able to secure the information without anyone in the Department knowing. . . . Also, very often, a certain memorandum has been sent to the FBI by an official in the Department of Justice. It often happens it is a very active case and the particular memorandum that is needed by the supervisor cannot be located in the FBI. After I contact Mrs. Donlan and give her the information that I am seeking, she calls for this particular file . . . and types for me a copy of the memorandum. . . . It is immediately handed to the [FBI] supervisor . . . and this of course does not delay further action on the pending case. . . .

The most outstanding work Mrs. Donlan has performed for me is . . . about three months ago . . . Mr. Keay's Section . . . [requested] a list . . . of all top officials in the Department, their rank, etc. [Hoover had requested this information in early January 1953 "to determine any soft spots" which he could use when briefing the new Republican attorney general Herbert Brownell.] I was told this was a most secretive matter and to be very careful how I got this information so as not to create suspicion in the Department. I knew the only way I could get this information was to contact Mrs. Donlan. After I explained to her fully what I wanted she said to me, "Chris, as you know, I am 100% for Mr. Hoover and the FBI and I will get this information for you as quickly as I can without anyone in the [Justice] Department knowing about it." In two days Mrs. Donlan handed me the list complete with all of the top officials down to the seventh man in rank in every Division in the Department. . . .

Several days ago while talking to Mrs. Donlan on some other matters, I mentioned the fact that the FBI and I were most appreciative for the wonderful help that she gives us and she mentioned at that time that I was not the only one she helps but that she also assists quite a number of Special Agents . . . [including nine in the Washington, D.C., field office]. She stated that at least three or four agents contact her every week in connection with cases they are working on.

Recommendation:

In view of the fact that I am certain that Mrs. Donlan is very loyal to the FBI and that she has helped me in so many ways, I would like to suggest that a letter signed by the Director be sent . . . thanking her for her fine cooperation and assistance to the FBI.

[Nichols's handwritten notation: "Let(ter) (signed by Hoover) to Mrs. Donlan 3/3/53."]

■ **Letter, Syndicated Columnist Drew Pearson to Donald Downes [Rome, Italy], June 5, 1953**

I have felt awfully bad at being such a poor correspondent. Life has been so hectic and I have been fighting on so many different fronts that I get unforgivably behind in my correspondence. Please forgive me.

I shall look forward to receiving your book and will write something that I hope will be helpful.

You probably won't believe what's happened to publishers in this country. I tried to get a book on Senator McCarthy published and took it up with some of the best publishing companies for whom I have worked in the past—Harper and Bros., Doubleday and Co. None of them would touch it even when I offered to write a special book for them in addition to the McCarthy book. It was finally published by Beacon Press [Jack Anderson and Roland May, *McCarthy: The Man, the Senator, the "Ism"*], the only publisher I know with any real courage.

I shall certainly be interested in hearing from you after the Italian elections. What is the inside dope on [Ambassador to Italy] Clare Luce's speech in Milan threatening to cut off American aid. It looked like a colossal boner, and the State Department was emphatic in saying that she did not consult them.

[It is unclear how the FBI obtained a copy of Pearson's letter to Downes and the air mail envelope in which it was mailed. The envelope bears a Washington, D.C., postmark stamped 9:30 p.m., confirming that the letter was intercepted after it had been mailed by Pearson.]

■ **Informal Memo, FBI Assistant Director Louis Nichols to FBI Associate Director Clyde Tolson, May 14, 1957**

[Syndicated Hearst columnist] George Sokolsky told me 5-13-57 that there is a rumor circulating in New York that [New York Times columnist] Arthur Krock actually wrote *Senator John Kennedy's book, "Profiles in Courage,"* which was on the best-seller list for more than a year but which *had not sold 100,000 copies and which received the Pulitzer Prize.* George told me that a group of New York people were working on this trying to get it verified and if the rumor is true, then the *charge of fraud will be made on the awarding of the Pulitzer Prize.*

■ **Memo, FBI Supervisor R. O. Allior to FBI Assistant Director Alan Belmont, August 17, 1960**

On 8-16-60 [FBI liaison agent Orrin] Bartlett . . . [learned from name withheld] in extreme confidence and for the Bureau's information only: [name withheld] is a close personal friend of Vice President [Richard] Nixon . . . [and] is working hard . . . to get Mr. Nixon elected and that he is busy contacting wealthy individuals to secure money for the campaign. [Name withheld] is hopeful that when the campaign "really gets under-way" in September that the Nixon forces will start to expose some of Senator [John] Kennedy's top advisors as "parlor pinks" and that this will probably have a lot of weight, particularly in the South.

If Senator Kennedy is elected, [name withheld] believes that the United States will slowly become a Socialist Government and that he plans to take a large chunk of his wealth and deposit it in a Swiss bank so if the United States follows the British pattern, at least he will have part of his wealth abroad where it cannot be touched. [Name withheld] commented, "This is a hell of a thing to do but I feel strongly about it." . . .

■ **Memo, FBI Supervisor G. H. Scatterday to FBI Assistant Director Alan Belmont, September 2, 1960**

The "Washington Post and Times Herald," August 31, 1960,

contained an article . . . [reporting] that Senator Kennedy had named a bipartisan committee to develop a new National Security Policy to be presented in the first one hundred days of the new Congress if he, Kennedy, is elected President. The group will be headed by Paul H. Nitze, former Chief of the State Department's Policy Planning Staff, and will include David K. E. Bruce, former Ambassador to France and Germany and one time Undersecretary of State; Roswell L. Gilpatric, New York attorney who worked on the Rockefeller study; and James A. Perkins, Vice President of the Carnegie Corporation. . . .

I thought you would be interested in the information contained in our files regarding the four above-mentioned individuals. . . .

■ **Memo, FBI Director J. Edgar Hoover to FBI Assistant Directors Clyde Tolson, Alan Belmont, William Sullivan, and Cartha DeLoach, January 14, 1965, Tolson File**

Judge Edward A. Tamm [former FBI assistant director] called and advised . . . that Congressman Don Edwards, who is described as a former FBI Agent, is very hostile to the Bureau and has introduced a bill or resolution to abolish the House Committee on Un-American Activities (HCUA). Judge Tamm continued that . . . present at the writing or drafting of the bill were [Frank] Wilkinson, a convicted communist, and Mr. and Mrs. [Carl] Braden, who formerly operated a communist school in Georgia. Judge Tamm stated it sounded so odd to him that an ex-FBI Agent would be associating with that kind of people. . . . He stated he could not understand why anybody who was mad at the FBI would think he was accomplishing anything by abolishing the HCUA. I inquired if he had mentioned the FBI in the bill and Judge Tamm stated that apparently he did not.

Judge Tamm stated that the name Wilkinson meant nothing to him and I stated he was convicted [of contempt of Congress for refusing to answer questions posed by HUAC] and the Bradens have always been active in communism. Judge Tamm stated the three are supposed to have collaborated with Edwards in a hotel room across from the House Office Building in writing the resolution and he thought that might be of interest to me.

I stated it is because there is an intensive drive to abolish the HCUA or to cut its appropriations materially. I stated they have already lined up 13 Congressmen in opposition to [HCUA] led by Jimmy Roosevelt, who has always opposed it. I stated there is a delegation coming down from New York week after next to try to line up Congressmen to abolish HCUA and we have already advised the Committee of that possibility. I stated I was glad to have this as there are three or four Congressmen, former Agents, who are high class fellows and from California and perhaps one of them can get to Edwards and try to pull his fangs.

Judge Tamm stated this information comes from a . . . former Assistant United States Attorney, with contacts on the Hill . . . [who] was not the type who would come to him with this type of thing if it were gossip and if it becomes essential he can pass the name on later. I stated it could be taken care of without bringing the Bureau or anybody else into the picture.

[DeLoach's handwritten notation: "(Summary) Memo 2/1—re C'man Edwards."]

[After Tamm's appointment to the federal district court in Washington, D.C., in 1948, he continued to forward to Hoover political intelligence, such as the above, which he thought might be of interest to the director. In this case, the FBI had already been active in trying to contain this political attempt to abolish the House committee. Dating from the 1940s, as documented in the Subversive Activities section, HUAC had been a useful conduit for disseminating FBI information. While sharing common political objectives, Hoover and the committee occasionally came into conflict— a conflict stemming from the committee's interest in publicity and its attendant downplaying of the FBI's role in the internal security area, as well as a certain carelessness in publicly suggesting FBI assistance.]

INCLUDED IN THE *section on John Kennedy is a July 13, 1960, summary memorandum on Kennedy, setting out whatever derogatory personal and political information the FBI had compiled on him. Prepared for Hoover's attention in view of Kennedy's anticipated success in gaining the Democratic presidential nomination (indeed, Kennedy won the nomination that day), this FBI report on the character and politics of liberal politicians was not exceptional. For example, on April 3 and July 24, 1952, and again on March 22, 1956, Hoover's aides had prepared similar summary memoranda on Adlai Stevenson, another liberal Democrat. As in Kennedy's case, the timing of these preparations was purposeful.*

On March 29, 1952, President Harry Truman announced his decision not to accept renomination as the Democratic presidential nominee, and Stevenson's name was cited as a likely candidate. At first Stevenson disavowed interest in the presidency. But after his electrifying welcoming speech at the Democratic National Convention in Chicago, he announced on July 24, 1952, that he would allow his name to be submitted for the nomination. Defeated in 1952, Stevenson remained the front-runner for the Democratic presidential nomination four years later, and by March 1956 he had lined up endorsements of major Democratic leaders for his renewed candidacy.

These three summary memoranda on Stevenson provided information about his attitudes toward law enforcement and the FBI. But the principal information in them bore on Stevenson's "subversive activities." The cited evidence, however, consisted exclusively of reports on his associations with suspect individuals and organizations. Readers today may find this "evidence" trivial and inconsequential, but it was this kind of "evidence" of "communist" associations that Senator Joseph McCarthy and the House Committee on Un-American Activities cited as documentation of "Communists in government."

I have not reprinted the three summary memoranda on Stevenson for considerations of space, but I have included a synopsis of the July 24, 1952, document to convey their essence.

More revealing of Hoover's interest in acquiring information which could serve his own bureaucratic and political interests, the FBI collected and maintained information alleging that Stevenson was a homosexual. (Indeed, Stevenson earned a place in the separately maintained "Sex Deviate" card file, a ready reference at FBI headquarters.) Hoover's interest in such information was not exceptional. In his secret office files, as we have seen, he retained information documenting the sexual indiscretions of prominent national leaders, including John Kennedy, Eleanor Roosevelt, Dwight Eisenhower, and various members of Congress (whose names the FBI has withheld).

The following documents show not only that such allegations were reported direct to Hoover but that further reports were welcomed and appropriately maintained. In Stevenson's case, when the FBI's interest in such information became known, FBI officials moved quickly to rebut the reports.

The Stevenson case was exceptional in one respect—the FBI director's willingness to share derogatory information with Stevenson's conservative political opponents. While not a

*comprehensive record of Hoover's assistance, the extant
documents confirm his interest in containing liberal politics.*

■ **Informal Memo, New York SAC Edward Scheidt to FBI Director
Hoover, April 17, 1952**

[Name withheld detective in New York district attorney's office] . . .
[reported] that last week he was assigned to go to Peoria, Illinois and bring
to New York the Bradley [University] basketball players who are under
indictment for a basketball fix.

In bringing the players back to New York, they advised [name withheld]
that the two best known *homosexuals* in the state were [Bradley University]
President [David] Owen and Governor Stevenson, and that Stevenson was
known as "Adeline." The basketball players were of the opinion that
Stevenson *would not* run for President because of this.

■ **Index Card, Sex Deviate Index Card File***

Stevenson, Adlai Ewing
Governor of Illinois
Sex Deviate
Memo from SAC Scheidt, NY, dated 4-17-52 (ans. 6-24-52)
94-4-980984 (April 17, 1952)

[Handwritten notation: "Removed from (Bradley University president
David) Owens card."]

■ **Informal Memo, FBI Assistant Director D. Milton Ladd to FBI
Director, June 24, 1952**

Pursuant to your request, there is attached hereto a blind memorandum
concerning Governor Stevenson, who, it has been alleged, is a known
homosexual. . . .

Attachment Blind Memo Re Adlai Ewing Stevenson

An official of the City of New York ascertained from an individual, as
well as from a public official, both from the State of Illinois, that Governor
Adlai Ewing Stevenson was one of the best-known homosexuals in the
State of Illinois. Stevenson was allegedly well-known as "Adeline."
Because of Stevenson's being a homosexual, it was the opinion of the

*Created in 1951 in response to Hoover's authorization of a special sex deviate
program, this index card file provided a centralized aid for identifying and
retrieving all reports of alleged homosexuality submitted since 1937.—Ed.

individuals who made this statement that he would not run for President in 1952.

■ **Informal Memo, FBI Supervisor Milton Jones to FBI Assistant Director Louis Nichols, July 24, 1952**

Purpose:

To synopsize the highlights of a detailed [nineteen-page] summary memorandum on Stevenson. . . .

Stevenson met [Alger] Hiss in 1933, in Washington when they were both employed by the Government. He also had contacts with Hiss during Hiss' service with the United Nations. . . . During the Hiss trial a deposition by Stevenson on behalf of Hiss' good character was read into the record by the Defense Counsel.

IV. *Association with Front Groups:*

Stevenson has allowed his name to be used as a sponsor by some groups which have been Communist controlled or infiltrated. They include a move to furnish economic aid to civilians of Loyalist Spain, 1938; and a society which sought cultural relations with Italy, 1947, and which was Communist inspired. In 1944, his name was discussed as a possible chairman of the Chicago Council of American Soviet Friendship, as a "progressive-thinking fellow."

The name of Stevenson also appeared in several documents of the Institute of Pacific Relations (IPR) which were in custody of Edward C. Carter, once its secretary. They do not reflect extent of his association other than that he was considered as one of numerous who had "contributed" to the work of the IPR. His name appears on a membership list of IPR in 1938.

V. *Miscellaneous:*

In 1949, Governor Stevenson vetoed bills in Illinois designed to outlaw the Communist Party and to set up a seditious activities investigating committee on the ground of existing Federal and Illinois laws on subversive activities.

In the April, 1952, issue of Harper's Magazine Bernard DeVoto in a laudatory article discussed Governor Stevenson as a strong candidate for the presidency of the United States stating the "independent voter sees in him just such a younger spokesman of liberal democracy as a compelling need demands."

VI. *Alleged Sexual Perversion*

In April, 1952, the New York Office received confidential information from a detective of the New York District Attorney's office to the effect that Adlai Stevenson and David B. Owen, President, Bradley University,

Peoria, Illinois, were two officials in Illinois who caused a great deal of trouble to law enforcement officers.

The detective had gone to Peoria to bring back basketball players who had been indicted in New York. The basketball players told the detective that the two best-known homo-sexuals in Illinois were Owen and Stevenson. According to the report, Stevenson was known as "Adeline."

■ **Memo, FBI Assistant Director D. Milton Ladd to FBI Director, August 15, 1952**

[Assistant SAC Washington] Fletcher . . . [reported having learned] that there was some high official alleged to be spreading word that [Adlai] Stevenson was a "queer"; that the FBI had a file on him. Further that the Democratic National Committee was very angry about the situation. . . .

I instructed ASAC Fletcher to have [name withheld Washington, D.C., police officer] immediately interviewed and instructed to "put up" or "shut up," and to run this matter back to its source in order to stop any such erroneous rumor.

[Name withheld] when interviewed . . . stated that he had overheard a conversation at the Mayflower Hotel among some men at an adjacent table, whose identity he did not know, and they indicated that they had heard that [Washington SAC] Guy Hottel had indicated the "FBI had a file indicating Mr. Stevenson to be a 'queer'." [Name withheld] states he knows Mr. Hottel and knows that Mr. Hottel was not at the table at the time he had heard this conversation. He stated he has not seen Mr. Hottel for some time.

Mr. Hottel was interviewed and a statement obtained from him. Mr. Hottel states that he knows [name withheld] but has not seen him for some time. He categorically denied having made such a statement to anyone and states in fact, he could not have made such a statement because he does not know whether the Bureau does or does not have such a file by reason of the fact that he is working in the Fingerprint Division and would have no access to Bureau files. . . .

■ **Personal and Confidential, Informal Memo, FBI Assistant Director Louis Nichols to FBI Director, August 29, 1952**

Milt Hill . . . is a very precautious type of individual, he is intensely anti-Communist, very loyal to the Bureau, and has been a friend of mine over a period of years. He is close to Arthur Summerfield [chairman] of the Republican National Committee and is doing leg work for Summerfield at the present time. He is also a personal friend of [Republican presidential nominee Dwight] Eisenhower. . . .

Hill recently advised me that he has been assigned to do the official Republican biography of Governor Stevenson. A former [FBI] Special Agent, Orval Yarger, who had a very good record in the Bureau, contacted the Republican National Committee and stated he had some information he desired to furnish. After considerable jockeying around, Hill saw him on August 28. Before [Yarger] talked to Hill he wanted a statement in writing to the effect that if anything is ever attributed to him, that if his name is ever used, that at no time would anyone associate him with the FBI or would there be any attempt to capitalize upon his prior Bureau background. . . .

Hill is to spend the next several days with Yarger compiling information which Yarger has. Although Yarger is short on documents, he is an eye witness to activities in the Purchasing Department of the State of Illinois [where he had been employed after retiring from the Bureau].

Milt, of course, has said nothing to Yarger about his acquaintenceship [sic] with me and Yarger has no suspicion that Hill is furnishing me details which Yarger is furnishing him. Hill emphasized he is furnishing me this information on a strictly personal and confidential basis. I assured him his confidence would be respected.

Hill has already furnished me with a copy of his first memorandum on his conversation [with Yarger]. He stated incidentally that four copies are made: one copy goes to Summerfield, one to a Bob McIlvane, Hill is keeping a third copy. He asked me to read and destroy the fourth copy. I think we must maintain Hill's confidence at any cost.

Hill stated . . . Yarger has an excellent attitude, he is a man of high principle, is very decent, is very intense in his feelings toward the situation in Illinois which he blames to Governor Stevenson.

Yarger has further told Hill that Stevenson is very bitter against the Director and it appears that the basic reason grew out of the fact that Stevenson came back to Washington shortly after he was elected [Governor of Illinois in 1948] to see the Director regarding the possibility of borrowing a former Agent named Randolph (Ross Randolph), that the Director would not see him although he was told the Director was out of town but someone else did see him and this apparently caused Stevenson considerable pique. Stevenson has referred to the Director as that "bastard in the Bureau." Yarger also told Hill that Stevenson's feelings might perhaps very well stem likewise from his old associations in the State Department.

The attached memorandum from Hill [not included in the file] is self-explanatory. There is nothing in here within our jurisdiction although Hill . . . recommends they might get someone after an investigation of these charges, to present the facts to the United States Attorney. I subsequently asked Hill how he would get this done, bearing in mind the United States Attorneys are Democratics. He stated that was a stupid observation of his, that what he meant was that some prosecuting attorney might precipitate a Grand Jury investigation.

Hill has further told me that Yarger is very cautious in what he says, that he has a very definite feeling Yarger is understating rather than overstating, that the material will have to be subjected to intensive investigation before it is used although Yarger furnished some of the material as an eye witness and has stated he is perfectly willing to stand up in court and testify to that which he furnishes Hill as fact.

Hill stated there was one item which Yarger labeled as "scuttlebutt" and would not reveal his source for it. He did say he had heard it from responsible sources. The information was that some years ago, presumably during the [Paul] O'Dwyer [mayoralty] regime in New York, Stevenson was arrested on a morals charge, put up bond, and elected to forfeit. Furthermore, that the articles which have recently been widely syndicated and which were reputedly based on interviews of Mrs. Stevenson, knocked down all of the whispers as to the reason for the divorce but never explained why she really divorced Stevenson. . . .

Since Hill furnished the attached memorandum to me on a personal basis, I am wondering if it wouldn't be advisable for me to return the memorandum to him (after, of course, making a photostatic copy which would not go to [the FBI's main] files).

■ **Memo, FBI Supervisor V. P. Keay to FBI Supervisor Alan Belmont, August 25, 1952**

I thought you would be interested in receiving the following information concerning [Adlai Stevenson], who is the Democratic nominee for President of the United States.

[Name withheld], Office of Naval Intelligence (ONI), advised on a highly confidential basis that while reviewing ONI's file on a [name withheld] it was noted that a memorandum was contained therein dated June 1, 1942, which presumably had been signed by Adlai E. Stevenson at the time he was acting as Special Assistant to the Secretary of the Navy in 1942. This communication dealt with the appeal of [this name withheld individual, at the time employed as a radio operator but who was dismissed on the basis of the Navy's ruling concerning his "alleged insubordination and un-American activities"] before a Naval board set up to deal with the qualifications of commercial radio operators. . . .

According to [the name withheld ONI official] it is not known whether Stevenson actually reviewed this matter; however, it was noted that Stevenson's signature appeared at the conclusion of this memorandum, . . . [and] the following is in substance what was contained in this memorandum. It stated the documents filed in this appeal had been examined and from what could be observed, they merely indicated that [name withheld] is an ardent and energetic trade unionist but produced no evidence reflecting upon [his] competency . . . or anything to substantiate the charge that he had been insubordinate in his behavior. It continued by stating that the only possible basis for disqualification . . . was the fact that [name withheld] was probably a Communist Party member or sympathizer. However, in the absence of creditable evidence of insubordination or other unfitnesses as a radio operator, . . . [name withheld] should be reinstated. . . .

Bureau files reflect that [name withheld was listed in the FBI's] Security Index since the latter part of December, 1941, after investigation . . . indicating that [name withheld] was possibly a dangerous Communist Party member. . . . Investigation since that date has been conducted by the Bureau and at the present time additional inquiries are being made relative to him. . . .

Action:

None. For your information.

■ **Memo, FBI Supervisor Alan Belmont to FBI Assistant Director D. Milton Ladd, January 19, 1953**

Mr. Donald Dawson, Administrative Assistant to the President [Harry Truman] . . . heard that the Bureau had investigated Adlai E. Stevenson and desired to obtain copies of the reports. He stated he would like the reports this afternoon as he would not be at the White House after today [with the inauguration of Dwight Eisenhower on January 20].

Bureau files reflect that the Bureau investigated Stevenson in 1937 as a Departmental applicant. This investigation failed to disclose any derogatory information concerning Mr. Stevenson. . . . There is also in the Bureau two miscellaneous files concerning Stevenson which contain various references to him but do not disclose any investigative reports having been made. The information in these latter two files is that type of information which is generally submitted to the Bureau by various persons on prominent personages.

Pursuant to the Director's instructions, [White House liaison Ralph] Roach contacted Mr. Dawson and informed him that it was not recalled that the Bureau had ever investigated Mr. Stevenson and that if he, Dawson, had reference to some old investigation that we had made, it would be necessary for the Bureau's files in the Archives to be checked. Dawson stated that he did not refer to an old investigation and that he had reference to an investigation that was allegedly conducted by the Bureau within the past four or five years. He was told by Mr. Roach that the Bureau had not conducted an investigation in recent years and that if it was desired, a further check would be made into the old records. Mr. Dawson stated this was not necessary. . . .

■ **Memo, FBI Assistant Director Louis Nichols to FBI Associate Director Clyde Tolson, November 1, 1956**
Miss Dorothy Donnelly of the Vice President's [Richard Nixon] office, whom I have known for many years called me. The Vice President had a letter from an individual in Chicago stating that [William Wirtz, one of Stevenson's speech writers, and a second name withheld speech writer who] was a Communist Party organizer. She wondered where she might verify this. I suggested that she check with the House Committee on Un-American Activities, as well as the Daily Worker.

[The second name withheld individual] who was in the Communist Party and now claims that he is out although his actions are dubious. A brief summary is attached.

[The summary ran five pages and detailed whatever derogatory personal and political information the FBI had compiled on Wirtz and this second individual.]

■ **Memo, FBI Assistant Director William Sullivan to FBI Assistant Director Alan Belmont, December 28, 1961**
You may be interested in the following information which was furnished to the Bureau. . . . [U.S. Ambassador to the United Nations Adlai] Stevenson visited La Paz [Bolivia] a few months ago and . . . became ill shortly after his arrival, which can be understood since this is a common affliction in view of the high altitude. Upon arrival at his hotel, he was confronted by a U.S. Marine who stated, "Governor I have been instructed to inform you that two Bolivian students have vowed to assassinate you." According to the Attache, Stevenson immediately began to tremble and practically staggered into the elevator. Once in the elevator, he began gasping for breath and almost fainted when the elevator became stuck between floors. The Military Attache, who was supplied with a small oxygen tank, immediately shoved the mask to the Governor's face. The door of the elevator finally opened but it was necessary to climb about three feet to the opening. Stevenson couldn't make it. The Attache was able to get under him and finally to throw and shove him to the floor level.

While in Lima [Peru], Stevenson made a point of visiting the National Museum of Archaeology, which has a collection of highly pornographic Inca statuettes. That particular collection is kept closely guarded and not available to the public. During his visit to the Museum, however, the

Director [of the museum] inquired if Stevenson would like to see the exhibit. Stevenson, however, declined in front of the other people who were with him but later returned to the Museum for a private viewing of the exhibit alone.

Action: For information.

■ **Informal Memo, FBI Supervisor William Cleveland to FBI Assistant Director Courtney Evans, October 31, 1964**

In accordance with the Director's request, there is enclosed herewith a copy of the summary memorandum concerning Stevenson. . . . We conducted the investigation in December, 1960, at the request of the Kennedy Administration [which had requested security checks of all senior-level appointees, including Stevenson's appointment as U.S. ambassador to the United Nations].

There was an allegation of homosexuality developed during the Stevenson investigation and information concerning that was included in the letter of transmittal which accompanied the summary when it was personally delivered to Lawrence O'Brien of Kennedy's staff on 12-29-60. The following summarizes information which was included in the transmittal letter and was not in the summary:

[Four lines withheld on sources and methods grounds.] One was that Stevenson and Owen were members of an elite homosexual group in New York where Stevenson had the feminine name Adelaide. The other version that the "Queens Morals Squad," or the "State's Attorney," Queens, New York, in 1950 or 1951 raided a gathering of homosexuals at an unknown place in New York City and Stevenson and Owen were found to be present. No arrests or charges reportedly were made.

[Two paragraphs, thirteen lines in length, withheld on sources and methods grounds.]

Rumors that Stevenson is a homosexual have been attributed to disgruntled officials of the Illinois State Police and former Bradley University basketball player Gene Melchiore. [Name withheld New York City detective] confidentially furnished information to [FBI] New York Office in 1950 [sic] indicating the rumors may have emanated from the Peoria, Illinois Police Department (PD) or Bradley University basketball players. . . .

HOOVER WAS NOT content to have his aides accumulate derogatory personal and political information which had no prosecutive value. When Congress in 1950 became alarmed over the security threat posed by "homosexuals in government," Hoover moved quickly to exploit this opportunity to utilize the FBI's burgeoning files (dating from 1937) identifying alleged homosexuals. In June 1951 he established a formal sex deviate program, first to purge the federal bureaucracy, later universities and police agencies, of alleged homosexuals.

■ **Memo, FBI Executives' Conference to Director, October 14, 1953, FBI 62-93875—Not Recorded**

The Executives' Conference . . . considered current policy relative to furnishing information from Bureau files outside of the Executive Departments and made recommendations as to future procedures. As the problem covers a wide area, it is broken down, as set forth below, under separate captions with the Executives' Conference recommendations as to each: . . .

(8) *Sex Deviates.*

Memorandum for Bureau Officials and Supervisors of June 20, 1951, set forth a uniform policy for furnishing information concerning allegations concerning present and past employees of any branch of the United States Government. In addition to specific instructions for furnishing information to the Executive Branch, specific individuals were designated to receive this information in the Legislative Branch, i.e., the United States Senate, the Botanical Gardens, the Library of Congress, the House of Representatives, General Accounting Office, and Government Printing Office. A specified individual was designated to receive information concerning sex deviates among employees of the Judicial Branch of the Government. In the past since the designation of this policy, dissemination has been made in accordance with the policy set forth.

Executives' Conference Recommendation:

The Executives' Conference unanimously recommended that we continue our policy in connection with the dissemination of information on sex deviates. . . .

[Hoover's handwritten notation: "OK."]

■ **Memo, FBI Assistant Director Leland Boardman to Director, October 28, 1954, FBI 62-93875-2503**
. . . *Sex Deviates*
Memorandum for Bureau Officials and Supervisors of June 20, 1951, sets forth a uniform policy for furnishing information concerning allegations as to sex deviate activities on the part of present and past employees of any branch of the United States Government. . . . This policy was continued after approval by the Executive Conference in October, 1953. In appropriate instances where the best interest of the Bureau is served, information concerning sex deviates employed either by institutions of higher learning or law enforcement agencies is disseminated to proper officials of such organizations. . . .

■ **Memo, [name withheld] FBI Agent to FBI Assistant Director Alex Rosen, October 22, 1954, FBI 62-93875—Not Recorded**
. . . There is no arrangement whereby [the FBI's Training and Inspection] Division, on a confidential basis, furnishes information to individuals or organizations. However: (1) On a few occasions the Director has instructed that we confidentially make available to George Washington University information concerning sex deviates or Communists employed as teachers there. However, there is no continuing program in this regard. (2) Although there is no continuing program with New York University, we have on one occasion within the recent past confidentially advised a contact at the University as to the sex deviate practices of an instructor who was involved in the Police Training Field and concerning whom there was a pending Security investigation which was later closed. (3) [five lines withheld on personal privacy grounds].
There is no continuing program of this type in the Training and Inspection Division. . . .
(4) *Sex Deviates* Information regarding sex deviates in the Legislative Branch is disseminated [by the FBI's domestic intelligence division] to designated individuals in the Senate, House, General Accounting Office, Government Printing Office, Library of Congress, and Botanical Gardens. Similar information furnished to person designated in Judicial Branch. Approved by Executives Conference 10/23/53. . . .
[The number of names in the FBI's sex deviate card file and the scope of its dissemination efforts cannot be determined because in 1977 FBI officials purposefully destroyed the three files at FBI headquarters which contained reports on alleged homosexuals and the operation of this program: 94-4-980 (Sex Degenerates and Sex Offenders), 105-34074 (Sex

Offenders Foreign Counterintelligence), and 105-12189 (Sex Perverts in Government Service). These files were massive—ninety-nine and a half cubic feet and approximately 300,000 pages—and contained all indexed reports of alleged homosexuality submitted between 1937 and 1977.]

15: The Obscene File

VIRTUALLY FROM THE time of his appointment as acting director of the FBI in May 1924, Hoover recognized the value of acquiring information about "obscene or indecent" activities. While he found pornography personally distasteful and feared its impact on the morals of his fellow citizens, he also recognized that his attitudes were shared by an influential constituency of religious and civic leaders. In March 1925 he authorized creation of a discrete Obscene File and devised a special submission procedure to ensure that "obscene or indecent" materials would be routed to this centrally maintained source. While the contents of the Obscene File consisted chiefly of pornographic films, literature, and other printed matter, FBI field offices also employed this special records procedure to forward sensitive information about illicit sexual activities.

Hoover's decision to create an Obscene File promoted his own and the Bureau's interests in a number of ways. First, the centralized depository ensured ready access and retrievability. Second, the strict collection procedure ensured that FBI employees would not have access to the obscene materials, fulfilling Hoover's puritanical bent. Third, the file could be used to further the FBI's bureaucratic interests—exemplified by the servicing of requests from other federal intelligence agencies. Finally, prosecutions for obscenity could ensure favorable publicity for the FBI.

■ **Letter, Director J. Edgar Hoover to All Special Agents in Charge, SAC Letter #512, March 24, 1925, FBI 66-04-X92**
It is my desire that the following methods be employed in the transmis-

sion through the mails, as well as in the filing, of all obscene matter such as booklets, leaflets, photographic prints, etc.

Whenever it becomes necessary to forward any obscene matter of any nature whatsoever, either to some other field office or to the Bureau, all exhibits of any kind or type which may properly be classified as obscene or improper should be placed in a separate envelope or package. Said envelope or package is to be sealed and there should be inscribed on the cover thereof in large type or letters the word "OBSCENE," in order that the nature of the contents may be noted at a glance. There should also appear on the cover of the envelope or package in question the title of the case to which the obscene exhibits or documents refer and the [FBI field] office of origin. Said envelope or package may then be attached to the report to which it pertains, or forwarded under separate cover.

The same method is to be observed in filing obscene matter in all field offices. It is not desired that any matter which may properly be classified as obscene or improper be forwarded to a field office or to the Bureau unsealed, or placed in the files of a field office in like manner.

Your strict compliance with the above rules is directed.

■ **Strictly Confidential Bureau Bulletin No. 37, Series 1946, July 10, 1946, FBI 66-03-759**

. . . (C) Interstate Transportation of Obscene Material—Submission of Obscene Exhibits to Bureau—Investigation of Cases—It is imperative that all obscene exhibits be immediately submitted to the Bureau at the earliest possible moment . . . [and] prior to presenting the facts and the exhibits to the appropriate U.S. Attorney for a prosecutive opinion. It is essential that all obscene exhibits be forwarded to the Bureau expeditiously in order that they may be

1. Reviewed at the Bureau with regard to their character as obscene exhibits.

2. Compared with specimens already obtained in the Obscene File of the FBI Laboratory in order that a laboratory report may be sent to the interested divisions relative to the source of the obscene literature.

3. Compared with specimens already in the Obscene File of the FBI Laboratory in order that a report may be submitted to the interested divisions relative to any indication known to the Bureau that this same type of obscene material has moved in interstate commerce.

4. Included as a permanent part of the Obscene File or destroyed where no purpose could be served by filing the exhibit.

All obscene material sent to the Bureau should be forwarded under obscene cover, marked for the attention of the FBI Laboratory. It should be accompanied by a cover letter identifying the exhibits and clearly stating the source of the material. . . . If they are further needed by the submitting division for use as evidence or as an investigative aid, such should be clearly indicated. In this instance the exhibits will be promptly returned to the field together with a laboratory report. If the exhibits are of no further value, a statement should be set forth indicating that the exhibits may be disposed of as deemed appropriate by the FBI Laboratory. In this instance representative copies will be maintained of all specimens while useless duplicates will be destroyed. It is to be remembered that in all cases exhibits returned to the submitting division must ultimately be returned to the FBI Laboratory for filing or destruction. No obscene material is to be permanently maintained in any division office.

Prosecution must proceed promptly in all obscene matter cases investigated by the Bureau where it has been established that the subject is transporting definitely obscene material in interstate commerce by means of express or common carrier in violation of Section 396, Title 18, U.S. Code. Unquestionably obscene exhibits are those which depict or describe activities which are clearly lewd, lascivious and licentious. Examples of true pornography would be so-called "stag" motion picture films of either the still or sound variety. . . . Other obscene exhibits have been found in the nature of printed pamphlets, free-hand drawings, comic strip cartoons, book novels, playing cards and photographs. Approximately one year ago the Post Office Department was considerably embarrassed when it revoked the second-class mailing privileges of Esquire Magazine. The U.S. Court of Appeals for the District of Columbia attacked the ruling of the Post Office Department in this so-called Varga Girl case and commented that it was the court's hope "that this is the last time that a government agency will attempt to compel the acceptance of its literary or moral standards relating to material admittedly not obscene." The Bureau must insist that each Special Agent in Charge closely follow the investigation of all obscene matter investigations undetaken [sic] by his division in order to insure that criticism does not result from the Bureau's investigation of cases which involve such items as pin-up pictures, art poses, nudist photographs or magazines, parlor novelties or other exhibits obviously not obscene or which are of highly questionable obscenity. The Bureau must make a common-sense view in these obscene matter cases, not a prudish one.

The Bureau is vitally interested in ascertaining the original source of obscene material. Examination of specimens submitted by the various divisions has resulted in determining by Laboratory Technicians that the bulk of this material emanates from a common source and is distributed by certain commercial purveyors of obscene materials. It is the general practice of such commercial exploiters to disseminate their products among school children and adults with perverted minds. For this reason it is extremely desirable that all field divisions submit samples of obscene material to the FBI Laboratory regardless of the source from which they are obtained. Even though no Federal violation exists, any material of this nature made available by local police agencies should be transmitted to the Bureau in order to increase the effectiveness of the Obscene Files.

Each obscene literature investigation possesses potential publicity value because of the very nature of the investigation. Every Special Agent in Charge should closely follow obscene matter investigations in order that consideration may be given to obtaining proper publicity in appropriate cases. Where it is contemplated that publicity will result from the Bureau's investigation of an obscene matter case, it is the responsibility of the Special Agent in Charge to make certain that the Bureau is notified in advance of any contemplated arrest, arraignment or other development prior to the time that any publicity is released.

During the course of the investigation . . . obscene material is generally obtained in Bureau cases through one of the following methods:

1. Voluntarily surrendering the exhibits by the subject in conjunction with an interview and the obtaining of a signed statement.

2. Through a search of the subject or his premises incidental to an arrest.

3. Through a written waiver consenting to a voluntary search of the subject's premises.

4. Through the authority of a formal search warrant.

The Bureau has experienced no difficulty in obtaining the necessary evidence in investigations of this character. However, there are certain individuals or their attorneys who may seek to embarrass the Bureau in the event the material is obtained improperly. Therefore, every precaution must be exercised by Special Agents to insure that all searches and seizures of evidence are accomplished in strict compliance with Federal law and Bureau regulations. Utmost care must be exercised to insure that no embarrassment will result to the Bureau and no action should be taken which will give the subject or his attorney grounds for challenging any investigative steps taken by the Agent because of the alleged employment of illegal or unconstitutional methods.

Juvenile delinquency is often encouraged by the distribution of obscene materials by commercial dealers. Local vice and crime is often stimulated through the circulation of pornography and in some instances racial agitation is inflamed. For these reasons the Bureau is anxious to develop for successful prosecution all cases involving the interstate transportation of obscene matter in violation of Section 396, Title 18, U.S. Code but all investigation undertaken must be conducted in strict compliance with the instructions set forth herein. . . .

■ **Memo, FBI Supervisor W. D. Griffith to FBI Assistant Director I. Conrad, July 11, 1966, FBI 66-3286—Not Recorded**

A review has been made of the physical and administrative files (80-622) relating to obscene material.

The physical file of obscene material is subdivided as follows: 1. Obscene and nude art motion picture films—1364; 2. Phonograph records—321; 3. Readers and pamphlets—3020; 4. Obscene books, nudist publications and questioned periodicals—898; 5. Cartoon booklets—5611; 6. Playing cards—183; 7. Miscellaneous cartoons, printed matter and novelties mounted on 373 cards; 8. Obscene and strip type photographs mounted on 1593 cards; 9. Advertising literature (by companies involved)—163.

The following index files are maintained as a part of the Obscene File: 1. Motion picture film titles, subtitles and categories; 2. Book titles; 3. Photograph code numbers; 4. Phonograph record titles; 5. Name of models who have posed for obscene and/or strip type photographs; 6. Advertising literature by company or producer names; 7. Opinions of the Department of Justice relative to obscenity of evidence.

A total of 10,458 specimens were received in the fiscal year of 1965–66 and searched in the Obscene File. . . .

It is noted that the bulk of the material in the Administrative file (80-662) consists of yellow [carbon] copies of [original] Laboratory reports. These copies are designated for 80-662 to afford a double check on the statistical record of identifications made. . . .

Recommendation:

1. The Obscene File be maintained in its present condition.

2. Discontinue adding yellow copies of Laboratory reports to 80-662 file and destroy yellow copies of Laboratory reports which are presently a part of 80-662 file.

■ **SAC Letter 69-19, March 29, 1966, FBI 66-3286—Not Recorded**

. . . (H) Maintenance and Destruction of Obscene Evidence—Interstate Transportation of Obscene Matter—Because of the large volume of obscene evidence received in the FBI Laboratory and the urgent need for careful handling, the basic rules for maintenance and destruction . . . are restated.

"Obscene material is submitted to the Laboratory in order that it may be: a. Reviewed at the Bureau with regard to its character as an obscene exhibit; b. Compared with specimens already in the obscene matter file of the FBI Laboratory, and any latent fingerprints developed thereon searched

through the obscene matter dealers section of the single fingerprint file, to
determine its source; c. Compared with specimens already in the obscene
matter file of the FBI Laboratory for information that may indicate that the
questioned obscene material has been moved in interstate commerce; d.
Included as a permanent part of the obscene matter file or destroyed where
no purpose could be served by filing the exhibit."

The [FBI] manual instructs that in all cases exhibits . . . must ultimately
be returned to the FBI Laboratory for filing or destruction and that no
obscene material is to be permanently maintained in any field office. There
are instances, however, involving huge quantities of pornography seized in
certain cases where there is considerable expense in shipping the evidence
back to the Laboratory for final disposition. . . . If little or none of the
bulky evidence is needed for the Obscene File and common sense suggests,
the Bureau may authorize destruction of the useless portion of the material
in the division office under rigid controls, personally supervised by the
SAC.

While obscene material which may arouse the curiosity of employees is
in the office, it must be maintained in either the gun vault or the SAC's
safe. At no time should it be kept in a place which is readily accessible to
other employees, such as the stock room or mail room.

While this material is in the office, it must not be shown to other
personnel of the office who have no need to observe it. . . . There should
be no undue curiosity about such filth.

■ **Obscene Letter, Portion of Transcript of Intercepted Conversation
Between John Vitale and [Name Withheld], January 27, 1954,
Nichols File**

With reference to [Herbert K.] Hyde (Phonetic) . . . following is a ver-
batim transcript of reference to Hyde.

[Name withheld]: Here's what he told me, John. He told me that Hyde
(Phonetic) is getting powerful all the time now Hyde's the General Trial
Attorney for General Services Adminstration.

Vitale: I follow ya.

[Name withheld]: Now—I told him "I can't see where him being that
can have anything to do with what we want."

Vitale: Uh Huh

[Name withheld]: Don't worry about it—he says he's [Hyde's] got a
good looking wife—he says Ike [President Eisenhower] has been trying to
get into her pants.

Vitale: Ain't that a dandy.

[The above document confirms that the Obscene Letter procedure was also employed to submit derogatory personal information. Because the reported information involved President Eisenhower, this letter was routed to FBI Assistant Director Louis Nichols's office file and produced the following response.]

■ **Memo, FBI Supervisor R. Price to FBI Assistant Director Alex Rosen, February 2, 1954, Nichols File**
. . . With respect to Hyde in the General Services Administration (GSA), there is one Herbert K. Hyde, an attorney, who is apparently assigned to the Office of the General Counsel. The [FBI] indices were checked for Herbert K. Hyde and numerous references were located. It was ascertained that in 1931, one Herbert K. Hyde was appointed U.S. Attorney for the Western District of Oklahoma. His date of birth was listed as August 5, 1898. A name check was requested by the GSA in October, 1953, regarding Herbert K. Hyde born, August 5, 1898. . . .

The Bufiles references on Herbert K. Hyde are being reviewed and a separate memorandum will be submitted.

[The ten-page memorandum on Hyde and recording FBI officials' follow-up actions was withheld on grounds of personal privacy, sources and methods, and internal personnel rules.]

■ **Confidential Memo, FBI Assistant Director D. Milton Ladd to FBI Director, June 26, 1944, FBI 62-116758**
Mr. Towell of OSS [Office of Strategic Services] has requested that permission be granted to a representative of OSS to come to the Bureau and select copies of obscene material, the purpose being that OSS has a project to combat the obscene material being disseminated by the Japs. He advises that the Japs are sending obscene photographs of American girls through India and other such countries in an effort to create the impression of lax morals on the part of Americans and the OSS is desirous of disseminating similar material with reference to Japanese girls through this same area.

The laboratory has a collection of 25 or 30 photographs of this nature.

It is suggested that OSS be permitted to obtain copies of a representative group of these photographs for their project.

In the event you approve, arrangements will be made for the OSS representative to call at the Bureau's Laboratory to look over this material.

[Hoover's handwritten notation: "O.K." Handwritten notation of un-identifiable FBI official having initials CDM: "Lt Shrewesbrey OSS was given this material on 6-29-44."]

■ **Informal Memo, FBI Assistant Director Louis Nichols to FBI Associate Director Clyde Tolson, April 21, 1953, Nichols File**

Reference . . . [to a request by Joseph Bryan III, an official in the CIA's psychological warfare division, to review the FBI's Obscene File at the FBI laboratory] relating to our efforts to pin down rare instances wherein the Obscene File in the FBI Laboratory had been viewed by outsiders. The Director stated, "I want to know more about these *rare instances* & who approved display of this material."

An unsuccessful check of Bureau files has been made to pin point those occasions when the file was viewed by outside persons. Since we lack specifics, to begin with and since the instances have been most infrequent, it has not been possible to find in writing in the files details of any visit together with necessary approval. Laboratory personnel recall during the past 2 years only the [name withheld] incident [a reference to Bryan's May 1951 review of the Obscene File]. They have no specific recollection of any other outsiders recently viewing the file. In going back, however, to the establishment of the OSS some ten years ago they recall that during World War II two OSS officers viewed the file with approval for official reasons [relating to anti-Japanese psychological warfare]. They do not recall who approved this viewing.

The only other recalled instance involved [three lines withheld on personal privacy grounds]. Laboratory and Investigative Division personnel do not recall who approved this viewing. [FBI assistant director] Harbo has been advised of the Director's instructions that the obscene file should not be exhibited to anyone outside the Bureau except upon specific approval of you or the Director.

16: Public Relations

UNDER HOOVER'S CLOSE supervision, the FBI developed a sophisticated and aggressive public relations operation. Responsibility for this activity was assigned to the FBI's Crime Records Division, and officials in that division and at all FBI field offices were required to monitor and clip all news stories pertaining to the FBI. Fully briefed on all positive and negative stories, Hoover oversaw a broad media campaign.

On the one hand, he demanded that all potentially critical stories be rebutted aggressively, by pressuring Justice Department or FBI officials to defend the Bureau's carefully crafted reputation of high professionalism and efficiency. On the other hand, Hoover had his aides leak selected information to "reliable" reporters, editors, and columnists in order to promote a positive image of the FBI. Hoover's aides prepared for him two lists of reporters: a "Special Correspondents" list (those deemed friendly and reliable) and a "Not to Be Contacted" list (those deemed hostile).

Those deemed reliable were carefully recruited and stroked. They benefited from well-orchestrated leaks on the condition that they not disclose the FBI as their source. In return, these journalists provided information of interest (see also Chapter 14, Political Intelligence) and were contacted to write needed "corrections" to unfavorable stories. The most extreme example of this cooperative relationship, based on a shared political conservatism, was that involving the commissioning, research, and writing of the best-seller history of the FBI, The FBI Story, *by reporter Don Whitehead.*

If Whitehead and William Hutchinson, among others, were the

*recipients of FBI assistance, others (Clayton Fritchey and
Jack Nelson) were regarded as enemies. Their reporting was not
to be assisted, and their character was to be impugned.
Hoover did not simply maintain derogatory information on
prominent newsmen in his secret office file. When it served
his interest, he shared this information with sympathetic
administration officials—as in the case of syndicated columnist
Joseph Alsop. (See also Chapter 12, Political Uses of the FBI.)*

*Never content just to monitor the media, Hoover also withheld
or provided assistance to local and state officials, depending
on their support of the FBI.*

*Hoover's public relations operation also entailed the purposeful
cultivation of prominent Americans. During World War II,
and again after the onset of the Korean War, Hoover initiated a
formal program to recruit so-called Special Service Contacts.
These businessmen, editors, and other influential citizens were
carefully selected on the basis of their prominence and their
shared conservatism— as in the recruitment of Joseph Kennedy in
1943. Suspect at the time because of his advocacy of
appeasing Nazi Germany during the late 1930s and early 1940s,
Kennedy's fervent anticommunism, even at the time when the
United States was allied with the Soviet Union against Nazi
Germany, nonetheless made him attractive to Hoover.*

*In Joseph Kennedy, Hoover found an ardent supporter whose
professional contacts could promote the director's political
interests—in reporting on communist influence in Hollywood or on
the deficiencies and objectives of the FBI's postwar rival, the
CIA. In return, Kennedy could tap the FBI's vast resources for
an array of personal needs. Hoover's assistance also extended
to other prominent Americans, including the millionaire John D.
Rockefeller III, Roosevelt aide Harry Hopkins, and Nixon's
attorney general John Mitchell. If other less favored Americans
had to hire private detectives, the Kennedys, Rockefellers,
Hopkinses, and Mitchells could tap the FBI's far superior
resources at taxpayers' expense. In return, Hoover was
assured of their continuing support for his directorship of the
FBI.*

■ **Memo, FBI Director J. Edgar Hoover to FBI Assistant Directors Clyde Tolson and Louis Nichols, December 8, 1948, Nichols File**

I am getting concerned about our public relations situation. We seem to be "going to seed." The attached* is an interesting article but we ought to be getting out some items like this ourselves. The CSC [Civil Service Commission] & [Loyalty Review Board Chairman] Seth Richardson have been giving out a lot about Loyalty Inv[estigations] whereas FBI which does the real work has been unusually silent. During the Hiss Chambers case we have not made any effort thru our contacts to protect our position. All of this quiescence on part of FBI in all its fields results in public & Congress losing interest in us. By the time we wake up it may be too late to regain our prestige.

■ **Do Not File Memo, FBI Assistant Director Edward Tamm to FBI Director, January 18, 1941**

I talked to [INS reporter] Bill Hutchinson about the issuance of a story along the lines that the President's well-worked out plan of having but a single investigative agency responsible for National Defense violations is being thwarted by the Bureaucrats who are attempting to establish in each of their agencies a so-called Fifth Column investigative agency. The story would point out that the Immigration and Naturalization Service is establishing an agency for the expressed purpose of handling Fifth Column matters, that the Civil Service Commission is asking for a large appropriation to handle investigations growing out of the National Defense problems, that it is reported that the State Department, the Nelson Rockefeller group and others are establishing investigative agencies. Mr. Hutchinson has talked to Congressman Joseph Martin and to Congressman John Taber about this situation and Martin or Taber will issue a statement to the press immediately after Inauguration.

*The referenced article reported the results of the Federal Employee Loyalty Program instituted under President Truman's executive order of March 1947 and seemed to document the effectiveness of this program in purging disloyal employees. The article was written immediately after dramatic disclosures in the Hiss-Chambers case, when Chambers had turned over to investigators from the House Committee on Un-American Activities the so-called "pumpkin papers."—Ed.

■ **Memo, FBI Assistant Director Louis Nichols to FBI Associate Director Clyde Tolson, May 10, 1955, FBI 77-68662-1X**

Don Whitehead, the Associated Press feature writer, who did the very excellent series on the Director a year ago, called me this morning. He stated he thinks now would be a very good time to do an article which would recount what had been done in the fight against Communism and what the Communists are now doing; what the position of the Party is; what the underground is doing and what has happened, with some speculative comment as to the future course of the Commies. He thought that a very good article could be done on the subject and in doing it he would like to have a few moments with the Director, as the Director's own personal observations would be what would make the article important.

I told Whitehead we would mull this over a little bit and let him know.

I think this is something that might be very much worthwhile and Whitehead has certainly established his reliability. It would be my recommendation we help him with such an article, however, I think that in a piece like this he should see the Director briefly.

[Tolson's handwritten notation: "Necessary data should be prepared." Hoover's handwritten notation: "Yes."]

■ **Informal Memo, FBI Assistant Director Louis Nichols to FBI Assistant Director Alex Rosen, August 29, 1955, FBI 77-68662-23**

. . . We are considering [Don] Whitehead for a special project [to provide him with controlled access to FBI files to write the authorized history of the FBI] which would necessitate a clearance for him and the Director has agreed that we should make a Special Inquiry type investigation. However, this should be handled on a very discreet basis and his present employers, namely, the Associated Press, should not be contacted. Should the question come up as to why investigation is being made, I think we should frankly state it is for the purpose of complying with an Executive Order for the purpose of granting him a security clearance. . . .

[The resulting FBI investigation, which involved interviewing thirty-five individuals, found Whitehead to be "a man of the highest caliber, honest, hard working, industrious, kindly, open-minded and as possessing a keen analytical mind . . . as having a fine grasp of current events and as reporting events exactly as they appear."]

■ **Memo, FBI Assistant Director Louis Nichols to FBI Associate Director Clyde Tolson, October 27, 1955, FBI 77-68662-25**

Don Whitehead will start devoting full time to the History of the Bureau on Tuesday, November 1st. In order to work out space for him to have an office, I am arranging to temporarily move the tour room from 5625. . . .

■ **Memo, FBI Director J. Edgar Hoover to FBI Assistant Directors Clyde Tolson and Louis Nichols, March 16, 1956, FBI 77-68662-26**

On Friday, March 9, I . . . [advised] Mr. Whitehead of my pleasure with the first four chapters of the "History of the FBI" which he has finished. . . .

■ **Informal Memo, FBI Assistant Director Louis Nichols to FBI Associate Director Clyde Tolson, June 21, 1956**

The Director asked for explanations and further details on several items appearing in [Chapter 29 of Don Whitehead's final draft of *The FBI Story*] which deals with the Loyalty-Security Programs.

[Nichols's memo runs five single-spaced typed pages and contains frequent insert comments by Hoover demanding further refinement or revision.]

. . . 2. The Director also raised the question as to why we did not go into the fact that Whitaker Chambers did not furnish us the information on the espionage activities of the Washington underground until 1948. Here, again, I felt it best to avoid getting into the Chambers background. After all, Chambers has written a book in which the Bureau comes out very good. There is little likelihood of stirring up the Chambers situation unless we were to come forward with some new information. . . .

On page 18 the Director raises the question as to whether [FBI informer Harvey] Matusow's contempt citation was not reversed. It was. That decision does not distract [sic] from the judges statement as to the motive of the motion for the new trial by the United Mine, Mill and Smelter Workers and we say nothing in the footnote regarding the contempt of Matusow. I thought that this was proper particularly since the Circuit Court of Appeals reversed the contempt citation on the ground that Matusow was entitled to a jury trial, the notice of contempt given him did not sufficiently inform him of the charges, he was not confronted with witnesses or accorded the right of cross examination and was not accorded the right of presumption of innocence to have his guilt established beyond doubt.

Since, however, the Director has raised a question as to the propriety and since we really didn't need it, it has been deleted. . . .

On pages 24 and 25 dealing with the Harry Dexter White case the Director felt that we should get in a reference to the way Truman never said that the shift of White was made to better keep him under surveillance like the leak stories had stated. This is deemed inadvisable and would bring on needless controversy since Truman did make the statement in his radio broadcast. . . .

On page 24, the text to the article states that the Attorney General [Herbert Brownell] stated that Truman had "appointed White . . . to the International Monetary Fund knowing that White was a Russian spy." This is a correct statement. The AG in his November 6, 1953, address after referring to White's background stated "Not withstanding all this, Harry Dexter White was a Russian spy . . . but I can now announce officially for the first time in public that the records in my Department show that White's spying activities for the Soviet government were reported in detail by the FBI to the White House by means of a report delivered to President Truman through his military aide. . . . Incredible though it may seem President Truman subsequently on January 23, 1946 nominated White. . . ." [Hoover's handwritten insert: "The language used—'knowing that White was a Russian spy'—is not accurate and A. G. [Attorney General Brownell] didn't exactly say that. What he said was reports were sent to W. H. [White House] and to General [Harry] Vaughan and then to [President] Truman. We don't know if latter ever happened. All we know is that we sent repts. [reports] to W. H."]

In this connection, the Director reported . . . "The AG called attention to the statement which he had made in the speech before the Executives' Club in Chicago last week wherein he stated that Harry Dexter White was a Russian spy." The bone of contention on the use of the term spy was that we did not call White a spy in our reports. The Director jumped the AG on this and the AG stated that this was so, that his referring to White as a spy was his own evaluation of the reports.

[Justice Department press officer] Mullen raised a point with me on the reference we have on page 25 wherein [Senate internal security subcommittee counsel Robert] "Morris was told he would have to take the matter up with the Attorney General, that Hoover wouldn't testify unless directed to do so. . . . The subcommittee's formal request then was made to the Department of Justice and Attorney General Brownell instructed Hoover on November 16 that he should testify in line with the committee request." Mullen argued the text, as it was phrased, placed the AG in a position of ordering the Director into the political arena, that he recalled the day before the Director testified the AG telling him that the Director wanted to testify. In this connection the text is being revised to follow the exact quotation which Whitehead used in his interview with the Director which appeared in the New York Herald Tribune on May 9, 1954, a copy of which is attached. . . .

[Hoover's handwritten notation: "Be certain that Mullen approves revised." Nichols later briefed Hoover that Mullen had approved and "is very happy" with revised version.]

■ **Memo, FBI Director J. Edgar Hoover to FBI Assistant Directors Clyde Tolson and Louis Nichols, July 2, 1956, FBI 77-68662—Not Recorded**

On June 26, 1956, I saw Mr. Don Whitehead and . . . told him that now that the chapters had been completed and I understood that [FBI assistant director Louis] Nichols and he were shortly to take the material to New York to discuss the same with [Whitehead's publisher] Bennett Cerf, I wanted to express to him my appreciation of his diligence and efforts to turn out a worthwhile product of credit to himself and to the FBI. . . .

I also mentioned to Mr. Whitehead my desire that whatever publicity was utilized in connection with the promotion of this book, I wanted to have the same dignified and passed upon by the Bureau in keeping with the general tone and character of the book which I considered had been done in a most dignified manner. I likewise stated that if any future serialization of the book or condensation were to be made, I desired to have him, Mr. Whitehead, personally handle it.

[FBI officials not only reviewed proposed publicity plans but actively promoted *The FBI Story*, including purchasing thousands of copies through FBI recreation association funds and ensuring favorable book reviews (notably by Harry Overstreet). *The FBI Story* became a best-seller and was made into a popular movie, allowing Whitehead to retire as a journalist and embark on a more leisurely and lucrative freelance career. He was able to rely on FBI assistance for many of his later articles and books about federal crime issues.]

HOOVER'S MEDIA OPERATIONS had a more aggressive side as well— the discrediting of hostile sources by raising questions about their loyalty and character. As the following examples demonstrate,

*Hoover was willing to promote prosecution, exploit the shared
political objectives of congressional witch-hunters, or leak
information to influential officials in order to achieve his ends.*

■ **Memo, FBI Director J. Edgar Hoover to Attorney General
Francis Biddle, February 7, 1942, Nichols File**

I am attaching hereto, for your information, a copy of an article
appearing in today's Washington Times-Herald, written by Chesly Manly.
This individual is the one who dug up the story which brought forth for
publication the [U.S.] War Plans prior to the declaration of war [on Japan].

The attached article is a gross fabrication and can be termed nothing
more nor less than a malicious tissue of lies . . . [and specifically Manly's
claim] that the Naval Communication Service and the Signal Service of the
Army kept commercial circuits between Tokyo and Honolulu under constant surveillance and gave copies of all messages to the FBI, and that he
[Manly] received this information from a meeting of a Government war
agency. It is noted that he doesn't state the identity of the Government war
agency from which the information emanated. I believe it is obvious why
he has not done so, because the information is absolutely untrue, but even
if true, it also means that the Army and Navy were fully aware of the
contents of these messages, and if so, why did they not act so as to avert
Pearl Harbor? He doesn't touch upon this very glaring fact. The Federal
Bureau of Investigation at no time was furnished any messages sent over
commercial radio circuits, and as a matter of fact, was refused such
messages when it requested them of the commercial radio companies.
There was no way for the Federal Bureau of Investigation to obtain these
messages because the Federal Communications Act prohibited the companies making such messages available, and it was impossible to obtain any
subpoenas because a subpoena would have to be issued from a Federal
Court and a case would have had to be pending in such a Court upon which
to predicate the subpoena.

It is therefore obvious that Manly's article is an absolute lie. I very
earnestly urge that consideration be given to the holding of a Grand Jury
proceeding incident to the unauthorized publication of the War Plans, at
which Manly and the other members of the Chicago Tribune, New York
Daily News and Washington Times-Herald staffs would be interrogated
under oath as to their utterly inexcusable actions in securing and publishing
that document, while at the same time that Manly be questioned concerning the attached article, because he cannot produce any proof to support his
allegations contained in the attached article. I think that some measure
should be taken to curb such "smear" tactics. The issuance of a denial

such as [Justice Department press official] Gilford did issue, and which Manly does carry in his article, is submerged in the middle of the article, whereas the headlines and the main portion of the article are not merely distortions of truth, but complete lies in themselves. Therefore, I do not believe that the mere statement of the facts upon our part will curb these very deliberate and malicious attacks and efforts to "smear" and discredit the Federal Bureau of Investigation.

I well realize your reluctance to take cognizance of such attacks upon the FBI in the belief that they are not particularly significant. However, it is obvious that there is a well planned "smear" campaign again afoot and that it will continue, and no doubt become intensified unless it is met and exposed for what it is.

[Attorney General Biddle was unwilling to initiate legal action against newspaper critics of the FBI and the Roosevelt administration. That action awaited the administration of President Nixon and the initiation of a suit first enjoining the *New York Times* from publishing the Pentagon Papers and then initiating legal action against reporter Neil Sheehan and the source of the leak, Daniel Ellsberg.]

■ **Memo, FBI Inspector Joseph Sizoo to FBI Supervisor Alan Belmont, December 9, 1953, FBI 62-88217-1299**

While talking with Ed Duffy [counsel] of the Jenner Committee [Senate internal security subcommittee] yesterday, he advised that some consideration is being given to the desirability of holding hearings concerning the general subject matter of Communist infiltration and domination of the publishing industry . . . [since] some of the men who are strongly anti-Communist are experiencing increasing difficulty in getting their books published. He stated that there seems to be some collusion among book reviewers to give favorable reviews to liberal writers and either refuse to review or give unfavorable reviews of individuals who are attacking Communists and Communist activities.

Several complaints along these lines have reached members of the Committee and some of the Senators are now quite interested in going into the field. They realize, however, that it will be a real battle but . . . are inclined to feel that it would be desirable for the Committee to explore the matter. Duffy stated that some representatives of the Committee would like to discuss the matter with [FBI assistant director Louis] Nichols. . . . [these being] Senators [Herman] Welker and [William] Jenner, [subcommittee counsels] Dick Arens, Frank Schroeder, and himself.

I have discussed this matter with Mr. Nichols, who stated that approximately a year and a half ago he talked with [subcommittee counsel] Jay Sourwine and attempted to interest the Committee in conducting hearings in this field but at that time they did not desire to do so. Mr. Nichols does not feel that we should go to any lengths in assisting the "Dick Arens" crowd at the Committee in connection with this matter although he did feel that if they had some plan of action, it might be well to see if we could be of assistance to them.

Recommendation:

That Duffy be advised that the Bureau does not have any particular desires or interests in the proposed hearings concerning communist infiltration in the publishing field; however, if the Committee has some plan or action in mind and wishes to discuss it with the Bureau, we will talk it over with them to see if we can be of assistance.

[Nichols's handwritten notation: "I agree." Hoover's handwritten notation: "OK."]

[Disturbed by the publication of Max Lowenthal's critical history of the FBI in 1950, the next year Hoover ordered his aides to approach the Senate internal security subcommittee about "the possibilities of the committee looking into the matter of Communist infiltration into the book publishing industry." Hoover wished to "counteract the left-wing element in the publishing business, which has been the source of the attacks on the Bureau . . . particularly the Max Lowenthal book, (Lowenthal's publisher) William Sloan(e) Associates, Merle Miller's *The Sure Thing*, and others." The subcommittee did not honor this request owing to the press of other matters, notably its investigation of the Institute of Pacific Relations. When the subcommittee sought to revive the matter in 1953, Hoover had lost interest, in part because the focus would not be on anti-FBI publications and also because "a year ago we had more time. Now we haven't."

In 1955, however, the subcommittee initiated hearings into the newspaper industry, focusing on the *New York Times* and the radical press. These hearings questioned the *Times*'s book reviewing practices and the loyalty of some of its employees. As Harrison Salisbury of the *Times* later discovered, the subcommittee's "main source of names was the raw unevaluated files of the FBI."]

■ **Informal Memo, FBI Director J. Edgar Hoover to FBI Assistant Directors Clyde Tolson, Cartha DeLoach, and Robert Wick, June 16, 1966, FBI 62-27585—Not Recorded**

Senator Robert C. Byrd of West Virginia . . . [inquired] if someone in the Bureau could prepare for him a little speech with reference to the Supreme Court [Miranda] ruling on Monday on police questioning of suspects.

I told the Senator I could get that done. I also told him there is a complication there which the Chief Justice [Earl Warren] tried to take care of in his opinion in that they are trying to claim there is no differentiation between the types of crime handled by the FBI and those of local authorities. I stated that, of course, is not entirely accurate because in Federal crimes, you generally have the case pretty well made before making an arrest and in local crimes you may have an attack or assault and the police officer has to make an arrest at once. I stated under the rulings we now have, a person had to be advised that he need not talk and can have a lawyer, et cetera, and therefore I think it will hit the local authorities harder than the Federal authorities, but I would get him up some notes on this.

Senator Byrd stated he would appreciate it as he would like to make a speech on the Senate floor hitting that ruling.

I spoke to Mr. Tolson about this matter and instructed that it be handled.

■ **Summary Memorandum Re Clayton Fritchey, FBI Supervisor Milton Jones to FBI Assistant Director Thomas Bishop, July 12, 1971**
The 7/2/71 issue of the "Louisville Times," Louisville, Kentucky, contained an article [critical of Hoover and the FBI] by [Fritchey] entitled "More of Keystone Cops Than Vaunted G-Men." In response to the Director's request ["Let me have summary on Fritchey"], our files were reviewed on Fritchey and they reveal the following.
Information in Bufiles:
An applicant-type investigation was conducted concerning Fritchey in 1951. . . . The investigation was generally favorable with the exception of information developed that his name appeared on a "membership list" of the Southern Conference for Human Welfare, which has been cited by the House Committee on Internal Security. Informants advised he was never active in the organization and was "anti-Communist." . . .

Bufiles further disclose that Fritchey was suspected of being responsible for leaking certain classified information appearing in the late Drew Pearson's column in 1950 and 1951. Fritchey at that time was employed by the Secretary of Defense and friendly with Pearson. Investigation failed to establish he was responsible. . . . [Jones then listed six further examples, all pertaining to Fritchey's articles which FBI compilers found politically suspect.] Files of the Director's Office reveal no data concerning Fritchey and no arrest data located identifiable with him.
Recommendation:
For information.

■ **Memo, FBI Assistant Director Cartha DeLoach to FBI Associate Director Clyde Tolson, February 27, 1970**

In accordance with the Director's instructions, I called SAC [Wesley] Grapp, Los Angeles, and reminded him of the shabby treatment the FBI had received from the Los Angeles "Times" and . . . that our treatment and feeling with regard to the "Times" should, of course, be guided by the way they treat us. I also told Grapp of the most recent warning we had, from Jack Landau, Departmental Information Officer, to the effect that the "Times" was out to get the Director, Mr. Tolson, me, and any other official they could pick up the slightest bit of gossip on.

SAC Grapp told me he would be guided accordingly. He stated the Los Angeles "Times" is a "melting pot of garbage" . . . [that] the officials of this newspaper believe they should print everything given to them, whether anonymous or otherwise. . . .

SAC Grapp also told me that one of the ruling officials of the Los Angeles "Times" is . . . Al Casey [who] was given his job by the late John F. Kennedy. One of Casey's assistants is Edwin Guthman, National Editor of the Los Angeles "Times" who was formerly a press agent for Bobby Kennedy.

Grapp stated the Los Angeles "Times" daily prints false stories concerning people in public life. It makes no difference to this paper whether the stories are true or not. He also stated that naturally Guthman and Casey have an intense hatred for the Director, his assistants, and the FBI as a whole. Grapp feels that the "Times" would print anything if it thought it would be damaging to the FBI.

■ **Airtel, SAC Birmingham to FBI Director, June 11, 1970**

[One and a half pages withheld on personal privacy grounds, but refers to *Los Angeles Times* reporter Jack Nelson's plans to write a critical article on FBI Director Hoover and the FBI.]

[Sentence withheld on personal privacy grounds, but refers to Nelson's inquiries about Hoover] Mr. Hoover was a "homosexual" and that he was planning to use this information in the article.

[Paragraph withheld on personal privacy grounds]

The above information is being furnished to the Bureau for whatever action they deem appropriate.

Information copies being furnished to Los Angeles and Washington Field Offices.

[Alerted to Nelson's plans, Hoover ordered a background check on

Nelson and prohibited FBI cooperation with *Times* reporters. He further-more sought to have Nelson fired. Arranging meetings with *Times* vice president and general manager Robert Nelson and *Times* Washington bureau chief David Kraslow, he cited instances of Jack Nelson's excessive drinking and quoted from a letter he had written to Attorney General John Mitchell in which he claimed that Jack Nelson had been given the "assignment of 'getting' me, and I have also been informed that he was assigned to the Washington bureau of the Los Angeles *Times* for this specific purpose." Kraslow and Robert Nelson denied Hoover's charges and demanded proof. Offered none, they left the meetings disturbed by Hoover's conduct. Jack Nelson's reputation and position with the *Times* remained secure.]

■ **Letterhead Memo Re [Syndicated Columnists] Joseph and Stewart Alsop, March 29, 1957**
    . . . Although nothing derogatory was developed during the course of an applicant-type investigation [of Joseph Alsop] for the Office for Emergency Management in 1943, it was determined that both Joseph and his brother, Stewart, are cousins of Eleanor Roosevelt. . . . Joseph Alsop has been described by editors of the "Saturday Evening Post" as an individual who, when in his early thirties, had seen more of life and more of the world than his fellow Groton and Harvard graduates see in generations. He was described as scornfully rejecting the more conventional careers to take up journalism.
    The afore-mentioned investigation revealed that Alsop joined the "New York Herald Tribune" as a cub reporter upon leaving Harvard, a position which was secured for him through family ties and influential friends. . . .
    Since the end of World War II, Joseph Alsop has coauthored with his brother, a [syndicated] column . . . [which] deals with all phases of the Washington scene, both domestic and international, and has frequently been critical of the FBI and the efforts being made by the FBI in the discharge of its responsibilities. . . .
Allegations of Homosexuality
    A confidential informant, formerly employed in the Foreign Service of the Department of State, confessed to engaging in homosexual activities and resigned. This informant furnished derogatory information regarding other Department of State employees which has been found to be reliable. He related on July 30, 1954, that while assigned to Germany he was introduced to Joe (Joseph) Alsop, the news correspondent, by [name and title withheld] now resigned. Alsop was allegedly visiting [name withheld] at that time. On one occasion informant stated [name withheld] advised that while Alsop was on a trip to Germany and a guest of [name withheld]

he, Alsop, asked [name withheld] to obtain for him the services of a "warmer" (homosexual). According to the informant, [name withheld] told him that he attempted to obtain a male prostitute for Alsop without success and that he, [name withheld], finally engaged in a homosexual experience with Joe Alsop to satisfy Alsop's desires. . . .

■ **Memo, FBI Director J. Edgar Hoover for Personal Files,**
April 14, 1959

The Attorney General [William] Rogers called to advise that he had been talking to Secretary of Defense, Neil H. McElroy, and he was amazed to learn that McElroy did not know about the Joseph Alsop incident in Russia wherein Alsop admitted to certain acts of homosexuality. The Attorney General . . . thought he should get together what we have on Alsop as he believed very few people knew of this and he was not sure that the President was aware of it. He then inquired if Alsop had signed the statement and when he was advised in the affirmative he indicated that he would like to have a copy of this statement. I told him that this would be done and I would also check on the dissemination of this information; that I did recall that we had sent a memorandum to [assistant to the president] Sherman Adams [in April 1957] but I did not know whether Adams had brought it to the attention of the President [Eisenhower] or whether [White House aide] General [Wilton] Persons knew of it or the people socially active in the White House. I also indicated that I would have a memorandum prepared of the information in our files concerning the incident in Russia involving Joseph Alsop.

The Attorney General then commented that he was going to see that certain individuals were aware of Alsop's propensities, namely, The President, Secretary of Defense McElroy, Under Secretary of State Herter, General Persons and Secretary to the Cabinet [Robert] Gray, who, he felt should be advised, but he would not take the responsibility for such information going any further.

[When briefing Adams and Attorney General Herbert Brownell two years earlier about Alsop's alleged homosexuality, Hoover justified this as "desirable for the White House to be informed of the Alsop case in view of the implications involved."]

HOOVER ALSO SOUGHT to promote his own and the Bureau's interests by cultivating prominent Americans.

■ **Letter, SAC Boston Edward Soucy to FBI Director, September 7, 1943**

Special Agent William H. Carpenter of this office is a personal friend of Joseph P. Kennedy, former Ambassador to London, and the latter has indicated he would be glad to assist the Bureau in any way possible should his services be needed.

Mr. Kennedy speaks very highly of the Bureau and the Director, and has indicated that if he were ever in a position to make any official recommendations there would be one Federal investigative unit and that would be headed by J. Edgar Hoover. He considers the Naval and Army Intelligence Services "amateurs" in comparison to the Bureau and regrets that they have often meddled in investigations coming within the jurisdiction of the Bureau.

However, no attempt will be made to develop Mr. Kennedy as a Special Service contact unless the Bureau so instructs.

■ **Letter, FBI Director J. Edgar Hoover to SAC Boston Edward Soucy, October 18, 1943**

. . . In the event you feel that Mr. Kennedy is in a position to offer active assistance to the Bureau such as is expected of Special Service Contacts, there is no objection to utilizing him in this capacity. If he can be made use of as a Special Service Contact, the Bureau should be advised as to the nature of the information he is able to provide, or the facilities he can offer for the Bureau's use. Every effort should be made to provide him with investigative assignments in keeping with his particular ability and the Bureau should be advised as to the nature of these assignments, together with the results obtained. . . .

■ **Letter, SAC Boston Edward Soucy to FBI Director, December 27, 1943**

Reference is made . . . to the offer by former Ambassador to London Joseph P. Kennedy to assist the Bureau in any possible manner. . . .

In the course of discussing the Bureau's project with Mr. Kennedy, Agent [William] Carpenter was informed by the former Ambassador that he, Kennedy, is still engaged in the liquor business in New York City and owns several moving picture houses there. He stated that he maintains very close connections, financial and otherwise, with the moving picture industry in California and presently fears that the Communists and their fellow travelers have succeeded in obtaining for themselves many key positions in the moving picture industry. Mr. Kennedy also stated that he has some very good connections in South America in the moving picture business and he added that most of the foreign managers of the moving picture industry are indebted to him in one way or another; also, that he could easily secure assistance from any of these individuals in the event this assistance would benefit the Bureau in any way.

Mr. Kennedy is a devout Catholic and is very well versed on Communism and what it might possibly mean to the United States. He has said that he has many Jewish friends in the moving picture industry who would furnish him, upon request, with any information in their possession pertaining to Communist infiltration in the moving picture industry. He feels also that he is in a position to secure any information the Bureau may desire from his contacts in the industry with reference to any individuals who have Communistic sympathies.

The Bureau is also reminded that, because of his diplomatic background, Mr. Kennedy also has innumerable contacts in the international diplomatic set and he is willing to use his entree into these circles for any advantage the Bureau might desire in this field.

From his contacts with former Ambassador Kennedy, Special Agent Carpenter is able to state that Mr. Kennedy thinks very highly of the Bureau. [Kennedy] has also had several contacts with Special Agent in Charge Richard Danner of the Miami Field Division Office and has entertained both the Director and Mr. Clyde Tolson of the Bureau at his estate in Palm Beach.

■ **Memo, SAC Boston to FBI Director, September 26, 1945**

. . . This office has been in contact with (Special Service contact) Joseph P. Kennedy, . . . [who] at the present time has expressed his fear of the impending threat of Communism to our democratic institutions. Mr. Kennedy has again advised this office that he is willing at any time to cooperate in any way possible with the Bureau, and has suggested that in the event any of his contacts in the industrial field or moving picture industry in the United States or South America can be of use to the Bureau in this connection, he will be glad to establish necessary contact.

This office . . . will continue to bear in mind the assistance [which the office's two Special Service contacts] may give to this office in securing information regarding matters which will be of interest to the office, either currently or for reference purposes in the future.

■ **Memo, FBI Section Chief Alan Belmont to FBI Assistant Director D. Milton Ladd, October 16, 1953**

The semiannual report for Special Service Contacts reflects there are presently 174 Service Contacts as compared to 180 on May 1, 1953, and 170 on October 1, 1952. . . . The Special Service Contacts are rendering valuable services to the Bureau including the furnishing of information on Security Index subjects, the saving of money and time in connection with transportation costs and installation of equipment, and the furthering of the good will toward the Bureau throughout the country.

Recommendation:

. . . While the Special Agents in Charge have been instructed not to engage in active solicitation of individuals as Special Service Contacts, they will continue to be encouraged to be alert to consider as such contacts influential persons who volunteer assistance or express unusual interest in the Bureau's work. . . .

A number of Special Service Contacts in the publication field have published articles favorable to the Bureau during this period. Mr. Joseph P. Kennedy, a Special Service Contact of the Boston Office, recently spoke to [syndicated columnist] Westbrook Pegler about his articles concerning civil rights cases in which he criticized the Bureau. Mr. Kennedy thereafter spoke to the Director about it. Several of the Special Service Contacts communicated with Governor Allan Shivers of Texas and others on behalf of the Bureau in connection with the recent challange [sic] to the Bureau's investigative action in civil rights matters. A large number of Special Service Contacts have been very helpful to the Special Agents in Charge in arranging luncheons and other affairs at which they introduced the Agents in Charge to other prominent and influential people in their respective field divisions. . . .

■ **Personal and Confidential Letter, SAC Boston H. G. Foster to FBI Director J. Edgar Hoover, July 2, 1954**

On July 1 I had the occasion to spend some time with Mr. [Joseph] Kennedy . . . [who] mentioned that President Eisenhower had requested the Hoover Commission to investigate the CIA. Mr. Kennedy advised that General Mark Clark would probably head up their investigative efforts. He also indicated he was leaving for Europe in just a little over a week and left the inference he expects to do some inquiring concerning CIA while he is abroad. He also advised it was his personal thought that President Eisenhower had asked the Hoover Commission to make this inquiry to forestall an investigation into CIA by Senator [Joseph] McCarthy. . . .

■ **Memo, FBI Director J. Edgar Hoover to FBI Assistant Directors Clyde Tolson, Leland Boardman, Alan Belmont, and Louis Nichols, February 16, 1956**

Yesterday, I saw the former American Ambassador to Great Britain, Mr. Joseph P. Kennedy, Sr., who has recently been named as a member of the President's Board of Consultants on Foreign Intelligence Activities.

Mr. Kennedy stated that he wished to just discuss with me generally the over-all picture concerning this matter and some of the ideas which he had in mind. He stated that he found at the first meeting held of this Board that there had been no definite program or plan set up as to how the Board would function. The Board has practically no staff and Mr. Kennedy said he, therefore, felt that the thing to do was to find out from CIA and the other agencies engaged in foreign intelligence activities what some of their problems were and then have these problems assigned to individual members of the Board to study and come up with recommendations for a solution.

He stated that he indicated at the first meeting that if the Board intended to do a thorough and complete job, all the Board members should take apartments in Washington and move here for a fulltime job until it was completed. This did not meet with the approval of the other members. Mr. Kennedy stated, therefore, during the last several days he has had conferences with CIA and has taken over the analysis of one problem, namely, that of duplication of coverage abroad by the Military, CIA and the State Department. He believes he has not only obtained the necessary facts, but has a solution for the same which he intends to explore during his present visit in Washington with representatives of the three agencies mentioned. Mr. Kennedy stated that this was the only procedure he believed could be followed if there was going to be full time given by the Commission as a whole over a period of some months.

I discussed with Mr. Kennedy generally some of the weaknesses which we have observed in the operations of CIA, particularly as to the organizational set-up and the compartmentation that exists within that agency.

■ **Memo, FBI Assistant Director Alex Rosen to FBI Assistant Director Nicholas Callahan, December 4, 1961**

[FBI agent] Edward Washholz . . . [called from Chicago that] Joseph P. Kennedy, the President's father, had called the Chicago Office from the Ambassador East Hotel. Mr. Kennedy, who had just checked in . . . said he thought his room was "bugged" and he wanted the FBI to check it out. His reason for believing it "bugged" was five minutes after he checked in, all kinds of people arrived at his room.

ACTION TAKEN:

The Chicago Office was instructed to comply with Mr. Kennedy's request.

[Chicago] SAC James Gale advised . . . that Mr. Kennedy's room had been thoroughly checked out . . . but no hidden microphones or other technical equipment was located.

Mr. Kennedy indicated that he was quite pleased at the way his request was handled by the Agents. He said that he intended to call Mr. Hoover on the morning of 12/4/61 to express his appreciation to him personally.

■ **Memo, SAC Miami to FBI Director, February 1, 1956**

Former Ambassador Joseph P. Kennedy, Palm Beach, Florida, yesterday gave me a letter addressed to his son-in-law, Sargent Schriver [sic, Shriver], . . .

Mr. Kennedy said this indicated a former maid of the Schrivers may be contemplating furnishing an article to some one of the new expose magazine, trying to embarrass the Kennedy family. He said someone, he could not recall who but may have been [radio commentator] Walter Winchell or someone else, had mentioned to him that a maid in his son-in-law's household was a dangerous character, and he had written Mr. Schriver to that effect. Subsequently, the Schrivers had discharged this maid, named [Kay Biddle].

Mr. Schriver sent Mr. Kennedy a letter postmarked Beverly Hills, California, 1/10/56, [by Kay Biddle] addressed to Mr. Sargent Schriver. . . .

Mr. Kennedy pointed out some of the things she claims to know could not be of the maid's own knowledge and indicates she may be around talking to hotel maids, trying to dig up information for the purpose of smearing someone.

Mr. Kennedy made no request for any action in connection with this but turned [Biddle's letter] over stating he felt we ought to have a record of this person. The original letter is being retained in the Miami file of this matter.

The Bureau is requested to advise Los Angeles and Chicago if it feels any discreet inquiries concerning the activities of this woman should be made. If so, Miami should be kept advised.

[Handwritten notation: "No record Bu(reau) Indices on Kay Biddle 2/2/56."]

■ **Memo, FBI Director to SAC Miami, February 8, 1956**

. . . You are to forward immediately the letter from [Kay Biddle] which Mr. Kennedy turned over to you, to the FBI Laboratory so that a photograph thereof may be made and retained in the Anonymous Letter File. Upon return of the original letter to you by the FBI Laboratory, you should return it to Mr. Kennedy. No mention should be made to Mr. Kennedy that the Bureau is retaining a copy of the letter.

No investigation is to be conducted in this matter; however, the Los Angeles and Chicago Offices should review their indices and advise the Bureau and Miami of any information in their files pertaining to [Kay Biddle].

■ **Memo, FBI Assistant Director Louis Nichols to FBI Associate Director Clyde Tolson, May 11, 1954**

Mr. Joseph P. Kennedy, former Ambassador to England, . . . [telephoned and] related that Jack Anderson of Drew Pearson's staff had contacted a Langdon Morben regarding a son Teddy, Edward M. Kennedy; further that his son Teddy had not been permitted to go to school at Camp Holabird, Maryland, because of an adverse FBI report which linked him to a group of "pinkos." Kennedy stated that he sent word to Drew Pearson that if he so much as printed a word about this that he would sue him for libel in a manner such as Drew Pearson had never been sued before. He further stated that he had . . . then contacted the Army; that the Army was incensed at the information which Anderson had. Apparently some of the information which Anderson had on his son's Army activities was accurate and Kennedy stated the Army was somewhat incensed over how the information got out. Kennedy stated . . . that he simply was not going to tolerate his son being victimized in any way, shape or form. . . .

I told Mr. Kennedy we would check into this matter immediately. Finding no identifiable information in the Bureau, I checked with ASAC Hargett of the Boston Office who likewise reported no identifiable record. I, accordingly, called Mr. Kennedy back and told him that I could find no record and that we certainly had not investigated his son; that this might be another case of throwing the name of the FBI around or of somebody confusing the FBI with some other investigative agency. Kennedy stated that he was certain that the FBI could not have disseminated such a report because his son has never had an opportunity to "get mixed up with pinkos." I told Mr. Kennedy that he was authorized to state, if need be, that he checked with the FBI and the FBI had not investigated his son. Kennedy further stated that Tim McInerney had talked to Pearson and Pearson did not contemplate using anything. . . .

■ **Letter, Kenneth Shirley [personal assistant to John D. Rockefeller, III] to FBI Director J. Edgar Hoover, March 6, 1940, Nichols File**
. . . My principal reason for stopping in Washington to see you was to see if it would not be possible to work out a date when you were planning to be in New York so that Mr. John D. Rockefeller, 3rd could have an opportunity to talk with you about the problem of his new home which he is building in Tarrytown [New York]. The matter is moving along to where he has to take some steps fairly soon and as you know, he has been quite anxious to talk with you about this. . . .
[Tolson's handwritten notation: "No ans[wer] required now as Mr. H. (indecipherable but refers to Hoover's personal contact with Rockefeller) 3/21."]

■ **Personal and Confidential Letter, FBI Inspector Myron Gurnea to FBI Director, March 30, 1940, Nichols File**
In compliance with your instructions, I interviewed John D. Rockefeller, III, in New York City, and went over with him numerous questions with relation to the protection of his home near Scarborough, New York.
The complete plans for the home were not available at that time and . . . I suggested that it would be advisable to consider the plans for the entire home, as well as making a survey of the premises on which it is to be erected. This seemed to please Mr. Rockefeller and he requested that the survey of the premises and subsequent study of the plans be made at such time as he could personally be present. He . . . inquired as to whether it would be possible for me to accompany him to Scarborough during the weekend of April 6 and 7. I advised him that, insofar as I knew at this time, your commitments for me would make it possible for me to be in New York on those dates. [Hoover's handwritten insert: "OK."]
Before leaving, I gave Mr. Rockefeller a list of the various plans, maps,

and charts that would be necessary. He advised that he would collect all of these and forward them to me at the Bureau.

While in New York City, I conferred with several manufacturers of burglar alarm systems for the purpose of compiling an authentic and up-to-date list of information on this matter. The representatives of these concerns were not advised, of course, as to the reason for the Bureau's interest in this type of equipment.

It was ascertained during the interviews with the manufacturers in New York that there are several large manufacturers of burglar alarm equipment in Chicago. In view of the fact that I have approximately one day's work to complete . . . in Chicago, it is suggested that I . . . interview one or two of the important manufacturers in that city. . . .

The foregoing arrangements are, of course, tentative, subject to your approval. I will proceed as outlined above, however, unless you advise to the contrary.

■ **Memo, FBI Assistant Director Edward Tamm to FBI Director, April 1, 1940, Nichols File**
I called Inspector Gurnea . . . and advised him that you had given your approval to his being in New York on the week-end of April 6th and 7th in connection with the protection of the home of John D. Rockefeller, III. I also advised him that you approved of his conducting interviews in Chicago with the manufacturers of burglar alarm equipment. . . .

■ **Letter, John D. Rockefeller 3rd to FBI Director J. Edgar Hoover, May 14, 1940, Nichols File**
Thank you very much for your letter of May 7 and Inspector Gurnea's report concerning the protection of my new house. I have read the report with a great deal of interest and find it exceedingly helpful. I do appreciate your kindness in having it prepared for me.

It was a pleasure meeting Inspector Gurnea and working with him in connection with my problem.

[Gurnea's report also provided the FBI's evaluation of the personnel and resources of the Briarcliff Manor, New York, police department as well as background information about Rockefeller's two neighbors, Albert L. Kennelly and George Ash.]

■ **Memo, Helen Gandy, Administrative Assistant to FBI Director Hoover, February 8, 1946**

Copies of "technical" [wiretap] reports which were furnished to [special assistant to the president] Harry L. Hopkins are maintained in the Official Confidential files in the Director's Office.

Should they continue to be maintained?

[Tolson's handwritten notation: "destroy duplicates" "destroy copies only." Hoover's handwritten notation: "At once" with the further instruction that Gandy should "See Me." Helen Boehm, a secretary in Hoover's office, reports that "Only duplicates were rough drafts in pencil of summaries from June 27 to July 18, 1945, inclusive. These were destroyed. 5-9-46."]

■ **Letter, White House Aide Harry Hopkins to Helen Gandy, December 23, 1944**

"Could you *shut the whole business* off at 3:30* this afternoon and give me the final findings at 5 at my office—east gate—this afternoon.

I do hope you have a very happy Christmas.

[Gandy's handwritten notation: "Done 12/23/44."]

■ **Memo, FBI Assistant Director John Mohr to FBI Associate Director Clyde Tolson, December 1, 1969**

. . . [Attorney General John Mitchell's secretary] stated that Mrs. Mitchell had told her that, while engaged in a telephone conversation with the

*Hopkins was referring to a particularly sensitive investigation he had requested: that the FBI both wiretap his residence and follow his wife in his absence. The FBI physical surveillance of Mrs. Hopkins began on December 6, 1944, while the tap on Hopkins's residence began on December 12. Either Hopkins suspected his wife was having an affair or, owing to her recent illness, wanted to ensure that she obeyed doctor's orders to remain at home. The FBI's surveillance ended whenever Hopkins returned home and uncovered no illicit activities on her part. While this surveillance was discontinued upon Hopkins's request on December 23, the wiretap on Hopkins's residence was reinstalled on April 6, 1945, and the physical surveillance resumed on April 9. On May 18, Hopkins telephoned Hoover's office and "asked that the reports be delivered to him" that morning. Hoover's administrative assistant, Helen Gandy, advised the FBI director that "this was done." On May 21, 1945, pursuant to Hopkins's instructions, the FBI's wiretap of the Hopkins residence was discontinued; there is no record when the physical surveillance was discontinued. The tap was reinstalled again on June 27, 1945, and continued through July 18. —Ed.

wife of Secretary of Commerce Maurice Stans, the conversation was interrupted by a third party. As a result of this incident, Mrs. Mitchell has requested a security check of her residence telephone lines.

. . . [The interrupted] telephone call had been placed to the Mitchell residence by Mrs. Stans from the Watergate Beauty Salon, Watergate East. The possibility exists, of course, that the interruption occurred when someone at the Watergate Beauty Salon attempted to use one of the telephone extensions.

A security check was made of the Mitchell's residence telephones by our Laboratory in September, 1969, at Mrs. Mitchell's request. No irregularities were found at the time of the survey. In view of Mrs. Mitchell's request, however, if the Director agrees, our Laboratory will make a determination whether any irregularities presently exist in connection with their residence telephones.

Recommendation:

If the Director approves, that a security check be made by our Laboratory of the residence telephones of the Mitchell residence.

[Hoover's handwritten notation: "O.K."]

■ **Memo, FBI Supervisor W. W. Bradley to FBI Assistant Director I. W. Conrad, December 3, 1969**

. . . [FBI] Laboratory personnel conducted a security survey of the Attorney General's residence telephone lines. . . . This involved the inspection of seven instruments, four lines and associated equipment in the apartment, in the telephone company exchange buildings, and at all points of access outside the above locations.

No evidence of tampering was observed at the time of the survey. Telephone company officials advised that no work had been done recently on any of the lines and equipment associated with Mr. Mitchell's residence telephone service.

Recommendation:

That the Attorney General and Mrs. Mitchell be advised of the results of the residence telephone security survey.

[Hoover's handwritten notation: "O.K." FBI Assistant Director John Mohr's handwritten notation: "Has been done 12/3."]

■ **Memo, FBI Director J. Edgar Hoover to FBI Assistant Directors Clyde Tolson, William Sullivan, and John Mohr, August 24, 1970, Tolson File**

At luncheon with the Chief Justice [Warren Burger] today, we covered many aspects of security, both of the Supreme Court Building as well as the security of the Chief Justice personally.

Chief Justice Burger is making many appearances before legal groups and will, no doubt, make some appearances before university assemblies.

I extended to him full cooperation of the FBI being of any assistance it could to him even in the way of personal protection, when he is on trips out of Washington, and the use of any automobiles which he may have occasion to utilize on such trips.

Any requests that are received from the Chief Justice along the above lines I desire to have promptly honored.

HOOVER UNHESITATINGLY ASSISTED prominent Americans, beyond the public relations value, when to do so furthered his own political objectives, as highlighted by the following request from Supreme Court Chief Justice Warren Burger. Because of the sensitivity of this request to help promote a more conservative judiciary, Burger did not approach Hoover directly. He asked former FBI assistant director and then federal judge Edward Tamm to explain the purpose of an apparently innocent request.

■ **Memo, FBI Director J. Edgar Hoover to FBI Assistant Directors Clyde Tolson, John Mohr, Nicholas Callahan, and Thomas Bishop, January 11, 1971, Tolson File**

Judge Edward A. Tamm called. He told me that I was going to get a call from Chief Justice of the Supreme Court Warren Burger sometime in the next few days and he, Tamm, thought if I had a little advance information about it, I would be a little better able to evaluate it. Judge Tamm said that as I knew, the Chief Justice has been instrumental in having this school created at the University of Denver for training of court executives . . . [and] there will be about 600 positions in the State and Federal Court systems which will open up in this area for trained people. Judge Tamm said the Chief Justice is going to call me to ask whether I would consider now and from time to time recommending to him or to Rowland Kirks of the Administrative Office FBI men who are retiring or are on the verge of retiring or are otherwise available who would go to this school in Denver for six months with all expenses paid and then become court executives.

Judge Tamm said he is thinking ultimately, he knows, in terms of 600 trained administrators in this area. Judge Tamm continued that the Chief Justice thinks men with FBI training would be admirably situated and his, Tamm's, interest is that he thinks men in these key positions could influence these judges who are so completely inexperienced and unlearned in the practicalities of law enforcement that aside from their executive duties, they could be a tremendous force for keeping some of these stupid appellate opinions from coming out. I commented I thought that was true plus the fact there is the opportunity for the man to ultimately become a judge.

Judge Tamm agreed and said . . . the financial opportunity is great, and as I said, there is the opportunity to become judges, but to him the important thing is to bring a sense of realism into some of these deliberations, which would be a worthwhile opportunity. I said it would be wonderful if it could be done. I said I think the administration of the courts is the greatest weakness as it exists today but by having somebody who will watch, no doubt a great deal of good could be done.

Judge Tamm commented that cases like Bobby Baker and Cassius Clay [the heavyweight boxing champ who changed his name to Muhammad Ali, and who was convicted for refusing to register for the draft] should have moved through in three or four months to the Supreme Court and disposed of, and a good executive could spot and get them and have them moving through and there is unlimited opportunity for good. . . .

I told Judge Tamm I would keep this in mind. Judge Tamm said the Chief Justice talked about this Saturday and he, Tamm, knew the Chief Justice was sitting today, but [Burger] had said he was going to call and talk it over with me so he, Tamm, thought if I had the background I could give it a little thought. I told him I was glad he called.

[If Burger did call the FBI director in the next day or two, Hoover created no record of this conversation—having already briefed senior FBI officials about the matter. Later that year Burger did call to request that Hoover expedite FBI clearances for these court executives.]

■ **Memo, FBI Director J. Edgar Hoover to FBI Assistant Directors Clyde Tolson, W. Mark Felt, Alex Rosen, William Cleveland, and Thomas Bishop, November 24, 1971, Tolson File**
Chief Justice of the Supreme Court Warren Burger . . . said I had been kind enough to have field examinations made for these Court Executives they clear through their Institute and they just sent, he thought, a dozen of them in. He said he did not want to ask for any earlier than normal treatment, but taking into consideration the Holidays that are forthcoming, he was wondering if at all possible if they could get them as soon after the

first of the year as possible. He said he thought he would mention this to me knowing that the Holidays slow up many things, as the Chief Justices of the Circuits are riding him to furnish them a list of available men. I said I would get after it and give it an extra push.

The Chief Justice asked if I needed the list, and I said it would be helpful. He said he would have Rowland Kirk send the list to me. I suggested he mark it "personal" and the Chief Justice said he would have it down later this afternoon. I said I would get at it personally and see that we get it done by the first of the year.

[Handwritten notation: "Memo (FBI supervisor) Martin to (FBI assistant director William) Cleveland 11-26-71."]

17: The Director

HOOVER USED THE increased power and autonomy of the FBI to cement and sustain his directorship. Covertly, he exploited the Bureau's vast resources (agents, informers, reporters, wiretaps) to ensure his continued tenure. For him, the FBI was really the Hoover Bureau of Investigation. It was no mere happenstance that his reign as FBI director lasted forty-eight years, ending only with his death in May 1972. Hoover's bureaucratic genius and the FBI's unparalleled resources assured this result.

Dating at least from February 1941, two recording devices were installed in the director's office. They provided a comprehensive and accurate record of particularly sensitive requests, whether from presidents, attorneys general, or prominent personalities. Hoover could use this information to safeguard himself and the Bureau from criticisms that the FBI was acting without authority—but it was also leverage to contain any challenge to his tenure. At the same time, Hoover employed FBI resources to keep tabs on rumors of proposed plans either to dismiss him or to limit the Bureau's power. Documents in the Political Intelligence chapter reveal his interest in monitoring personnel and policy changes within the federal bureaucracy and the administration in power. Hoover's interest exploded whenever he learned of efforts to curb the Bureau's power or limit its gains. He never hesitated to raise questions about any rival and thus neutralize any challenge.

Most revealingly, Hoover also used the FBI's resources to combat criticism of his personal life. Rumors that he was homosexual incensed him, and he insisted that FBI agents

*monitor and vigorously contain such allegations. These
activities underscore the FBI's massive attention to noncriminal
activities within American society and the forging of the
Bureau into Hoover's personal instrument.*

■ **Memo, FBI Assistant Director W. R. Glavin to FBI Director,
February 25, 1941**
In compliance with your instructions, . . . the Bureau at present time
possesses five telephone recording instruments. . . .
2 instruments in the Director's office (1—Miss [Helen] Gandy's Office;
1—Telephone Room of the Director's Office). . . .
1 Instrument in the Technical Laboratory. . . . The Laboratory Technicians use it so that as a result of experimentations by them, adjustments,
replacements and improvements can be made on the Director's sets with a
minimum loss of time.

*VINCENT ASTOR, a cousin of President Roosevelt, was appointed
in June 1940 as the president's liaison to the Special
Interagency Committee in New York assigned to monitor German
activities in the United States and the Western Hemisphere.
Composed of representatives from those departments having
intelligence responsibilities, including the FBI, this joint
committee operated with great secrecy, in part because the
United States was formally neutral. At the conclusion of one
of the committee's meetings on July 3, 1941, Astor approached
the FBI's representative, Thomas Donegan, to relay a
specially sensitive presidential request that the FBI investigate
Kermit Roosevelt, the president's cousin and son of former
president Theodore Roosevelt. Kermit Roosevelt was involved in
an affair with a masseuse, Herta Peters, and had seemingly
disappeared. His wife, fearing a scandal and concerned over her
husband's health (he had contracted a venereal disease),
sought President Roosevelt's assistance to locate her husband
and sever this relationship.*

Donegan agreed to Astor's request, but when his superior, FBI assistant director P. E. Foxworth, advised Hoover of this development, the director disapproved. He considered it politically risky for the FBI to monitor a relative of the president without FDR's explicit authorization.

Eventually, Astor arranged for the president's personal secretary, Grace Tully, to contact Hoover, and the FBI reinstituted the investigation. Kermit Roosevelt was located and kept under FBI surveillance for a month. The nature of the president's request, and Astor's inept handling of this matter, helped increase Hoover's leverage as director.

■ **Transcript, Recorded Telephone Conversation FBI Director J. Edgar Hoover and Vincent Astor, July 5, 1941, 12:15 P.M., Nichols File**

. . . Astor: . . . I want to talk over this little problem of ours.

Hoover: What problem is that?

Astor: Well about the man [FBI agent Thomas Donegan] I have on this particular fellow [Kermit Roosevelt] you know, that the big chief [President Roosevelt] is interested in.

Hoover: Well, of course everything is being done on that Vincent that can be done.

Astor: Yes, I just thought—if you'd been around here I'd have liked to have given you all the dope and background. I thought you might have some ideas that probably nobody else would think of.

Hoover: Well, I have instructed the New York Office to put everybody on it that they possibly can with the effort of trying of course to find out where this fellow is. . . . I have been in touch with them and have told them that I wanted all the resources of the Bureau there to be applied to it.

Astor: Yes, of course in a small way, Edgar, because we've got to be awfully careful that it doesn't get out.

Hoover: That was what my concern was the other night. Very frankly, Vincent, I was pretty angry the other night.

Astor: Well, apparently you were, Edgar. I honestly think there's a misunderstanding—I don't quite see what it was all about.

Hoover: The thing about it was, that made me quite angry were some of the things that you said, I mean about this idea of having a new Director come into the Bureau—

Astor: I never said anything of the sort.

Hoover: Well, that's what [FBI assistant director and head of the FBI's New York office P. E.] Foxworth told me.

Astor: Well, listen, what I said was that there was darn bad coordination—

Hoover: No, Vincent, I think the whole thing could have been very readily handled if, when this request was made of you, you had gotten in touch with us at Washington, it wouldn't have taken us ten minutes to have cleared it, you see. The thing about it is that in a matter like this, as you say it is quite a delicate matter, its a matter that we don't want any publicity on, we don't want it to, of course, get out. A thing like that ought not be given directly to our New York Office. As a matter of fact if you'd called me or called Washington in the first instance I would have arranged to put a special on right away, in other words, I would have had somebody probably fly from Washington by plane so that nobody in our New York Office would necessarily know about it. . . . I know how a story like this if it got out by any chance would just be terribly embarrassing to the big boss [President Roosevelt]. Its a kind of case that we usually handle in a little different way, that is, where there is a personal angle involved I generally will send in some personal representative directly from Washington so he can go ahead and handle it without anybody locally knowing what it is all about you see. . . . [Astor then explained why he had handled it the way he had, reporting the instructions from the president; the pressures from Mrs. Kermit Roosevelt; the absence of SAC New York Ed Sackett, and thus his decision to contact Donegan; and his discovery, through Donegan, that the FBI surveillance squad had been called off, which led him to chastise Foxworth.]

Hoover: The thing that I took particular exception to is this, is the conversation that you had with Foxworth. . . . You made some statement to him that he wasn't so hot and it might not be bad to have a change in his place. (Astor interrupting)

Astor: I happen to be very fond of him. I may have said that the handling of this situation is not so hot.

Hoover: What was the statement made about the need for a change in the Directorship?

Astor: Oh no I did not at all. I said here is an example where we need a lot better coordination. . . .

Hoover: The thing about it is, when I got that message, frankly, of course, I think as you probably know this job doesn't mean so much to me anyway.

Astor: Why sure it does Edgar. You've got as good a job as there is—

Hoover: And its a terrible headache and if anybody wants it—

Astor: I am quite sure I did not say some of those things—

Hoover: And if anybody ever wants this job they can have it merely for the asking because I am not very keen about it anyway.

Astor: Well, Edgar I don't think you should talk about giving up your job just at a time—the situation of—the country is in now—

Hoover: Right. That's the only thing that has held me because of this national situation but of course on the other hand I just don't intend to have anybody, I don't care who it is, indicating that they are going to make a change in the Directorship with any idea they are going to be able to get me to do something or not to do something, you know.

Astor: (interrupting)—Sam got a little excited himself if he said that. And—

Hoover: And then there was some statement about Colonel [William] Donovan [the current head of OSS] needing to do this and that, etc. Now I don't know anything about the Colonel Donovan situation and I, of course, care less. But the point about it is if they want Colonel Donovan to come in or if they want you to come in or if they want Smith or Brown . . . when I was told of these things that you had said which, of course, made me very angry and I, as I told Sam, I said, 'Hell, I'll wire my resignation tonight if that's the way the President feels about it.' And I said, 'It doesn't make one damn bit of difference to me, nobody is going to talk to me like that and think I am going to stand for it.' I said, 'The job doesn't mean enough to me.'

Astor: Well now, Edgar, honestly there is a great deal of exaggeration and misunderstanding and . . . then about the larger (?) thing, your being angry and I being angry, let's just forget about that, shall we? There was obviously great overstatement—

Hoover: I'm perfectly willing to—

Astor: Anything that I said which may have been improper, I was mad that night myself. All I can do, I apologize to you in blank. . . .

In February 1940, FBI agents in Detroit and Milwaukee conducted midnight raids leading to the arrest of radical activists. Three years earlier these radicals had recruited volunteers to fight on behalf of the Spanish government against the fascist-led forces of General Francisco Franco. That same month Hoover flew to Miami to lead highly publicized arrests of individuals charged with violating the White Slave Traffic Act. The combination of these events—one involving radical activists and the other involving morals charges— precipitated press and congressional criticism of the FBI: that the Bureau was acting like a "Gestapo," that the director was

*engaged in a publicity campaign to enhance the Bureau's
authority, and that First Amendment and privacy rights were
threatened. Some critics demanded an investigation of FBI
activities.*

*Oversensitive to criticism and fearful that these attacks (which
Hoover termed a "smear campaign") threatened his tenure as
FBI director, Hoover moved quickly to contain the political
damage. He was especially concerned about rumors that
Thomas Corcoran, an influential Roosevelt adviser, and the
respected Republican senator from Nebraska, George Norris,
were leading this campaign. In contrast to Corcoran, Norris
emerged as a highly visible public critic who, in a series of
speeches in the Senate, laid out his case for curbing Hoover's
power.*

*Eager to blunt this challenge, Hoover directed his agents to
monitor Norris's activities. The Bureau not only clipped press
stories and followed the congressional debate, it also attempted
to uncover Norris's plans and strategy. This highly risky effort
succeeded in acquiring sensitive information about Norris's plans
from a "reliable source on the Hill." In view of the kind of
confidential information this source provided to the FBI, one of
three questionable methods had to have been employed: (1) an
informer had been recruited on Norris's office staff; (2) FBI
agents had broken into Norris's office and read or copied his
correspondence and internal staff memoranda; or (3) FBI agents
had opened Norris's mail and tapped his phone.*

■ **Memo, FBI Assistant Director Edward Tamm for the File,
February 20, 1940, Nichols File**

I called [assistant to the attorney general Ugo] Carusi and told him the
Director just called from Miami and stated that a newspaper story came in
there to the effect that the recent "smear Hoover" campaign has been
prompted by some administration officials in an effort to remove Mr.
Hoover from the FBI prior to the forthcoming political campaign; that one
of the moving figures behind this is Thomas Corcoran. I told Mr. Carusi
that the story is similar to Earl Godwin's [radio] broadcast . . . [and] that
his authority for this was an International News Service story which stated
that according to a high administration official this was an attempt on the

part of Mr. Thomas Corcoran to make the FBI free of J. Edgar Hoover for political uses during the next year.

I told Mr. Carusi that the Director . . . has made no comment whatsoever about [this story] and obviously cannot as he is totally in the dark as to what this is all about; that the newspapers, however, are assuming that the story is correct because no one has commented upon it; that he does not know what the Attorney General's feeling is about this particular situation, however, he did want him to know about it because he is afraid that these stories are building up a growing wave of comments that there is some breach between the Attorney General and himself or some very wide rift within the Department; that being a subordinate official it is not for him to make any comment about it . . . [but] is very much concerned about this.

[Carusi] stated he would tell the Attorney General [Robert Jackson].

■ **Memo, FBI Assistant Director Edward Tamm to FBI Director, March 1, 1940, Nichols File**

. . . [Reports in detail his contacts with Justice Department officials, including Attorney General Robert Jackson, in an effort to secure a press release refuting allegations of a rift between Hoover and Jackson, and to secure a public response to Senator Norris's criticisms of FBI conduct.]

Mr. Jackson stated that he had been very dubious of Mr. Hoover's policies in operating the Bureau when he became Attorney General and that his doubt in this regard was prompted in no small degree by statements which had been made to him from time to time by former Attorney General Frank Murphy. The Attorney General stated that Mr. Murphy had on one occasion informed him that the Bureau had an investigative file upon Tommy Corcoran, one on Mr. Jackson and most of the government officials in Washington; that the Bureau kept Tommy Corcoran under surveillance and that the Bureau maintained taps upon the telephone of some of the more prominent Government officials. I told the Attorney General that these statements were absolutely false and untrue; . . . [Tamm proceeded to refute them in detail and to explain FBI investigative conduct].

The Attorney General then stated that although he had considerable doubt in his mind concerning Mr. Hoover and the policies of the Bureau, his recent discussion with Mr. Hoover had considerably clarified the matter. . . . [Thereafter Tamm reported further discussions pertaining to the drafting of a letter responding to Senator Norris's criticisms, including Jackson's rejection of Hoover's proffered resignation.]

■ **Do Not File Memo, FBI Assistant Director Louis Nichols to FBI Director, November 14, 1940, Nichols File**

[Chicago] SAC [W. S.] Devereaux . . . [reported on] an article in the Chicago Herald American . . . entitled "New Deal Purges Planned" by William K. Hutchinson, INS [International News Service]. . . . The article pointed out that the inner circle of the New Deal planned an ambitious program bringing about sweeping changes in the Government and referred to [Roosevelt brains trusters] Tommy Corcoran and Ben Cohen as heading the program and stated they would like to see:

. . . 4. An earlier smear campaign resuming, to force the retirement of J. Edgar Hoover, Director of the FBI, and the naming of a new dealer to assume this position.

The foregoing is the substance of the article.

■ **Do Not File Memo, FBI Assistant Director Hugh Clegg to FBI Director, May 30, 1940, Nichols File**

Senator [Pat] McCarran of Nevada . . . does not like, he stated, the attitude of [Senators] Norris and [Burton] Wheeler. They are on the floor now, he said, criticizing the Bureau and Mr. Hoover. Senator Norris has been on the floor for a long time, citing instances occurring in his State of Nebraska, trying to bring tears to the eyes of those who will listen. [McCarran] wants Mr. Hoover to know that he has some friends in the Senate who would like to defend his organization. . . . If Mr. Hoover has been wrong, then it ought to be brought out; if Mr. Hoover has not done wrong, Mr. Hoover ought to defend himself and furnish information to his friends in the Senate who would be glad to defend him. . . . If Mr. Hoover was wrong, it ought to be brought out and if he was right he wanted to defend Mr. Hoover at the time when he defends himself.

I expressed appreciation and told him that he would be furnished with any facts which were pertinent to the criticism.

■ **Confidential Memo, FBI Assistant Director Hugh Clegg to FBI Director, April 3, 1940, Nichols File**

[Name and title withheld] advised that the office of Senator Norris has received a large volume of mail. A large number of complaints are of mishandling cases and violations of civil rights are alleged in this mail, although there is a volume of mail favorable to the Bureau. . . . [describes three examples of these allegations].

The office of Senator Norris was not particularly interested in the allegations concerning the Director being in Florida [to lead the vice raid].

The office of Senator Norris was not particularly concerned about wire tapping allegations. They were not especially interested but believed the law should be changed, but as long as the law was in existence it should be obeyed and understood. Mr. Hoover admitted violating this law [the Federal Communications Act of 1934, which contained a section banning wire-tapping] since its passage, evidently referring to the Federal Communications Act, but there was an admission if their child was kidnapped they would advise the use of wire tapping.

The office of Senator Norris is somewhat aggravated because Attorney General Jackson had made a blanket denial of allegations without investigation. They believed the Attorney General was too hasty.

The office of Senator Norris believed Bureau Agents used chains and violated civil rights, instead of U.S. Marshals or others.

[Six-line paragraph withheld on grounds that its release would reveal FBI sources and methods—describing how the FBI obtained the above information on Norris's plans.]

It was suggested that Senator Norris' office would not insist upon a congressional investigation. . . .

■ **Memo, FBI Supervisor R. C. Hendon to FBI Assistant Director Clyde Tolson, September 3, 1940, Nichols File**
With reference to the attached letter [to Hoover, dated August 3, 1940, from the head of the FBI's Omaha field office] indicating in paragraph three that Senator George Norris was involved in a questionable election at the time he was running for District Judge in Nebraska some years ago and that the proceedings are set out in *46 Nebraska 669*, please be advised that this case was briefed and it failed to substantiate the contention as set forth in the letter. . . . [Sets out in detail the facts of this 1895 election contest which Norris won and the resultant inquiry which refuted charges that Norris had engaged in electoral misconduct.]

■ **Memo, FBI Assistant Director Edward Tamm to FBI Director, December 2, 1940, Nichols File**
[Name withheld] called to advise that he had received information from a confidential source at the Capitol to the effect that Senator Norris during the past weeks has personally been making a private examination of the

Attorney General's reports since 1911; that his purpose in doing this is to compile data and secure information to use in an attack upon you.

[Name withheld] stated his informant is in a position to know of this matter and he is also reliable. He will inform me as to the identity of the informant when he can call me from a private phone.

■ **Do Not File Memo, FBI Assistant Director Edward Tamm to FBI Director, December 6, 1940, Nichols File**

On Monday afternoon, December 2nd [name withheld] advised me by telephone that he had learned from a reliable source on the Hill that Senator Norris was engaged in preparing material for a blast at the Bureau and that he had been reviewing all of the annual reports of the Attorney General back as far as 1911 in order to secure material for this blast. According to [name withheld] the information was "very hush hush" and the Senator was taking careful steps to prevent anyone knowing what he was working on. [Name withheld] said he would check into the matter further as soon as possible and determine further facts.

On December 3rd [seven lines withheld identifying how the following information had been obtained]. This employee furnished the information to [name withheld] with the suggestion that it be transmitted to the FBI. According to this clerk, Senator Norris, his secretary and one other person in the Senator's office, have been working on this matter for from three to four weeks. The matter has been handled in a most secretive manner and Senator Norris' office would deal only with this one clerk in the [Senate] document room, refusing to make inquiry for any material desired through anyone else. . . . [The remainder of the memo describes the specific documents requested by Norris's office.]

■ **Do Not File Memo, FBI Director J. Edgar Hoover to FBI Assistant Directors Clyde Tolson and Edward Tamm, September 23, 1941**

While discussing another matter with [name withheld] he told me that . . . there is presently in progress a movement to remove me from the position as Director of the FBI . . . [and] that [Francis] Biddle accepted the position of Attorney General with the understanding that I would be removed from the FBI. [Name withheld] told me that [name withheld, a former member of former Republican President Herbert Hoover's cabinet] also claimed that Vincent Astor and ONI [Office of Naval Intelligence] are behind this movement. [This former Hoover cabinet member] did not supply . . . any further details but he will be in Washington again within the next week to see if he can obtain any more information.

[Name withheld] also . . . has learned . . . I will be re-appointed as Director and that a fellow by the name of [Charles] Fahy, who is half-Irish and half-Jewish, will be named Solicitor General.

■ **Strictly Personal and Confidential Letter, FBI Director J. Edgar Hoover to Harry Vaughan [Military Aide to President Truman], June 13, 1945**

I have just received certain information from a newspaper source on the Pacific Coast [in fact a wiretap on Thomas Corcoran]. . . .

A William O'Connor, who is . . . the nephew of Federal Judge J. F. T. O'Connor of Los Angeles, in contact with a party on the Pacific Coast claimed close friendship with the President, and in fact showed several letters addressed to him on White House stationery bearing the signature of the President. O'Connor in discussion with this party . . . made reference to the fact that he had recently been in Washington and had visited with the President, . . . [that the] President contemplated the removal of the present Director of the Federal Bureau of Investigation . . . [and] had expressed a critical attitude toward the present Director's administration of the FBI, with particular reference to the newspaper publicity which has resulted from time to time concerning the Bureau's work. According to O'Connor, the President did not approve of such publicity and he contemplated a replacement of the Director of the Bureau.

Further, according to O'Connor, the President . . . would not immediately effect this change because of the possibility of some public protest but that it would be arranged by some program covering a period of six months to one year.

Further, according to O'Connor, the President expressed dissatisfaction with the alleged closeness between Mr. Hoover and Walter Winchell and indicated that he would in due course also "take care" of Winchell.

I would not bring the above to your attention but for the fact that I thought you should know of the loose talk being engaged in by a person who at least claims to be in touch with the President, both by letter and in person, and particularly when such statements are made to a newspaper man.

I, of course, do not know of the reliability of the substance of the remarks made by O'Connor, but I can certainly assure you that in so far as Mr. Winchell is concerned he is but one of many newspaper men whom I know in my professional capacity and neither he nor any one else has any particular entree into the Bureau. As regards the publicity which has been accorded the Bureau by the press from time to time, it has always been my consistent policy not to hold any press conferences. The only information reaching the press concerning the activities of the Bureau emanates through the regular press channels of the Attorney General's Office or through the handling of cases in the courts of law.

■ **Transcript, Intercepted Telephone Conversation, Henry Grunewald to Thomas Corcoran, June 14, 1945, 10:56 AM**
. . . Grunewald: Well, listen, fine. I spoke to somebody [Justice Department attorney James McInerney], you know. . . . A friend of that guy . . . J. E. [Hoover], you know.
Corcoran: Yeah.
Grunewald: That s.o.b. is out gunning for you now. He figured that [Attorney General Francis] Biddle has gone out, you know, and that . . . well, it is his chance, you know, see, see what I mean; and that this fellow told me, he's a very good friend of his, they're having some kind of luncheon today at the Statler Hotel, I don't know what it is but he's going to be there and he has invited this particular fellow I know over there.
Corcoran: This is J. E.?
Grunewald: That's the s.o.b. That's right. He said he's gunning for you see, and so you better tell that new fellow [Attorney General Tom Clark] he's gotta straighten himself out with that guy [Hoover] and put him where he belongs from the very beginning.
Corcoran: Yeah.
Grunewald: That's very important, see, you know.
Corcoran: Yeah.
Grunewald: Don't handle him with any kid gloves or anything.
Corcoran: Yeah. . . .

■ **Transcript, Intercepted Telephone Conversation, Thomas Corcoran to Henry Grunewald, June 14, 1945, 11:55 AM**
Corcoran: What did you know about this fellow J. E. [Hoover]?
Grunewald: Well, that fellow [Justice Department Attorney] Jimmy [McInerney] called me—you know—he said he met him [Hoover]—you know—and that they were having some kind of luncheon there today and etc. He had been invited in through some other friends that would be there, but not by J. E.—you see—but in the course of the conversation etc, his resentment was very strong. You know what I mean along that line, and as long as the other guy [former attorney general Francis] (Biddle) was gone

there will be a different situation now so I told the guy [McInerney] you will have an occasion, see, to talk but you just tell [then Democratic National Committee chairman and President Truman's appointee as post-master general later that month] Bob [Hannegan] right back again—tell him that he is absolutely plum nuts for even thinking anything like that for the simple reason the same guy [Attorney General] (Tom Clark) who is there now is a very dear friend of yourself and so is "top Bob" (Hannegan). And tell him [Hoover] also that such guys like [Secretary of Commerce] Jesse Jones, [Under Secretary of State] Sumner Welles and guys like that, you know, were asked to step out. The same thing can happen to him so pull in his strings a little bit and not blow off at the mouth.

■ Do Not File Memo, FBI Assistant Director Louis Nichols to FBI Associate Director Clyde Tolson, July 13, 1949, Nichols File

. . . [Name withheld] confided in [syndicated columnist Drew Pearson] the President [Harry Truman] had made up his mind to let the Director go, that the [name withheld] told the President that before he is talked into anything rash, he should face certain facts, namely the Director is tremendously popular throughout the country and that if the President did anything which would cause the Director to leave, it would reflect adversely on the elections in 1950 and 1952. The President stated he guessed this was so. . . .

■ Undated Blind Memo, Nichols File

On memo for Director Feb. 3, 1954 by [FBI assistant director F. O.] Holloman advising of dinner at [Washington] Press Club and conversations with various Cong.

Set out that Cong. Jamie Whitten took position that Director's [November 1953] appearance [before Senate internal security subcommittee supporting Attorney General Herbert Brownell's charge that former Democratic President Harry Truman had ignored FBI reports when nominating Harry Dexter White to the International Monetary Fund] ill-advised & he thought that when Democrats regained control of Cong that efforts would be made, on part of Democrats, to take action to remove Director from his position.

[Hoover's handwritten notation: "If that be the price one must pay for telling the truth, it is alright with me." Hoover's further handwritten notation: "I am not interested in politics. I was required to appear by the Committee. Was I supposed to refuse? I doubt that a Bureau Chief is immune to subpoenas. In appearing I confined myself to the facts. For that (Southern Democratic congressmen and Senators James) Eastland, Whitten & (William) Winstead think I am wrong. I was under oath and was not going to lie to serve political expediency."]

■ **Informal Memo, FBI Assistant Director Stanley Tracy to FBI Director, April 1, 1954**

Former Special Agent Hu Finzel and I had lunch today with H. L. Edwards, Administrative Assistant to Senator Olin Johnston (D-S.C.), and during the conversation, Edwards informed me that a serious situation has developed in that certain Senators are determined if and when the Democrats get back in power to make every effort to remove the Director . . . the reason was mainly the Director's appearance in the "Truman affair" [Hoover's appearance before the Senate internal security subcommittee] and that the Democrats will not accept the explanation that Attorney General [Herbert] Brownell forced Mr. Hoover's appearance. The reaction is that Mr. Hoover had avoided appearing on Capital Hill on many occasions in the past and that he could have avoided that particular appearance.

On further questioning, Edwards stated the reaction could be phrased . . . "It was hitting below the belt and Mr. Hoover was party to it." . . .

Edwards was not anxious to name names; however, he made it very clear that Senator Olin Johnston was positively not a party to it, that he has the highest of respect and admiration for the Director. . . .

On still further questioning Edwards stated that some of the Senators involved were from the South while others were from the North, that it was not solely a Southern Democrat matter.

Hu Finzel is going to contact Edwards . . . and make every effort to get the names of the Senators or at least the leaders. In the event he is unsuccessful in getting Edwards to name names . . . Finzel will be making out the Maryland and District of Columbia income tax returns for four or five of the employees in Senator Johnston's office, including the Senator himself, and he will again at that time bring up the subject and secure as much information as possible.

■ **Informal Memo, FBI Assistant Director Gordon Nease to FBI Associate Director Clyde Tolson, January 22, 1958**

I spent most of the afternoon with H. L. Edwards, administrative assistant to Senator Olin Johnson. . . . I inquired of Edwards if the information I had sent over to him . . . concerning [proposed legislation before the Senate Post Office and Civil Service Committee, chaired by Senator Johnston, to increase by 1,800] the super grades in F.B.I. was sufficient . . . and I noticed that he was somewhat non-committal. . . .

I promptly discussed this matter with [Edwards] again and he stated he wanted to be entirely candid with me. . . . He has already discussed this matter briefly with Senator Johnston . . . [who] had more or less been in one of his moods wherein the mention of the FBI set him off. . . . [Edwards] did not intend to indicate this was hopeless; however, because at other times the Senator was very favorable to us. . . . He wanted us to know that the Bureau was rapidly losing prestige in the South; that while the South had always been one of the staunchest Bureau supporters, the civil rights question has people thinking in an unreasonable manner; and that some of their constituents are continuously getting to the Senator and blaming the Bureau for investigating civil rights matters which they feel are strictly of local concern, and that we are being made pawns of the NAACP.

Edwards further stated that many of the Southern Senators have not forgotten the Director's testimony in the Harry Dexter White case, although if they stop to reason it out they all understand why we must investigate civil rights matters and why the Director had to appear in the Harry Dexter White matter. . . . At the time of the White matter, however, the feeling was so great that definite steps had been taken to attempt to have the Director removed from his job . . . that a meeting had been held by various representatives on the Hill but that the matter had gradually calmed down. This coupled with the present unrest in the South on civil rights matters has made many reasonable people take an unreasonable attitude. . . .

During this discussion, I went over in great detail . . . the part the Bureau plays in civil rights matters and the reasons for it, and also what we had attempted to do to educate the public as to our jurisdiction and responsibilities. I also again discussed with him in detail the Director's position on the Harry Dexter White case and . . . our participation in the Little Rock High School incident. There is no misunderstanding in his mind concerning either of these matters. . . .

I told Edwards I appreciate his discussing this matter with me in some detail and . . . his interest in attempting to straighten out those persons who are under a misconception as to our responsibilities. In conclusion, he assured me if there is anything he could do to include the additional super grades in the current pay raise bill, he would do so and he will let me know. I told him that we did not want to push the matter under the circumstances and that he should use his own good judgment. . . .

[Tolson's handwritten notation: "I think we might as well forget the additional super grades." Hoover's handwritten notation: "I concur. It is amazing how utterly unobjective some individuals get. We have a job to do & we will do it."]

THE SALE OF film rights to his own and the Bureau's exploits presented delicate situations relating to Hoover's personal profit.

■ **Letter, Louis de Rochemont to J. Edgar Hoover, July 13, 1951**
   This letter will supplement and become a part of the Agreement . . . by which you [Hoover] are conveying to me the motion picture rights to your article entitled "The Crime of the Century."
   1. . . . The right thereby granted shall extend only to the making of one motion picture version or adaptation of your work and shall not include the right to make any remakes or other motion pictures based thereon.
   2. . . . The television and radio rights thereby granted shall include only the right to televise the motion picture to be based upon your work and the right to broadcast by television, radio and other methods for the purpose solely exploiting the motion picture.
   3. The sum of $15,000 payable to you . . . shall be paid within ninety (90) days after the first general release of the motion picture.
   4. . . . Any and all depictions or portrayals of the activities of the Federal Bureau of Investigation or any of its personnel will be submitted in advance to you or a representative designated by you, and will require your approval or that of your representative. Such approval shall be required not only in the case of the motion picture but also for any exercise of the radio, television or other subsidiary rights granted by the Agreement in which use is made of your name or the name of the Federal Bureau of Investigation. . . .
   5. Any assignment of the rights granted . . . by the Agreement . . . will, of course, be made subject to the provisions of this letter.
   If this letter supplement and amendment to the purchase agreement . . . is satisfactory, will you please let me know.

[Although willing at first to accept a $15,000 payment for motion picture rights, Hoover had second thoughts. Seventeen months later he asked de Rochemont to amend the contract "that I do not desire to accept any payment for the said motion picture rights."]

■ **Letter, Benjamin Kalmens [Executive Vice President, Warner Brothers Studio] to FBI Assistant Director Cartha DeLoach, December 11, 1964**

In accordance with our conversation in Washington last night, I am confirming herewith that we will purchase the worldwide motion picture, television and other allied rights in a book entitled "MASTERS OF DECEIT" by J. Edgar Hoover . . . for the sum of seventy-five thousand dollars ($75,000). In addition, we will pay, in accordance with your direction, $500, for each original TV episode produced for television telecasting during the second and each subsequent year thereafter.

We will have the right to distribute such TV series for network TV syndication worldwide and theatrical if possible.

You in turn agree and the Federal Bureau of Investigation consents and authorizes us, on an exclusive basis, to produce such television series and to use the title "THE F.B.I. STORY" or other title or titles that we can mutually agree upon. It is also agreed that we will mutually cooperate in the production of the series and in the publicity and advertising as pertains to all of its phases. . . .

AGREED TO:
FEDERAL BUREAU OF INVESTIGATION
Signed by: FBI Assistant Director Cartha DeLoach

[Once again Hoover was willing to profit from his position as FBI director, but once again he concluded that disclosure could affect his continued tenure. Sixteen months later he asked Warner Brothers to assign payments to the FBI Recreation Association.]

ANY ALLEGATION, NO *matter how nebulous, that Hoover was homosexual was conscientiously reported by FBI agents. They*

*knew that their failure to do so might lead to a reprimand and
jeopardize their career in the Bureau.*

■ **Personal and Confidential Letter, SAC New York E. E. Conroy
to FBI Director, January 21, 1944, Nichols File**

At the regular [FBI] Supervisors' Conference . . . I commented very
forcefully about the fact that there had just been called to my attention two
instances where scandalous and scurrilous remarks of a vicious nature had
been made by persons in New York City concerning the Director; that such
had become known to Agents and two Supervisors of the office without
that information being called to my attention for a considerable period of
time thereafter. Shortly after the conference, Supervisor [Agent No. 1]
inquired as to whether I would be available for a conference with
him . . . and stated that he felt that I had been talking about him. He stated
that approximately two months previous, Special Agent [No. 2] had
informed him that some person had referred to the Director as a "fairy."
He stated that he had had this Agent [No. 2] get the address of the
individual who had made the remark, but that during a later discussion
with this Agent it was felt that as the statement of the individual was so
ridiculous that he felt that it was unwise to pursue the matter further. He
suggested to the Agent the matter be dropped.

Agent [No. 1] was advised by me that he had displayed extremely
poor judgment; that I considered this matter to be a direct attack on the
character of the Director; that it was a matter that should have been
handled without delay and that in his position as a Supervisor he should
have called the matter to my attention immediately after he received the
information from Agent [No. 2]. I instructed him to the effect that he and
Agent [No. 2] should immediately submit memoranda setting forth complete
details. . . .

I have impressed on Agents [No. 1] and [No. 2], and particularly Agent
[No. 1], my extreme displeasure in the way this matter was handled, and
have informed them both that the matter is being submitted to the Bureau
for appropriate action.

[Following the submission of reports on the original allegation, the
individual alleged to have made the remark about Hoover was interviewed.
This individual, a prominent Republican, responded to the aggressive
nature of the FBI interview by reporting the matter "to two of his
acquaintances who are at the present time members of the Republican
National Association. The men hearing the story made the remark that
they were displeased with the fact that agents of the FBI were being

used to investigate such statements when there were so many subversive matters to investigate." While FBI officials contained this situation, Hoover remained incensed over the earlier dereliction of the agents who had first heard of these remarks. Accordingly, the supervisor was reprimanded for his failure to have acted on the report of FBI Agent No. 2, while Agent No. 2 was commended for his action in reporting this information to his superior.]

■ **Letter, SAC New York E. E. Conroy to FBI Director J. Edgar Hoover, March 1, 1946, Nichols File**

Yesterday morning, [FBI associate director Clyde] Tolson called regarding . . . [name withheld] who was alleged to have been making scurrilous remarks about you and Mr. Tolson. Mr. Tolson suggested that I have some Agent contact [name withheld] in order to put an end to the rumors he apparently was spreading.

There is attached hereto a memorandum dated February 28, 1946 by [two names withheld, FBI agents] setting forth the results of their interview with [name withheld] that same morning. These two Agents, incidentally, are well capable of being able to handle themselves under almost any circumstances. From what I can gather in personal conversations with them, they were rather vigorous in the treatment of [name withheld] much more so than their memorandum would indicate.

■ **Memo, [Two Names Withheld, FBI Agents], February 28, 1946, Nichols File**

. . . [Reports on interview with the name withheld individual, interrogating him whether he had ever heard or made derogatory statements regarding Hoover and Tolson, and this individual's denial.]

He was advised in no uncertain terms that in the event there was a recurrence or if there were any word ever received that he had made remarks or was the instigator of any remarks concerning Bureau officials, he would be libel [sic] for slander, amongst other things.

[Name withheld] advised that he had nothing but the greatest respect for the FBI and its Director. He was told by the writers that it was felt that he had indeed made the statements about the Director and that anything he said to the contrary was not believed by the writers. It should be noted that throughout the interview [name withheld] acted in a very nervous manner, he changed color when confronted with statements allegedly made by him and continuously wet his lips and when the writers left, it was their opinion that he was in a rather nervous state of mind and that there would never be any further necessity for interviewing Mr. [name withheld] on a matter such as this.

■ **Personal and Confidential Do Not File Memo, FBI Assistant Director Robert Hendon to FBI Assistant Director Clyde Tolson, June 30, 1943**

As a matter of record, [New Orleans] SAC Guerin . . . advised that [name withheld], Cleveland, Ohio is an aunt of [an FBI agent] . . . [who reported] that on June 11, 1943, a bridge party was held at her home in Cleveland. . . .

During the course of the bridge party the Director's name was mentioned at which time [name withheld] made the statement that the Director was a homosexual and kept a large group of young boys around him. . . . One person in the party immediately took [name withheld] to task for this statement pointing out that it just did not line up with the responsibilities and reputation of the Director.

After advising the Director of this matter telephonically, I contacted SAC L. V. Boardman at Cleveland and instructed him to vigorously take [name withheld] to task for her gossip. SAC Boardman [later] advised me [that he] . . . called [name withheld] into his office and severely chastised her, pointing out that he personally resented such a malicious and unfounded statement as she had made and that he could not understand what would lead her to make any such libelous statement concerning a man in such a responsible position as the Director. . . .

[Name withheld] was deeply sorry and . . . explained that while on a trip with her husband in the fall in 1941 they were eating in Millers Restaurant in Baltimore. At an adjoining table were several young men who were having a riotous time and . . . one of them said that on that day he had seen J. Edgar Hoover of the FBI go through Baltimore with his chauffeur. To this one of the men stated that the chauffeur was Mr. Hoover's sweetheart and that Hoover was queer.

[Name withheld] claimed that she never said anything about this nor had she thought anything about it until the day of this bridge party. She said during the course of the bridge party there was the ordinary small talk and some mention was made of the Director. One of the girls pointed out that the Director was a bachelor and she wondered why. To this [name withheld] said that she replied she understood Mr. Hoover was queer. She said there was no discussion of this and immediately after she made the statement she thought it should not have been made and she could not

understand why she had made it. She stated that those in attendance at the
bridge party had been gathering like this for a period of eleven years and
she was going to point out to each of those present that her statement was
not founded on fact and that she was deeply sorry that she had made it and
it should not have been made at all. She is going to advise Boardman when
this has been done.

Boardman emphasized that he had chastised her most vigorously and
that she thoroughly understood the untruth of her statements and the serious
nature of her action in having made them.

[Hendon's handwritten notation: "Director fully advised."]

■ **Highly Confidential Memo, [Name Withheld FBI Agent] to SAC
New York, January 18, 1944, Nichols File**
 In connection with [an OPA bribery investigation of John Monroe]
. . . on December 17, 1943, one [name withheld] appeared in the New
York Office at which time he furnished information indicating that [John
Monroe] had agreed, for a certain consideration, to make arrangements
through his alleged friend, Congressman [name withheld] to have an OPA
suit against the Berke Cake Company in Brooklyn, dismissed.
 . . . [During an interview with name withheld, he] reported [Monroe]
to have made a statement to him to the effect that he had no fear of the
FBI as he knew the Director to be a homosexual, and further that he
had no fear of the Attorney General as he, [was intimate with the niece of
Biddle]. . . .

■ **Strictly Confidential Letter, SAC New York E. E. Conroy to FBI
Director, January 19, 1944, Nichols File**
 . . . In connection with the [report concerning Monroe's allegations that
Hoover was a homosexual, and that he, Monroe, was "intimate" with
Biddle's niece], there are being transmitted herewith memoranda . . . dated
January 18, 1944. In connection therewith, it will be noted that although
this matter dates back to December 17, 1943, that same was not called to
my attention until January 18, 1944. . . .

The Director may be assured that the series of situations of this type are
being called to the attention of the Supervisors at the meeting today, and to
the Agents at the next Agents' conference, with the warning that information of this nature should be conveyed to the Special Agent in Charge of
the office immediately upon its receipt.

■ **Memo, FBI Director J. Edgar Hoover to FBI Assistant Directors Clyde Tolson, Edward Tamm, D. Milton Ladd, and Alex Rosen, undated but ca January 19, 1944, Nichols File**

This was grossly mishandled. I note nothing in [name withheld, FBI agents] memos as to why these matters were not reported from Dec. 17 to Jan. 18. This is significant that none sees fit to explain that & [New York SAC] Conroy doesn't insist upon it. I want vigorous action taken for failure to promptly & properly report this. I also want steps taken to make Monroe "put up or shut up" both as to his statements re A.G. [Attorney General Biddle] & myself.

[The agent who received the information from the FBI's informer was chastised for failing to submit a report and "warned that there should be no repetition of any such derelictions in the future." The agent's immediate supervisor was also reprimanded and advised that his "dereliction is most serious. In the event there is a repetition of such, drastic disciplinary action will be recommended." A second agent who learned of this information from the first agent was also chastised for failing to file a report and was advised that "your dilatory handling of this serious matter, which was also most delicate, reflects on your capabilities. No repetition will be tolerated."

In addition, FBI assistant director Louis Nichols was instructed to "talk to" Monroe and to "dress down on both stments crim slander unless can prove."]

■ **Do Not File Memo, FBI Assistant Director Louis Nichols to FBI Associate Director Clyde Tolson, January 24, 1944**

. . . I talked to [Washington, D.C.-based businessman and influence peddler] John Monroe . . . [about] the report [that] had come to us that he had made the statement that he feared no prosecution in view of the association which he had with Gladys Drexel, the Attorney General's niece, over a period of ten years, and in view of certain information he had concerning the Director. Monroe, asked if he made this statement, immediately stated that it was "a contemptible lie." He then stated he is suing [syndicated columnist] Drew Pearson for a million dollars, along with 600 newspapers, and that every tactic known to discredit a man is being directed at him, that while he cannot prove that Drew Pearson is back of these tricks, he . . . thought possibly Pearson was the source of the report to the Director.

He then stated that about four or five weeks ago he had gone to . . . Congressman [James H.] Morrison of Louisiana, to find out why the Director was angry with him, as he had a report the Director was angry and had stated that he, Monroe, was a very vindictive individual. A few days later Congressman Morrison reported back that the Director was angry because Monroe was author of the statement which I told Monroe had been attributed to him. . . . He then asked me to call Congressman Morrison . . . and ask him if it was a fact that he, Monroe, had requested to find out why the Director was mad at him and ask Morrison just what he had reported back to Monroe. He also stated he had gone to other friends with a view of finding out why the Director was angry. . . . [and] in each instance he asked the individual to find out why the Director was mad at him, and he denied that he ever said it was because of the slanderous remark which had been made against the Director and about which we asked him. He stated he knew this was not true, claiming he had a great admiration of the manner in which the Director had taken hold of the organization and built it into something that was a great credit, and that he had great personal admiration for the Director, although he admitted he had been mad at him some months ago. . . .

Monroe then swore . . . that he was not the author of the statements, that he would not say bad things about people, that he, himself, was the victim of all kinds of rumors. He stated he thinks Congressman Morrison does know the source, that he, of course, feels it is Drew Pearson. I told him it was not Drew Pearson. I then told him since he stated he was not the author of the statement that he would not object to putting it in writing. He accordingly dictated the attached statement. . . .

Attachment: Signed statement of John Monroe to Louis Nichols, January 24, 1944:

"I would be glad to be very helpful in finding the sources of the two vicious rumors that are obviously made to discredit me and cause friction against me.

One, . . . I do not know of and to the best of my knowledge, [Attorney General] Biddle has no niece named Gladys. I have never said that I have had any intercourse or relationship of any kind with a relative of Mr. Biddle's, either social or business, and I have not made any disparaging statement of any kind against Mr. Hoover's private life. On the contrary, I have admired the job he has done. I believe that being engaged in a very difficult litigation with certain sources that these are being planted not only with Mr. Hoover but with others, obviously to discredit me and to cause me mental discomfort.

Regarding my making the statement that I do not fear prosecution, on various times that I have heard I was to be prosecuted for this, that, or the other thing, I have said I do not fear prosecution from any place because I do nothing wrong and you cannot prosecute someone who does nothing wrong. Now, if that statement has been warped in any way for the purpose of hurting me, I have no control over it."

[Monroe contacted Nichols twenty-one months later to inquire whether Hoover still believed that he had claimed the director was a homosexual and whether he "has given instructions in every way possible to do a job on me." Monroe's concern stemmed from the fact that FBI agents, when interviewing his clients, were "telling them I am under investigation," and this was hurting his business. While Nichols denied that Monroe had been targeted, in fact Monroe was the subject of a criminal investigation to determine if he was violating the OPA statute. Ironically, one week after he telephoned Nichols, on September 18, 1945, Monroe was arrested (and was later convicted) on a charge of violating OPA price ceilings.]

■ **Memo, FBI Assistant Director Louis Nichols to FBI Associate Director Clyde Tolson, June 20, 1951**

. . . Mrs. [Hazel] Baxter [an employee of the FBI records section] stated that yesterday afternoon she went to the [name withheld beauty shop]. . . .

[Woman No. 1, the owner of this shop] then stated to Mrs. Baxter that she was a matron in the Eastern Star and . . . that her husband was a Mason. Mrs. Baxter stated that there were a large number of Masons in her family and stated as a matter of fact her "Boss" was also a Mason. [Woman No. 1] then asked who this was and Mrs. Baxter stated it was the Director.

[Woman No. 1] immediately made the remark "That S—O—B—is no credit to the Masons." She also stated that the Director was a "two-faced S—O—B—" at which point Mrs. Baxter asked her whether she was referring to politics. [Woman No. 1] stated she was not talking about politics and then stated all of the bookies in Washington turned in money to the Director and paid him off.

Mrs. Baxter challenged [Woman No. 1] on this statement and reprimanded her for engaging in idle gossip. [Woman No. 1] then replied that everyone in Washington knew that the Director was being paid off by the bookies. [Woman No. 1] then stated that the Director was a sissy, liked men, and was "queer." Mrs. Baxter again challenged [Woman No. 1] and stated that such statements were uncalled for and that there was strictly nothing to such statements and that as a matter of fact such activity on the part of [Woman No. 1] in saying such things regarding the Director, was merely something that the Communists would like to engage in and it was strictly to the advantage of the Communists for such tactics to be followed.

At the time that [Woman No. 1] referred to the Director as a "queer," the beautician [Woman No. 2] . . . stated that she had also heard this about the Director.

Mrs. Baxter reprimanded both of these people for these remarks and advised them that they should not engage in such idle gossip. [Woman No. 1] then replied that it was not gossip, nor was it hearsay and she could back up every statement she had made regarding the Director. . . .

Mrs. Baxter stated she did not know why [Woman No. 1] had made these statements and that they were all uncalled for and she had challenged [Woman No. 1] in regard to them. She stated that she, of course, gave no credence to these remarks. . . .

A check of our files failed to reflect any identical information concerning her. It is recommended that in view of the statements made by this woman that she be appropriately contacted and confronted with the statements.

[Nichols's handwritten notation: "I suggest (FBI agents) Holloman and Suttler both Masons take this scandal monger and liar on. Also suggest Mrs. Baxter be commended." Tolson's handwritten notation: "Yes 6/20." Hoover's handwritten notation: "Yes."]

■ **Memo, FBI Assistant Director Louis Nichols to FBI Associate Director Clyde Tolson, June 22, 1951**

. . . In compliance with instructions, Mr. Suttler and [FBI assistant director] Holloman interviewed [Woman No. 1] this morning at her place of business. She received Suttler and Holloman without incident and appeared to be very frank and above board during the interview. She unhesitatingly and categorically denied making the statements attributed to her. She advised that she had not referred to the Director in the manner indicated and as a matter of fact she does not use such obscene language. She was closely questioned concerning each and every allegation and in each instance she, without hesitation, denied them.

[Woman No. 1] stated that she does recall stating to Mrs. Baxter in passing that one of her customers, [name withheld] had told her on one occasion that the Director had acted as a honorary pallbearer for her husband . . . [who] was a bookie and had been one all of his life. [Woman No. 1] stated that she was merely repeating what [the customer] had told her and made no further comments and definitely did not say that the Director received a payoff from the bookies in Washington.

The beauty operator, [Woman No. 2], was interviewed separately and later with [Woman No. 1]. She also denied that such remarks had been made. Both [Woman No. 1] and [Woman No. 2] denied that such remarks were made in the beauty salon at all and stated as a matter of fact, Mrs. Baxter had made the remark that certain people thought that the Director was "queer" but she did not believe this to be true and thought that people only said it because the Director only associated with men and did not associate with women. [Woman No. 1] . . . got the impression from Mrs.

Baxter that Mrs. Baxter was defending the Director in the matter but stated that there was no further discussion of the matter and again denied making any statements or entering into the discussion further. [Woman No. 1] denied that she made any such statements concerning the Director as attributed to her. . . .

Suttler and Holloman vigorously questioned both of these people and they stuck to their story and contended that they did not make any such statements.

Mr. Suttler and Holloman upon their return to the Bureau interviewed Mrs. Baxter again and confronted her with [these] denials. Mrs. Baxter stated that the original information given by her was true, that she had furnished only the truth and she was persistent in sticking to this story. She stated that she would be willing to confront [Woman No. 1] and would be willing to testify to the facts she had given. . . .

I have been advised that [Woman No. 1] fully realizes the seriousness of the situation at this point and that there is very little likelihood of any repetition of such acts on her part. Holloman has suggested that we proceed cautiously as these women have so little to lose in the matter, and it is always difficult to catch up with gossiping rumormongers.

Both Holloman and Suttler feel that while this matter should be pursued vigorously caution should also be exercised and that . . . [they] have Mrs. Baxter at the beauty parlor when it opens tomorrow morning before customers come in and merely ask Mrs. Baxter to repeat what she has told us these women said, and tell these women they believe Mrs. Baxter who has no motive for lying in the matter, and that she is willing to testify in court under oath to these matters, and it is expected both . . . women will be given an opportunity to testify before a grand jury as to exactly what they did or didn't say.

[Tolson's handwritten notation: "OK 6/22." Hoover's handwritten notation: "OK."]

[This confrontation was arranged for the morning of June 23. While both women again denied having stated that Hoover was homosexual, they were "advised in no uncertain terms that such statements . . . would not be countenanced." Hoover was further advised that the beauty shop owner "fully realizes the seriousness of her accusations and it is not believed that she will ever be guilty of such statements." "In view of the above," FBI assistant director Louis Nichols recommended that "no further action be taken" as "nothing will be gained by further pursuit of this matter."]

■ **Personal and Confidential Letter, SAC Louisville M. W. McFarlin to FBI Director J. Edgar Hoover, July 14, 1944, Nichols File**
. . . [Reports having learned from Louisville police officers that one of

four individuals arrested on a perversion charge claimed to have been employed as an FBI file clerk and "knew several employees of the FBI who are sexually perverted and also stated that you were homosexual and he knew your seventeen year old lover." McFarlin thereupon had FBI agents interview this individual and obtained a signed statement that the above statements "were untrue without any basis in fact."]

It is unfortunate that you were made the subject of such a vile and dastardly attack; however, persons occupying high public offices are frequently exposed to the mouthings of liars and vermin.

You may be assured that so long as there is a Federal Bureau of Investigation that those associated with you will exert every means in their power to protect you from malicious lying attacks and throw the lies down the throats of those who utter them.

It is a privilege to be associated with you in your great contribution to our country at war.

Conclusion:
<u>The Hoover Legacy</u>

THE ACTIVITIES DESCRIBED in this book illustrate how J. Edgar Hoover exploited the FBI's resources to serve the political interests of the White House and to advance his own bureaucratic, political, and moralistic agenda during forty-eight years as director. Hoover's ability to maintain the secrecy of selected FBI records helps to explain why the Bureau was able to operate in this fashion. Recent developments—including 1968 legislation which limits the tenure of the FBI director to ten years; 1974 amendments to the Freedom of Information Act which promote the public release of FBI records; and changes in public and congressional attitudes toward the presidency and the intelligence agencies in the wake of the Watergate affair—make more difficult the repetition of the abuses that occurred under Hoover.

This does not mean, though, that Hoover's legacy of a politicized agency with minimal disclosure of its questionable activities has been repudiated. The lesson of Hoover's directorship—that a quasi-autonomous secret police agency can undermine democratic principles—has not been effectively addressed by Congress or the executive, and recent events confirm that FBI abuses did not die with Hoover.

One example is the Bureau's program on sex deviates. My research in FBI policy files uncovered the existence of this program, which was formally instituted in 1951. This discovery then led to the FBI's admission in 1990 that in 1977, more than five years after Hoover's death, the Bureau had destroyed all records pertaining to the sex deviate program and its indexing of allegations of homosexuality. Had I not found these sketchy references, we might never have known that the FBI had accumulated 300,000 pages of sex deviate information and later destroyed them.

The FBI's interest in hiding Hoover-era abuses was not confined to sex deviate records. Far more disturbing were the misleading responses of FBI officials to a series of inquiries about FBI break-ins.

In 1974, responding to a General Accounting Office (GAO) inquiry into FBI "domestic security" investigations, FBI officials agreed to prepare written summaries of selected cases rather than open their files to GAO inspection. Although one of the cases had involved an FBI break-in, FBI officials withheld this information in their report to the GAO.

In 1973 the Socialist Workers Party (SWP) filed suit against the government, seeking damages for FBI harassment and misconduct. SWP attorneys demanded the release of FBI records documenting break-ins of the party's offices, but U.S. attorneys, relying on FBI information, denied the existence of any such records. In March 1976, however, the Justice Department backtracked, advising the court and SWP attorneys that it had recently discovered FBI records documenting at least ninety-four break-ins involving the SWP.

In 1975 the Senate Select Committee on Intelligence Activities, investigating FBI activities, was told by FBI officials that they could not provide accurate statistics on break-ins because there were no files, documents, or index that recorded them. Based on the "recollections" of FBI agents, FBI officials presented figures which implied that break-ins had been sparingly used, and that the few targets were related to the Bureau's counterintelligence responsibilities. In fact, FBI officials misled the committee. Special files which I later obtained confirm that a great many break-ins had been conducted, and that the targeted organizations included the American Youth Congress, the National Lawyers Guild, the Chicago Committee to Defend the Bill of Rights (a branch of the national committee seeking the abolition of the House Un-American Activities Committee), and a number of other left-liberal and radical organizations having no possible relation to counterintelligence.

The Senate Select Committee investigation found that FBI "subversive activities" investigations had no law-enforcement purpose, that FBI officials decided the initiation and length of such noncriminal investigations, and that their object was information about the plans, financing, and membership of radical organizations.

To end such activities, in March 1976 Attorney General Edward Levi issued new guidelines governing FBI "domestic security" investigations. Levi was willing to allow FBI officials some discretion in initiating investigations without hard evidence of criminal conduct. Thus he authorized "preliminary" investigations in the "domestic security" area based merely on "allegations or other information that an individual or group may be engaged in activities which involve or will involve the violation of federal law." But Levi limited this discretionary authority by stipulating that such investigations could last only ninety days and could only verify or refute the "allegation or other information."

Levi imposed tighter restrictions on ongoing ("full") investigations. They required the advance approval of the attorney general and had to be based on "specific and articulable facts giving reason to believe that an individual or group is or may be engaged in activities which involve or will involve the use of force or violence and which involve or will involve the violation of federal law." The "results" of these investigations were to be reviewed at least annually by the Justice Department, which then was to "determine in writing whether continued investigation is warranted" and again in writing approve continuance "beyond one year."

Levi's aim of ending FBI surveillance of dissident political activities was not shared by the Reagan administration. To encourage the FBI to monitor these (renamed) "terrorist" activities, Ronald Reagan's attorney general, William French Smith, on March 7, 1983, rescinded the Levi guidelines. Under new and more permissive standards, FBI "domestic security/ terrorist" investigations were authorized "when the facts or circumstances reasonably indicate that two or more persons are engaged in an enterprise [to further] political or social goals wholly or in part through activities that involve force or violence and a violation of the criminal law of the United States." Smith directed FBI officials to "anticipate or prevent crime" and to initiate investigation whenever individuals or organizations "advocate criminal activity or indicate an apparent intent to engage in crime, particularly crimes of violence."

Smith also rescinded Levi's carefully crafted oversight requirements. The FBI director or a designated assistant director was now allowed to initiate a "domestic security/terrorist" investigation for 180 days, after which the same official could reauthorize the investigation. Setting aside Levi's requirements of annual review and written authorization by the Justice Department, Smith instead required that the FBI need only "notify" the department's Office of Intelligence Policy when instituting a "domestic security/terrorism" investigation. He reduced the attorney general's role to "may, as he deems necessary, request the FBI to prepare a report on the investigation." The Justice Department need not stipulate in writing that continued investigation was warranted, or approve in writing the continuance of the investigation.

Under Reagan administration pressure, FBI officials returned to their former role as agents of the White House, targeting critics of the administration's foreign policy for investigation, in this case opponents of Central America policy. As in the past, the FBI's investigations uncovered no evidence of criminal activity.

The crisis precipitated by the Iraqi annexation of Kuwait in August 1990, with the imminent possibility of U.S. involvement in armed conflict with Iraq, provided another example that Hoover-inspired criteria continue to inform FBI conduct. On January 7, 1991, with the approach of the Bush administration's January 15 deadline for the withdrawal of Iraqi troops from Kuwait, FBI officials announced they would interview two hundred Arab American leaders, ostensibly to obtain information of (1) violations of the civil rights of Arab citizens, and (2) planned "terrorist" activities. The FBI's program provoked immediate criticism from Arab Americans and civil libertarians as having a chilling effect on political dissent and serving indirectly to legitimize public intolerance toward Arab Americans during a period of national crisis. Some critics darkly recalled memories of the internment of Japanese Americans during World War II.

The FBI's abuses in the post-Hoover era bear a strong similarity to earlier activities: investigations are not confined to law enforcement, nor, with the exception of the brief period between Edward Levi's attorney generalship and that of William French Smith, are they tightly monitored and explicitly authorized by the attorney general. The Hoover abuses and more recent FBI activities make a powerful case for the enactment of an FBI legislative charter, one which defines the parameters of FBI investigative authority and ensures that congressional committees are provided with the information necessary to their oversight mission. By defining the scope and purpose of the FBI's "domestic security" investigations, Congress can ensure that political criteria will no longer define FBI activities and that FBI investigations will no longer be triggered by the political and policy objectives of either the FBI director or the White House.

Given the unwillingness of attorneys general to monitor FBI activities, Congress should also require that the FBI report annually (1) the number of domestic security investigations it has conducted, (2) the number of individuals and organizations about whom information was received, and (3) the duration of each investigation. Such data can alert congressional investigators to potential problems, at the same time helping to deter abusive inquiries. It was, and is, folly to rely on the self-restraint of either FBI or administration officials.

A Note on Hoover's Important Aides

■ **Clyde Tolson**

Tolson joined the FBI in 1928 and, after serving in field offices, was brought to headquarters in Washington in 1930 with the rank of inspector. He was promoted to assistant director in January 1931 and assigned responsibility for inspection of FBI field offices. Developing a close friendship with Hoover, Tolson handled administrative and personnel matters and was formally appointed associate director in 1947. He served as Hoover's liaison with the heads of divisions in Washington and chaired FBI executive conference meetings, where major policy matters were discussed and changes recommended. Hoover's closest friend and confidant, Tolson resigned within twenty-four hours of Hoover's death in May 1972. He inherited the bulk of Hoover's estate.

■ **Louis Nichols**

Nichols joined the FBI in 1934 after graduating from Washington University Law School. He was brought to FBI headquarters in 1935 and soon headed the Crime Records Division, where he served as Hoover's liaison to the media and Congress. A powerful assistant director, Nichols was ordered by Hoover in October 1941 to create a special office file to maintain specially sensitive communications sent by senior FBI officials to Hoover. He was appointed assistant to the director in 1947 and held the position until he retired in 1957 to accept an appointment as executive vice president for Schenley Industries. Despite his retirement from the Bureau, Nichols continued to work with Hoover and to promote the FBI's interests; in 1965 he convinced Louis Rosenstiel, president of Schenley, to establish and endow the J. Edgar Hoover Foundation.

■ **Edward Tamm**

Tamm joined the FBI in 1930 as a young graduate of Georgetown University Law School. A diligent agent who demonstrated superior administrative abilities, he was brought to FBI headquarters in 1934 to help assistant director Harold Nathan supervise criminal investigations. Promoted to inspector in 1935, Tamm handled the delicate administrative and public relations responsibilities of a series of highly publicized investigations, notably the John Dillinger case. He became a general troubleshooter and was promoted to assistant director in 1937 with responsibility for criminal investigations. With the outbreak of war in Europe in September 1939, Tamm was transferred to head the FBI's General Intelligence Division where he supervised and directed internal security investigations. In January 1941 Hoover appointed him to the newly created post of assistant to the director, with the more general responsibility to handle FBI investigative and liaison functions. In 1948 Tamm resigned from the Bureau to accept appointment as a federal district judge, but he stayed in close touch with Hoover, periodically providing intelligence about political, legislative, and judicial developments.

■ **Cartha DeLoach**
While still attending Stetson Law School in 1942, DeLoach sought an appointment with the FBI. He resigned it to serve in the armed forces but afterward returned to the Bureau. DeLoach's service in counterintelligence resulted in his transfer to FBI headquarters in 1951 to serve as liaison to the CIA. In 1953, however, he was promoted to inspector and assigned as an aide to assistant director Louis Nichols in the Crime Records Division. With Nichols's retirement, DeLoach was promoted to assistant director in 1959 and head of crime records. His prominence in the American Legion led Hoover to name him liaison to that organization in 1953, and his close friendship with Senator Lyndon Johnson led to his appointment as Hoover's liaison to the Johnson White House after President Kennedy's assassination. Retiring at the age of fifty in June 1970 to accept an appointment as vice president for Pepsico, Inc., DeLoach at the time was the third most powerful official in the FBI, having succeeded to Nichols's title as assistant to the director.

■ **William Sullivan**
Sullivan joined the FBI in 1941. He had graduated from American University with a B.A. in education and taught English while working for the Internal Revenue Service and studying for a master's degree. Assigned to various field offices, predominantly in the Southwest, Sullivan developed contacts with Mexican police and focused on foreign intelligence matters. In 1945 he was promoted and brought to FBI headquarters as supervisor in the research section. For his work on internal security matters Sullivan won a series of promotions, culminating with his appointment as assistant director in charge of the Intelligence Division in 1961. The FBI's

resident "expert" on communism, Sullivan prepared various position papers and ghost wrote many of Hoover's articles and books on the subject. As assistant director he was the driving force behind the expansion of the FBI's COINTELPRO from a narrower concern with the Communist party to include militant civil rights, segregationist, and youth organizations during the 1960s. With Richard Nixon's election in 1968, Sullivan replaced DeLoach as Hoover's liaison to the White House, and, with DeLoach's retirement, was appointed assistant to the director in 1970. In this liaison capacity he performed extremely sensitive tasks on behalf of the Nixon White House. In his office he kept the FBI's copies of the wiretap records involving those members of the White House and National Security Council staffs, and the Washington press corps, who were tapped at the request of President Nixon and his national security adviser Henry Kissinger in 1969 in an effort to determine the source of leaked information.

Sullivan was bothered by Hoover's obsession with the Communist party and his relative unconcern with the more militant New Left. Sullivan worked covertly with Nixon White House aide Tom Charles Huston in June-July 1970 to convince the president to lift Hoover's restrictions on the monitoring of civil rights and anti–Vietnam War activists. Hoover was not aware of Sullivan's insubordination, nonetheless relations between the two men deteriorated in the summer of 1971, and Hoover demanded that Sullivan apply for retirement. Earlier that summer, Sullivan had contacted Assistant Attorney General Robert Mardian to advise him of the sensitive wiretap records he maintained in his office and the prospect that Hoover might use them to "blackmail" the president to keep him on as director. Later, in 1973, White House aide John Dean contacted Sullivan, in the midst of the developing Watergate crisis, to solicit his assistance. Sullivan briefed Dean on the political services that Hoover had performed for the Roosevelt and Johnson administrations; Dean used the information to rebut criticisms of the Nixon administration's political uses of the FBI.

■ Thomas Bishop, Milton Jones, John Mohr, Courtney Evans, D. Milton Ladd, and Alan Belmont

Bishop succeeded Cartha DeLoach as assistant director in charge of the Crime Records Division after DeLoach's retirement in 1970.

Milton Jones, a supervisor in the Crime Records Division, served as both Nichols's and then DeLoach's key aide during the 1950s and 1960s.

John Mohr served in the same capacity to Clyde Tolson but earned promotion to assistant director for administrative matters. In 1972 he was the FBI official who assisted Helen Gandy in transferring Hoover's Personal and Confidential File to the director's home following his death. There this file was reviewed and then destroyed by Gandy.

Courtney Evans was a section chief in the Criminal Division who served as liaison to the Senate Labor Committee during its investigation of the influence of organized crime in the trade union movement. He developed a close working relationship with Senator John Kennedy and committee counsel Robert Kennedy. In 1961 Evans was promoted to assistant director and served as Hoover's liaison to Attorney General Robert Kennedy.

D. Milton Ladd headed the Domestic Intelligence Division of the FBI during World War II and the early Cold War years.

Alan Belmont succeeded Ladd as a supervisor in that division. He later was appointed an assistant director and head of domestic intelligence.

Appendix: Secret Files, Secret Records Systems

CREATING AND MAINTAINING *secret office files demanded procedures to preclude the possible discovery that FBI records were being purposefully withheld. Normally, all FBI records were indexed and serialized in the Bureau's central records system. This created a retrievable record of the contents of a particular case file (e.g., gaps in the consecutively numbered file would confirm the existence of a withheld document). To circumvent this problem, dating from 1940 FBI Director Hoover devised special records procedures to be employed when sensitive communications were not to be indexed or filed in the central records system and could thus either be safely destroyed (as no record had been created of their existence) or separately maintained.*

■ **Memo, FBI Director J. Edgar Hoover to FBI Assistant Director Clyde Tolson, all 14 other FBI Assistant Directors, Helen Gandy [Hoover's Executive Assistant], April 11, 1940, FBI 66-3665-544**
In the future, memoranda written merely for informative purposes, which need not be retained for permanent filing, should be prepared without abstracts and without carbon copies on a blue inter-office memorandum form attached hereto [the memos contained the following printed notation: INFORMATIVE MEMORANDUM NOT TO BE SENT TO FILES SECTION]. . . . It will be understood that in the event any of these blue inter-office memoranda reach the Files Section, they will not be filed but will be returned to [FBI Assistant Director Stanley] Tracy in the Director's Office for appropriate disposition.
[The extensive use of blue memoranda, combined with the Department

of Justice's decision to require the use of blue paper for all intra-departmental communications, led Hoover to revise this procedure. FBI officials were to reduce the use of this procedure and were to use pink paper containing the following printed notation: THIS MEMORANDUM IS FOR ADMINISTRATIVE PURPOSES TO BE DESTROYED AFTER ACTION IS TAKEN AND NOT SENT TO FILES. The FBI's use of pink memoranda for documents which were to be destroyed became known during the Judith Coplon trial. In response, Hoover suspended this procedure and verbally directed FBI officials henceforth to report such information either through "personal notes or informal memoranda... which were never intended by the author for permanent retention in our filing system."]

BLUE/PINK/INFORMAL MEMORANDA were either maintained in Hoover's office files or, on return to the sender of the memorandum, placed in his office files. To minimize the possibility that such records might be publicly compromised, Hoover spelled out a specific schedule for their destruction.

■ **Memo, FBI Director J. Edgar Hoover to FBI Associate Director Clyde Tolson and 11 named FBI Assistant Directors, March 19, 1953, FBI 66-2095-100**
Re: Retention of Original Memoranda
From time to time original memoranda are prepared at [FBI Headquarters] or by me directed to a Bureau official concerning matters affecting the Bureau or a particular division [of the FBI]. In the past there has been no rule with respect to the length of time for which these memoranda should be retained.
In view of the fact that a yellow copy is prepared of such memoranda and is made a part of the Bureau's files,* it is not desired that these

---

* Not all "original memoranda" prepared by FBI assistant directors were made part of the Bureau's files—blue/pink/informal memoranda were not included in the Bureau's files nor were Do Not File memoranda authorizing break-ins. Under Hoover's 1953 order, the original memorandum in these cases was destroyed, ensuring that the only permanently maintained record was filed in Hoover's office files.—Ed.

memoranda be retained for an indefinite period of time. I desire that henceforth you periodically review these memoranda and destroy them as promptly as possible but in no case shall they be retained in excess of six months. . . .

DESPITE HOOVER'S specific order, not all office files maintained by FBI assistant directors were regularly destroyed. FBI Assistant Director Louis Nichols's office file escaped this ordered records destruction as did portions of the office files of FBI Associate Director Clyde Tolson (covering the years 1965–1972) and FBI Assistant Director D. Milton Ladd (covering the years 1941–1946). These failures of compliance created unanticipated problems for FBI officials in 1975 when the Senate Select Committee on Intelligence Activities launched its investigation into FBI practices and demanded that the FBI temporarily cease all records destruction.

■ **Blue Memo, FBI Director J. Edgar Hoover to [name withheld] FBI assistant directors, October 1, 1941, reprinted in Hearings into Inquiry into the Destruction of Former FBI Director J. Edgar Hoover's Files and FBI Recordkeeping, pp. 154–155**
As you are no doubt aware, there is presently maintained in the office of Miss [Helen] Gandy a confidential file in which are kept various and sundry items believed inadvisable to be included in the general files of the Bureau. Among this material are certain items such as confidential information on [name withheld], Communist infiltration into the Department of Justice, etc., which, if they are to be of value, must be properly indexed and filed. . . . It is my desire that a confidential file be maintained in the office of [FBI Assistant Director Louis] Nichols, under his direction and supervision, and hereafter any material which should be placed in this file will be forwarded to Mr. Nichols for his attention.

It is further my desire that the confidential file in Miss Gandy's office be restricted to confidential items of a more or less personal nature of the

Director's and items which I might have occasion to call for from time to time, such as memoranda to the Department on the Dies Committee, etc. . . .

■ **Memo, FBI Assistant Director John McDermott to FBI Assistant Director Thomas Jenkins, June 11, 1975, FBI 66-17404-94**

There are now temporarily maintained in my office six volumes of original memoranda dictated by former Director Hoover to Mr. Tolson and other Bureau officials from 1-14-65 through 4-26-72. . . . The question has now been raised as to what disposition should be made of these six volumes of original memoranda. [Handwritten insert: "Should have been destroyed in 6 months per Ex(ecutive) Conf(erence memo of) 3/5/53 and Hoover memo 3/19/53."]

These memoranda most probably should have been destroyed by Mr. Tolson or his staff prior to his retirement since they were never intended for inclusion in the Bureau's permanent records collection. It is observed, however, that Senate Majority Leader Mike Mansfield and Senate Minority Leader Hugh Scott have requested that no Bureau records having any bearing on the subject matter of Senate Resolution 21 [creating the Special Senate Committee on Intelligence Activities to investigate the activities of the federal intelligence agencies, including the FBI] be destroyed. Since Senate Resolution 21 is susceptible to extremely broad interpretation it would be difficult in many instances to distinguish which memoranda fall within the ambit of the Resolution. Should it become necessary to produce any particular memo in the future the yellow file copy should suffice; however, questions might be raised as to the location or disposition of the originals which contain Director Hoover's holographic signatures or initials and occasionally a holographic postscript. To avoid any question by the Senate Select Committee or others concerning the destruction of such originals, it is suggested they be retained in the Special File Room of the Files and Communications Division until at least the Senate hearings are concluded. . . .

THE JUDITH COPLON CASE *not only led Hoover to replace pink memoranda with informal memoranda, but to authorize two additional special records procedures: Administrative Pages and JUNE Mail.*

■ **Strictly Confidential Bureau Bulletin No. 34, Series 1949, July 8, 1949, FBI 66-03-996**

... The information which is considered suitable for distribution to outside agencies is to be included in the regular report [submitted by FBI agents] as at present, and the information which is not to be distributed to agencies outside the Bureau should be placed on administrative pages attached to the regular report.... As a general rule, therefore, Special Agents in preparing reports should prepare them with the understanding that the regular part of the report will probably be distributed to agencies outside the Bureau and the information which should not be sent to outside agencies will be set forth in the administrative pages at the conclusion of the report, which will be detached before distribution....

Types of information not to be disseminated—to be included in the administrative pages of the report:

(1) Gossip, rumor or any information that could *unjustifiably* embarrass any person or organization.

(2) Verified or unverified information, the pertinency of which has not been established, but may be the basis for future investigation....

(3) Unconfirmed and uncorroborated information concerning associates, relatives, or organizations to which the subject may belong, who are alleged to be subversive.

(4) Facts and information which are considered of a nature not expedient to disseminate, or which could cause embarrassment to the Bureau, if distributed....

Examples—Internal Security:

(1) An anonymous complainant alleges A ... is a member of the Communist Party and further that A is a man of loose morals, a heavy drinker living with a known prostitute.... The allegation of Communist Party membership should be included in the investigative section while the allegation concerning loose morals should be included in the administrative section....

Examples—Criminal and Other Types of Cases: ...

(7) During the legal search in a white slave traffic act investigation there is found an address book containing data identifying prominent public officials. Unless the names appearing therein are material to the investigation, this type of information should be placed in the administrative section....

■ **Personal Attention Strictly Confidential SAC Letter No. 69, Series 69, June 29, 1949, FBI 66-1372-1**

... (B) CONFIDENTIAL INFORMANTS—LISTING IN REPORTS—

SPECIAL COMMUNICATION—When information is received from some highly confidential source and such source of information or informant is of such a confidential character that the information should not appear in the file of a case, it is desired that the identification of such a highly confidential source be communicated to the Bureau by letter, . . . sealed in an envelope bearing the code word "June" and then placed in the envelope addressed to the Director "Personal and Confidential."

These letters received at the Bureau will be filed in a separate confidential file maintained under lock and key. The copies of such letters in the field offices are to be maintained in a confidential file by the Special Agent in Charge and this file, too, shall be retained under lock and key. . . .

The above-described letter is to be used only for the most secretive sources, such as Governors, secretaries to high officials who may be discussing such officials and their attitude, or when referring to highly confidential or unusual investigative techniques. . . .

■ **JUNE Memo, FBI Supervisor W. Raymond Wannall to FBI Assistant Director William Sullivan, January 17, 1969, FBI 66-1372-49**

. . . 1. It is noted that all sources utilized in the criminal and criminal intelligence type investigations and where the code word "June" is utilized were sources illegal in nature [wiretaps, bugs, break-ins, mail opening] and, of course, to protect those sources all information is included in the June file together with field office requests and [FBI Headquarters] responses with respect to authority for installation. . . .

In view of the foregoing, it is believed important that full security be maintained with respect to these files which are even now in some instances subject to inquiry by the Department [of Justice] because of disclosure considerations in matters pending before the courts. . . .

Index

A Note on the Editor

ATHAN THEOHARIS was born in Milwaukee and studied history at the University of Chicago, where he received A.B., A.M., and Ph.D. degrees. He has taught at Texas A&M University, Wayne State University, and the City University of New York, and is now Professor of History at Marquette University. For more than a decade Mr. Theoharis has been one of the most diligent critics of the Federal Bureau of Investigation, based upon his intensive research in the Bureau's files under the Freedom of Information Act. His other books include *The Boss: J. Edgar Hoover and the Great American Inquisition, Beyond the Hiss Case, Spying on Americans, The Specter, Seeds of Repression, The Yalta Myths,* and *Anatomy of Anti-Communism*. He has received the H. L. Mencken Award of the Free Press Association and the Binkley-Stephenson Award of the Organization of American Historians. Mr. Theoharis is married and the father of three children, and lives in Milwaukee.

ELEPHANT PAPERBACKS

American History and American Studies
Stephen Vincent Benét, *John Brown's Body,* EL10
Henry W. Berger, ed., *A William Appleman Williams Reader,*
    EL126
Andrew Bergman, *We're in the Money,* EL124
Paul Boyer, ed., *Reagan as President,* EL117
Robert V. Bruce, *1877: Year of Violence,* EL102
George Dangerfield, *The Era of Good Feelings,* EL110
Clarence Darrow, *Verdicts Out of Court,* EL2
Floyd Dell, *Intellectual Vagabondage,* EL13
Elisha P. Douglass, *Rebels and Democrats,* EL108
Theodore Draper, *The Roots of American Communism,* EL105
Joseph Epstein, *Ambition,* EL7
Paul W. Glad, *McKinley, Bryan, and the People,* EL119
Daniel Horowitz, *The Morality of Spending,* EL122
Kenneth T. Jackson, *The Ku Klux Klan in the City, 1915–1930,*
    EL123
Edward Chase Kirkland, *Dream and Thought in the Business
    Community, 1860–1900,* EL114
Herbert S Klein, *Slavery in the Americas,* EL103
Aileen S. Kraditor, *Means and Ends in American Abolitionism,*
    EL111
Leonard W. Levy, *Jefferson and Civil Liberties: The Darker Side,*
    EL107
Seymour J. Mandelbaum, *Boss Tweed's New York,* EL112
Thomas J. McCormick, *China Market,* EL115
Walter Millis, *The Martial Spirit,* EL104
Nicolaus Mills, ed., *Culture in an Age of Money,* EL302
Roderick Nash, *The Nervous Generation,* EL113
William L. O'Neill, ed., *Echoes of Revolt: The Masses,
    1911–1917,* EL5
Glenn Porter and Harold C. Livesay, *Merchants and
    Manufacturers,* EL106
Edward Reynolds, *Stand the Storm,* EL128
Geoffrey S. Smith, *To Save a Nation,* EL125
Bernard Sternsher, ed., *Hitting Home: The Great Depression in
    Town and Country,* EL109
Athan Theoharis, *From the Secret Files of J. Edgar Hoover,* EL127
Nicholas von Hoffman, *We Are the People Our Parents Warned
    Us Against,* EL301
Norman Ware, *The Industrial Worker, 1840–1860,* EL116
Tom Wicker, *JFK and LBJ: The Influence of Personality upon
    Politics,* EL120
Robert H. Wiebe, *Businessmen and Reform,* EL101
T. Harry Williams, *McClellan, Sherman and Grant,* EL121
Miles Wolff, *Lunch at the 5 & 10,* EL118